מסורה

ArtScroll Mesorah Series®

Rabbi Nosson Scherman / Rabbi Meir Zlotowitz

General Editors

באור על פרקי אבות לרבי עובדיה ספורנו

COMMENTARY ON PIRKEI AVOS

Published by

ArtScroll®
Mesorah Publications, ltd

SFORNO

Translation and explanatory notes
by Rabbi Raphael Pelcovitz

FIRST EDITION
First Impression . . . May 1996
Second Impression . . . February 2001
Third Impression . . . April 2006
Fourth Impression . . . April 2012

Published and Distributed by
MESORAH PUBLICATIONS, Ltd.
4401 Second Avenue
Brooklyn, New York 11232

Distributed in Europe by
LEHMANNS
Unit E, Viking Business Park
Rolling Mill Road
Jarrow, Tyne & Wear NE32 3DP
England

Distributed in Israel by
SIFRIATI / A. GITLER — BOOKS
6 Hayarkon Street
Bnei Brak 51127

Distributed in Australia & New Zealand by
GOLDS WORLD OF JUDAICA
3-13 William Street
Balaclava, Melbourne 3183
Victoria Australia

Distributed in South Africa by
KOLLEL BOOKSHOP
Ivy Common 105 William Road
Norwood 2192, Johannesburg, South Africa

ARTSCROLL MESORAH SERIES
SFORNO — COMMENTARY ON PIRKEI AVOS

ISBN 10: 0-89906-388-8 / ISBN 13: 978-0-89906-388-1

Typography by CompuScribe at ArtScroll Studios, Ltd.

Printed in the United States of America by Noble Book Press
Bound by Sefercraft Quality Bookbinders, Ltd., Brooklyn, NY

◆ Acknowledgments

The author wishes to acknowledge with heartfelt thanks the dedicated efforts of the following, who have a significant share in this important work.

MOSHE SHAPIRO, of Jerusalem, for his careful editing of the manuscript and most valuable suggestions, a number of which are incorporated in the final version of the *Sforno* on *Mesechta Avos.*

FRIEDA LAPIDES, executive secretary of Congregation Kneseth Israel, Far Rockaway, for her readiness to help with the typing of the manuscript and her kindness and patience during the correcting and revising period, which is always a difficult, tedious time.

RABBI NOSSON SCHERMAN, for his usual competent, perceptive and inimitable editorial touch and wise guidance, and RABBI MEIR ZLOTOWITZ whose wisdom and dedication make the ArtScroll Series possible.

MAX SEPTIMUS, who graciously made available his priceless copy of *Machzor Roma* for inclusion in this work. This volume is a fitting memorial for his beloved parents, יוסף דוב ב״ר ישראל יהודה and חנה בת ר׳ אליעזר צבי, נכד החסיד הצדיק ר׳ מנדל׳ה הוזיר. May *Hashem* grant him many healthy years to enjoy the rare, unique *seforim* which adorn his library shelves, and may he be *zocheh* to *Yiddishe nachas* from his entire family.

ETHEL GOTTLIEB, my beloved, talented daughter, for her meticulous final reading of the manuscript, ensuring that the completed work be a whole and faithful one, as befits a *sefer* of Torah.

To RABBI SHEAH BRANDER, SHMUEL BLITZ, RABBI MOSHE ROSENBLUM, ELI KROEN, AVROHOM BIDERMAN, YOSEF TIMINSKY, MRS. FAYGIE WEINBAUM, MRS. CHAYA GITTY LOEVY, and the entire ArtScroll/Mesorah Publication staff I express my sincere thanks.

And, *acharon acharon chaviv,* last but not least, my dear, devoted wife SHIRLEY תחי׳ for her encouragement, support and wise counsel over the years.

R.P.

◆§ Preface

Unlike the *Sforno's* commentary on Torah, which was popularized over the years through its inclusion in the standard version of the *Mikraos Gedolos Chumash,* his commentary on *Pirkei Avos* is known to but a small number of Torah scholars and students. It was first published in *Machzor Roma* in the year 1540 (5300) but never became widely known, as did the commentary of other *Rishonim* (early commentators) on this tractate, such as *Rashi, Rambam* and *Ovadiah MiBartenura.* With the passage of time, *Pirkei Avos* became beloved by *Klal Yisrael* and is included in practically every *siddur,* but the commentary of the *Sforno* remained relatively unknown. The Mosad Harav Kook reprinted his commentary on *Avos* in 1983 as part of *Kisvei HaSforno,* which also includes *Sforno's* commentary on *Tehillim* and some books of *Nach,* as well as his philosophical writings. This English translation of the *Sforno* on *Mesechta Avos* will not only introduce his masterful commentary to a larger public, but hopefully the explanatory notes will explain and elucidate this important work, thereby increasing the appreciation of the reader for this classic of one of the Torah giants of the 16th century.

Rabbi Ovadiah Sforno was born in Cesena, Italy in 1470 and lived in Rome and Bologna until his death in 1550. He was a physician and philosopher, as well as a confidant of kings and churchmen, but it is as Torah commentator that his fame endures.

In 1987, we published the English translation of the *Sforno* on the Five Books of Torah with explanatory notes. That work introduced many of our generation to the *Sforno;* for those who knew of him before, but found his work difficult to comprehend, the English treatment helped them gain a clearer understanding of his commentary.

This translation of *Pirkei Avos* will, it is hoped, find as wide an audience as did the *Sforno* on Torah. As we wrote in the Introduction to that work: "Many exegetes of the early 16th century do not appeal to the 20th-century reader. Not so the *Sforno.* His intellectual clarity, philosophical insights and religious fervor . . . are as fresh and meaningful today as then." Our time, in many ways, parallels his, and he speaks as compellingly to us today as he did over 450 years ago.

I am appreciative to Rabbi Meir Zlotowitz and Rabbi Nosson Scherman for recognizing the importance of bringing the *Sforno's* teachings on *Pirkei Avos* to this generation, and I am confident that this work will be a welcome addition to their historic contribution to the dissemination of Torah in our time.

Foreword

The *Sforno's* commentary on *Mesechta Avos* was published thirty-seven years before his monumental commentary on the Torah. His commentary on *Avos* was published during his lifetime, whereas his commentary on Torah was published seventeen years after his passing. It is strange, therefore, that his earlier work on *Pirkei Avos* never gained the popularity of his later work on the Torah. One might speculate that the study of *Pirkei Avos* was never as widespread as that of *Chumash,* since it did not have the advantage of being part of the weekly practice of public reading and private review (שְׁתַּיִם מִקְרָא וְאֶחָד תַּרְגּוּם).

However, from his introduction to *Pirkei Avos* we see that he was attracted to this tractate, which he characterizes as being one that is "lovely and delightful, teaching us ways that are pleasant, through which we will find favor in the eyes of God and man." We know that the *Sforno* was not only a great Torah scholar, physician and philosopher, but also a man who greatly admired and appreciated the aesthetic aspect of Torah. This character trait of the *Sforno* is reflected in his commentary on the Torah, as we remarked in the introduction to the English edition of the *Sforno* on *Chumash.* It is important to remember that the *Sforno* lived at the time of the Renaissance and, as a physician and confidant of leading figures of the country, he was exposed to great art, classical music and literature, and this enhanced his appreciation of, and sensitivity for, the aesthetic. The "Sayings of the Fathers" appeals to this aesthetic nature of man, which is an integral part of man's soul, as well as informing his ethical sensibilities. Together they shape the Jew's interior moral landscape. As such, the *Sforno* put much of his own poetic, sensitive soul into this commentary and thereby gave his generation, and future generations, a deeper, more meaningful understanding of the teachings of our Sages, as expressed in this fascinating *Mesechta.*

The maxims, principles of conduct, and moral teachings of the Sages, collected together in *Pirkei Avos,* have their origin or parallel in the Written Torah (תּוֹרָה שֶׁבִּכְתָב). One can also find many parallels of these teachings in the Talmud and Midrash (תּוֹרָה שֶׁבְּעַל פֶּה) as well. The *Sforno* skillfully uses Scriptural verses and Talmudic teachings to elucidate the succinct sayings of our fathers, while expanding and expounding upon their instructive and inspiring lessons. The style and methodology of the *Sforno,* in his commentary on this tractate, is a forerunner of his approach in his *Chumash* commentary. It is succinct, precise and clear. It is simple, yet elegant, and always presents an intellectual challenge. His prodigious, encyclopedic knowledge of *Tanach* and *Chazal* is used to explain the terminology, as well as the sense of the Tanna's teaching. In the original Hebrew there is constant use of the phrase כְּאָמְרוֹ ("as it is said"), as well as the expression אמרו ז"ל ("as our Sages, of blessed memory, said"), the former referring to the Written Torah and the latter referring to the Oral Torah, which indicates how he was careful to build his commentary on the foundation of Torah itself. This is the method of all *Rishonim* (early Torah commentators) who attempted to understand every aspect of Torah teaching from within the Torah itself. This, however, does not restrict any *Rishon* from bringing a unique, original, innovative approach to his understanding of Torah, be it the written or the oral tradition.

The *Sforno's* commentary on *Pirkei Avos* is a perfect example of this power of *chiddush* (innovative thinking). His explanation of Mishnah 5:7 is a good example of his original and unique approach in understanding the meaning of the Mishnah:

> שִׁבְעָה דְבָרִים בְּגֹלֶם וְשִׁבְעָה בְּחָכָם
>
> *"Seven traits characterize an uncultured person and seven a learned one."*

His commentary is based on the story of Job and his companions, and he brilliantly demonstrates that these positive and negative traits are reflected in their discussions with Job, and his response to them.

His philosophical and theological prowess can be seen in his commentary on 3:19-20, where he discusses man's freedom of choice and G-d's foreknowledge, as well as the concept of reward and punishment. Also, in 4:18, he goes to great lengths to explain the dilemma confronting the man of faith, which also puzzled our Sages, as to why the righteous suffer while the wicked flourish. In 4:28 we find a most intricate commentary on a complex Mishnah regarding man's purpose in life. Although the normal approach of the *Sforno* is to be brief and concise, he does at times depart from this style, as we see from his commentary on these *Mishnahs.*

From time to time, he explains the words of the Tanna from a historical perspective, personal experience, or as reflecting the time in which the Tanna lived. Examples of this are 1:9, 1:15, and 4:13. The first example reflects a tragic personal episode in the life of Shimon ben Shetach, which prompted his cautionary instruction, הֱוֵי מַרְבֶּה לַחֲקוֹר, "interrogate the witnesses extensively." In the second instance, he explains that Shammai was speaking specifically to Menachem, his predecessor as head of the court. Rabbi Yochanan HaSandler, in chapter 4, felt the need, given the spiritual climate of his time, to caution his disciples to distinguish between a gathering "for the sake of Heaven," as opposed to one which is not motivated by pure considerations.

The appeal of the *Sforno* has not diminished with the passage of time. Each generation has come to appreciate his unique contribution to Torah commentary. Just as his concise style, penetrating analysis of Torah phraseology, and ability to capture the ethical lessons to be derived from Biblical events intrigued Bible scholars and students for the past four centuries, so will his special contribution to the understanding of *Pirkei Avos* appeal to the Torah students and scholars of our generation. In many cases, I have refrained from commenting on his words, for I believe they are self-explanatory. However, there are times when his commentary is overly brief or cryptic, and it is then that I explain and elaborate what I believe his intention to be. I also include in the Notes the full text and context of the verses and מַאֲמָרֵי חז״ל quoted by him, for only in this manner can the reader fully appreciate what the *Sforno* is saying to us.

Our translation of the *Sforno's* commentary is not a literal one. We have attempted to adapt his 16th-century phraseology to make it more understandable to the 20th-century reader. We have tried, however, to capture the essence and spirit of his commentary, while retaining the flavor of his phraseology. It is our hope that this English translation of the *Sforno's* commentary on *Pirkei Avos* will open the door to the masterful work of one of the great Torah scholars of the Middle Ages, while the explanatory Notes will surely be of assistance even to those who are conversant with the original Hebrew text, which is printed in this edition together with the English translation. Incidentally, the *Sforno's* Hebrew text is taken from the *Machzor* Roma edition that was published in his lifetime.

Traditionally, we recite the last Mishnah of *Mesechta Makkos* at the conclusion of each chapter. That Mishnah, in turn, quotes a verse from *Sefer Yeshayahu,* which ends with the phrase, יַגְדִּיל תּוֹרָה וְיַאְדִּיר, *that the Torah be made great and glorious* (*Isaiah* 42:21). Our intent and purpose in undertaking this project was motivated by our desire to expand the reader's knowledge and appreciation of *Pirkei Avos,* so that God's Torah be made great and that glory be brought to His Name. That will be the greatest reward for our efforts. We pray that the Almighty will grant us years of good health, strength of mind and spirit, so that we may be *zocheh* to study and teach and disseminate Torah, לְהַגְדִּיל תּוֹרָה וּלְהַאֲדִירָהּ.

Raphael Pelcovitz

אייר תשנ״ו

הקדמת אביר הרופאים מורינו
הרב רבינו עובדיה מספורנו יצ״ו
Sforno's Introduction to Pirkei Avos

אם שלמים וכן רבים הרבו אמרי שפר בפירוש המסכתא הזאת הנקראת מסכת אבות שכלה מחמדים מגידים דרכי נעם למצוא חן בעיני אלקים ואדם כאמרם ז״ל האי מאן דבעי למהוי חסידא לקיים מילי דאבות הן רבים עתה מפרטי דברים היו בעיני קצת קדמוני המפרשים כמבוארים בעצמם עד כי עצרו במלין מלדבר בם וקצתם האריכו למעניתם במאמר רחב רב הכמות היה לטורח בעיני מביני זמננו ואמרו הנה מתלאה:

לכן שעפי הואילו פנו להגיד המושג אצלי בה כמלקט בשבלי גדולי חקרי לב הלא כה דברי ודברי זולתי יכונו יחדו לעיני זקני עמנו ישפוטו הם איזה יכשר להתיר כל ספק וחפץ יי בידם יצלח ועלימו אטיף מלתי

אני עובדיה בכ״מא״ר יעקב מספורנו יצ״ו בקצר מלין כפי האפשר לברר וללבן כוונת המחבר הואלתי לדבר בחלוקת פרקי זאת המסכתא וסדרם כפי המושג אצלי:

וזה כי אמנם התחיל המחבר בפרק הראשון ממנה לספר דברי הקודמים נשיאי ואבות בית דין מראשית בנין בית שני כפי סדר הדורות המה אנשי השם אשר עמדו לנס עמים בדורותם והיו למאורות להבין ולהורות לחכמים ותלמידיהם במה יזכו את ארחם במדו׳ ובמושכלות להעלות נר תמיד:

ובפרק השני סדר דברי נשיאים וזולתם כמו כן על סדר הדורות במאמרים מורים גם להמון זהירות מביאה לידי זריזות ולכן חזר אל דברי הלל הקדמון אחר שהשלים סדר דורות התנאים אשר ישבו על כסא דין

Chapter One relates the teachings of the *Nessiyim* (communal leaders) and heads of the court from the beginning of the Second Temple period, according to the sequence of their generations. These were men of renown who guided their generations, serving as luminaries in teaching and imparting understanding to the wise and their disciples, that they might refine their ways in ethical and intellectual pursuits, and thereby kindle and guard the eternal light.

In Chapter Two, the words of the *Nessiyim* and others are set forth — again, according to the sequence of their generations — in statements which address also the general populace, in the spirit of [the Sages' adage], זְהִירוּת מְבִיאָה לִידֵי זְרִיזוּת, "*Watchfulness brings to zeal*" (*Avodah Zarah* 20b). This explains why he

NOTES

In the preface to the *Sforno*'s formal introduction, where he explains the order and sequence of *Pirkei Avos,* he acknowledges the commentaries written by outstanding Torah scholars before him. He praises their work written on this tractate, which the Talmud (*Bava Kamma* 30a) recommends as a manual for piety, stating, האי מאן דבעי למהוי חסידא לקיים מילי דאבות, *He who wishes to be a man of utmost piety should fulfill the teachings of Pirkei Avos.*

Nonetheless, the *Sforno* intimates that there are certain shortcomings in the works of earlier commentaries, and he proceeds to present his own version. He begins with a brief explanation of the order and divisons of the five chapters, which are Mishnaic in time and character. As far as the sixth chapter is concerned, since it is a collection of *beraisos* [non-Mishnaic literature] which were merely written in the style of the Mishnah, the *Sforno* does not discuss its

ונשיאות ולא שתם על שאר דברי הלל עצמו אשר בפרק הקודם:
ובפרק השלישי ספר דברי גדולי הדורות כמו כן על סדר דורותם מיוסדים על אדני זריזות גם להמון מעוררים לחזות בנעם אמרי אל ודעת עליון ושמור דרכו לרצון להם לפני יי׳:
ובפרק הרביעי סדר המחבר כמו כן על סדר הדורות אמרות טהורות מורות אורחות יושר לקנות ולהשיג זהירות וזריזות במועצות ודעת וזה בששים האדם מגמת פניו לכבוד האל יתברך בכל מעשיו ולהשמר מכל מה שיהיה נגד כבודו או שיהיה בו חלול שם קדשו ח״ו:
ובפרק החמישי הגדיל ענין העיון והמעשה בהודיעו מה יקרו המחזיקים בם ונמאסו מורדי אור את פני האדון דיין ובעל דין הוא יושיענו יודיענו אורח חיים יאר פניו ואתנו סלה:

[i.e., the author of *Avos*] goes back to the words of Hillel (who was a Tanna, and lived in an earlier era), after having completed the sequence of the Tannaim and why he did not insert them among the rest of Hillel's own words in the previous chapter.

In Chapter Three, we are taught the teachings of the great scholars [of later day], also according to the sequence of their generations. These are structured on the basis of religious zeal (זְרִיזוּת), and directed also to the masses, urging them to witness the pleasantness of God's words and to appreciate the knowledge of the One above, while guarding His ways according to His will.

In Chapter Four, the author [of *Avos*] sets forth — also according to the sequence of the generations — pure sayings which teach the ways of uprightness, [that one may] acquire and attain "watchfulness and zeal" (זְהִירוּת וְזְרִיזוּת) through good counsel and understanding. This is accomplished when man sets out to honor God through all his deeds, and is careful to guard against that which diminishes His honor, or contains an element of desecration of His holy Name, heaven forbid.

In Chapter Five, the theme of analytical thought and its implementation through practical deeds is discussed at length. The author teaches how honored are those who support Torah, and how abhorrent are those who conceal the light of the Master and Judge of the Universe. May He grant us salvation, teach us the way of life, and let His countenance shine upon us, *selah*!

NOTES

internal structure or placement.

According to the *Sforno,* Chapter One is addressed exclusively to the elite — the leaders and teachers of Israel — whereas Chapter Two is directed also to the common folk, the masses. This answers the question of why Hillel, who lived in the generation of scholars mentioned in Chapter One, is quoted again in Chapter Two. Whereas in Chapter One he addresses only the leaders and teachers, in Chapter Two he speaks also to the masses, because these teachings are of universal application.

The importance of זְהִירוּת, *watchfulness,* and זְרִיזוּת, *zeal,* mentioned by the *Sforno* in his introduction, is based upon the famous statement of Rav Pinchas ben Yair (end of *Sotah; Avodah Zarah* 20b). This statement is also used by R' Moshe Luzatto as the basis of his classic work *Mesillas Yesharim.* The text reads, תּוֹרָה מְבִיאָה לִידֵי זְהִירוּת, זְהִירוּת מְבִיאָה לִידֵי זְרִיזוּת..., *Torah study leads to watchfulness, watchfulness leads to zeal. . .*

באור על פרקי אבות לרבי עובדיה ספורנו

SFORNO

COMMENTARY ON PIRKEI AVOS

פרק א

Chapter One

כָּל יִשְׂרָאֵל יֵשׁ לָהֶם חֵלֶק לָעוֹלָם הַבָּא, שֶׁנֶּאֱמַר: „וְעַמֵּךְ כֻּלָּם צַדִּיקִים, לְעוֹלָם יִירְשׁוּ אָרֶץ, נֵצֶר מַטָּעַי, מַעֲשֵׂה יָדַי לְהִתְפָּאֵר.״

All Israel has a share in the World to Come, as it is said: "And your people are all righteous; they shall inherit the land forever; they are the branch of My planting, My handiwork, in which to take pride."

א [א] **מֹשֶׁה** קִבֵּל תּוֹרָה מִסִּינַי, וּמְסָרָהּ לִיהוֹשֻׁעַ,
א וִיהוֹשֻׁעַ לִזְקֵנִים, וּזְקֵנִים לִנְבִיאִים,
וּנְבִיאִים מְסָרוּהָ לְאַנְשֵׁי כְנֶסֶת הַגְּדוֹלָה. הֵם

פירוש לרבי עובדיה ספורנו

א:א. כבר באר האל יתברך שספרו מתחלק אל עיוני ומעשי, כאמרו „והתורה והמצוה אשר כתבתי להורותם״. כי אמנם החלק העיוני ממנו, אשר ענינו לדעת את האל יתברך, ותכלית זה ליראה ולאהבה אותו – הוא יקרא תורה באמת, וכאשר חדלו תופשי התורה מהתבונן בזה החלק העיוני קצף האל יתברך, באמרו „ותופשי התורה לא ידעוני״, והחלק המעשי ממנו יקרא מצוה בלי ספק. וכבר אמרו „אין דורשים במעשה בראשית בשנים ולא

SFORNO'S COMMENTARY

1:1

מֹשֶׁה קִבֵּל תּוֹרָה מִסִּינַי — *Moses received the Torah from Sinai.* The Almighty explained that [the Torah] can be divided into two categories: the philosophical (חֵלֶק עִיּוּנִי) and the practical (חֵלֶק מַעֲשִׂי). As the verse says, *Hashem said to Moses,* עֲלֵה אֵלַי הָהָרָה וֶהְיֵה שָׁם וְאֶתְּנָה לְךָ אֶת לֻחֹת הָאֶבֶן וְהַתּוֹרָה וְהַמִּצְוָה אֲשֶׁר כָּתַבְתִּי לְהוֹרֹתָם, *"Ascend to Me to the mountain and remain there, and I shall give you the stone Tablets,* and *the Torah and the commandment that I have written, to teach them"* (*Exodus* 24:12).

The philosophical aspect of Torah consists of knowing the Almighty, its ultimate purpose being to revere and love Him. Indeed, [this category] is referred to as "the Torah" [by the above verse]. Hence, when Torah scholars ceased to contemplate the philosophical aspect of the Torah, God grew angry, as the verse says, וְתֹפְשֵׂי הַתּוֹרָה לֹא יְדָעוּנִי, *And they that grasp the law did not know Me* (*Jeremiah* 2:8). As for the practical aspect of Torah, it is undoubtedly [what the above verse] refers to as "the commandment."

NOTES

1:1

מֹשֶׁה קִבֵּל תּוֹרָה מִסִּינַי, וּמְסָרָהּ — *Moses received the Torah from Sinai and transmitted it.* It is no coincidence that the *Rambam's Mishneh Torah* begins with *Sefer Mada* (Book of Knowledge), which elucidates the theme of "knowing God," (יְדִיעַת הַשֵּׁם) for this knowledge is of paramount importance in Torah *hashkafah.*

The term "to know God," has two meanings: First, it means to discern His ways and attributes, which enables one to emulate Him. This was Moses' intention when he beseeched Hashem, הוֹדִעֵנִי נָא אֶת דְּרָכֶךָ, *Make known to me Your ways* (*Exodus* 33:13). Second, it means to recognize His will, which enables one to fulfill His commandments. These two meanings of the term "to know God" correspond to the two aspects of Torah mentioned by the *Sforno* — the philosophical (עִיּוּנִי) and the practical (מַעֲשִׂי).

The verse from *Jeremiah,* where God laments over the fact that the Torah scholars of that era "did not know Him," illustrates their neglect in striving to attain this knowledge of God.

The two passages from Tractate *Chagigah* stipulate the prerequisites that are necessary to study and understand two major esoteric areas of Jewish theology — מַעֲשֵׂה בְרֵאשִׁית, or the Divine process of Creation, and מַעֲשֵׂה מֶרְכָּבָה, the works of the Divine Chariot. The latter theme is described in detail by both Isaiah (Ch.6) and Ezekiel (Ch.1), who glimpsed these secrets in prophetic visions. Both prophets depict the heavenly

1 **1.** *Moses received the Torah from Sinai and trans-*
1 *mitted it to Joshua; Joshua to the Elders; the Elders to the Prophets; and the Prophets transmitted it to the Men of the Great Assembly. They [the Men of the*

פירוש לרבי עובדיה ספורנו

במרכבה ביחיד אלא אם כן היה חכם ומבין מדעתו", ואמרו שמוסרים ראשי פרקים כאלה לאב בית דין וכולי. אמר אם כן זה המחבר שמשה רבינו היה כל כך מבין מדעתו שקבל זה החלק העיוני הנקרא תורה מסיני, וזה שמאותן הדברים שנאמרו לו בסיני קבל והבין את כל החלק העיוני בזולת שימסור לו האל יתברך שום ראשי פרקים כלל. והוא אחרי כן מסרה ליהושע שהיה נשיא בדורו ואולי אב בית דין בימי משה, וכן מדור לדור עד אנשי כנסת

SFORNO'S COMMENTARY

Now, our Sages have stated, אֵין דּוֹרְשִׁים בְּמַעֲשֵׂה בְרֵאשִׁית בִּשְׁנַיִם וְלֹא בְמֶרְכָּבָה בְּיָחִיד אֶלָּא אִם כֵּן הָיָה חָכָם וּמֵבִין מִדַּעְתּוֹ, "*It is prohibited to expound upon the story of Creation with [only] two [disciples], or upon the Divine Chariot with [only] one, unless he is wise and capable of attaining understanding on his own*" (*Chagigah* 11b). The Sages added, "[However,] a general outline of these topics *may* be transmitted to the head of the court, as well as to other such serious-minded individuals" (ibid., 13a).

The author [of *Pirkei Avos*] teaches that Moses' ability to "attain understanding on his own" was so great that he received the philosophical aspect called "the Torah" [directly] *from Sinai* (מֹשֶׁה קִבֵּל תּוֹרָה מִסִּינַי). In other words, Moses received and understood *the entire philosophical aspect of Torah* solely on the basis of the things he was told at Sinai, without Hashem having to transmit to him "a general outline of these topics."

Moses then transmitted this knowledge to Joshua, for he [subsequently] became the leader of his generation, and probably served as the head of the religious court in the days of Moses.

This [transmission] continued from generation to generation until the period of the People of the Great Assembly.

NOTES

host and the image of God seated upon His throne. According to our Sages, such esoteric traditions may only be transmitted by *Kaballah* masters to select students.

Moses was able to fully grasp these mysteries. However, even though he himself transmitted these teachings to Joshua, and Joshua in turn transmitted them to the elders, Moses' vast well of knowledge did not remain intact. As our Sages said, "The face of Moses was like the sun, while the face of Joshua was like the moon" (*Bava Basra* 75a). This conveys that a measure of Divine knowledge was somehow lost in the transfer from Moses to Joshua: Just as the moon has no light of its own, but merely reflects that of the sun, so too, the radiance of Joshua's intellectual brilliance was a mere reflection of Moses' teaching.

Nonetheless, *Mesorah* — the transmission of knowledge — *did* take place. And although it is undeniably true that the knowledge Moses originally imparted to Joshua became more and more diluted with each passing generation, vast stores of wisdom were still being transmitted from teacher to student, and we are all the beneficiaries of the teachings recorded in this *Mesechta.*

א אָמְרוּ שְׁלֹשָׁה דְבָרִים: הֱווּ מְתוּנִים בַּדִּין, וְהַעֲמִידוּ
ב תַלְמִידִים הַרְבֵּה, וַעֲשׂוּ סְיָג לַתּוֹרָה.

[ב] **שִׁמְעוֹן** הַצַּדִּיק הָיָה מִשְּׁיָרֵי כְנֶסֶת הַגְּדוֹלָה. הוּא הָיָה אוֹמֵר: עַל שְׁלֹשָׁה דְבָרִים הָעוֹלָם עוֹמֵד: עַל הַתּוֹרָה, וְעַל הָעֲבוֹדָה, וְעַל גְּמִילוּת חֲסָדִים.

פירוש לרבי עובדיה ספורנו

הגדולה. והם שראו בקלקול דורם ששכחו רובם את התורה והמצוה בגלות בבל הזהירו על שלשה דברים לתקן זה המעוות, ואמרו לחכמי הדור: הוו מתונים בדין, על הפך גויי הארץ דדייני בגיוותא, שאף על פי שבא דין כזה לפניכם כבר ונגמר דינו מכל מקום שאו ותנו בזה הדין בעצמו, כי אמנם נשתנו העדים ובעלי הדין וטענותיהם. והעמידו תלמידים הרבה עד יצא כנגה איזה מהם שיעלה למדרגת חכם ומבין מדעתו או שיהיה ראוי למסור לו ראשי פרקים. ועשו סייג לתורה לענוש את החוטאים להוראת

SFORNO'S COMMENTARY

הֵם אָמְרוּ שְׁלֹשָׁה דְבָרִים — *They [the Men of the Great Assembly] said three things.* The Men of the Great Assembly, in turn, observed the deterioration of their generation: The majority of [the people] had forgotten the "Torah and the commandment" during the Babylonian exile. Hence, they warned [the people] to correct "three things" in order to rectify their shortcomings. They advised the wise men of the generation to:

1. **הֱווּ מְתוּנִים בַּדִּין** — *Be deliberate in judgment,* unlike gentile judges, who dispense justice arrogantly and [enforce it] with physical force. They urged the Jewish judges to carefully deliberate each case, even if a similar case had previously come before them and a verdict had been reached. For [each case is different]: The witnesses vary, as do the litigants and their claims.

2. **וְהַעֲמִידוּ תַלְמִידִים הַרְבֵּה** — *Develop many disciples,* so that some will excel and attain the level of "one who is wise and capable of attaining understanding on his own," or at least, become sufficiently worthy to be taught "a general outline of these topics."

3. **וַעֲשׂוּ סְיָג לַתּוֹרָה** — *Make a protective hedge around the Torah.* They

NOTES

וַעֲשׂוּ סְיָג לַתּוֹרָה — *And make a protective hedge around the Torah.* The *Sforno's* interpretation of the clause עֲשׂוּ סְיָג לַתּוֹרָה is certainly unique, but it is firmly based on the Gemara in *Yevamos* 90b. There, the Sages establish the concept of לְמִיגְדַּר מִילְּתָא — the need to implement strong punitive measures, even at the expense of stretching the bounds of the law, when the times call for it.

An example of this concept is the encounter between Elijah and the false prophets of Baal (see *I Kings* Chap. 18): Elijah brought an offering upon the altar on Mt. Carmel, which, strictly speaking, comprised a viola-

Great Assembly] said three things: Be deliberate in judgment; develop many disciples; and make a protective hedge around the Torah.

2. *Shimon the Righteous was among the survivors of the Great Assembly. He used to say: The world [of Israel] depends on three things — on Torah study, on the service [of God], and on kind deeds.*

פירוש לרבי עובדיה ספורנו

שעה, כענין אמרם ז״ל ,,אמר רבי אליעזר בן יעקב שמעתי שבית דין מכין ועונשין שלא כדין ולא לעבור על דברי תורה אלא לעשות סייג לתורה״.

א:ב. אמר שהעולם של ישראל, והוא שיהיה ענינם באופן שתשרה שכינה בתוכם ויהיו לרצון, עומד על שלשה דברים המשרים שכינה בישראל. כי אמנם על ידי העבודה

SFORNO'S COMMENTARY

urged the court to take punitive measures against transgressors as dictated by the needs of the time. As the Sages said אָמַר ר׳ אֱלִיעֶזֶר בֶּן יַעֲקֹב שָׁמַעְתִּי שֶׁבֵּית דִּין מַכִּין וְעוֹנְשִׁין שֶׁלֹּא מִן הַתּוֹרָה וְלֹא לַעֲבוֹר עַל דִּבְרֵי תּוֹרָה אֶלָּא לַעֲשׂוֹת סְיָג לַתּוֹרָה, "*Rabbi Eliezer ben Yaakov said: 'I heard that the court may administer lashings and punishments without any legal basis — not in defiance of the Torah, but rather to make a protective hedge around the Torah'* " (*Yevamos* 90b).

1:2

עַל שְׁלֹשָׁה דְבָרִים הָעוֹלָם עוֹמֵד — *The word [of Israel] depends on three things.* "The world" that is Israel's, in which the Divine Presence (שְׁכִינָה) dwells when they find favor before Him, stands upon the "three things" that draw the Divine Presence to dwell among them:

NOTES

tion of a Torah-ordained law (offerings may not be brought upon altars [שְׁחוּטֵי חוּץ] other than the one situated in the Holy Temple).

The Talmud brings other examples, such as the severe punishments meted out by the court against violators of rabbinically ordained Sabbath prohibitions, and against a certain married couple who behaved indecently in public. According to the strict letter of the law these violations did not call for such stringent punishment, but since the integrity of the Torah was at stake, the Sages judged them harshly.

This is what the Mishnah means by, עֲשׂוּ סְיָג לַתּוֹרָה, *make a protective hedge around the Torah*: When the times call for it, strong steps must be taken to safeguard the integrity of Torah.

1:2

עַל שְׁלֹשָׁה דְבָרִים הָעוֹלָם עוֹמֵד — *The world [of Israel] depends on three things.* The *Sforno* explains that the word "world" refers to the special "world of Israel." Shimon the Righteous teaches us that the existence of this "world" is conditional upon the Divine Presence residing among the Jewish People. This, in turn, is contingent on three factors:

א
ג

[ג] אַנְטִיגְנוֹס אִישׁ סוֹכוֹ קִבֵּל מִשִּׁמְעוֹן הַצַּדִּיק. הוּא הָיָה אוֹמֵר: אַל תִּהְיוּ כַּעֲבָדִים הַמְשַׁמְּשִׁין אֶת הָרַב עַל מְנָת לְקַבֵּל פְּרָס; אֶלָּא הֱווּ כַּעֲבָדִים הַמְשַׁמְּשִׁין אֶת הָרַב שֶׁלֹּא עַל מְנָת לְקַבֵּל פְּרָס; וִיהִי מוֹרָא שָׁמַיִם עֲלֵיכֶם.

פירוש לרבי עובדיה ספורנו

תשרה שכינה כאמרו „עולת תמיד לדורותיכם וכו׳ ונועדתי שמה לבני ישראל״, ובתורה ובגמילות חסדים יהיו ישראל בצלמו כדמותו ויהיו ראויים להקרא בניו והוא כאב את בן ירצה אותם לשכנו בתוכם:

א:ג. הנה העובד מיראה יקרא עבד והעובד מאהבה יקרא בן, כאמרו „בנים אתם לה׳ אלהיכם״, ובהיות היראה על אחד משני פנים — אם יראת עונש והפסד שכר, אם הכנעה כאשר יכיר העבד מעלת רבו ויירא אותו לא

SFORNO'S COMMENTARY

עַל הַתּוֹרָה, וְעַל הָעֲבוֹדָה, וְעַל גְּמִילוּת חֲסָדִים — *On Torah study, on the service [of God], and on kind deeds.* Indeed, the Divine Presence comes to reside [among us] because of עֲבוֹדָה, or sacrificial "service." As the verse says, עֹלַת תָּמִיד לְדֹרֹתֵיכֶם . . . וְנֹעַדְתִּי שָׁמָּה לִבְנֵי יִשְׂרָאֵל, *As a continual elevation offering, for your generations. . . .and I shall set My meeting there with the Children of Israel* (*Exodus* 29:42-43).

In addition, through "Torah" and "kind deeds" Israel fulfills the intent of the verse נַעֲשֶׂה אָדָם בְּצַלְמֵנוּ כִּדְמוּתֵנוּ, *Let us make Man in Our image, after Our likeness* (*Genesis* 1:26), and thereby are deemed worthy to be called "His children." In turn, Hashem, like a father with a son, will find favor in them and dwell in their midst.

1:3

אֶלָּא הֱווּ כַּעֲבָדִים הַמְשַׁמְּשִׁין אֶת הָרַב שֶׁלֹּא עַל מְנָת לְקַבֵּל פְּרָס; וִיהִי מוֹרָא שָׁמַיִם עֲלֵיכֶם *— Instead be like servants who serve their master not for the sake of receiving a reward. And let the awe of Heaven be upon you.*

An individual whose service of Hashem is motivated by יִרְאָה, or *fear,* is referred to as an עֶבֶד, "a servant," but he whose service of Hashem is motivated by אַהֲבָה, or *love,* is referred to as a בֵּן, "a son." As the verse says, בָּנִים אַתֶּם לַה׳

NOTES

עַל הַתּוֹרָה, וְעַל הָעֲבוֹדָה, וְעַל גְּמִילוּת חֲסָדִים — *On Torah study, on the service [of God], and on kind deeds.* One is עֲבוֹדָה, the Divine service in the Holy Temple. The other two are Torah and kind deeds, which mold and refine the character of a person, enabling him to attain the ideal state that Hashem had in mind when He first created Man בְּצַלְמוֹ כִּדְמוּתוֹ, *in His image and likeness.* When we attain this exalted spiritual level, we are truly worthy of being called God's children. God then treats us as lovingly as a father would treat his own son, and he craves to dwell in our midst, as the verse states, וּכְאָב אֶת בֵּן יִרְצֶה, *even as a Father delights in His son* (*Proverbs* 3:12). In turn, by dwelling in our midst, the Divine Presence ensures the stability and security of the "world of Israel."

1:3

וִיהִי מוֹרָא שָׁמַיִם עֲלֵיכֶם — *And let the awe of Heaven be upon you.* We are commanded by

3. *Antigonus, leader of Socho, received the tradition from Shimon the Righteous. He used to say: Be not like servants who serve their master for the sake of receiving a reward; instead be like servants who serve their master not for the sake of receiving a reward. And let the awe of Heaven be upon you.*

פירוש לרבי עובדיה ספורנו

את ענשו ולא את הפסד שכרו, לפיכך אמר זה החכם אל תהיו אתם כאותם עבדים שמשמשין את הרב מיראת הפסד השכר, אבל היו כאותם עבדים שמשרתים את הרב על צד ההכנעה, וזה בהכירכם את פרשת גדלת המלך הקדוש. ובזה האופן יהיה עליכם אותו מורא שמים שצוה בתורת קדשו, כאמרו ,,מה יי אלהיך שואל מעמך כי אם ליראה וזה המין מהיראה הוא המיוחס לאבות עולם כאמרו כי עתה ידעתי כי ירא אלהים אתה, ועל זה הצד נקראו עבדים, כאמרו ,,זכור לאברהם ליצחק ולישראל עבדיך",

SFORNO'S COMMENTARY

אֱלֹהֵיכֶם, *You are* ***children*** [בָּנִים] *to Hashem, your God* (*Deuteronomy* 14:1).

Now there are two kinds of יִרְאָה: One is fear of punishment or loss of reward. The other, the subservience of a servant who acknowledges the superiority of his master and reveres him, and does not [serve him merely] out of fear of punishment or loss of reward.

Therefore, this Sage [Antigonus] said, "Do not be like those servants who serve their master out of fear of losing their reward. Rather, be like those servants who serve their master out of subservience. Recognize the extent of the Holy King's (הַמֶּלֶךְ הַקָּדוֹשׁ) greatness! In this manner, you shall experience the awe of Heaven that He commanded [to you] in the holy Torah, as it is written, וְעַתָּה יִשְׂרָאֵל מָה ה׳ אֱלֹהֶיךָ שֹׁאֵל מֵעִמָּךְ, כִּי אִם לְיִרְאָה אֶת ה׳ אֱלֹהֶיךָ, *Now, O Israel, what does Hashem, your God, ask of you? Only to fear Hashem, your God . . .*" (ibid. 10:12).

This is the kind of יִרְאָה that our Patriarchs experienced, as the verse says [of Abraham], כִּי עַתָּה יָדַעְתִּי כִּי יְרֵא אֱלֹהִים אַתָּה, *For now I know that you are a God-fearing man*" (*Genesis* 22:12). This explains why the [Patriarchs] were called עֲבָדִים, or "servants," as the verse says, זְכֹר לְאַבְרָהָם לְיִצְחָק וּלְיִשְׂרָאֵל

NOTES

the Torah to love Hashem, as the first *parashah* of the *Shema* states: וְאָהַבְתָּ אֵת ה׳ אֱלֹהֶיךָ, *and you shall love Hashem your God* (*Deuteronomy* 6:5). The *Sforno* cites the verse וְעַתָּה יִשְׂרָאֵל מָה ה׳ אֱלֹהֶיךָ שֹׁאֵל מֵעִמָּךְ כִּי אִם לְיִרְאָה אֶת ה׳ אֱלֹהֶיךָ, *Now, O Israel, what does Hashem, your God, ask of you? Only to fear Hashem, your God . . .* (ibid. 10:12), which teaches that God also requires us to fear Him.

Antigonus explains that there are two kinds of fear. One is the plain, visceral fear of punishment which deters a person from displeasing his Master. The second is on a much higher level. It is a sense of awe and reverence engendered by one's recognition of the superiority and greatness of Hashem. Antigonus urges us to develop the latter kind of יִרְאָה, *fear of God.*

The *Sforno* posits that the Patriarchs, beginning with Abraham at the *Akeidah,* as well as Isaac and Jacob, all possessed this superior level of יִרְאַת שָׁמַיִם, *fear of Heaven.*

[ד] **יוֹסֵי** בֶּן יוֹעֶזֶר אִישׁ צְרֵדָה וְיוֹסֵי בֶּן יוֹחָנָן אִישׁ יְרוּשָׁלַיִם קִבְּלוּ מֵהֶם. יוֹסֵי בֶּן יוֹעֶזֶר אִישׁ צְרֵדָה אוֹמֵר: יְהִי בֵיתְךָ בֵּית וַעַד לַחֲכָמִים, וֶהֱוֵי מִתְאַבֵּק בַּעֲפַר רַגְלֵיהֶם, וֶהֱוֵי שׁוֹתֶה בַצָּמָא אֶת דִּבְרֵיהֶם.

[ה] **יוֹסֵי** בֶּן יוֹחָנָן אִישׁ יְרוּשָׁלַיִם אוֹמֵר: יְהִי בֵיתְךָ פָּתוּחַ לָרְוָחָה, וְיִהְיוּ עֲנִיִּים בְּנֵי

פירוש לרבי עובדיה ספורנו

כי אמנם אותה היראה אשר היא יראת עונש או יראת הפסד שכר היא יראה גרועה מיוחדת לעבד איש מקנת כסף או שכיר:
א:ד. אמר שאלו השנים קבלו משמעון הצדיק ואחריו קבלו מאנטיגנוס. ובאמרו „יהי ביתך" רצונו תדירות ישיבתך, אמר אם כן יהי שבתך תדיר במקום אשר הוא בית ועד לחכמים, והוי מתאבק בעפר רגליהם אפילו חוץ מבתי

SFORNO'S COMMENTARY

עֲבָדֶיךָ, *Remember for the sake of Abraham, Isaac and Israel,* ***your servants*** (*Exodus* 32:13).

However the kind of יִרְאָה that stems from fear of punishment or loss of reward is a lowly יִרְאָה, characteristic of a bought slave or hired worker.

1:4

יוֹסֵי בֶּן יוֹעֶזֶר . . . וְיוֹסֵי בֶּן יוֹחָנָן . . . קִבְּלוּ מֵהֶם . . . — *Yose ben Yoezer . . . and Yose ben Yochanan . . . received the tradition from them . . ..* The [Mishnah] says that these two [sages, Yose ben Yoezer and Yose ben Yochanan,] received [their Torah] from Shimon the Righteous, and subsequently from Antigonus.

יְהִי בֵיתְךָ בֵּית וַעַד לַחֲכָמִים — *Let your residence be in the meeting place of sages.* The expression "let your residence be in" means "spend most of your time there." In other words, you should spend most of your time in a place that is a meeting place of scholars [i.e. in the *beis midrash* setting].

NOTES

1:4

יְהִי בֵיתְךָ בֵּית וַעַד לַחֲכָמִים — *Let your residence be in the meeting place of sages.* The *Sforno* digresses from the conventional interpretation of this Mishnah.

Rather than rendering the first clause "let *your house* be a meeting place for sages," he interprets it as, "let your residence be in the meeting place of sages" — i.e., in the House of Study. In other words, spend the majority of your time there, reminiscent of David's request, אַחַת שָׁאַלְתִּי מֵאֵת ה' אוֹתָהּ אֲבַקֵּשׁ; שִׁבְתִּי בְּבֵית ה' כָּל יְמֵי חַיַּי, *One thing I asked of Hashem that shall I seek: That I dwell in the House of Hashem all the days of my life* (*Psalms* 27:4).

וֶהֱוֵי מִתְאַבֵּק בַּעֲפַר רַגְלֵיהֶם — *Follow in the dust of their feet.* Rather than rendering the second clause "*sit* in the dust of their feet," meaning to listen to their teachings, he interprets it to mean that the devoted, sincere disciple should *follow* his teacher, and all scholars, wherever they may be found, so as to constantly be in their company.

1
4-5

4. *Yose ben Yoezer, leader of Tz'redah, and Yose ben Yochanan, leader of Jerusalem, received the tradition from them. Yose ben Yoezer, leader of Tz'redah, says: Let your residence be in the meeting place of sages; follow in the dust of their feet; and drink in their words thirstily.*

5. *Yose ben Yochanan, leader of Jerusalem, says: Let your house be open wide; let the poor be as*

פירוש לרבי עובדיה ספורנו

המדרש והועד, כענין אלישע, כאמרו ,,ויקם וילך אחרי אליהו״. והוי שותה בצמא את דבריהם אפילו שיחה שלהם, כאמרם ז״ל ,,שיחה שלתלמידי חכמים צריכה תלמוד״:

א:ה. פתוח לרוחה לצריכים הראוים לכך שיהנו די מחסורם בזולת שיצטרכו לשאול כדי שלא יתביישו. ויהיו עניים בני ביתך לשרתך בשכר ויתפרנסו בנקיות. ואל תרבה

SFORNO'S COMMENTARY

וֶהֱוֵי מִתְאַבֵּק בַּעֲפַר רַגְלֵיהֶם — *Follow in the dust of their feet.* The statement "follow in the dust of their feet" [is to be understood to mean that] even when you are away from the study halls and meeting places, [you should still pursue the wise men and associate with them,] similar to the practice of Elisha, of whom it is written, וַיָּקָם וַיֵּלֶךְ אַחֲרֵי אֵלִיָּהוּ, *And he arose and went after Elijah* (*I Kings* 19:21).

וֶהֱוֵי שׁוֹתֶה בַצָּמָא אֶת דִּבְרֵיהֶם — *And drink in their words thirstily.* The statement "drink in all their words thirstily" [teaches us to pay attention] even to their mundane conversation, as our Sages say, "The [mundane] conversation of Torah scholars is worthy of study" (*Succah* 21b).

1:5

יְהִי בֵיתְךָ פָּתוּחַ לָרְוָחָה — *Let your house be open wide.* "Let your house be open wide" for the needy who are worthy, that their needs might be met without them having to ask, in order that they not feel embarrassment.

וְיִהְיוּ עֲנִיִּים בְּנֵי בֵיתֶךָ — *Let the poor be as members of your household.* And "let the poor be as members of your household" — i.e., employ them, so that they might earn their livelihood honestly.

NOTES

וֶהֱוֵי שׁוֹתֶה בַצָּמָא אֶת דִּבְרֵיהֶם — *And drink in their words thirstily.* And as for the statement "drink in their words thirstily," he interprets דִּבְרֵיהֶם, "their words," to mean not their formal words of Torah, but their informal, seemingly ordinary speech. It should not be treated lightly, for one can learn wisdom even from their דִּבְרֵי חוֹל, their mundane words, as the Talmud states in *Succah* 21b, which the *Sforno* cites in his commentary.

1:5

וְיִהְיוּ עֲנִיִּים בְּנֵי בֵיתֶךָ — *Let the poor be as members of your household.* The *Sforno* interprets the teaching "let the poor be as members of your household" to mean that

א ביתֶךָ, וְאַל תַּרְבֶּה שִׂיחָה עִם הָאִשָּׁה. בְּאִשְׁתּוֹ אָמְרוּ,
ו קַל וָחֹמֶר בְּאֵשֶׁת חֲבֵרוֹ. מִכַּאן אָמְרוּ חֲכָמִים: כָּל הַמַּרְבֶּה שִׂיחָה עִם הָאִשָּׁה – גּוֹרֵם רָעָה לְעַצְמוֹ, וּבוֹטֵל מִדִּבְרֵי תוֹרָה, וְסוֹפוֹ יוֹרֵשׁ גֵּיהִנֹּם.

[ו] **יְהוֹשֻׁעַ** בֶּן פְּרַחְיָה וְנִתַּאי הָאַרְבֵּלִי קִבְּלוּ מֵהֶם. יְהוֹשֻׁעַ בֶּן פְּרַחְיָה אוֹמֵר: עֲשֵׂה לְךָ רַב,

פירוש לרבי עובדיה ספורנו

שיחה אפילו עם אשתך אף על פי שראוי לדבר עמה בעסקי הבית, כאמרם ז״ל „אתתך גוצא גחון ולחוש לה״, מכל מקום אל תרבה אותה השיחה. מכאן אמרו כיון שאין סבת ההמנע משיחת האשה מפני חשש ערוה שהרי הזהיר מזה גם באשתו אם כן היתה זאת האזהרה ממנה מפני איבוד הזמן שלא ירגיש האדם בו ובזה גורם רעה לעצמו בעסקי חיי שעה ובוטל מדברי תורה באבוד הזמן וטרדת הכח המחשבי שיפנה אחרי ההבל וסופו

SFORNO'S COMMENTARY

וְאַל תַּרְבֶּה שִׂיחָה עִם הָאִשָּׁה. בְּאִשְׁתּוֹ אָמְרוּ — *And do not converse excessively with a woman. They said this even about one's own wife.* [When the Tanna teaches us,] "do not converse excessively with a woman," even with one's own wife, [he means that] although it is proper to converse with her regarding household matters, as our Sages say, "If your wife is of short stature, bend over and whisper to her" (*Bava Metzia* 59a), nonetheless, do not overly indulge even in such conversation.

מִכַּאן אָמְרוּ חֲכָמִים: כָּל הַמַּרְבֶּה שִׂיחָה עִם הָאִשָּׁה – גּוֹרֵם רָעָה לְעַצְמוֹ, וּבוֹטֵל מִדִּבְרֵי תוֹרָה — *Consequently, the Sages said: Anyone who converses excessively with a woman causes evil to himself, neglects Torah study.* Now, since the reason for avoiding excessive conversation with a woman is not because of immodesty [or to deter immorality], since the Tanna cautions one to avoid this even with one's own wife, if so, the reason must be because of wasting time, which most people are not aware of. Through this [vice] a man "causes

NOTES

one should employ disadvantaged individuals in order to help them regain their dignity. This interpretation is similar to that of R' Ovadiah Bartenura in his commentary on this Mishnah.

וְאַל תַּרְבֶּה שִׂיחָה עִם הָאִשָּׁה — *And do not converse excessively with a woman.* Out of concern that the reader misinterpret Rabbi Yose's warning against conversing excessively with one's own wife as a denigration of women's intelligence and judgment, the *Sforno* reminds us that the Sages have always encouraged consulting with one's wife. Rabbi Yose's *only* concern was that excessive idle conversation robs one of precious time which could be used more productively.

גּוֹרֵם רָעָה לְעַצְמוֹ . . . וְסוֹפוֹ יוֹרֵשׁ גֵּיהִנֹּם — *Causes evil to himself . . . and will eventually inherit Gehinnom.* The Gemara cited by the *Sforno* (*Shabbos* 105) depicts the clever misleading ways of the יֵצֶר הָרָע, *the Evil Inclination.* The exact text reads, כָּךְ אֻמָּנוּתוֹ שֶׁל יֵצֶר הָרָע. הַיּוֹם אוֹמֵר לוֹ עֲשֵׂה כָּךְ וּלְמָחָר אוֹמֵר לוֹ עֲשֵׂה כָּךְ, עַד שֶׁאוֹמֵר לוֹ עֲבוֹד ע״ז וְהוֹלֵךְ וְעוֹבֵד, "*Such is the treacherous way of the Evil*

members of your household; and do not converse excessively with a woman. They said this even about one's own wife; surely it applies to another's wife. Consequently, the Sages said: Anyone who converses excessively with a woman causes evil to himself, neglects Torah study and will eventually inherit Gehinnom.

6. *Yehoshua ben Perachyah and Nittai of Arbel received the tradition from them. Yehoshua ben Perachyah says: Accept one teacher upon yourself;*

פירוש לרבי עובדיה ספורנו

יורש גהינם, שכך דרכו של יצר הרע להוציא מרעה אל רעה כאמרם ז״ל שכך דרכו של יצר הרע „שנאמר לא יהיה בך אל זר ולא תשתחוה לאל נכר איזהו אל זר שהוא בגופו של אדם הוי אומר זה יצר הרע״:

א:ו. עשה לך רב שתהיה כל קבלתך ממנו, וכבר גנו מי שלמד על הפך זה כאמרם ז״ל „יוסף ב״ר חייא מכולי עלמא גמר״.

SFORNO'S COMMENTARY

evil to himself" in his temporal endeavors, and "neglects Torah study" by wasting time and squandering his mental powers in the pursuit of vanity.

וְסוֹפוֹ יוֹרֵשׁ גֵּיהִנֹּם — *And will eventually inherit Gehinnom.* "[He] will eventually inherit Gehinnom," for this is the way of the Evil Inclination — to lead one from evil to evil, as our Sages said, "That is the way of the Evil Inclination. Commenting on the verse, לֹא יִהְיֶה בְךָ אֵל זָר, וְלֹא תִשְׁתַּחֲוֶה לְאֵל נֵכָר, *There shall be no strange gods among you* [בְךָ, lit. "within you"], *nor shall you worship any foreign deity* (*Psalms* 81:10), they explain, אֵיזֶהוּ אֵל זָר שֶׁהוּא בְּגוּפוֹ שֶׁל אָדָם, הֱוֵי אוֹמֵר זֶה יֵצֶר הָרָע, "*What strange god [resides] within man's body? This refers to the Evil Inclination*" (*Shabbos* 105b).

1:6

עֲשֵׂה לְךָ רַב — *Accept one teacher upon yourself.* "Accept one teacher upon yourself" so that all your tradition of Torah knowledge come from him. For [our Sages] have already criticized those who learned in the opposite

NOTES

Inclination: Today he says to one 'do this' and tomorrow 'do that,' until he eventually tells one 'worship idols,' and the man obeys." This statement of the Sages is based on the verse in *Psalms* 81:10, as quoted by the *Sforno.*

It is interesting to note that in his commentary on *Tehillim,* the *Sforno* interprets this verse differently. There, he writes that the "strange god in man" refers to the alienation and rejection of the Divine image in man, and not to the Evil Inclination. In truth, however, there is no contradiction between this interpretation and that of our Sages in Tractate *Shabbos.* Since nature abhors a vacuum, once the Divine image in man abandons him, the **יצר הרע** enters to take its place.

1:6

עֲשֵׂה לְךָ רַב — *Accept one teacher upon yourself.* Although we should be willing to learn from everyone (as the Sages say, "I

וּקְנֵה לְךָ חָבֵר, וֶהֱוֵי דָן אֶת כָּל הָאָדָם לְכַף זְכוּת. א

ז

[ז] **נִתַּאי** הָאַרְבֵּלִי אוֹמֵר: הַרְחֵק מִשָּׁכֵן רָע, וְאַל תִּתְחַבֵּר לָרָשָׁע, וְאַל תִּתְיָאֵשׁ מִן הַפֻּרְעָנוּת.

פירוש לרבי עובדיה ספורנו

וקנה לך חבר דומה לך וראוי להתחבר עמך, כאמרם „כל עוף למינו ישכון ובן אדם לדומה לו". והוי דן את כל האדם לכף זכות כי בזולת זאת המדה לא יתקיים שום ריעות, כי אמנם ברוב המאמרים יוכל השומע לדון המדבר לכף חובה ובזה יתבטל כל ריעות בלי ספק:

א:ז. הרחק, לא בלבד תמנע מהתחבר עם

SFORNO'S COMMENTARY

manner [and studied under a number of teachers], as the Talmud states: "Yosef son of Chiya received [learned Torah] from everyone [and therefore his testimony is unreliable]" (*Chullin* 18b).

וּקְנֵה לְךָ חָבֵר — *Acquire a friend similar to yourself.* "Acquire a friend [who is] similar to you", and hence, fitting to be your companion, as it is said, כָּל עוֹף לְמִינוֹ יִשְׁכּוֹן וּבֶן אָדָם לְדוֹמֶה לוֹ, "*Every bird flocks with his kind, and man with those who are of one mind*" (*Ben Sira,* cited in *Bava Kamma* 92b).

וֶהֱוֵי דָן אֶת כָּל הָאָדָם לְכַף זְכוּת — *And judge everyone favorably.* "Judge everyone favorably" because without this trait friendship will not endure. For in the majority of statements, the listener can judge a speaker in a negative light. And this [attitude] will unquestionably annul all friendship.

NOTES

gained knowledge from all my teachers, and most of all from my disciples"), nevertheless, when it comes to Torah direction and halachic decisions, it is important to have a single mentor and teacher whom we accept as a final legal authority (פּוֹסֵק). To prove this point, the *Sforno* cites *Chullin* 18b, which discusses a question regarding ritual slaughter (שְׁחִיטָה). There, Rabbi Zeira comments that a certain statement transmitted by Yosef bar R' Chiya is not authoritative, since he was known to accept Torah and halachic decisions from a number of sages.

In regards to this issue, the *Bartenura* differentiates between סְבָרָא, "reasoning," which we *should* accept from various authorities, and halachic decisions, which we should only accept from a single authority.

וּקְנֵה לְךָ חָבֵר, וֶהֱוֵי דָן אֶת כָּל הָאָדָם לְכַף זְכוּת — *Acquire a friend similar to yourself, and judge everyone favorably.* Regarding companionship, the *Sforno* advises one to make friends with "one's like," for there must be common interests and values if there is to be a common bond. He cites the Talmud in *Bava Kamma* 91, which speaks of the folk saying, "Like meets like." One proof brought by the Sages for this truism is the verse in Ben Sira 13, "Every bird flocks with his kind, and man, with those who are of one mind."

He also explains the link between R' Yehoshua ben Perachyah's statement "ac-

1 *acquire a friend similar to yourself, and judge everyone*
7 *favorably.*

7. *Nittai of Arbel says: Distance yourself from a bad neighbor; do not associate with a wicked person; and do not rule out the possibility of retribution.*

פירוש לרבי עובדיה ספורנו

אדם רע לבריות אבל הרחק גם כן משכונתו בהיותו מועד להזיק. ואל תתחבר לרשע בעל עבירות אף על פי שהיה חכם ובלתי מזיק לבריות. ואל תתיאש מללקות עם הרשע כענין יהושפט עם אחזיהו, כאמרו ,,בהתחברך את אחזיהו פרץ יי את מעשיך״:

SFORNO'S COMMENTARY

1:7

הַרְחֵק מִשָּׁכֵן רָע — *Distance yourself from a bad neighbor.* Not only should you desist from associating with a person who is wicked towards his fellow men, but you should also "distance yourself" from his vicinity, for he is מוּעָד לְהַזִּיק, *a confirmed menace,* [and he will surely harm you].

וְאַל תִּתְחַבֵּר לָרָשָׁע — *Do not associate with a wicked person*. I.e., with a sinner, even if he is a wise man, and does not harm his fellow men.

וְאַל תִּתְיָאֵשׁ מִן הַפֻּרְעָנוּת — *And do not rule out the possibility of retribution.* I.e., [do not rule out the possibility] that you will be punished along with the wicked one, as occurred with Jehoshaphat and Ahaziah, as the verse says, בְּהִתְחַבֶּרְךָ עִם אֲחַזְיָהוּ פָּרַץ ה׳ אֶת מַעֲשֶׂיךָ, *Because you joined yourself with Ahaziah, Hashem will destroy what you* [Jehoshaphat] *have done* (*II Chronicles* 20:37).

NOTES

quire a friend similar to yourself" and the next phrase, "judge everyone favorably." Unless one judges others favorably, he will find himself isolated and alone, for it will be difficult for him to find friends, even among people "of his own kind."

1:7

הַרְחֵק מִשָּׁכֵן רָע, וְאַל תִּתְחַבֵּר לָרָשָׁע, וְאַל תִּתְיָאֵשׁ מִן הַפֻּרְעָנוּת — *Distance yourself from a bad neighbor; do not associate with a wicked person; and do not rule out the possibility of retribution.* The first part of this Mishnah speaks of a שָׁכֵן רָע, *a bad neighbor,* and the second part, of a רָשָׁע, *a wicked companion.* On the basis of these different terms, the *Sforno* interprets the former admonition as urging one to distance oneself physically from evil (רָע) individuals, for one's own safety and security. As for the latter admonition, it warns against associating with a wicked person (רָשָׁע, as opposed to רָע), who does not represent a direct threat to one's physical well being, but rather endangers one's spiritual and moral values. Hence, even though he is a potential חָבֵר, *companion,* the Mishnah warns against developing a relationship with him (אַל תִּתְחַבֵּר, "Do not associate with a wicked person"). An alliance between a צַדִּיק (righteous person) and a רָשָׁע (wicked person) will eventually result in both sharing a common fate, as proven from the alliance forged between Jehoshaphat, the righteous king of Judah, and Achaziah, the wicked king of Israel.

[ח] **יְהוּדָה** בֶּן טַבַּאי וְשִׁמְעוֹן בֶּן שָׁטַח קִבְּלוּ מֵהֶם. יְהוּדָה בֶּן טַבַּאי אוֹמֵר: אַל תַּעַשׂ עַצְמְךָ כְּעוֹרְכֵי הַדַּיָּנִין; וּכְשֶׁיִּהְיוּ בַּעֲלֵי הַדִּין עוֹמְדִים לְפָנֶיךָ, יִהְיוּ בְעֵינֶיךָ כִּרְשָׁעִים; וּכְשֶׁנִּפְטָרִים מִלְּפָנֶיךָ, יִהְיוּ בְעֵינֶיךָ כְּזַכָּאִין, כְּשֶׁקִּבְּלוּ עֲלֵיהֶם אֶת הַדִּין.

[ט] **שִׁמְעוֹן** בֶּן שָׁטַח אוֹמֵר: הֱוֵי מַרְבֶּה לַחֲקוֹר אֶת הָעֵדִים; וֶהֱוֵי זָהִיר בִּדְבָרֶיךָ, שֶׁמָּא מִתּוֹכָם יִלְמְדוּ לְשַׁקֵּר.

פירוש לרבי עובדיה ספורנו

א:ח. אל תעש עצמך אפילו חוץ לבית דין כאותם שעורכים טענות ודינים של בעלי דין לדיינים ומלמדים טענות לבעלי הדין. יהיו בעיניך כרשעים, שלא תאמין לדברי שום אחד מהם אבל תחוש שאולי כל אחד מהם טוען שקר, ובזה לא תשא שמע שוא כלל. יהיו בעיניך כזכאים אפילו התברר לך שטענו שקר שניהם או אחד מהם לא יהיו

SFORNO'S COMMENTARY

1:8

אַל תַּעַשׂ עַצְמְךָ כְּעוֹרְכֵי הַדַּיָּנִין — *Do not act as a lawyer organizing the case for a party.* "Do not act [as a lawyer organizing the case for a party]" even outside the courtroom, as is the wont of those who arrange the claims and legal charges of litigants [before] the judges, and coach them to present their arguments.

וּכְשֶׁיִּהְיוּ בַּעֲלֵי הַדִּין עוֹמְדִים לְפָנֶיךָ, יִהְיוּ בְעֵינֶיךָ כִּרְשָׁעִים — *When the litigants stand before you, consider them both as untruthful.* I.e., [at the outset,] do not believe the words of any one of them. Rather, suspect that each of them is making a false claim. In this manner, [you shall not violate the prohibition] לֹא תִשָּׂא שֵׁמַע שָׁוְא, *Do not accept a false report* (*Exodus* 23:1) to any extent.

NOTES

1:8

וּכְשֶׁיִּהְיוּ בַּעֲלֵי הַדִּין עוֹמְדִים לְפָנֶיךָ, יִהְיוּ בְעֵינֶיךָ כִּרְשָׁעִים; וּכְשֶׁנִּפְטָרִים מִלְּפָנֶיךָ יִהְיוּ בְעֵינֶיךָ כְּזַכָּאִין — *When the litigants stand before you, consider them both as untruthful; but when they are dismissed from you, consider them both as honest.* The *Sforno* reconciles the seeming contradiction in Yehudah ben Tabbai's words — at first he advises judges to regard all litigants as untruthful, and then he bids them to regard them as meritorious. The *Sforno* explains that the reason why judges must initially treat both litigants with skepticism and suspicion is in order to avoid the Torah-ordained violation of לֹא תִשָּׂא שֵׁמַע שָׁוְא, *Do not accept a false report* (*Exodus* 23:1) — even if a person believes a deleterious claim against another person for a fleeting moment, he is regarded as having violated this commandment.

By the same token, even if the judges are *absolutely certain* that one of the litigants has lied, they should still judge him favorably (לְכַף זְכוּת) as long as he shows a

8. *Yehudah ben Tabbai and Shimon ben Shatach received the tradition from them. Yehudah ben Tabbai says: Do not act as a lawyer organizing the case for a party; when the litigants stand before you, consider them both as untruthful; but when they are dismissed from you, consider them both as honest, provided they have accepted the judgment.*

9. *Shimon ben Shatach says: Interrogate the witnesses extensively; and be cautious with your words, lest they learn to lie.*

פירוש לרבי עובדיה ספורנו

חשודים בעיניך לעבירות, שלפעמים יטעון האדם שקר לא לגזול את חבירו אבל לדחותו לאיזה זמן כאמרם ז״ל אשתמוטי קא משתמיט סבר עד דהוו לי זוזי ופרענא ליה: א:ט. אמר כל אלה להשמר ממה שקרה בענין בנו, שנהרג במצות בית דין על פי עדים

SFORNO'S COMMENTARY

וּכְשֶׁנִּפְטָרִים מִלְּפָנֶיךָ, יִהְיוּ בְעֵינֶיךָ כְּזַכָּאִין — *But when they are dismissed from you, consider them both as honest.* [Meaning, that] even if you have determined that one or both have made a false claim, do not suspect them of [committing other] transgressions, for at times a man will make a false statement, not with the intent of defrauding his fellow Jew, but simply to stall for time, as our Sages say, דְּאִשְׁתַּמּוּטֵי הוּא דְּקָא מִשְׁתַּמֵּיט לֵיהּ סָבַר עַד דְּהָווּ לִי זוּזֵי וּפָרַעְנָא לֵיהּ, *He is postponing and delaying; he thinks I will eventually have money and be able to repay him* (*Gittin* 51b).

1:9

הֱוֵי מַרְבֶּה לַחֲקוֹר אֶת הָעֵדִים; וֶהֱוֵי זָהִיר בִּדְבָרֶיךָ, שֶׁמָּא מִתּוֹכָם יִלְמְדוּ לְשַׁקֵּר — *Interrogate the witnesses extensively; and be cautious with your words, lest they learn to lie.* He addressed all these [cautionary statements to the judges] in order to prevent [a repetition of] the incident involving his own son, who was executed by order of the court on the basis of testimony that he had

NOTES

willingness to submit to the judgment of the court. For it is possible that he did not lie maliciously, but only to stall for time and delay his financial obligation. However, he had full intention of eventually fulfilling his responsibility.

1:9

הֱוֵי מַרְבֶּה לַחֲקוֹר אֶת הָעֵדִים; וֶהֱוֵי זָהִיר בִּדְבָרֶיךָ, שֶׁמָּא מִתּוֹכָם יִלְמְדוּ לְשַׁקֵּר — *Interrogate the witnesses extensively; and be cautious with your words, lest they learn to lie.* The Talmud (*Yerushalmi, Sanhedrin* 6:3) relates that Rabbi Shimon ben Shatach's son was falsely accused of murder by the relatives of a certain group of witches who had been put to death by Shimon ben Shatach. On the basis of this testimony, his son was sentenced to death by the court. Moments before the execution was to take place, one of the false witnesses recanted. Technically, however, the witness' retraction had no legal validity, and even though Rabbi Shimon wanted to stop the execution, his son

[י] **שְׁמַעְיָה** וְאַבְטַלְיוֹן קִבְּלוּ מֵהֶם. שְׁמַעְיָה אוֹמֵר: אֱהַב אֶת הַמְּלָאכָה, וּשְׂנָא אֶת הָרַבָּנוּת, וְאַל תִּתְוַדַּע לָרָשׁוּת.

[יא] **אַבְטַלְיוֹן** אוֹמֵר: חֲכָמִים, הִזָּהֲרוּ בְדִבְרֵיכֶם, שֶׁמָּא תָחוֹבוּ חוֹבַת גָּלוּת וְתִגְלוּ לִמְקוֹם מַיִם הָרָעִים, וְיִשְׁתּוּ הַתַּלְמִידִים הַבָּאִים אַחֲרֵיכֶם וְיָמוּתוּ, וְנִמְצָא שֵׁם שָׁמַיִם מִתְחַלֵּל.

פירוש לרבי עובדיה ספורנו

שהעידו בפניהם שהרג את הנפש והעדים עצמן הכחישו את עצמן בסוף:
א:י. אהוב את המלאכה כדי לעסוק בתורה, כענין הלל תלמידו שקרה לו שעשה כן והצליח. ושנא את הרבנות וכו׳ שמזה ימשך הסתלק האדם מחיי עולם לחיי שעה כמו שקרה למנחם תלמידו שיצא לעבודת המלך:

SFORNO'S COMMENTARY

committed murder. The witnesses themselves ultimately contradicted each other and were proven to be unreliable [see *Talmud Yerushalmi, Sanhedrin* 6:3].

1:10

אֱהַב אֶת הַמְּלָאכָה — *Love work.* "Love work" so that you will [have the wherewithal] to study Torah, as with Hillel, his student, who did so and was successful [see *Yoma* 35b].

וּשְׂנָא אֶת הָרַבָּנוּת, וְאַל תִּתְוַדַּע לָרָשׁוּת — *Despise lordliness; and do not become overly familiar with the government.* "Despise lordliness," since it may cause one to forsake "eternal life" for "transitory life," as happened to Menachem, his student, [who left his position as *Av Beis Din*] and went to serve the king [see *Chagigah* 16b].

NOTES

would not permit it. Rabbi Shimon's son felt that making an exception in his case would set a dangerous precedent, for according to the law, only two witnesses may effect a legal decision, a principle that Rabbi Shimon had always championed.

Now, had the court initially examined the witnesses properly, they would have never issued the sentence against Rabbi Shimon's son. For this compelling reason he strongly exhorts the judges to carefully interrogate the witnesses, and to be extremely cautious in their cross-examination, in order to prevent a similar miscarriage of justice.

1:10

אֱהַב אֶת הַמְּלָאכָה, וּשְׂנָא אֶת הָרַבָּנוּת, וְאַל תִּתְוַדַּע לָרָשׁוּת — *Love work; despise lordliness; and do not become overly familiar with the government.* The *Sforno* regards Hillel — a disciple of Shemayah and Avtalyon — as a perfect example of someone who applied the principle אֱהַב אֶת הַמְּלָאכָה, "Love work." He would labor each day to earn a half *dinar.* With half of this sum he would support his family, and with the other half, he would pay the admission fee to the *beis midrash.*

In contrast, Menachem, a colleague of Hillel who served as the *Av Beis Din* (head of the Rabbinical Court), personifies the nega-

10. *Shemayah and Avtalyon received the tradition from them. Shemayah says: Love work; despise lordliness; and do not become overly familiar with the government.*

11. *Avtalyon says: Scholars, be cautious with your words, for you may incur the penalty of exile and be banished to a place of evil waters [heresy]. The disciples who follow you there may drink and die, and consequently the Name of Heaven will be desecrated.*

פירוש לרבי עובדיה ספורנו

א:יא. הזהיר על זה משרבו המינים המפרשים דברי התורה ודברי חכמים וחידותם כפי דיעותם הרעות ובאמרו חובת גלות רצונו הגלות מעיר לעיר, ואמר יקרה שתגלו לעיר מושב המינים שיפרשו דבריכם גם כן כפי דיעותם הנפסדות, וישתו התלמידים שיחשבו שזה דעתכם אלא שאינכם רוצים לפרסמו, ונמצא שם

SFORNO'S COMMENTARY

1:11

חֲכָמִים, הִזָּהֲרוּ בְדִבְרֵיכֶם — *Scholars, be cautious with your words.* He cautioned [the wise to be careful with their words] when the heretics grew in number and they misinterpreted the words of the Torah and the Sages, and their esoteric teachings, according to their own corrupt beliefs.

שֶׁמָּא תָחוּבוּ חוֹבַת גָּלוּת וְתִגְלוּ לִמְקוֹם מַיִם הָרָעִים — *For your may incur the penalty of exile and be banished to a place of evil waters [heresy].* When he speaks of "the penalty of exile," he means being exiled from town to town. [In essence] he says, "You may be exiled to a city of heretics, who will also interpret your words according to their distorted ideology."

וְיִשְׁתּוּ הַתַּלְמִידִים הַבָּאִים אַחֲרֵיכֶם וְיָמוּתוּ — *The disciples who follow you there may drink and die.* For they will erroneously conclude that you embrace [this distorted ideology], but that you have chosen not to express your opinion publicly.

NOTES

tive consequences of embracing the trait of "lordliness" — he abandoned his office to accept a position in the king's court. This decision on his part greatly displeased his teachers, and thus, they urged their students not to emulate him. Nevertheless, the Talmud tells us in *Chagigah* 16b that eighty pairs of students ultimately did follow Menachem's example.

1:11

חֲכָמִים, הִזָּהֲרוּ בְדִבְרֵיכֶם, שֶׁמָּא תָחוּבוּ חוֹבַת גָּלוּת וְתִגְלוּ לִמְקוֹם מַיִם הָרָעִים — *Scholars, be cautious with your words, for you may incur the penalty of exile and be banished to a place of evil waters [heresy].* Avtalyon admonished scholars to be extremely careful in their teachings because he noticed a sharp increase in the number of heretics emerging from among the disciples of the wise. These students misquoted their righteous teachers and mislead their fellow students by claiming that their own heretical teachings represented those of their mentors.

If the masters would be present, they

[יב] **הִלֵּל** וְשַׁמַּאי קִבְּלוּ מֵהֶם. הִלֵּל אוֹמֵר: הֱוֵי מִתַּלְמִידָיו שֶׁל אַהֲרֹן, אוֹהֵב שָׁלוֹם וְרוֹדֵף שָׁלוֹם, אוֹהֵב אֶת הַבְּרִיּוֹת וּמְקָרְבָן לַתּוֹרָה.

[יג] **הוּא** הָיָה אוֹמֵר: נְגִיד שְׁמָא אֲבַד שְׁמֵהּ, וּדְלָא מוֹסִיף יָסֵף, וּדְלָא יַלִּיף קְטָלָא

פירוש לרבי עובדיה ספורנו

שמים מתחלל על ידכם, שיחשבו גם ההמון שאותו הדעת הנפסד הוא דעתכם:

א:יב. שלא תהיה קפדן כשמאי, כמו שספרו רבותינו זכרונם לברכה באותן גרים שנזדמנו למקום אחד ואמרו קפדנותו של שמאי בקשה לטרדנו מן העולם ענותנותו של הלל קרבתנו תחת כנפי השכינה:

א:יג. נגד שמא המשתדל למשוך שמו בעולם להשיג כבוד — אבד שמיה, שהכבוד בורח ממנו, כאמרו „עינים רמות

SFORNO'S COMMENTARY

וְנִמְצָא שֵׁם שָׁמַיִם מִתְחַלֵּל — *And consequently the Name of Heaven will be desecrated.* Through you, for the masses will conclude that this distorted opinion is yours [and inadvertently, you will be the cause of this חִלּוּל הַשֵּׁם, *desecration of God's Name*].

1:12

הִלֵּל אוֹמֵר: הֱוֵי מִתַּלְמִידָיו שֶׁל אַהֲרֹן, אוֹהֵב שָׁלוֹם וְרוֹדֵף שָׁלוֹם, אוֹהֵב אֶת הַבְּרִיּוֹת וּמְקָרְבָן לַתּוֹרָה — *Hillel says: Be among the disciples of Aaron, loving peace and pursuing peace, loving people, and bringing them closer to the Torah.*

Do not be as impatient and as strict as Shammai. As our Sages of blessed memory recount, three proselytes met in one place and said, "The harshness of Shammai threatened to remove us from the [eternal] world, while the humility of Hillel brought us under the [sheltering] wings of the Divine Presence" (see *Shabbos* 31a).

1:13

נְגִיד שְׁמָא אֲבַד שְׁמֵהּ — *He who seeks to make known his name loses his reputation.* "He who seeks to make known his name" in the world in order to attain

NOTES

would be able to refute these distortions, but if they would be sent into exile, they would be totally unaware of the degree to which their words were being misinterpreted, and thus, they would be incapable of rectifying the situation. Hence, Avtalyon warns his disciples to teach their own disciples with great caution.

1:12

הִלֵּל אוֹמֵר . . . אוֹהֵב אֶת הַבְּרִיּוֹת, וּמְקָרְבָן לַתּוֹרָה — *Hillel says . . . loving people, and bringing them closer to Torah.* In *Shabbos* 31a, the Sages recount three different episodes of heathens who came to the Sages expressing a desire to convert to Judaism. However, each one attached a condition to his conversion:

The first heathen expressed a desire to convert on condition that he be permitted to accept only the Written Law, but not the Oral Law. The second, that he be taught the whole Torah "while standing on one foot," and the third, that he be appointed High Priest.

12. *Hillel and Shammai received the tradition from them. Hillel says: Be among the disciples of Aaron, loving peace and pursuing peace, loving people, and bringing them closer to the Torah.*

13. *He used to say: He who seeks to make known his name loses his reputation; he who does not increase [his hours of Torah learning] decreases [his life]; he who refuses to teach [Torah knowledge]*

פירוש לרבי עובדיה ספורנו

תשפיל״. ודלא מוסיף יסוף, תני רב יוסף „דלא מוסיף אורין תקבריניה אמיה״, כי אמנם כשלא ישתדל האדם להוסיף דעת אינו ראוי לחיי שעה שאין ענינם אלא לחיי עולם, כאמרם ז״ל „העולם הזה דומה לפרוזדור בפני העולם הבא״.

SFORNO'S COMMENTARY

honor "loses his reputation," for honor shall flee from him, as it is written, וְעֵינַיִם רָמוֹת תַּשְׁפִּיל, *haughty eyes You bring down* (*Psalms* 18:28).

וּדְלָא מוֹסִיף יָסֵף — *He who does not increase [his hours of Torah learning] decreases [his life].* [In reference to the teaching,] "He who does not increase [his hours of Torah learning] decreases [his life]," [the Sages say,] "R' Yosef taught: 'He who does not increase his hours of Torah study, his mother shall bury him" (*Taanis* 31a; *Bava Basra* 121b). For if one does not apply himself to increase his knowledge, he is not deserving of transitory life, since its only purpose is [to enable one to prepare] for eternal life. As the Sages say, הָעוֹלָם הַזֶּה דּוֹמֶה לִפְרוֹזְדוֹר בִּפְנֵי הָעוֹלָם הַבָּא, *This world is but an antechamber to the World to Come* (below 4:21).

NOTES

When each of these individuals came before Shammai, he understandably rebuffed them. Hillel, on the other hand, addressed them cordially, and gently persuaded each one that his condition could not be met without compromising the integrity of Torah law. In this manner, he convinced all three individuals to accept conversion unconditionally.

The *Sforno* cites this Gemara as an example of Hillel practicing what he taught in this Mishnah — to love people and thereby bring them close to Torah.

1:13

נְגִיד שְׁמָא אֲבַד שְׁמֵהּ, וּדְלָא מוֹסִיף יָסֵף — *He who seeks to make known his name loses his reputation; he who does not increase [his hours of Torah learning] decreases [his life].* In his commentary on this Mishnah, *the Sforno* paraphrases two Talmudic sayings, one from *Eruvin* 13b, and the other from *Taanis* 31a. The former, relating to a person's pursuit of fame, is based on the aphorism, כָּל הַמְחַזֵּר עַל הַגְּדוּלָּה גְּדוּלָּה בּוֹרַחַת מִמֶּנּוּ, "*whoever pursues greatness, greatness will flee from him.*" As for the latter, it is based on a statement regarding one's failure to pursue growth through constant Torah study: וּדְלָא מוֹסִיף יֶאֱסֵף — מַאי יֶאֱסֵף? אָמַר רַב יוֹסֵף תִּקְבְּרֵיהּ אִימֵּיהּ, "[The Mishnah says,] *'He who does not increase decreases it.' What does '[he] decreases it' mean? R' Yosef said, '[It means,] "Let his mother bury him!" [i.e., he will die prematurely at a young age.]'* "

חַיָּב, וּדְאִשְׁתַּמַּשׁ בְּתָגָא חֳלָף.

[יד] **הוּא** הָיָה אוֹמֵר: אִם אֵין אֲנִי לִי, מִי לִי? וּכְשֶׁאֲנִי לְעַצְמִי, מָה אֲנִי? וְאִם לֹא עַכְשָׁו, אֵימָתָי?

פירוש לרבי עובדיה ספורנו

ודלא יליף, ומי שאינו מלמד דעת את העם, בהיותו מונע בר – קטלא חייב, כאמרו „מונע בר יקבוהו לאום״. ודאשתמש בתגא, שיהיה תכליתו בתורה להשיג בה כבוד ותועלת בחיי שעה – חלף, ראוי למות כמחלל את הקדש ומשתמש בו בדברי חול, כאמרו „ומתו בו כי יחללוהו״. אבל יהיה התועלת הנמשך ממנה בחיי שעה מכוון שיוכל להשתדל בהשגת חיי עולם, כענין „לתת מנת הכהנים והלוים למען יחזקו בתורת יי״:

א:יד. מי לי, שלא יוכל אדם לקנות חלק

SFORNO'S COMMENTARY

וּדְלָא יַלִּיף קְטָלָא חַיָּב — *He who refuses to teach [Torah Knowledge] deserves death.* "He who refuses to teach" — he who refrains from teaching knowledge to the people, by withholding the "grain" [i.e. knowledge], "deserves death," as it is written, מֹנֵעַ בָּר יִקְּבֻהוּ לְאוֹם, *He who withholds grain, the nation shall curse him* (*Proverbs* 11:26; see *Sanhedrin* 91b).

וּדְאִשְׁתַּמַּשׁ בְּתָגָא חֳלָף — *And he who exploits the crown of Torah for self-aggrandizement shall fade away.* "He who exploits the crown of Torah," whose purpose in studying Torah is to attain honor and fulfillment in this transitory life, "shall fade away" — i.e., is worthy of death, as one who has desecrated the holy and used it for a profane purpose, as it is written, וּמֵתוּ בוֹ כִּי יְחַלְּלֻהוּ, [They shall protect My charge and not bear a sin thereby] *and die because of it, for they will have desecrated it* (*Leviticus* 22:9).

Rather, the benefits of [Torah study] which manifest themselves in this temporal world should be directed towards enabling one to make efforts to attain eternal life, as we find [in the verse], לָתֵת מְנָת הַכֹּהֲנִים וְהַלְוִיִּם לְמַעַן יֶחֶזְקוּ בְּתוֹרַת ה׳, [He ordered the people, the inhabitants of Jerusalem,] *to give a*

NOTES

וּדְאִשְׁתַּמַּשׁ בְּתָגָא חֳלָף — *And he who exploits the crown of Torah for self-aggrandizement shall fade away.* The concluding admonition of Hillel in this Mishnah against "exploiting the crown of Torah" is explained by the *Sforno* as an extension of מְעִילָה, or making mundane use of possessions which have been consecrated for holy use: Just as the *Kohanim* and Levites may not abuse the gifts and tithes that were granted to them to enable them to serve Hashem and teach Torah to the people, so too, a Torah scholar may not abuse the God-given sustenance that is honorably granted to him in this world by those who support Torah. Since these privileges are given to him for the express purpose of enabling him to delve into Torah study, if he accepts the honor given to him but is lax in this duty and does not fulfill his responsibility to the people, then he is also guilty of מְעִילָה.

This commentary of the *Sforno* echoes the teachings of the Sages in *Nedarim* 62a: "R' Yochanan said: 'Whoever puts the crown of Torah to profane use is uprooted from the world.' " R' Yochanan derived this principle

deserves death; and he who exploits the crown of Torah for self-aggrandizement shall fade away.

14. *He used to say: If I am not for myself, who will be for me? And if I am for myself, what am I? And if not now, when?*

פירוש לרבי עובדיה ספורנו

בחיי עולם על ידי שליח כמו שיקרה בקנינים המדומים שיקנה האדם אותם לפעמים על יד משרתיו, לפיכך יפה אמרתי דלא מוסיף יסוף. וכשאני לעצמי, משתדל להשלים עצמי בלבד ולא אשתדל ללמד לאחרים להשלים כוונת האל יתברך ברב עם – מה אני חשוב שישלם בי לבדי רצון קוני, ולכן יפה אמרתי דלא יליף קטלא חייב, כיון שלא חשש להגדיל כבוד קונו במה שבידו לעשות, כמו שקרה בענין מי מריבה,

SFORNO'S COMMENTARY

portion to the Kohanim and Levites in order that they may grow strong in the Torah of Hashem" (*II Chronicles* 31:4).

1:14

אִם אֵין אֲנִי לִי, מִי לִי — *If I am not for myself, who will be for me?* "[If I am not for myself,] who will be for me?" A man cannot acquire a portion in the World to Come through an envoy, unlike material things, which one can at times acquire through one's servants. Therefore, I have correctly said, "He who does not increase [his hours of Torah learning] decreases [his life]" (*Mishnah* 13).

וּכְשֶׁאֲנִי לְעַצְמִי, מָה אֲנִי — *And if I am for myself, what am I?* "And if I am for myself" — i.e., if I make an effort only to perfect myself, but do not try to teach others to fulfill the intent of Hashem among the multitudes — then, "what am I?" Of what importance am I that the will of my Creator be fulfilled by me alone? Hence, I have correctly said, "He who refuses to teach [Torah knowledge] deserves death" (ibid.), for [such an individual] is not concerned to increase the honor of his Creator to the best of his ability. Indeed, this was the sin at Meribah, as the verse says, "[Because you trespassed against Me among the Children of Israel at the waters of Meribath-kadesh, in the

NOTES

from the episode of Belshazzar, who used the holy vessels of the Temple and was consequently uprooted from the world, even though they had already been used once before for profane reasons, and had thus "lost their sanctity." Based on this episode, the Talmud draws the following conclusion: "How much more [severe is the punishment of] he who makes profane use of the crown of Torah!"

1:14

אִם אֵין אֲנִי לִי, מִי לִי? וּכְשֶׁאֲנִי לְעַצְמִי, מָה אֲנִי? — *If I am not for myself, who will be for me? And if I am for myself, what am I?* Masterfully, the *Sforno* links the first part of this Mishnah to the previous Mishnah. The rhetorical question, "If I am not for myself, who will be for me?" ties in with the previous Mishnah's teaching, "he who does not increase [his Torah learning] decreases it." Similarly, the

[טו] **שַׁמַּאי** אוֹמֵר: עֲשֵׂה תוֹרָתְךָ קֶבַע, אֱמֹר מְעַט וַעֲשֵׂה הַרְבֵּה, וֶהֱוֵי מְקַבֵּל אֶת כָּל הָאָדָם בְּסֵבֶר פָּנִים יָפוֹת.

[טז] **רַבָּן גַּמְלִיאֵל** הָיָה אוֹמֵר: עֲשֵׂה לְךָ רַב, וְהִסְתַּלֵּק מִן הַסָּפֵק,

פירוש לרבי עובדיה ספורנו

כאמרו „על אשר לא קדשתם אותי". ואין התנצלות למתרשל מהוסיף דעת או מללמד שיעשה זה בימים באים, כי אמנם זה הזמן האובד אין לו תשלומים לעולם בהיות החיים קצרים לרגל המלאכה, וזה הוא אמרו ואם לא עכשו אימתי:

א:טו. כבר ספרו ז"ל שיצא מנחם לעבודת המלך ויצאו עמו שמנים תלמידים לובשי סריקון של זהב ואז נכנס שמאי במקום מנחם. ובכן אמר, אף על פי שיצאת אתה

SFORNO'S COMMENTARY

wilderness of Zin;] עַל אֲשֶׁר לֹא קִדַּשְׁתֶּם אוֹתִי, *because you did not sanctify Me* [among the Children of Israel] (*Deuteronomy* 32:51).

וְאִם לֹא עַכְשָׁיו, אֵימָתָי — *And if not now, when?* And there is no excuse for an indolent person to refrain from increasing his [Torah] knowledge, or from teaching others, by claiming he will do it at some future time, for the time that he squanders cannot ever be replaced, being that life is short and never long enough to complete [God's] work. This is what is meant by "And if not now, when?"

1:15

שַׁמַּאי אוֹמֵר: עֲשֵׂה תוֹרָתְךָ קֶבַע, אֱמֹר מְעַט וַעֲשֵׂה הַרְבֵּה, וֶהֱוֵי מְקַבֵּל אֶת כָּל הָאָדָם בְּסֵבֶר פָּנִים יָפוֹת — *Shammai says: Make your Torah study a fixed practice; promise little and do much; receive everyone with a cheerful face.* Our Sages told us (as mentioned above in the commentary to Mishnah 10) that Menachem left [his position as *Av Beis Din*] to enter into the service of the king, and that he was joined by eighty pairs of scholars "who wore the golden garments." Then, Shammai replaced Menachem.

Therefore, [Shammai in effect said to him:]

"Menachem, although you have left to enter into the service of the king,

NOTES

question "and if I am for myself, what am I?" merges with the teaching of the previous Mishnah, "he who refuses to teach [Torah knowledge] deserves death."

1:15

עֲשֵׂה תוֹרָתְךָ קֶבַע, אֱמֹר מְעַט וַעֲשֵׂה הַרְבֵּה, וֶהֱוֵי מְקַבֵּל אֶת כָּל הָאָדָם בְּסֵבֶר פָּנִים יָפוֹת — *Make your Torah study a fixed practice; promise little and do much; receive everyone with a cheerful face.* According to the *Sforno,* Shammai's words are directed not to the scholars and students in general, but specifically to his predecessor, Menachem, who served as *Av Beis Din,* as mentioned in Mishnah 10. Shammai, who succeeded him, was concerned lest his colleague, who left the world of Torah study and law to join

15. *Shammai says: Make your Torah study a fixed practice; promise little and do much; receive everyone with a cheerful face.*

16. *Rabban Gamliel used to say: Accept a teacher upon yourself and remove yourself from uncertainty;*

פירוש לרבי עובדיה ספורנו

מנחם לעבודת המלך ראוי לך לקבוע עתים לתורה, ובהנהגת שררתך בבית המלך אין ראוי לך להתנהג כשאר בני הרשות שאומרים הרבה ועושים מעט, כאמרם ז״ל „נראין כאוהבים בשעת הנייתן ואין עומדים לו לאדם בשעת דחקו״, אבל אתה בעל תורה ראוי לך שתעשה הפך זה אבל תאמר מעט ותעשה הרבה, ושתקבל את האדם בסבר פנים יפות לא בגאוה ובוז כמנהג בני הרשות:

א:טז. אף על פי שאמרו הרוצה לעשות כדברי בית שמאי עושה כדברי בית הלל עושה מפני שאלו ואלו דברי אלקים חיים מכל מקום ראוי לך שתעשה לך איזה רב

SFORNO'S COMMENTARY

you should designate fixed times for Torah study. And when you exercise authority in the house of the king, do not conduct yourself in the manner of the other men of power, who promise much and do little, as our Sages say: 'They act friendly when it benefits them, but they do no stand by someone in his time of need' (below, 2:3). Instead, you, who are a Torah scholar, should do the opposite — 'promise little and do much.' Also, 'receive everyone with a cheerful face,' not with pride and contempt, as is the wont of those in power."

1:16

רַבָּן גַּמְלִיאֵל הָיָה אוֹמֵר: עֲשֵׂה לְךָ רַב, וְהִסְתַּלֵּק מִן הַסָּפֵק — *Rabban Gamliel used to say: Accept a teacher upon yourself and remove yourself from uncertainty.* Even though the Talmud states, הָרוֹצֶה לַעֲשׂוֹת כְּדִבְרֵי בֵית שַׁמַּאי עוֹשֶׂה, כְּדִבְרֵי בֵית הִלֵּל עוֹשֶׂה, מִפְּנֵי שֶׁאֵלוּ וְאֵלוּ דִּבְרֵי אֱלֹקִים חַיִּים "*Whoever wants to follow the decision of Beis Shammai may do so, and whoever wishes to follow that of Beis Hillel may do so, for both are the words of the living God,*" nonetheless, it is fitting for you to choose one particular teacher whose decisions and

NOTES

the ranks of government, would neglect his own Torah study. Thus, he urged him to designate fixed times for Torah study. Shammai was also concerned that the surroundings and trappings of the king's court would have a detrimental effect on Menachem's moral and ethical character, so he urged him to have empathy for those who would seek him out, and to be honest and courteous to them. Hence he said, "Promise little and do much," and "receive everyone with a cheerful face," unlike the behavior of the average government official in his dealings with the people.

1:16

עֲשֵׂה לְךָ רַב, וְהִסְתַּלֵּק מִן הַסָּפֵק — *Accept a teacher upon yourself and remove yourself from uncertainty.* At first glance, the advice of Rabban Gamliel to "accept a teacher" seems repetitious, since Yehoshua ben Perachyah already advised to do this in Mishnah 6. The *Bartenura* explains that our Mishnah refers to choosing a single hala-

א

וְאַל תַּרְבֶּה לְעַשֵּׂר אֻמָּדוֹת.

יז

[יז] **שִׁמְעוֹן** בְּנוֹ אוֹמֵר: כָּל יָמַי גָּדַלְתִּי בֵּין הַחֲכָמִים, וְלֹא מָצָאתִי לְגוּף טוֹב אֶלָּא שְׁתִיקָה. וְלֹא הַמִּדְרָשׁ הוּא הָעִקָּר, אֶלָּא הַמַּעֲשֶׂה. וְכָל הַמַּרְבֶּה דְבָרִים מֵבִיא חֵטְא.

פירוש לרבי עובדיה ספורנו

מיוחד שתעשה לעולם כפי דעתו ותורה כפי הוראתו, ובזה תסתלק מן הספק של מחלקת באופן שלא יטה לבך לעשות לפעמים כדברי זה, ופעמים כדברי זה שעל כמו זה אמרו ז״ל „עליו הכתוב אומר הכסיל בחשך הולך״. ואל תרבה לעשר אומדות, אף על פי שאמרו מדד ואחר כך ברך הרי זו תפלת שוא שאין הברכה מצויה בדבר המדוד, ובשביל זה אולי יעלה על לבבך לעשר באומד ובמחשבה כענין בתרומה – אל תרבה לעשות זה, שמא תטעה ותאכל טבל ויצא שכרך בהפסדך:

SFORNO'S COMMENTARY

rulings you will always follow. In this manner, you will "remove yourself from the uncertainty" of [*halachic*] disagreements, so that you will not sometimes follow the decision of one authority, and at other times, follow the decision of the other, for in regards to such an individual the Sages (*Eruvin* 13b) said, "Regarding him the verse says, וְהַכְּסִיל בַּחֹשֶׁךְ הוֹלֵךְ, *A fool walks in darkness*" (*Ecclesiastes* 2:14).

וְאַל תַּרְבֶּה לְעַשֵּׂר אֻמָּדוֹת — *And do not make a habit of taking tithes by estimating [instead of measuring].* Even though the Sages said, "If one measures his produce and then invokes God's blessing, it is a prayer in vain, for blessing is never found in that which has been measured" (*Taanis* 8b), which might lead one to conclude that [it is *preferable*] to tithe by estimating and assessing, as with *terumah,* [the Mishnah nevertheless warns,] "Do not make a habit" of this, lest you estimate incorrectly and eat untithed produce (טֶבֶל), and lose more than you gained.

NOTES

chic authority from whom to receive פְּסַק הֲלָכָה (practical legal rulings), while the earlier Mishnah urges one to choose a single person from whom to learn Torah.

The *Sforno,* however, links this Mishnah with the preceding ones which cite the words of Hillel and Shammai. Therefore, he interprets the advice of Rabban Gamliel as referring to the historic halachic division between these two major schools of thought. The Mishnah teaches that although the opinions of both the schools of Hillel and Shammai are well-founded and authoritative, one may not choose to follow the rulings of one school of thought for certain issues, and the rulings of the other for different issues. Rather, one must accept one or the other school of thought *fully,* and regard it as the ultimate authority regarding all areas of Torah law.

וְאַל תַּרְבֶּה לְעַשֵּׂר אֻמָּדוֹת — *And do not make a habit of taking tithes by estimating [instead of measuring].* The *Sforno* explains Rabban Gamliel's warning against estimating the amount of tithes to take from one's crops, which seemingly is a contradiction of the rabbinic dictums, עַשֵּׂר בִּשְׁבִיל שֶׁתִּתְעַשֵּׁר, *Tithe* *and do not make a habit of taking tithes by estimating [instead of measuring].*

17. *Shimon his son says: All my days I have been raised among the Sages and I have found nothing better for oneself than silence; not study, but practice is the main thing; and one who talks excessively brings on sin.*

פירוש לרבי עובדיה ספורנו

א:יז. כי אמנם רבים חשבו שהכח הדברי באדם הוא הנכבד מכל כחתיו עד שאמרו קצתם שהאדם נכבד משאר בעלי חיים בכח הדברי, וכן האדם נכבד מחברו כפי מה שיגדל עליו בחכמת הדבור, הנה אמר זה החכם שהדבור עם כל מעלתו לא יועיל לגוף כלל, כמו שנראה בשאר בעלי חיים המאריכים ימים ומתפרנסים שלא בצער בלתי דבור כלל, אבל יהיה תועלת הדבור בעסקי השכל המעשי במדיניות ובענין

SFORNO'S COMMENTARY

1:17

שִׁמְעוֹן בְּנוֹ אוֹמֵר . . . וְלֹא מָצָאתִי לְגוּף טוֹב אֶלָּא שְׁתִיקָה. וְלֹא הַמִּדְרָשׁ הוּא הָעִקָּר, אֶלָּא הַמַּעֲשֶׂה. וְכָל הַמַּרְבֶּה דְּבָרִים מֵבִיא חֵטְא — *Shimon his son says . . . I have found nothing better for oneself than silence; not study, but practice is the main thing; and one who talks excessively brings on sin.*

Many are of the opinion that man's power of speech is his greatest attribute, to the point that some say that it is the gift of speech that makes him superior to all other living creatures. Therefore, the individual who speaks most eloquently is considered superior to his fellow man.

However, Shimon tells us that in spite of the importance of speech, it is of absolutely no benefit to the body. For we see that other living creatures live long and obtain a livelihood painlessly even though they completely lack the power of speech.

Rather, the true benefits of speech are in the arena of practical intellectual applications such as social administration, and in areas of analytical

NOTES

so that you may become wealthy (*Taanis* 9a) and אֵין הַבְּרָכָה מְצוּיָה אֶלָּא בַּדָּבָר הַסָּמוּי מִן הָעַיִן, *Blessing is to be found only in that which is hidden from the eye* (*Taanis* 8b) — A person may therefore conclude that it would be preferable to tithe by estimating, rather than by measuring, since according to the Sages, an exact count actually diminishes the blessing that will reside upon one's crops! Therefore, Rabban Gamliel teaches us that the laws of tithing demand that one measure the amount, since estimating may result in a serious infraction of *Halachah* and cause one to eat טֶבֶל, or untithed food.

1:17

שִׁמְעוֹן בְּנוֹ אוֹמֵר . . . וְלֹא מָצָאתִי לְגוּף טוֹב אֶלָּא שְׁתִיקָה. וְלֹא הַמִּדְרָשׁ הוּא הָעִקָּר, אֶלָּא הַמַּעֲשֶׂה — *Shimon his son says . . . I have found nothing better for oneself than silence; not study, but practice is the main thing.* *Onkelos* interprets the verse "And Hashem God formed the man of dust from the ground, and He blew into his nostrils the soul of life, and man became a living being

א
יח

[יח] **רַבָּן** שִׁמְעוֹן בֶּן גַּמְלִיאֵל אוֹמֵר: עַל שְׁלשָׁה דְבָרִים הָעוֹלָם קַיָּם – עַל הַדִּין וְעַל הָאֱמֶת וְעַל הַשָּׁלוֹם, שֶׁנֶּאֱמַר: „אֱמֶת וּמִשְׁפַּט שָׁלוֹם שִׁפְטוּ בְּשַׁעֲרֵיכֶם.״

פירוש לרבי עובדיה ספורנו

השכל העיוני ללמד לזולתו. ועם כל זה התועלת – לא המדרש והדבור הוא העקר והתכלית המכוון, אבל המכוון הוא המעשה הנמשך ממנו במדיניות או בלמוד המושכלות. וגם באלה ייטב מעוט הדבור והלמוד בדרך קצרה, שכל המרבה דברים מביא חטא, כי יפול בהם יותר ספק וטעות שכחה. ומכל זה יתחייב שהדבור אינו שלמות מצד עצמו כלל, אבל הוא בלי ספק כלי להשיג תכלית מכוון במדיניות ובמושכלות להודיע מחשבת הלב אל הזולת, וזה במיעוט הדבור כפי האפשר, הפך מה שיקרה בכל מה שהוא שלמות בעצמו שהוא אמנם כל מה שירבה יהיה יותר טוב:

SFORNO'S COMMENTARY

thought such as teaching others.

Nonetheless, in spite of the importance [of the gift of speech], it is not the expression and exposition of [man's thoughts] that is of paramount importance and [man's] ultimate goal and purpose, but the deeds which result from it as they affect society and the intellectual pursuit of knowledge. And even in these [noble endeavors], it is best to use words sparingly and be concise in one's studies, for "one who talks excessively brings on sin." For [excessive words] promote uncertainties and errors of forgetfulness.

From all this we see that speech (דִּבּוּר) is not at all inherently perfect (שָׁלֵם). Rather, it is merely an instrument for achieving a specific objective in social administration and intellectual pursuits — namely, to convey the thoughts of one man to another. And this is best accomplished through the greatest possible brevity. This is contrary to the nature of something that is inherently perfect, about which the general rule is "the more, the better."

NOTES

[וַיִּפַּח בְּאַפָּיו נִשְׁמַת חַיִּים וַיְהִי הָאָדָם לְנֶפֶשׁ חַיָּה] to mean, "*and He blew into his nostrils the soul of life, and it became in man* לְרוּחַ מְמַלְּלָא, *the spirit of speech*" — i.e., the gift of language which permits man to formulate his thoughts and communicate (*Genesis* 2:7).

Nevertheless, Rabbi Shimon cautions us to use this gift sparingly, for like many forces in nature, this power can be beneficial or harmful. The *Sforno* finds it necessary, therefore, to stress that even though silence is praised by the Tanna, measured and thoughtful speech is also praiseworthy, providing, of course, that one appreciates the fact that the ultimate goal of all speech — even of *divrei Torah* — is action and deed as regarding the performance of God's commandments.

1:18

רַבָּן שִׁמְעוֹן בֶּן גַּמְלִיאֵל אוֹמֵר: עַל שְׁלשָׁה דְבָרִים הָעוֹלָם קַיָּם – עַל הַדִּין וְעַל הָאֱמֶת וְעַל הַשָּׁלוֹם — *'Rabban Shimon ben Gamliel says: The world endures on three things — justice, truth, and peace.* In Mishnah 2, Shimon HaTzaddik tells us that "The world stands on three things — on Torah study, on the service [of God], and on kind deeds." In this *mishnah,* however, Shimon ben Gamliel

1
18

18. *Rabban Shimon ben Gamliel says: The world endures on three things — justice, truth, and peace, as it is said: "You shall adjudicate the verdict of truth and peace at your gates."*

פירוש לרבי עובדיה ספורנו

א:יח. אמר שעל אלה יתקיים המדיניות, על האמת, שיוכל האדם להשען על דברי חברו, על הפך אמרו ,,מרמה דבר, בפיו שלום את רעהו ידבר ובקרבו ישים ארבו״, ועל הדין ועל השלום, כי על שלש אלה הזהיר זכריה הנביא בייעודו לטוב ישראל ולקיומם, כאמרו ,,דברו שלום איש את רעהו אמת ומשפט שלום שפטו בשעריכם״ כי אמנם שפטם אמת תהיה שורת הדין ובשפטם משפט שלום תהיה הפשרה, כאמרם ז״ל ,,איזהו משפט שיש עמו שלום הוי אומר זו פשרה״, ומזה התבאר כח השלום בקיום המדיניות, שגם בענין הדין אשר בנטייה ממנו יקרה עול בלי ספק מכל מקום תהיה הפשרה נאהבת מפני השלום:

SFORNO'S COMMENTARY

1:18

עַל שְׁלֹשָׁה דְבָרִים הָעוֹלָם קַיָּם — *The world endures on three things.* [Rabban Shimon ben Gamliel says] that the perpetuation of organized society is dependent on the following [traits]:

עַל הַדִּין וְעַל הָאֱמֶת וְעַל הַשָּׁלוֹם — *Justice, truth, and peace.* "Truth" — i.e., that a person may rely on the word of his fellow, as opposed to [the Prophet's] lament, מִרְמָה דִבֵּר בְּפִיו שָׁלוֹם אֶת רֵעֵהוּ יְדַבֵּר וּבְקִרְבּוֹ יָשִׂים אָרְבּוֹ [Their tongue] *speaks deceit; one speaks peaceably to his neighbor with his mouth, but in his heart he lies in wait for him* (*Jeremiah* 9:7).

And "justice. . .and peace" — For these are the three elements about which Zechariah the Prophet warned Israel in his mission to ensure their well-being and continuing existence. He stated, דַּבְּרוּ אֱמֶת אִישׁ אֶת רֵעֵהוּ אֱמֶת וּמִשְׁפַּט שָׁלוֹם שִׁפְטוּ בְּשַׁעֲרֵיכֶם, *Let every man speak truth to his neighbor; execute the judgment of truth and peace in your gates* (*Zechariah* 8:16). "The judgment of truth" refers to following the letter of the law, while "the judgment of peace" refers to reaching compromise, as our Sages say, אֵיזֶהוּ מִשְׁפָּט שֶׁיֵּשׁ עִמּוֹ שָׁלוֹם, הֱוֵי אוֹמֵר זוֹ פְּשָׁרָה, *What is judgment that carries with it peace? The answer is: Compromise* (*Sanhedrin* 6b).

From this [saying of the Sages] we may appreciate the power of peace in ensuring the stability of organized society. For even though deviating from judgment will undoubtedly result in injustice, nonetheless, compromise is to be cherished, for it fosters peace [among people].

NOTES

teaches us that the world depends on three things — on justice, on truth, and on peace. Many commentators address this apparent contradiction and give a variety of answers to reconcile these two Mishnahs.

The *Sforno,* however, sees no difficulty at all. The earlier Mishnah speaks of the special, particular "world of Israel," while this Mishnah discusses the world of universal man. The "world of Israel" exists only if the

רַבִּי חֲנַנְיָא בֶּן עֲקַשְׁיָא אוֹמֵר: רָצָה הַקָּדוֹשׁ בָּרוּךְ הוּא לְזַכּוֹת אֶת יִשְׂרָאֵל, לְפִיכָךְ הִרְבָּה לָהֶם תּוֹרָה וּמִצְוֹת, שֶׁנֶּאֱמַר: „יהוה חָפֵץ לְמַעַן צִדְקוֹ, יַגְדִּיל תּוֹרָה וְיַאְדִּיר.״

פירוש לרבי עובדיה ספורנו

אמר שכדי שיהיה לכל אחד מישראל איזה חלק לעולם הבא הרבה להם תורה ומצוות שבאחת מהם שיקיים לשמו יקנה בה איזה חלק לחיי עולם כאמרם ז״ל בביאור מה שנאמר „לכן הרחיבה שאול נפשה ופערה פיה לבלי חק״ למי שלא קיים אפילו חוק

SFORNO'S COMMENTARY

רָצָה הקב״ה לְזַכּוֹת אֶת יִשְׂרָאֵל . . . — *The Holy One, Blessed is He, wished to confer merit upon Israel . . .* The Tanna says that in order for each Israelite to have some portion in the World to Come, "He gave them Torah and *mitzvos* in abundance," for if one fulfills but one of them in God's Name, he will acquire some portion of eternal life. Our Sages say, explaining the verse, לָכֵן הִרְחִיבָה שְׁאוֹל נַפְשָׁהּ וּפָעֲרָה פִיהָ לִבְלִי חֹק, *Therefore Sheol has expanded her desire and spread wide her mouth without measure* (*Isaiah* 5:14), that this

NOTES

שְׁכִינָה dwells in its midst, which necessitates the presence of Torah, Godly service, and kind deeds. In contrast, the world at large — the society of man — needs justice, peace, and truth in order to continue existing.

רָצָה הקב״ה לְזַכּוֹת אֶת יִשְׂרָאֵל — *The Holy One, Blessed is He, wished to confer merit upon Israel . . .*

It is customary to recite this Mishnah at the conclusion of the study of *each* chapter of *Pirkei Avos*, when recited on Shabbos afternoons.

The *Sforno's* interpretation of this Mishnah is similar to that of the *Rambam*'s commentary, in his פֵּירוּשׁ הַמִּשְׁנָיוֹת on Tractate *Makkos*. The reason for the multiplicity of *mitzvos* is not to increase the burden of responsibility placed on the Jewish people. On the contrary, it is to give an opportunity to every Jew to earn a share in the World to Come, since among the multitude of *mitzvos*, there is bound to be one that a son or daughter of Israel will fulfill properly during the course of his or her lifetime!

This explanation, however, is only valid

Rabbi Chanania ben Akashia says: The Holy One, Blessed is He, wished to confer merit upon Israel; therefore He gave them Torah and mitzvos in abundance, as it is said: "HASHEM desired, for the sake of its [Israel's] righteousness, that the Torah be made great and glorious."

פירוש לרבי עובדיה ספורנו

אחד והביא ראיה על זה ממה שנאמר „יי חפץ למען צדקו יגדיל תורה ויאדיר" כלומר שכדי לצדק את ישראל חפץ להגדיל את התורה ולהרבות את המצוות למען יצדק כל אחד מהם באיזה חלק מהתורה והמצוות ויהיו כלם זוכים לחיי העולם הבא:

SFORNO'S COMMENTARY

refers to one who has not even observed one Torah law. He then brings proof to his thesis from the verse, ה׳ חָפֵץ לְמַעַן צִדְקוֹ יַגְדִּיל תּוֹרָה וְיַאְדִּיר, *Hashem desired, for the sake of [Israel's] righteousness, that the Torah be made great and glorious* (ibid. 42:21) — meaning, that in order to grant merit to Israel, He expanded Torah and gave abundant *mitzvos*, so that each Jew be capable of gaining merit by fulfilling some portion of Torah and *mitzvos*, and as a result, all will merit life in the World to Come.

NOTES

in accordance with Rabbi Yochanan, who interprets the verse in *Isaiah* (5:14), cited by the *Sforno*, to mean, *"Even if one learned (or fulfilled) no more than a single law, he will be spared the punishment of Sheol"* ["the underworld"] (*Sanhedrin* 111). Resh Lakish, however, disagrees and is of the opinion that the verse teaches us that "Whoever leaves even a single law unfulfilled," will descend into Sheol. The *Sforno*'s commentary is in accordance with Rabbi Yochanan. He stresses, however, that the performance of that one *mitzvah* must be done לִשְׁמָהּ, *for the sake of heaven,* and not perfunctorily, or for personal gain or honor.

By including the concept of עוֹלָם הַבָּא, "the World to Come," in his commentary, the *Sforno* links the concluding Mishnah in Tractate *Makkos*, read after each chapter, to the Mishnah in *Sanhedrin* 90a, which is recited as an introduction to each chapter of *Avos,* where we are taught that *"All Israel has a share in the World to Come."* That Mishnah reveals to us the reward in store for the Children of Israel. Our Mishnah explains how readily it can be attained.

פרק ב

Chapter Two

כָּל יִשְׂרָאֵל יֵשׁ לָהֶם חֵלֶק לָעוֹלָם הַבָּא, שֶׁנֶּאֱמַר: „וְעַמֵּךְ כֻּלָּם צַדִּיקִים, לְעוֹלָם יִירְשׁוּ אָרֶץ, נֵצֶר מַטָּעַי, מַעֲשֵׂה יָדַי לְהִתְפָּאֵר.״

All Israel has a share in the World to Come, as it is said: "And your people are all righteous; they shall inherit the land forever; they are the branch of My planting, My handiwork, in which to take pride."

ב א

[א] **רַבִּי** אוֹמֵר: אֵיזוֹ הִיא דֶרֶךְ יְשָׁרָה שֶׁיָּבֹר לוֹ הָאָדָם? כָּל שֶׁהִיא תִּפְאֶרֶת לְעֹשֶׂהָ וְתִפְאֶרֶת לוֹ מִן הָאָדָם. וֶהֱוֵי זָהִיר בְּמִצְוָה קַלָּה כְּבַחֲמוּרָה, שֶׁאֵין אַתָּה יוֹדֵעַ מַתַּן שְׂכָרָן שֶׁל מִצְוֹת. וֶהֱוֵי מְחַשֵּׁב הֶפְסֵד מִצְוָה כְּנֶגֶד שְׂכָרָהּ, וּשְׂכַר עֲבֵרָה כְּנֶגֶד הֶפְסֵדָהּ. הִסְתַּכֵּל בִּשְׁלֹשָׁה דְבָרִים, וְאֵין אַתָּה בָא לִידֵי עֲבֵרָה; דַּע מַה לְּמַעְלָה מִמְּךָ — עַיִן רוֹאָה, וְאֹזֶן שׁוֹמַעַת, וְכָל מַעֲשֶׂיךָ בְּסֵפֶר נִכְתָּבִים.

פירוש לרבי עובדיה ספורנו

ב:א. אמר שממיני ההשתדלות בחיי שעה יבור לו האדם מהאפשרים אצלו אותו המין שהוא תפארת למי שיתעסק בו ולא יבור לו השתדלות בזוי, כאמרם ז"ל „אשרי מי שאומנותו בשם אוי לו למי שאומנותו בורסי", ועם זה יבור לו איזה מין השתדלות שימצא עצמו מוכן להיות יותר שלם בו באופן שישיג בו תהלה ותפארת מן האדם כי בו יצליח יותר. הוי מחשב הפסד מצוה שתפסיד בעשייתה מעסקי חיי שעה שהוא דבר בעל תכלית בלי ספק כנגד שכרה לחיי עולם שהוא דבר בלתי בעל תכלית, וכן

SFORNO'S COMMENTARY

2:1

אֵיזוֹ הִיא דֶרֶךְ יְשָׁרָה שֶׁיָּבֹר לוֹ הָאָדָם? כָּל שֶׁהִיא תִּפְאֶרֶת לְעֹשֶׂהָ וְתִפְאֶרֶת לוֹ מִן הָאָדָם — *Which is the proper path that a man should choose for himself? That which brings glory to himself and earns him the esteem of fellow men.* The Tanna teaches that of all the numerous occupations which are available to a person in this transitory life, "a man should choose" — from among those which are within his reach — the type which "brings glory" to the one who pursues it. One should not, however, choose an occupation which is regarded with disdain. As our Sages say, "Happy is he who works as a perfumer, woe to he who works as a tanner" (*Kiddushin* 82b).

In addition, a person should choose an occupation in which he is capable of excelling and thereby earn the praise and "esteem of his fellow men," for he will have more success in this [line of work].

וֶהֱוֵי מְחַשֵּׁב הֶפְסֵד מִצְוָה כְּנֶגֶד שְׂכָרָהּ, וּשְׂכַר עֲבֵרָה כְּנֶגֶד הֶפְסֵדָהּ — *Calculate the loss of a mitzvah against its reward, and the reward of a sin against its cost.* "Calculate the loss of a *mitzvah.*" [That is, assess] the loss that a

NOTES

2:1

כָּל שֶׁהִיא תִּפְאֶרֶת לְעֹשֶׂהָ וְתִפְאֶרֶת לוֹ מִן הָאָדָם — *That which brings glory to himself and earns him the esteem of fellow men.* The *Sforno* interprets Rabbi's dictum, "That which brings glory to himself and earns him the esteem of fellow men," as establishing two criteria by which a person should choose his occupation: First, it should be an occupation that is dignified and satisfying, which gives one a sense of self-respect. Second, the individual should take pride

2
1

1. *Rabbi said: Which is the proper path that a man should choose for himself? That which brings glory to himself and earns him the esteem of fellow men. Be as scrupulous in performing a "minor" mitzvah as in a "major" one, for you do not know the reward given for the respective mitzvos. Calculate the loss of a mitzvah against its reward, and the reward of a sin against its cost. Consider three things and you will not come into the grip of sin: Know what is above you — a watchful Eye, an attentive Ear and all your deeds are recorded in a Book.*

פירוש לרבי עובדיה ספורנו

שכר עבירה והתועלת המושג בעשייתה בחיי שעה כנגד ההפסד הנמשך ממנה לחיי עולם, שאין ביניהם יחס ערך או הדמות בלי ספק בהיות זה נצחי וזה נפסד. דע מה למעלה ממך, דע פרשת גדלת המלך אשר תמרה את פיהו בהיותך עובר עבירה, וגם כן דע שעם כל גדלתו לא יחדל מהשגיח באלה השפלים כלל, אבל אמנם עין רואה וכולי, וגם כן דע שאין עונש העבירה בא לאלתר ולא יטעך האיחור כי אמנם כל מעשיך בספר נכתבים ולגמול ולענוש עליהם:

SFORNO'S COMMENTARY

mitzvah-performance will cause you in your temporal affairs — even though [such temporal concerns] undoubtedly serve a purpose — against the eternal reward you will gain by [performing] the *mitzvah,* which is infinite.

Also, [calculate] "the reward of a sin" — i.e., the perceived benefit in worldly terms that one gains by performing [a sin] — against the resulting loss in the World to Come. For there is undoubtedly no comparison or likeness between [them], since this one is eternal, while the other is ephemeral.

דַּע מַה לְּמַעְלָה מִמְּךָ – עַיִן רוֹאָה, וְאֹזֶן שׁוֹמַעַת, וְכָל מַעֲשֶׂיךָ בְּסֵפֶר נִכְתָּבִים — *Know what is above you — a watchful Eye, an attentive Ear and all your deeds are recorded in a Book.* "Know what is above you." Realize the greatness of the King against Whom you are rebelling when you commit a sin. Know also that in spite of His grandeur, He does not refrain from observing the deeds of lowly [mortal beings]. Rather, "an Eye observes, [an Ear listens]. . ."

Know also that [heavenly] punishment for a transgression does not come immediately. Do not let this postponement mislead you, for "all your deeds are recorded in a Book," and ultimately you will be rewarded or punished for them.

NOTES

in his profession and strive to excel so that others will recognize his excellence. This will encourage him to retain superiority in his field of endeavor and improve upon it. In the Talmudic passage (*Kiddushin* 82b) cited by the *Sforno,* various occupations are discussed, and although they are all utilitarian and productive, some are considered praiseworthy, while others are not.

ב
ב

[ב] **רַבָּן** גַּמְלִיאֵל בְּנוֹ שֶׁל רַבִּי יְהוּדָה הַנָּשִׂיא אוֹמֵר: יָפֶה תַלְמוּד תּוֹרָה עִם דֶּרֶךְ אֶרֶץ, שֶׁיְּגִיעַת שְׁנֵיהֶם מַשְׁכַּחַת עָוֹן. וְכָל תּוֹרָה שֶׁאֵין עִמָּהּ מְלָאכָה, סוֹפָהּ בְּטֵלָה וְגוֹרֶרֶת עָוֹן. וְכָל הָעוֹסְקִים עִם הַצִּבּוּר, יִהְיוּ עוֹסְקִים עִמָּהֶם לְשֵׁם שָׁמַיִם, שֶׁזְּכוּת אֲבוֹתָם מְסַיַּעְתָּם, וְצִדְקָתָם עוֹמֶדֶת

פירוש לרבי עובדיה ספורנו

ב:ב. כבר אמרו ז״ל ,,אומה זו כגפן נמשלה זמורות שבה אלו בעלי בתים״ אשר השתדלותם בחיי שעה פרטי וכללי לקיום המדינות בגולה, ולכן נתן זה החכם עצתו להם בענין השתדלותם הפרטי ובענין השתדלותם הכללי. ואמר כי אמנם אף על פי שהשתדלותם הפרטי הוא על הרוב לקנות ממון לחיי שעה – יפה להם שעם זה יהיה להם איזה זמן מיוחד ללמוד תורה, ואע״פ שיחשבו עצמן בלתי מוכנים לזה הנה יגיעת שניהם תסיר מלבם כל מחשבת עון, והפך זה יהיה אם בסורם מן

SFORNO'S COMMENTARY

2:2

יָפֶה תַלְמוּד תּוֹרָה עִם דֶּרֶךְ אֶרֶץ, שֶׁיְּגִיעַת שְׁנֵיהֶם מַשְׁכַּחַת עָוֹן. וְכָל תּוֹרָה שֶׁאֵין עִמָּהּ מְלָאכָה, סוֹפָהּ בְּטֵלָה וְגוֹרֶרֶת עָוֹן — *Torah study is good together with an occupation, for the exertion of them both makes sin forgotten. All Torah study that is not joined with work will cease in the end, and leads to sin.* Our Sages have already said, אוּמָּה זוּ כְּגֶפֶן נִמְשְׁלָה, זְמוֹרוֹת שֶׁבָּהּ אֵלּוּ בַּעֲלֵי בָתִּים, "*This nation is compared to a vine: The twigs are the laymen*" (*Chullin* 92a), whose efforts in worldly matters — individually and collectively — sustain our communities in the Diaspora. Therefore, this Sage gave them his advice regarding [both] their personal and communal efforts.

He said that although their personal efforts are primarily for the purpose of obtaining material wealth for their temporal existence, nonetheless, it would be appropriate that they also designate a set time to study Torah. And even though they may feel ill-prepared for this, still "the exertion of them both [makes sin forgotten]" — i.e., it will remove from their hearts all sinful thoughts. Otherwise, when they take time out from their business, they will occasionally turn to vain pursuits.

NOTES

2:2, 3, 4

יָפֶה תַלְמוּד תּוֹרָה עִם דֶּרֶךְ אֶרֶץ . . . וְכָל הָעוֹסְקִים עִם הַצִּבּוּר . . . לְשֵׁם שָׁמַיִם . . . וְאַתֶּם, מַעֲלֶה אֲנִי עֲלֵיכֶם שָׂכָר הַרְבֵּה . . . עֲשֵׂה רְצוֹנוֹ כִּרְצוֹנְךָ, כְּדֵי שֶׁיַּעֲשֶׂה רְצוֹנְךָ כִּרְצוֹנוֹ — *Torah study is good together with an occupation . . . All who exert themselves for the community should . . . for the sake of Heaven . . . as for you, I [God] will bestow upon you as great a reward . . . Treat His will as if it were your own will, so that He will treat your will as if it were His will.* The *Sforno* treats these three *mishnayos* as one unit. He interprets the words of Rabban Gamliel as being directed to lay Jewish leaders. They are admonished not to neglect the study of Torah in

2
2 **2. R**abban Gamliel, the son of Rabbi Judah HaNassi, *says: Torah study is good together with an occupation, for the exertion of them both makes sin forgotten. All Torah study that is not joined with work will cease in the end, and leads to sin. All who exert themselves for the community should exert themselves for the sake of Heaven, for then the merit of the community's forefathers aids them and their righteousness endures*

פירוש לרבי עובדיה ספורנו

העסקים לעתים יפנו אל הבטלה. ואמר שלא יהיה זה נמנע אצלם שיהיה האדם משתדל בחיי שעה ועם זה יעסוק בתורה, כי אמנם כל תורה שאין עמה מלאכה סופה בטלה וכולי. אמנם בדבר הנהגתם הכללית אמר, הנה ראוי שכל העסוקים בצרכי צבור תהיה כונתם לא להתכבד ולהשתרר אבל תהיה לשם שמים, שאף על פי שצרכי צבור רבים ויקשה לכל להתעסק בם כאמרם ז״ל „הטל עליהם צרכי צבור והם כלים מאליהם״, מכל מקום כשיתעסקו בהם לשם שמים תהיה זכות אבותם של צבור מסייעת למתעסקים וצדקתם של מתעסקים עומדת לעד.

SFORNO'S COMMENTARY

He also said that they should not think it impossible for a man to combine worldly pursuits with Torah study, for indeed, "All Torah study that is not joined with work will cease in the end. . ."

וְכָל הָעוֹסְקִים עִם הַצִּבּוּר, יִהְיוּ עוֹסְקִים עִמָּהֶם לְשֵׁם שָׁמַיִם, שֶׁזְּכוּת אֲבוֹתָם מְסַיַּעְתָּם, וְצִדְקָתָם עוֹמֶדֶת לָעַד — *All who exert themselves for the community should exert themselves for the sake of Heaven, for then the merit of the community's forefathers aids them and their righteousness endures forever.* As for their communal leadership, [R' Gamliel] said that it is fitting that "All who exert themselves for the community" should not intend to gain honor and authority. Rather, [their efforts] should be "for the sake of Heaven." And even though the needs of the community are numerous, and everyone finds it difficult to deal with them, as our Sages said, "Cast communal duties upon them, and they will automatically be destroyed" (*Sanhedrin* 17a), nonetheless, when they do so "for the sake of Heaven," "the merit of the community's forefathers will aid" those who manage the community's affairs, and "their righteousness shall endure forever."

NOTES

spite of their personal and communal burdens of responsibility; he recognizes the difficulties encountered by those occupied in communal endeavors and encourages them to tenaciously work on behalf of the Jewish People, and never be deterred or discouraged in the face of failure, for Hashem recognizes their efforts and will generously reward them. What they must believe is that if they fulfill God's Will, He will certainly fulfill their will as well. Rabban Gamliel also admonishes Jewish leaders to be sincere, dedicated and altruistic, for only in this manner will they be successful and be rewarded by the Almighty even in the realm of their personal lives.

ב
ג־ד

לָעַד. וְאַתֶּם, מַעֲלֶה אֲנִי עֲלֵיכֶם שָׂכָר הַרְבֵּה כְּאִלּוּ עֲשִׂיתֶם.

[ג] **הֱווּ** זְהִירִין בָּרָשׁוּת, שֶׁאֵין מְקָרְבִין לוֹ לְאָדָם אֶלָּא לְצֹרֶךְ עַצְמָן; נִרְאִין כְּאוֹהֲבִין בִּשְׁעַת הֲנָאָתָן, וְאֵין עוֹמְדִין לוֹ לָאָדָם בִּשְׁעַת דָּחֳקוֹ.

[ד] **הוּא** הָיָה אוֹמֵר: עֲשֵׂה רְצוֹנוֹ כִּרְצוֹנְךָ, כְּדֵי שֶׁיַּעֲשֶׂה רְצוֹנְךָ כִּרְצוֹנוֹ. בַּטֵּל רְצוֹנְךָ מִפְּנֵי רְצוֹנוֹ, כְּדֵי שֶׁיְּבַטֵּל רְצוֹן אֲחֵרִים מִפְּנֵי רְצוֹנֶךָ.

פירוש לרבי עובדיה ספורנו

אמנם אתם בעלי בתים המשתדלים בגולה להציל את הצבור מגזרות העמים, גם שלפעמים לא תשיגו כל הצריך בחרות אפם בנו – מחשב אני עליכם שאתם ראוים לשכר הרבה כאלו עשיתם והשגתם את כל הצריך לצבור:

ב:ג. אמנם בהשתדלותכם הוו זהירין ברשות שאף על פי שיסבירו לכם פנים וידרו נדרים להיטיב אל תבטחו בזה כלל, כי אינם מקרבים אתכם ומסבירים פנים אלא לצורך עצמם לקבל פרס מכם:

ב:ד. עשה רצונו כרצונך, לא בלבד ראוי

SFORNO'S COMMENTARY

וְאַתֶּם, מַעֲלֶה אֲנִי עֲלֵיכֶם שָׂכָר הַרְבֵּה כְּאִלּוּ עֲשִׂיתֶם — *Nevertheless, as for you, I [God] will bestow upon you as great a reward as if you had accomplished it on your own.* "Nevertheless, as for you," the laymen who make efforts in the Diaspora to save the community from the [evil] decrees of the nations, even though at times you do not completely achieve your goal, due to their anger against us, nevertheless, "I [God]" regard you as being worthy of much reward, as though you *had* attained all that was necessary for the community.

2:3

הֱווּ זְהִירִין בָּרָשׁוּת, שֶׁאֵין מְקָרְבִין לוֹ לְאָדָם אֶלָּא לְצֹרֶךְ עַצְמָן — *Beware of rulers, for they befriend someone only for their own benefit.* Nevertheless, in your efforts [on behalf of the community], "beware of rulers," for even though they act cordially towards you and promise to benefit [your people], do not rely on this. "For they befriend" and act cordially towards you "only for their own benefit" — i.e., in order to obtain a reward from you.

2
3-4 *forever. Nevertheless, as for you, I [God] will bestow upon you as great a reward as if you had accomplished it on your own.*

3. *Beware of rulers, for they befriend someone only for their own benefit; they act friendly when it benefits them, but they do not stand by someone in his time of need.*

4. *He used to say: Treat His will as if it were your own will, so that He will treat your will as if it were His will. Nullify your will before His will, so that He will nullify the will of others before your will.*

פירוש לרבי עובדיה ספורנו

לך להשתדל לשם שמים כמשועבד אליו וירא מענשו, אבל ראוי שתעשה רצונו זה להשתדל בעד עמו כמו רוצה וחפץ ושמח בזה כדי שישיג רצונו, כי אז יעשה הוא רצונך שתשיג מה שאתה רוצה וחפץ להשיג כרצונו כי חפץ חסד הוא ומודד מדה כנגד מדה. ובהשתדלותך זה בטל רצונך החפץ בתענוגים ובמנוחה וזולתם כדי להשיג רצונו זה להציל את עמו, כי אז למדה כנגד מדה יבטל רצון אחרים מפני רצונך וכל חפצך תשלים גם בעסקיך:

SFORNO'S COMMENTARY

2:4

עֲשֵׂה רְצוֹנוֹ כִּרְצוֹנְךָ, כְּדֵי שֶׁיַּעֲשֶׂה רְצוֹנְךָ כִּרְצוֹנוֹ — *Treat His will as if it were your own will, so that He will treat your will as if it were His will.* It is only proper that your efforts be "for the sake of Heaven," as a subject of the Almighty, who is fearful of His retribution. [Additionally] it is [also] fitting that you regard "His will" — i.e., to make efforts on behalf of His people — as one who wants and desires and rejoices in this goal, "as if it were your own will."

For then, "He will treat your will as if it were His will" — i.e., you will attain that which you desire to attain. For He loves lovingkindness, and rewards a person in accordance with his deeds [measure for measure].

בַּטֵּל רְצוֹנְךָ מִפְּנֵי רְצוֹנוֹ, כְּדֵי שֶׁיְּבַטֵּל רְצוֹן אֲחֵרִים מִפְּנֵי רְצוֹנֶךָ — *Nullify your will before His will, so that He will nullify the will of others before your will.* And in your efforts [on behalf of the community], "Nullify your will" — i.e., the desire for pleasure and rest — for the sake of achieving "His will" — namely, to save His people. For then, measure for measure, "He will nullify the will of others before your will," and all your desires will be fulfilled, including in your personal affairs.

ב
ה

[ה] **הִלֵּל** אוֹמֵר: אַל תִּפְרוֹשׁ מִן הַצִּבּוּר, וְאַל תַּאֲמִין בְּעַצְמְךָ עַד יוֹם מוֹתְךָ, וְאַל תָּדִין אֶת חֲבֵרְךָ עַד שֶׁתַּגִּיעַ לִמְקוֹמוֹ, וְאַל תֹּאמַר דָּבָר שֶׁאִי אֶפְשָׁר לִשְׁמוֹעַ, שֶׁסּוֹפוֹ לְהִשָּׁמַע. וְאַל תֹּאמַר לִכְשֶׁאֶפְּנֶה אֶשְׁנֶה, שֶׁמָּא לֹא תִפָּנֶה.

פירוש לרבי עובדיה ספורנו

ב:ה. אחר שהשלים את כל התנאים עד הדור האחרון מהם הנזכר במשנה התחיל בדברי הלל שהיה קדמון, וספר מה שאמר בדבר הזהירות שהוא ענין זה הפרק כאשר התבאר. אמר זה החכם אל תפרוש מן הצבור כמו שעשה יוחנן כהן גדול שנעשה צדוקי ולא קבל שמנה עשרה דבר שגזרו בית שמאי או זולתם אעפ״י שקבלום עלהם שאר הצבור, ואל תאמן בעצמך אל תבטח שלא תשנה טעמך שהרי יוחנן כהן גדול שמש בכהנה גדולה שמונים שנה ולא פרש מדרכי צבור כלל אבל התקין תקנות כדאיתא בסוף

SFORNO'S COMMENTARY

2:5

הִלֵּל אוֹמֵר — *Hillel said.* After completing [the teachings of] the *Tannaim,* including their last generation as recorded in the [previous] Mishnah, [the author of *Avos*] begins with the words of Hillel, who lived in an earlier era. He tells us what [Hillel] said in regards to [the trait of] זְהִירוּת, or "watchfulness," which is the main topic of this chapter, as has been explained [see *Sforno*'s introduction].

אַל תִּפְרוֹשׁ מִן הַצִּבּוּר — *Do not separate yourself from the community.* This Sage stated: Do not separate yourself from the community, as did Yochanan the High Priest when he became a *Tzaduki* and refused to accept the eighteen decrees (י״ח גְּזֵרוֹת) issued by the House of Shammai — or, for that matter, any others — even though the rest of the community accepted them.

וְאַל תַּאֲמִין בְּעַצְמְךָ — *Do not believe in yourself.* Do not be certain that you will never change your beliefs, for Yochanan the High Priest served for eighty years in the High Priesthood and did not deviate from the ways of the community in any way. [On the contrary,] he himself issued decrees, as we are taught in the end of *Sotah* [47a], yet in the end, he became a *Tzaduki.*

NOTES

2:5

אַל תִּפְרוֹשׁ מִן הַצִּבּוּר . . . וְאַל תָּדִין אֶת חֲבֵרְךָ עַד שֶׁתַּגִּיעַ לִמְקוֹמוֹ, וְאַל תֹּאמַר דָּבָר שֶׁאִי אֶפְשָׁר לִשְׁמוֹעַ — *Do not separate yourself from the community . . . do not judge your fellow until you have reached his place; do not make a statement that cannot be easily understood.* The *Sforno* interprets the cautionary words of Hillel in this Mishnah as being directed to a tragic figure among the *Tannaim*: Yochanan the High Priest, who lived in Hillel's time. He served with distinction for 80 years during the Second Temple era, only to become a *Tzaduki* in the last years of his life. In Tractate *Shabbos* (13, 18), the Talmud enumerates the eighteen decrees which were at issue between Hillel and Shammai, and which were put to a vote in the *beis midrash.* The decision was in Shammai's favor, and the school of Hillel, who opposed the decrees, accepted this decision. The only exception was Yochanan

2
5

5. *Hillel said: Do not separate yourself from the community; do not believe in yourself until the day you die; do not judge your fellow until you have reached his place; do not make a statement that cannot be easily understood on the ground that it will be understood eventually; and do not say, "When I am free I will study," for perhaps you will not become free.*

פירוש לרבי עובדיה ספורנו

סוטה, ולבסוף נעשה צדוקי. ואל תדין את יוחנן כהן גדול לרשע בזה עד שתגיע למקומו ותבין ענינו, כי אולי אם היית בימיו היית פורש כמוהו ובלתי מקבל אותן הגזרות. ואל תאמר דבר שאי אפשר לשמוע בתחלת העיון להיות המאמר בלתי מבואר וצריך פירוש, כמו שעשו הגוזרי שמנה עשרה דבר שאמרו שקצתם גזרו משום דבר אחר ואותו דבר אחר משום דבר אחר ואולי בזה הולידו ספיקות בלב רבים. ואל תאמר אתה ההמוני המתעסק בתורה באי זה מעתות הפנאי לכשאפנה אשנה, אלא קבע עתים:

SFORNO'S COMMENTARY

וְאַל תָּדִין אֶת חֲבֵרְךָ עַד שֶׁתַּגִּיעַ לִמְקוֹמוֹ — *Do not judge your fellow until you have reached his place.* But "do not judge" Yochanan the High Priest and regard him as a wicked person "until you have reached his place" and understand his situation. For perhaps, had you lived in his days, you may also have separated yourself from the community and refused to accept those decrees.

וְאַל תֹּאמַר דָּבָר שֶׁאִי אֶפְשָׁר לִשְׁמוֹעַ — *Do not make a statement that cannot be easily understood.* Initially, because it is unclear and requires clarification, as did the Sages who issued the eighteen decrees, who said that certain decrees were issued because one action might lead to another, and that one in turn to another, because of a different matter [i.e., they prohibited their bread because of their oil; their oil because of their wine and their wine because of their daughters, for fear of intermarriage, see *Shabbos* 17b]. Perhaps this is what elicited doubts in the minds of many [which led them to reject these decrees].

וְאַל תֹּאמַר לִכְשֶׁאֶפְּנֶה אֶשְׁנֶה — *And do not say, "When I am free I will study."* "And do not say" — i.e., you, one of the masses, who occupies himself with Torah study infrequently during his free time — "when I am free I will study." Rather designate set times for Torah study.

NOTES

the High Priest, who left the ranks of the Sages and cast his lot with the *Tzadukim.*

The *Sforno* interprets the words of Hillel, "do not separate yourself from the community," as being directly linked to Yochanan's action, since Hillel himself, although he disagreed with Shammai's decrees, nevertheless accepted the decision of the majority. Even so, Hillel cautions us not to judge Yochanan too harshly, for had we been there at the time, we might have felt just as strongly as he did against these decrees. Perhaps we, too, would have found them unjustified and liable to confuse people. For Yochanan was not opposed in principle to issuing decrees, since he himself issued a number of them regarding work on *Chol Hamoed,* tithes (מַעַשְׂרוֹת), and certain funeral practices, as recorded in *Sotah* 47.

ב ו [ו] **הוּא** הָיָה אוֹמֵר: אֵין בּוּר יְרֵא חֵטְא, וְלֹא עַם הָאָרֶץ חָסִיד, וְלֹא הַבַּיְּשָׁן לָמֵד, וְלֹא הַקַּפְּדָן מְלַמֵּד, וְלֹא כָל הַמַּרְבֶּה בִסְחוֹרָה מַחְכִּים, וּבְמָקוֹם שֶׁאֵין אֲנָשִׁים הִשְׁתַּדֵּל לִהְיוֹת אִישׁ.

פירוש לרבי עובדיה ספורנו

ב:ו. הנה יפה אמרתי לך ההמוני שתקבע אי זה עת לתורה ולא תאמר לכשאפנה אשנה, כי גם שלא תקוה להשיג את החלק העיוני ממנה לא ימנע שתשיג בה החלק המעשי, כי אמנם אין בור ירא חטא אף על פי שיזהר מאי זה חטא, וכן עם הארץ אינו חסיד אף על פי שיגמול חסד לפעמים, כי זה יקרה להם בהיותם אוחזים מנהג אבותיהם בידיהם על צד ההרגל. ואתה כשתקבע אי זה עת ללמוד אל תבוש לשאול בלי ספק, שלא הבוישן למד, כאמרו „אם נבלת בהתנשא" ודרשו ז"ל „אם נבלת בה –

SFORNO'S COMMENTARY

2:6

אֵין בּוּר יְרֵא חֵטְא, וְלֹא עַם הָאָרֶץ חָסִיד — *A boor cannot be fearful of sin; an unlearned person cannot be scrupulously pious.* Behold, man of the masses, I gave you sound advice when I told you to designate some set time for Torah study, and not claim, "When I have time, I will study"! For even though you may not aspire to master the חֵלֶק הָעִיּוּנִי, *philosophical* (intellectual) aspect of Torah, nonetheless, it is not beyond you to acquire the חֵלֶק הַמַּעֲשִׂי, *practical* aspect [of Torah].

For "a boor cannot be fearful of sin" even though he may be careful not to transgress certain sins, and "an unlearned person cannot be scrupulously pious" even though he may at times perform acts of lovingkindness. For he does this because he follow the customs of his forefathers, by rote. As for you, when you will designate some time to study [Torah], do not be ashamed to ask questions, for "the bashful person cannot learn, as it is written, אִם נָבַלְתָּ בְהִתְנַשֵּׂא, *If you have acted foolishly by lifting yourself up* (*Proverbs* 30:32) — in reference to this the Sages said, אִם נָבַלְתָּ בָּהּ – תִּנַּשֵּׂא,

NOTES

2:6

וְלֹא עַם הָאָרֶץ חָסִיד — *An unlearned person cannot be scrupulously pious.* The *Sforno* links this Mishnah, which is a continuation of Hillel's teachings, to the concluding section of the previous Mishnah. Whereas the first part of that Mishnah is directed primarily — if not exclusively — to the intellectual and scholarly segment of the populace, the admonition to set aside time for Torah study on a daily basis is aimed at the general populace, those whom the *Sforno* calls "men of the masses."

It is this person whom Hillel continues to address in this Mishnah. He urges the average Jew to pursue Torah knowledge in order to perfect that area which the *Sforno* calls חֵלֶק הַמַּעֲשִׂי, the *practical* aspect of Torah — namely, *mitzvah* observance, as he posits in Mishnah 1:1. Only by increasing one's knowledge of this aspect of Torah can one avoid performing *mitzvos* by rote,

6. *He used to say: A boor cannot be fearful of sin; an unlearned person cannot be scrupulously pious; the bashful person cannot learn, and the quick, impatient person cannot teach; anyone excessively occupied in business cannot become a scholar; and in a place where there are no leaders, strive to be a leader.*

פירוש לרבי עובדיה ספורנו

תנשא", וכן השמר מללמוד מאיש קפדן, שאין הקפדן מוכן ללמד. ולא המרבה בסחורה מחכים, ולכן ראוי שתקבע אי זה עת לתורה שלא ימנעך רבוי ההשתדלות בסחורה. וגם שתשיג אי זה דבר בתורה אל תשתדל להיות איש מורה ומדריך זולתך במקום שיש גדולים, כאמרם ז"ל ,,באתר דאית גבר תמן לא תהוי גבר", אבל השתדל בזה במקום שאין אנשים תופשי התורה:

SFORNO'S COMMENTARY

"If you are willing to make yourself a fool in it [Torah study], you will be lifted up" (*Berachos* 63b).

וְלֹא הַקַּפְּדָן מְלַמֵּד — *And the quick, impatient person cannot teach.* Also, be careful not to study with a teacher who is impatient, for "the quick, impatient person cannot teach."

וְלֹא כָּל הַמַּרְבֶּה בִסְחוֹרָה מַחְכִּים, וּבִמְקוֹם שֶׁאֵין אֲנָשִׁים הִשְׁתַּדֵּל לִהְיוֹת אִישׁ — *Anyone excessively occupied in business cannot become a scholar; and in a place where there are no leaders, strive to be a leader.* "Anyone excessively occupied in business cannot become a scholar." Therefore, it is fitting that you set aside some time for Torah study so that your numerous business responsibilities do not impede you [from studying]. And even if you do study and gain some Torah knowledge, do not attempt to become a teacher and a guide to others in a community where there are great Torah scholars, as our Sages say, בְּאַתְרָא דְּאִית גְּבַר תַּמָּן לֹא תֶהֱוֵי גְּבַר, "*In a town where there is a [wise] man, there you should refrain from being a [wise] man*" (*Berachos* 63b). However, "in a place where there are no leaders, strive to be a leader."

NOTES

and improve the quality and standards of his *mitzvah* observance.

וְלֹא הַבַּיְשָׁן לָמֵד, וְלֹא הַקַּפְּדָן מְלַמֵּד . . . וּבְמָקוֹם שֶׁאֵין אֲנָשִׁים הִשְׁתַּדֵּל לִהְיוֹת אִישׁ — *The bashful person cannot learn, and the quick, impatient person cannot teach . . . and in a place where there are no leaders, strive to be a leader.* As the *Sforno* explains, Hillel offers practical advice to the "man of the masses" regarding Torah study, be it in his conduct as a student, or the personality of the teacher he chooses. He also cautions the lay student to recognize his own shortcomings and not arrogate authority to himself when a religious decision is to be made, or even when teaching Torah to those who are less educated. Circumstances and good judgment should dictate when to assume the role of teacher and when to accept the role of student.

[ז] **אַף** הוּא רָאָה גֻּלְגֹּלֶת אַחַת שֶׁצָּפָה עַל פְּנֵי הַמָּיִם. אָמַר לָהּ: „עַל דְּאַטֵּפְתְּ אַטְפוּךְ, וְסוֹף מְטַיְּפָיִךְ יְטוּפוּן.״

[ח] **הוּא** הָיָה אוֹמֵר: מַרְבֶּה בָשָׂר, מַרְבֶּה רִמָּה; מַרְבֶּה נְכָסִים, מַרְבֶּה דְאָגָה; מַרְבֶּה נָשִׁים, מַרְבֶּה כְשָׁפִים; מַרְבֶּה שְׁפָחוֹת, מַרְבֶּה זִמָּה;

פירוש לרבי עובדיה ספורנו

ב:ז. הנה זה החכם ראה גלגלת של אדם נודע אצלו לאיש דמים, וידע שנהרג ולא נמסרו הורגיו לבית דין, ואמר, הנה אתה נפלת ביד הורגים שהציפו נבלתך במים על דאטפת שהרגת אחרים והצפת אותם על פני המים כמוך היום, וסוף גם ההורגים שלא הרגוך לענשך, אבל הרגוך בעברת זדון – סופם שיהרגום לסטים או המלכות וישליכו נבלתם במים מדה כנגד מדה, כאמרם ז״ל „מי שנתחייב הריגה או נמסר למלכות או לסטים באין עליו:״

ב:ח. הנה הדבר אשר הוא בעצמו שלמות

SFORNO'S COMMENTARY

2:7

„עַל דְּאַטֵּפְתְּ אַטְפוּךְ, וְסוֹף מְטַיְּפָיִךְ יְטוּפוּן״ — *"Because your drowned others, they drowned you; and those who drowned you will be drowned eventually."* This wise man [Hillel] saw the skull of a person whom he knew to be a murderer. He knew that he had been murdered, and that his killers had not been brought to justice, so he said: "Behold, you have been killed by murderers, who cast your body upon the waters 'because you drowned others' — i.e., because you yourself murdered others and cast [their bodies] upon the waters, as it has befallen you today. Eventually, however, also those who killed you — not in order to punish you, but out of willful malice — will also be eliminated, either by thieves or by the authorities, who will cast their carcasses upon the waters, measure for measure, as our Sages said, **מִי שֶׁנִּתְחַיֵּב הֲרִיגָה אוֹ נִמְסָר לַמַּלְכוּת אוֹ לִסְטִים בָּאִין עָלָיו**, *"He who has been condemned to death [by a Torah court] will either be handed over to the authorities or set upon by thieves"* (*Sotah* 8b).

2:8

מַרְבֶּה בָשָׂר, מַרְבֶּה רִמָּה — *The more flesh, the more worms.* The more something is inherently perfect (שָׁלֵם), the better. In contrast, that which is

NOTES

2:8

מַרְבֶּה בָשָׂר, מַרְבֶּה רִמָּה; מַרְבֶּה נְכָסִים, מַרְבֶּה דְאָגָה . . . מַרְבֶּה תוֹרָה, מַרְבֶּה חַיִּים — *The more flesh, the more worms; the more possessions, the more worry . . . [However] the more Torah, the more life.* In this lengthy Mishnah, which incorporates the concluding remarks and observations of Hillel, a number of important points are made by the *Sforno*:

2
7-8

7. *He also saw a skull floating on the water; he said to it: "Because you drowned others, they drowned you; and those who drowned you will be drowned eventually."*

8. *He used to say: The more flesh, the more worms; the more possessions, the more worry; the more wives, the more witchcraft; the more maidservants, the*

פירוש לרבי עובדיה ספורנו

כל מה שירבה יהיה יותר טוב אמנם מה שאינו בעצמו שלמות אף על פי שיהיה כלי הכרחי לאי זה שלמות יהיה הרבוי ממנו מותר ומזיק, ולכן אמר זה החכם שאף על פי שבריאות הגוף וכן הקנינים המדומים הם הכרחיים לעוסק בתורה, מכל מקום אם ירבה בשר ירבה לחות מותרי מוכן אל העפוש והרמה, וכן מרבה נכסים ומשתדל בקנינים מאד תרבה דאגתו להפסידם ובזה יטריד מחשבתו מהשתדל בחיי עולם כלל, וכן הנשים אף על פי שחברת האשה תועיל בחיי שעה, כאמרו „אעשה לו עזר כנגדו,, – הנה רבוי הנשים ירבה כשפים, שכל אחת מהן תבקש בכשפיה להטות אליה לב הבעל.

SFORNO'S COMMENTARY

not inherently perfect — even though it may well be a necessary means by which to attain some type of perfection — is superfluous and harmful, when excessive.

Therefore this wise man [Hillel] said that although a healthy body and material possessions are vital [requirements] for Torah study, nevertheless, "the more flesh" the more will be the excess moisture [of his body], which [in the grave] will bring on decay and maggots.

מַרְבֶּה נְכָסִים, מַרְבֶּה דְאָגָה — *The more possessions, the more worry.* So too, a person who increases his possessions greatly increases his worries for fear of losing them. He occupies his mind on this instead of striving to attain eternal life.

מַרְבֶּה נָשִׁים, מַרְבֶּה כְשָׁפִים — *The more wives, the more witchcraft.* The same can be said of women. Even though a relationship with a woman [i.e., one's wife] benefits one in this temporal world, as the verse states, אֶעֱשֶׂה לּוֹ עֵזֶר כְּנֶגְדּוֹ, *I will make him a helper corresponding to him* (*Genesis* 2:18), nevertheless, "the more wives, the more witchcraft" — each one will attempt to gain her husband's favor and attention through witchcraft.

NOTES

Excess, in and of itself, is not a vice or inherently wicked; everything depends on the nature of one's activities. In general the rule of thumb is: In the realm of the physical, "more is less" — i.e., excess is dangerous, harmful and self-destructive. This includes indulging in physical pleasures, wealth, and material possessions. Not so in the realm of knowledge and the spiritual domain. Here, the rule is, "the more, the better" — to increase is beneficial and productive, for it enhances the

ב מַרְבֶּה עֲבָדִים, מַרְבֶּה גָזֵל. מַרְבֶּה תוֹרָה, מַרְבֶּה
ח חַיִּים; מַרְבֶּה יְשִׁיבָה, מַרְבֶּה חָכְמָה; מַרְבֶּה עֵצָה,
מַרְבֶּה תְבוּנָה; מַרְבֶּה צְדָקָה, מַרְבֶּה שָׁלוֹם. קָנָה שֵׁם
טוֹב, קָנָה לְעַצְמוֹ; קָנָה לוֹ דִבְרֵי תוֹרָה, קָנָה לוֹ חַיֵּי
הָעוֹלָם הַבָּא.

פירוש לרבי עובדיה ספורנו

אמנם מרבה תורה מרבה מרבה חיים לעד, כאמרו „כי הוא חייכם״, אם כן כל מה שתרבה התורה תרבה מעלת החיים, וכן מרבה ישיבה ומעמיד תלמידים הרבה וזה בשלמות שכלו המתעורר להבין ולהורות, הנה כל מה שירבה זה השלמות יהיה יותר טוב, כי בו תרבה חכמת המורה כאמרם ז״ל ומתלמידי יותר מכלם, וכן מרבה עצה להתבונן לעשות המעשיות בשלמות מרבה תבונה להתבונן בטעמן, כי אמנם המעורר אל המעשה הטוב הוא שלמות אהבת האל יתברך ויראתו, וכל מה שירבה זה ירבה התבוננות לדעת תכלית רצון קונו בזה, וכמו כן מרבה צדקה והוא התעוררות הנפש להיטיב לזולת והוא שלמות תכונה בה מרבה שלום לעצמו ולזולתו, וזה כי

SFORNO'S COMMENTARY

מַרְבֶּה תוֹרָה, מַרְבֶּה חַיִּים; מַרְבֶּה יְשִׁיבָה, מַרְבֶּה חָכְמָה — *The more Torah, the more life; the more study, the more wisdom.* However, [in contrast,] "The more Torah, the more [eternal] life," as it is written, כִּי הוּא חַיֵּיכֶם, *for it is your life* (*Deuteronomy* 32:47). Hence, to the extent that you increase your Torah study, your quality of life shall increase. Similarly, "the more [one] studies" (יְשִׁיבָה) and cultivates numerous students — through the perfection of one's mind and its awakening to understand and teach — here more is better, for it will increase the teacher's own wisdom, as our Sages said, וּמִתַּלְמִידַי יוֹתֵר מִכֻּלָּם, *"And from my students [I learned] the most"* (*Taanis* 7a).

מַרְבֶּה עֵצָה, מַרְבֶּה תְבוּנָה — *The more counsel, the more understanding.* So too, "the more counsel" — i.e., the more one reflects upon performing [*mitzvos*] with perfection — "the more understanding" — the deeper one's understanding of the reasons behind these commandments. For aspiring to do good deeds is the epitome of love and reverence of the Almighty. And the more one increases [this aspiration], the more he will reflect upon and know God's purpose in [commanding] this [*mitzvah*].

מַרְבֶּה צְדָקָה, מַרְבֶּה שָׁלוֹם. קָנָה שֵׁם טוֹב, קָנָה לְעַצְמוֹ — *The more charity, the more peace. One who has gained a good reputation has gained it for his own benefit.*

NOTES

quality of one's life in both this world and the next.

מַרְבֶּה יְשִׁיבָה, מַרְבֶּה חָכְמָה . . . מַרְבֶּה צְדָקָה, מַרְבֶּה שָׁלוֹם. קָנָה שֵׁם טוֹב, קָנָה לְעַצְמוֹ . . . קָנָה לוֹ חַיֵּי הָעוֹלָם הַבָּא — *The more study, the more wisdom . . . the more charity, the more peace. One who has gained a good reputation has gained it for his own benefit . . . has gained himself the life of the World to Come.* The *Sforno* goes on to skillfully explain the logical progression of the Mishnah:

The more a person studies Torah, the more he will add to his eternal life; the

2 *more lewdness; the more manservants, the more thiev-*
8 *ery. [However] the more Torah, the more life; the more study, the more wisdom; the more counsel, the more understanding; the more charity, the more peace. One who has gained a good reputation has gained it for his own benefit; one who has gained himself Torah knowledge has gained himself the life of the World to Come.*

פירוש לרבי עובדיה ספורנו

מצד מה שקנה שם טוב בהיטיבו לזולת ובהשתדלו להשבית מדנים שהוא מפעלות הצדקה יוכל על זה בהיותו נשוא פנים מצד השם טוב כענין איוב באמרו וריב לא ידעתי אחקרהו. וכמו כן מרבה שלום במה שקנה לעצמו תכונת ההיטיב לזולת בהרבותו אותה, ובזה ידמה ליוצרו ויקנה שלום במנוחתו מכל מקטרג כחוק מדה כנגד מדה, כאמרו „והיה מעשה הצדקה שלום". אמנם בקנותו דברי תורה והוא החלק העיוני ממנה קנה לו חיי העולם הבא, כאמרו „כי הוא חייכם", כי אמנם מין החיות השכלי הוא הנכבד במיני החיים והנה חיי השכל הכחיי הוא היותו משכיל

SFORNO'S COMMENTARY

Similarly, "the more charity" — meaning, the [more one increases] one's desire to do good unto others — the more one will engender "peace" in both one's own self [i.e., peace of mind], as well as in one's relationships with others. For as a result of benefiting others, one will "gain a good reputation" — i.e., credibility and status. This will enable one to succeed in resolving disputes, a function of צְדָקָה, or "charity." As we find regarding Job, who said, וְרִב לֹא יָדַעְתִּי אֶחְקְרֵהוּ, *And the dispute which I knew not, I investigated* (Job 29:16).

One also "increases peace" by acquiring and frequently practicing the trait of bestowing good unto others. For in this manner one emulates one's Creator, and thereby will find peace from all accusers when one shall be put to rest, consistent with the rule of "measure for measure," as it is written: וְהָיָה מַעֲשֵׂה הַצְּדָקָה שָׁלוֹם, *The work of righteousness shall be peace* (Isaiah 32:17).

קָנָה לוֹ דִבְרֵי תוֹרָה, קָנָה לוֹ חַיֵּי הָעוֹלָם הַבָּא — *One who has gained himself Torah knowledge has gained himself the life of the World to Come.* However, "one who has gained himself Torah knowledge" — referring to the intellectual aspect of Torah — "has gained himself the life of the World to Come," as it is written: כִּי הוּא חַיֵּיכֶם, *for it is your life* (Deuteronomy 32:47). For the life of the intellect is superior to all other forms of life, and the life of the intellect's

NOTES

more students he will attract, the better and deeper will his understanding of Torah be; the greater his desire to improve the quality of his *mitzvos*, the more he will appreciate them, and the more intense will be his love and reverence of the Almighty.

Through one's willingness to help others, one increases one's own sense of inner peace, and spreads peace among one's society. He also establishes a good reputation which will benefit him and grant him life in the World to Come.

[ט] **רַבָּן** יוֹחָנָן בֶּן זַכַּאי קִבֵּל מֵהִלֵּל וּמִשַּׁמַּאי. הוּא הָיָה אוֹמֵר: אִם לָמַדְתָּ תּוֹרָה הַרְבֵּה, אַל תַּחֲזִיק טוֹבָה לְעַצְמְךָ, כִּי לְכָךְ נוֹצָרְתָּ.

[י] **חֲמִשָּׁה** תַלְמִידִים הָיוּ לוֹ לְרַבָּן יוֹחָנָן בֶּן זַכַּאי, וְאֵלּוּ הֵן: רַבִּי אֱלִיעֶזֶר בֶּן הֻרְקְנוֹס, רַבִּי יְהוֹשֻׁעַ בֶּן חֲנַנְיָא, רַבִּי יוֹסֵי הַכֹּהֵן, רַבִּי שִׁמְעוֹן בֶּן נְתַנְאֵל, וְרַבִּי אֶלְעָזָר בֶּן עֲרָךְ. הוּא הָיָה מוֹנֶה שִׁבְחָן: (רַבִּי) אֱלִיעֶזֶר בֶּן הֻרְקְנוֹס, בּוֹר סוּד שֶׁאֵינוֹ מְאַבֵּד טִפָּה; (רַבִּי) יְהוֹשֻׁעַ בֶּן חֲנַנְיָא, אַשְׁרֵי יוֹלַדְתּוֹ; (רַבִּי) יוֹסֵי הַכֹּהֵן, חָסִיד; (רַבִּי) שִׁמְעוֹן בֶּן נְתַנְאֵל, יְרֵא חֵטְא; וְ(רַבִּי) אֶלְעָזָר בֶּן עֲרָךְ, כְּמַעְיָן הַמִּתְגַּבֵּר.

פירוש לרבי עובדיה ספורנו

בפעל. ומכל זה התבאר שבחלק העיוני ממנה תתן לנפש חיי עולם ובחלק המעשי ממנה תתן חן בעיני אלקים, ובזה יהיו אותם החיים מאושרים באור פני מלך חיים:

ב:ט־י. אם למדת תורה הרבה יותר מחביריך אל תיחס זה אל רב השתדלותך ולמעוט השתדלותך חביריך, כי אמנם יקרה זה גם בהיות ההשתדלות שוה

SFORNO'S COMMENTARY

potential is fulfilled in its active functioning. From all this it is evident that the intellectual aspect of Torah (חֵלֶק הָעִיּוּנִי) grants eternal life to the soul, while the practical aspect of Torah (חֵלֶק הַמַּעֲשִׂי) grants one "favor in the eyes of God." In this manner, that "life" will be joyous in the light of the countenance of the living God.

2:9-10

רַבָּן יוֹחָנָן בֶּן זַכַּאי . . . הָיָה אוֹמֵר: אִם לָמַדְתָּ תּוֹרָה הַרְבֵּה, אַל תַּחֲזִיק טוֹבָה לְעַצְמְךָ, כִּי לְכָךְ נוֹצָרְתָּ. חֲמִשָּׁה תַלְמִידִים הָיוּ לוֹ . . . הוּא הָיָה מוֹנֶה שִׁבְחָן — *Rabban Yochanan ben Zakkai . . . used to say: If you have studied much Torah, do not take credit for yourself, because that is what you were created to do . . . [he] had five*

NOTES

2:9-10

רַבָּן יוֹחָנָן בֶּן זַכַּאי . . . הָיָה אוֹמֵר: אִם לָמַדְתָּ תּוֹרָה הַרְבֵּה, אַל תַּחֲזִיק טוֹבָה לְעַצְמְךָ, כִּי לְכָךְ נוֹצָרְתָּ. חֲמִשָּׁה תַלְמִידִים הָיוּ לוֹ . . . הוּא הָיָה מוֹנֶה שִׁבְחָן — *Rabban Yochanan ben Zakkai . . . used to say: If you have studied much Torah, do not take credit for yourself, because that is what you were created to do . . . [he] had five [primary] disciples . . . He used to enumerate their praises.* The *Sforno* links the statement of Rabban Yochanan ben Zakkai regarding a person who has studied much Torah with the following *mishnayos,* which describe

9. *Rabban Yochanan ben Zakkai received the tradition from Hillel and Shammai. He used to say: If you have studied much Torah, do not take credit for yourself, because that is what you were created to do.*

10. *Rabban Yochanan ben Zakkai had five [primary] disciples. They were: Rabbi Eliezer ben Hyrkanos, Rabbi Yehoshua ben Chanania, Rabbi Yose the Kohen, Rabbi Shimon ben Nesanel, and Rabbi Elazar ben Arach. He used to enumerate their praises: (Rabbi) Eliezer ben Hyrkanos is like a cemented cistern that loses not a drop; (Rabbi) Yehoshua ben Chanania, praiseworthy is she who bore him; (Rabbi) Yose the Kohen is a scrupulously pious person; (Rabbi) Shimon ben Nesanel fears sin; and (Rabbi) Elazar ben Arach is like a spring flowing stronger and stronger.*

פירוש לרבי עובדיה ספורנו

כשתהיה ההכנה ביצירה בלתי שוה, ולכן תיחס זה אל מה שנוצרת מוכן לכך יותר מחביריך. ולקיום דבריו אלה מנה שבח גדולי תלמידיו שהיה ההשתדלות בעיון ובמעשה שוה בכלן אמנם מדרגת המעלות הנקנות בהם היה בלתי שוה וזה בהיות הכנתם ביצירה בלתי שוה:

SFORNO'S COMMENTARY

[primary] disciples . . . He used to enumerate their praises. "If you have studied" more Torah than your peers, do not attribute this to a greater effort on your part and a lesser effort on their part. For if your innate aptitudes and theirs are unequal, this [disparity] may occur, even if both your efforts are equal. Therefore, attribute it to the fact that you were created with a greater propensity [for Torah study] than were your companions.

To prove this point, [Rabban Yochanan] enumerates the praises of his greatest disciples; although they all made an equal effort in Torah scholarship and practical deeds, their attainments of excellence varied due to their differing innate tendencies.

NOTES

his five outstanding disciples, their special qualities, and their relative strengths.

He interprets R' Yochanan's statement as referring to the wide variance in mental faculties and intellectual talents with which people are born. These differing natural inclinations are the reason why one Torah scholar gains superiority over others, rather than the amount of effort each dedicated to his studies.

To prove this theory, he cites the diverse qualities of his pupils, each of whom excelled in a different area. One was blessed with a prodigious memory, another with a tendency to piety, and another was inclined to dialectics.

[יא] **הוּא** הָיָה אוֹמֵר: אִם יִהְיוּ כָּל חַכְמֵי יִשְׂרָאֵל בְּכַף מֹאזְנַיִם, וֶאֱלִיעֶזֶר בֶּן הֻרְקְנוֹס בְּכַף שְׁנִיָּה, מַכְרִיעַ אֶת כֻּלָּם. אַבָּא שָׁאוּל אוֹמֵר מִשְּׁמוֹ: אִם יִהְיוּ כָּל חַכְמֵי יִשְׂרָאֵל בְּכַף מֹאזְנַיִם, וְ(רַבִּי) אֱלִיעֶזֶר בֶּן הֻרְקְנוֹס אַף עִמָּהֶם, וְ(רַבִּי) אֶלְעָזָר בֶּן עֲרָךְ בְּכַף שְׁנִיָּה, מַכְרִיעַ אֶת כֻּלָּם.

[יב] **אָמַר** לָהֶם: צְאוּ וּרְאוּ אֵיזוֹ הִיא דֶּרֶךְ טוֹבָה שֶׁיִּדְבַּק בָּהּ הָאָדָם. רַבִּי

פירוש לרבי עובדיה ספורנו

ב:יא. הנה לפי דעת תנא קמא שבח את בור סיד הבקי שהיה תלמודו בידו, כאמרם ז״ל „שלחו מתם סיני ועוקר הרים סיני עדיף דהכל צריכין למרי חטייא״, וזה יתאמת בלי ספק לצריכים לדברי קבלה שאין דרך לקנותה בסברא כי אמנם טוב להם להושיב בראש את הבקי הנקרא סיני שיודיעם דברי קבלה יותר מן המפולפל הנקרא עוקר

SFORNO'S COMMENTARY

2:11

הוּא הָיָה אוֹמֵר: . . . וֶאֱלִיעֶזֶר בֶּן הֻרְקְנוֹס מַכְרִיעַ אֶת כֻּלָּם: אַבָּא שָׁאוּל אוֹמֵר . . . וְרַבִּי אֶלְעָזָר בֶּן עֲרָךְ . . . מַכְרִיעַ אֶת כֻּלָּם — *He used to say: . . . and Eliezer ben Hyrkanos . . . he would outweigh them all. Abba Shaul said . . . (Rabbi) Elazar ben Arach . . . would outweigh them all.* According to the opinion of the first Tanna, [Rabban Yochanan] praised the erudite "cemented cistern" (Eliezer ben Hyrkanos) whose knowledge was at his disposal, as our Sages said: **שָׁלְחוּ מִתָּם סִינַי וְעוֹקֵר הָרִים, סִינַי עָדִיף דְּהַכֹּל צְרִיכִים לְמָרֵי חִטַּיָּא**, "*They sent an answer from Eretz Yisrael — [Between] Sinai* (one with vast Torah knowledge) *and an 'uprooter of mountains* (one whose understanding of Torah is deeper),' *Sinai is preferable, for all need 'the one who owns the wheat'* " (*Berachos* 64a). This truth is self-evident to those who require transmitted knowledge, for it cannot be attained through speculation and reasoning. Hence, it is better for them to appoint as their leader (רֹאשׁ הַיְשִׁיבָה) a sage who will teach them transmitted

NOTES

2:11

הוּא הָיָה אוֹמֵר . . . וֶאֱלִיעֶזֶר בֶּן הֻרְקְנוֹס . . . מַכְרִיעַ אֶת כֻּלָּם אַבָּא שָׁאוּל אוֹמֵר . . . וְרַבִּי אֶלְעָזָר בֶּן עֲרָךְ . . . מַכְרִיעַ אֶת כֻּלָּם — *He used to say . . . Eliezer ben Hyrkanos . . . he would outweigh them all. Abba Shaul said . . . (Rabbi) Elazar ben Arach . . . he would outweigh them all.* The *Sforno* cites various rabbinic sources in the Talmud to clarify the argument between the two Tannaim in this Mishnah as to whether Rabbi Eliezer ben Hyrkanos or Rabbi Elazar ben Arach was the greater sage.

In the first quote, the Sages of the Talmud speculate which quality should be sought for in a teacher — the gift of memory, or talent for logic and reasoning. The term they use for an individual possessing the former trait is "Sinai" — a metaphor for accumulated knowledge — while the

11. *He used to say: If all the sages of Israel were on one pan of a balance-scale, and Eliezer ben Hyrkanos were on the other, he would outweigh them all. Abba Shaul said in his name: If all the sages of Israel, with even (Rabbi) Eliezer ben Hyrkanos among them, were on one pan of the balance-scale, and (Rabbi) Elazar ben Arach were on the other, he would outweigh them all.*

12. *He said to them: Go out and discern which is the proper way to which a man should cling.*

פירוש לרבי עובדיה ספורנו

הרים, שהרי בידם להתבונן ולפלפל בענין רב כהנה ורב אסי תלמידי דרב דלגמריה הוו צריכי. לסבריה לא הוו צריכי אמנם בבחינת אמתות כל דבר ודבר בלי טעות ובהבנת דבר מתוך דבר יותר משובח העוקר הרים מן הסיני, כאמרם ז״ל „טבא פילפלא חריפא ממלא צנא דקרי״:

ב:יב. דרך טובה מישרת האדם אל מעלות

SFORNO'S COMMENTARY

knowledge — whom the Sages call a "Sinai" — rather than a master of dialectics (מְפַלְפֵּל), whom the Sages call "an uprooter of mountains" (עוֹקֵר הָרִים) for the students are capable of analyzing and examining [what they are taught on their own], as we find regarding Rav Kahana and Rav Assi, the students of Rav, "who required instruction in transmitted knowledge (גְּמָרָא), but did not require direction in analytical deduction" (see *Sanhedrin* 36b).

However, to understand the true meaning of every [Torah concept] without error, and to deduce one concept from another, an "uprooter of mountains" is preferable over a "Sinai," as our Sages said, טָבָא חֲדָא פִּלְפְּלָא חֲרִיפָא מִמְּלֹא צַנָּא דְקָרֵי, "*Better one sharp pepper seed than a basketful of gourds*" (*Yoma* 85b).

2:12

אֵיזוֹ הִיא דֶרֶךְ טוֹבָה שֶׁיִּדְבַּק בָּהּ הָאָדָם — *Go out and discern which is the proper way to which a man should cling.* A proper way of life guides one [on a path] towards the qualities of [superior] ethical character traits and concepts.

NOTES

latter trait is characterized by the term עוֹקֵר הָרִים, literally "an uprooter of mountains."

Our Mishnah uses different terms for these two types of individuals: "a cistern that loses not a drop" refers to the former, while a "spring flowing stronger and stronger" refers to the latter. The difference of opinion in the Talmud as to which of these attributes is superior is reflected in our Mishnah in the different opinions expressed by the first Tanna and by Abba Shaul.

The *Sforno* explains the advantages of each of these strengths: For the sharp student, "Sinai" is preferable, whereas for the purpose of clear understanding and reaching an accurate *halachic* decision, the attribute of "a spring flowing stronger and stronger" is preferred. Thus, it is possible that the first Tanna and Abba Shaul do not disagree with each other, but are merely expressing their opinion regarding different areas of Torah scholarship.

ב אֱלִיעֶזֶר אוֹמֵר: עַיִן טוֹבָה. רַבִּי יְהוֹשֻׁעַ אוֹמֵר: חָבֵר
יג טוֹב. רַבִּי יוֹסֵי אוֹמֵר: שָׁכֵן טוֹב. רַבִּי שִׁמְעוֹן אוֹמֵר: הָרוֹאֶה אֶת הַנּוֹלָד. רַבִּי אֶלְעָזָר אוֹמֵר: לֵב טוֹב. אָמַר לָהֶם: רוֹאֶה אֲנִי אֶת דִּבְרֵי אֶלְעָזָר בֶּן עֲרָךְ מִדִּבְרֵיכֶם, שֶׁבִּכְלַל דְּבָרָיו דִּבְרֵיכֶם.

[יג] **אָמַר** לָהֶם: צְאוּ וּרְאוּ אֵיזוֹ הִיא דֶּרֶךְ רָעָה שֶׁיִּתְרַחֵק מִמֶּנָּה הָאָדָם. רַבִּי אֱלִיעֶזֶר אוֹמֵר: עַיִן רָעָה. רַבִּי יְהוֹשֻׁעַ אוֹמֵר: חָבֵר רָע. רַבִּי יוֹסֵי אוֹמֵר: שָׁכֵן רָע. רַבִּי שִׁמְעוֹן אוֹמֵר: הַלֹּוֶה וְאֵינוֹ מְשַׁלֵּם. אֶחָד הַלֹּוֶה מִן הָאָדָם כְּלֹוֶה מִן הַמָּקוֹם, שֶׁנֶּאֱמַר: „לֹוֶה רָשָׁע וְלֹא יְשַׁלֵּם,

פירוש לרבי עובדיה ספורנו

המדות והמושכלות. עין טובה, שלא יקנא ותרבה חמדתו לאין תכלית כי בסור זה יפנה לבו אל מה שהוא הטוב באמת. חבר טוב, יבחר להתחבר עם אדם בעל מעלות מדות ומושכלות כי בחברתו יקנה אותם אל נקלה ותקבענה בנפשו. שכן טוב, לא בלבד צריך לזה חבר טוב אבל יצטרך עם זה שכונת הטובים. הרואה את הנולד,

SFORNO'S COMMENTARY

עַיִן טוֹבָה — *A good eye.* "A good eye" means that one should not be jealous nor nurture his desires *ad infinitum,* for by shunning these [undesirable inclinations which serve no meaningful purpose], a person will focus his mind on that which is truly good.

חָבֵר טוֹב — *A good friend.* "A good friend" [means] to choose as a friend someone who possesses good qualities, [and superior] character traits and ethics. For by befriending him, one will readily attain these [qualities], and they will become a permanent part of his character.

שָׁכֵן טוֹב — *A good neighbor.* "A good neighbor" [means] that it is not sufficient to have a good friend, but also to reside among good neighbors.

NOTES

2:12-13

רַבִּי אֶלְעָזָר אוֹמֵר: לֵב טוֹב . . . רוֹאֶה אֲנִי אֶת דִּבְרֵי אֶלְעָזָר בֶּן עֲרָךְ — *Rabbi Elazar says: A good heart . . . I (Rabban Yochanan ben Zakkai) prefer the words of Elazar ben Arach.* When Rabban Yochanan ben Zakkai praises the words of Rabbi Elazar ben Arach, he does not mean that his statement is preferable to that of the other disciples. Rather, he is teaching us that without "a good heart" — i.e., the proper intentions which motivate and shape one's actions — the character traits enumerated by the other disciples are meaningless, be it a good eye, a good companion, a good neighbor, or foresight.

אֵיזוֹ הִיא דֶּרֶךְ רָעָה שֶׁיִּתְרַחֵק מִמֶּנָּה . . . רַבִּי אֶלְעָזָר אוֹמֵר: לֵב רַע . . . רוֹאֶה אֲנִי אֶת דִּבְרֵי אֶלְעָזָר בֶּן עֲרָךְ — *Which is the evil path from which a*

Rabbi Eliezer says: A good eye. Rabbi Yehoshua says: A good friend. Rabbi Yose says: A good neighbor. Rabbi Shimon says: One who considers the outcome of a deed. Rabbi Elazar says: A good heart. He [Rabban Yochanan ben Zakkai] said to them: I prefer the words of Elazar ben Arach to your words, for your words are included in his words.

13. *He said to them: Go out and discern which is the evil path from which a man should distance himself. Rabbi Eliezer says: An evil eye. Rabbi Yehoshua says: A wicked friend. Rabbi Yose says: A wicked neighbor. Rabbi Shimon says: One who borrows and does not repay; one who borrows from man is like one who borrows from the Omnipresent, as it is said: "The wicked one borrows and does not repay,*

פירוש לרבי עובדיה ספורנו

המשוה לנגדו תמיד את הטוב הנמשך לפועל הטוב ואת הרע הנמשך לפעל הרע. לב טוב, שתהיה כוונת האדם לכבוד קונו בכל אשר יפנה שם. רואה אני את דברי רבי אלעזר בן ערך מדבריכם, כי אמנם דבריכם לא יתאמתו שיהיו דרכים טובים בזולת דברו, אבל דברו יתאמת שיהיה דרך טוב גם בזולת דבריכם:

SFORNO'S COMMENTARY

הָרוֹאֶה אֶת הַנּוֹלָד — *One who considers the outcome of a deed.* "One who considers the outcome of a deed" [refers to] one who constantly sees the benefits that result from a good deed, and the evil which results from a bad deed.

לֵב טוֹב — *A good heart.* "A good heart" [means] that a person's intent should ever be to bring honor to his Maker, in all his deeds.

רוֹאֶה אֲנִי אֶת דִּבְרֵי אֶלְעָזָר בֶּן עֲרָךְ מִדִּבְרֵיכֶם, שֶׁבִּכְלַל דְּבָרָיו דִּבְרֵיכֶם — *I prefer the words of Elazar ben Arach to your words, for words are included in his words.* "I prefer the words of Elazar ben Arach to your words," for your words will not be realized without heeding his advice [i.e., the need for a good heart], whereas his advice *can* be realized as the "proper way" even in the absence of your suggestions.

NOTES

man should distance himself . . . Rabbi Elazar said: A wicked heart . . . I (Rabban Yochanan ben Zakkai) prefer the words of Elazar ben Arach. The *Sforno* also explains why Rabbi Yochanan saw it necessary to ask his students to define the "evil path" to be shunned even though they clearly expressed their opinion of what constitutes the "good way." He answers that "evil" is not always the reverse of "good," for once

ב וְצַדִּיק חוֹנֵן וְנוֹתֵן." רַבִּי אֶלְעָזָר אוֹמֵר: לֵב רָע.
יד אָמַר לָהֶם: רוֹאֶה אֲנִי אֶת דִּבְרֵי אֶלְעָזָר בֶּן עֲרָךְ
מִדִּבְרֵיכֶם, שֶׁבִּכְלַל דְּבָרָיו דִּבְרֵיכֶם.

[יד] **הֵם** אָמְרוּ שְׁלשָׁה דְבָרִים. רַבִּי אֱלִיעֶזֶר אוֹמֵר: יְהִי כְבוֹד חֲבֵרְךָ חָבִיב עָלֶיךָ כְּשֶׁלָּךְ, וְאַל תְּהִי נוֹחַ לִכְעוֹס; וְשׁוּב יוֹם אֶחָד לִפְנֵי מִיתָתְךָ; וֶהֱוֵי מִתְחַמֵּם כְּנֶגֶד אוּרָן שֶׁל חֲכָמִים, וֶהֱוֵי זָהִיר בְּגַחַלְתָּן שֶׁלֹּא תִכָּוֶה —

פירוש לרבי עובדיה ספורנו

ב:יג. רבי אליעזר אומר עין רעה וכולי. אף על פי שאמר הרב שכל מה ששבחו לטוב לא יתאמת בלתי לב טוב, חשבו שבזה לא ימנע שיהיה הדבר רע בזולת לב רע בהיותו בעצמו רע, והשיב להם הרב ואמר שגם מה שיראה רע בעצמו לא יהיה רע באמת אם לא יהיה עם לב רע, כאמרם ז"ל „גדולה עברה לשמה ממצוה שלא לשמה" כאשר התבאר בענין יעל ותמר וזולתם:

SFORNO'S COMMENTARY

2:13

רַבִּי אֶלְעָזָר אוֹמֵר: לֵב רַע. אָמַר לָהֶם: רוֹאֶה אֲנִי אֶת דִּבְרֵי אֶלְעָזָר בֶּן עֲרָךְ מִדִּבְרֵיכֶם, שֶׁבִּכְלַל דְּבָרָיו דִּבְרֵיכֶם — *Rabbi Elazar said: A wicked heart. He [Rabban Yochanan ben Zakkai] said to them: I prefer the words of Elazar ben Aruch to your words, for your words are included in his words.* Although the master [Yochanan ben Zakkai] already stated that all the [traits the other disciples] had praised as being good could not become actual without "a good heart," nonetheless, they [incorrectly] concluded that this does not rule out the possibility of a wicked trait existing even in the absence of "a wicked heart."

The master answered them by saying that even that which appears to be intrinsically evil is not truly evil if there is an absence of "a wicked heart," as our Sages said, גְּדוֹלָה עֲבֵרָה לִשְׁמָהּ מִמִּצְוָה שֶׁלֹּא לִשְׁמָהּ, "*Greater is a transgression*

NOTES

again, everything depends on a person's intentions.

As he proves from the Sages' statement which he cites, an apparent sin may actually be a virtuous act, while an apparent *mitzvah* may in reality constitute a sin.

Yael was the virtuous woman who invited Sisera, the captain of the Canaanite army fleeing Barak's men, into her tent. There she killed him and saved Israel (see *Judges* 4).

Tamar was the daughter-in-law of Yehudah. She sat at the crossroads and acted the role of a harlot in order to conceive a child from Yehudah. In this manner, she brought forth the אוֹרוֹ שֶׁל מָשִׁיחַ, "the light of the Messiah," through Peretz, the child born from this union.

Both of these events demonstrate that an apparent transgression, when committed "for the sake of heaven," can result in a triumph for Israel and the sowing of the seeds of *Moshiach.*

2 but the Righteous One is gracious and gives." Rabbi
14 Elazar said: A wicked heart. He [Rabban Yochanan ben Zakkai] said to them: I prefer the words of Elazar ben Arach to your words, for your words are included in his words.

14. They each said three things. Rabbi Eliezer says: (a) Let your fellow's honor be as dear to you as your own, and do not anger easily; (b) repent one day before your death; and (c) warm yourself by the fire of the sages, but treat their glowing coal with care, lest

פירוש לרבי עובדיה ספורנו

ב:יד. אמר הנה להשיג מעלת בור סיד שהשגתי לא קדמני אדם בבית המדרש ולא הנחתי אדם בבית המדרש ויצאתי. ולעשות זה צריך שלא ידחוהו חבריו, וזה בהיותו נוח לחבריו בהזהרו בכבודם ובהיותו בלתי נוח לכעוס עליהם. שנית שאם יקרה שלפעמים יגבר יצרו ויכעס – שיחזור בו תכף. שלישית שיקרב

SFORNO'S COMMENTARY

for the sake of Heaven than a mitzvah which is not for the sake of Heaven" (*Nazir* 23b). This is evident from the incident of Yael, Tamar and others.

2:14

יְהִי כְבוֹד חֲבֵרְךָ חָבִיב עָלֶיךָ כְּשֶׁלָּךְ, וְאַל תְּהִי נוֹחַ לִכְעוֹס; וְשׁוּב יוֹם אֶחָד לִפְנֵי מִיתָתְךָ — *Let your fellow's honor be as dear to you as your own, and do not anger easily, repent one day before your death.* Rabbi Elazar said: In order to acquire the quality of "a cemented cistern," which I attained, לֹא קְדָמַנִי אָדָם בְּבֵית הַמִּדְרָשׁ וְלֹא הִנַּחְתִּי אָדָם בְּבֵית הַמִּדְרָשׁ וְיָצָאתִי, "*No one preceded me to the study hall, and I never left [with] another person [still] in the study* hall" (*Succah* 28a). And in order to do this, one must not be rebuffed by one's colleagues. This is accomplished by behaving pleasantly towards one's colleagues, by being respectful of their honor, and by not being quick to grow angry against them.

Second, even if a person's [evil] inclination occasionally overpowers him and he does become angry, he should recant immediately.

NOTES

2:14

יְהִי כָבוֹד חֲבֵרְךָ חָבִיב עָלֶיךָ כְּשֶׁלָּךְ, וְאַל תְּהִי נוֹחַ לִכְעוֹס . . . וֶהֱוֵי מִתְחַמֵּם כְּנֶגֶד אוּרָן שֶׁל חֲכָמִים — *Let your fellow's honor be as dear to you as your own and do not anger easily . . . and warm yourself by the fire of the Sages.* The *Sforno* interprets the following statements of Rabbi Yochanan's outstanding disciples as natural extensions of their distinguishing attributes. For instance, Rabbi Eliezer, whose strength lay in his prodigious memory, tells us that he was not simply born with this gift, but developed it through his behavior and conduct in the בֵּית הַמִּדְרָשׁ, *study hall,* and through his relationship with other Torah scholars.

Similarly, Rabbi Yehoshua, Rabbi Yose, Rabbi Shimon and Rabbi Elazar each ex-

שֶׁנְּשִׁיכָתָן נְשִׁיכַת שׁוּעָל, וַעֲקִיצָתָן עֲקִיצַת עַקְרָב, וּלְחִישָׁתָן לְחִישַׁת שָׂרָף, וְכָל דִּבְרֵיהֶם כְּגַחֲלֵי אֵשׁ.

[טו] **רַבִּי** יְהוֹשֻׁעַ אוֹמֵר: עַיִן הָרָע, וְיֵצֶר הָרָע, וְשִׂנְאַת הַבְּרִיּוֹת מוֹצִיאִין אֶת הָאָדָם מִן הָעוֹלָם.

[טז] **רַבִּי** יוֹסֵי אוֹמֵר: יְהִי מָמוֹן חֲבֵרְךָ חָבִיב

פירוש לרבי עובדיה ספורנו

לחכמים ללמוד מהם, אבל לא יגיס לבו בהם, שנשיכתן והיא הנזיפה היא רעה ועקיצתן והיא הנדוי רעה ממנה ולחישתן והיא השמתה רבת ההיזק מכלן, ועם כל זה צריך שיתקרב האדם אליהם תמיד ללמוד מהן, שכל דבריהם כגחלי אש המאיר ומחמם, שאפילו שיחה שלהם צריכה תלמוד:

SFORNO'S COMMENTARY

וֶהֱוֵי מִתְחַמֵּם כְּנֶגֶד אוּרָן שֶׁל חֲכָמִים, וֶהֱוֵי זָהִיר בְּגַחַלְתָּן שֶׁלֹּא תִכָּוֶה – שֶׁנְּשִׁיכָתָן . . . וַעֲקִיצָתָן . . . וּלְחִישָׁתָן . . . וְכָל דִּבְרֵיהֶם כְּגַחֲלֵי אֵשׁ — *Warm yourself by the fire of the Sages, but treat their glowing coal with care, lest you be burnt — for their bite . . . their sting . . . their hiss . . . and all their words are like fiery coals.* Third, a person should come close to wise men in order to learn from them, but he must not act arrogantly in their presence. For their "bite" — i.e., rebuke — is harsh, and their "sting" — i.e., ban — is even harsher, and their "hiss" — i.e., excommunication — is harshest of all. Nonetheless, a person should become close with Torah scholars so as to learn from them constantly, for "all their words are like fiery coals," which illuminate and warm, to the extent that "even their [mundane] conversation requires study" (*Succah* 21b).

NOTES

plain how they reached perfection in their particular field of expertise, be it a pleasant personality, piety, reverence, or dialectic adroitness.

Rabbi Yehoshua did so through his ethical generous spirit; Rabbi Yose, through his spirit of empathy, application to Torah study and commitment to fulfill God's Will; Rabbi Shimon, through his constant awareness of God's omnipotence and omniscience; and Rabbi Elazar developed his mastery of Torah dialectics and became like a "spring flowing stronger and stronger" through his unusual diligence in the pursuit of Torah study.

וֶהֱוֵי זָהִיר בְּגַחַלְתָּן שֶׁלֹּא תִכָּוֶה – שֶׁנְּשִׁיכָתָן . . . וַעֲקִיצָתָן . . . וּלְחִישָׁתָן . . . וְכָל דִּבְרֵיהֶם כְּגַחֲלֵי אֵשׁ — *But treat their glowing coal with care, lest you be burnt — for their bite . . . their sting . . . their hiss . . . and all their words are like fiery coals.* Regarding the care one must exercise in his dealings with the wise, the *Sforno* explains the choice of the three phrases used by Rabbi Eliezer, i.e. "bite," "sting," and "hiss." Each is progressively more severe; they represent three degrees of punishment leveled by the court against those who are disrespectful to Torah scholars, ranging from a rebuke, which is the lightest, to excommunication, the most severe. Interestingly, he does not interpret the concluding part of the Mishnah, as additional cautionary advice, but rather as words of encouragement to the student, to

2 15-16 *you be burnt — for their bite is the bite of a fox, their sting is the sting of a scorpion, their hiss is the hiss of a serpent, and all their words are like fiery coals.*

15. *Rabbi Yehoshua says: (a) An evil eye, (b) the evil inclination, and (c) hatred of other people remove a person from the world.*

16. *Rabbi Yose says: (a) Let your fellow's money be as dear to you as your own; (b) apply*

פירוש לרבי עובדיה ספורנו

ב:טו. עין הרע בשל אחרים וחמדת ממונם, ויצר הרע והוא תאות התענוגים, ושנאת הבריות מחמת קנאה – מוציאין את האדם מכל מדה ממוצעת ומאושרת ששבח אותי הרב באמרו אשרי יולדתו:

ב:טז. הנה מדת החסידות ששבח הרב, והיא בהיטיב לזולת – תעלה בידך בהיות ממון חברך חביב עליך כשלך באהבתך את

SFORNO'S COMMENTARY

2:15

רַבִּי יְהוֹשֻׁעַ אוֹמֵר: עַיִן הָרָע — *Rabbi Yehoshua says: (a) An evil eye.* "An evil eye" means [envying] others and coveting their money.

וְיֵצֶר הָרָע — *(b) The evil inclination.* "The evil inclination" means lusting after physical pleasures.

וְשִׂנְאַת הַבְּרִיּוֹת — *(c) Hatred of other people.* "Hatred of other people" [refers to] jealousy-induced [hatred].

מוֹצִיאִין אֶת הָאָדָם מִן הָעוֹלָם — *Remove a person from the world.* These [negative attributes] "remove a person" — i.e., they remove one from every favorable attribute of moderation for which my teacher praised me when he said, **אַשְׁרֵי יוֹלַדְתּוֹ**, "*Praiseworthy is she who bore him*" (Mishnah 10).

2:16

רַבִּי יוֹסֵי אוֹמֵר: יְהִי מָמוֹן חֲבֵרְךָ חָבִיב עָלֶיךָ כְּשֶׁלָּךְ — *Rabbi Yose says: (a) Let your fellow's money be as dear to you as your own.* The attribute of "piety" — i.e., being kind to others — for which the master praised me will be attained when "your fellow's money will be as dear to you as your own" — that is, when you will become truly concerned for his well-being.

NOTES

cultivate his relationship with the wise, and draw closer to them, for there is much to be gained by being in their company and observing their behavior.

2:16

יְהִי מָמוֹן חֲבֵרְךָ חָבִיב עָלֶיךָ כְּשֶׁלָּךְ, וְהַתְקֵן עַצְמְךָ לִלְמוֹד תּוֹרָה. . . מַעֲשֶׂיךָ יִהְיוּ לְשֵׁם שָׁמָיִם — *(a) Let your fellow's money be as dear to you as your own; (b) apply yourself to study Torah . . . and (c) let all your deeds be for the sake of Heaven.* According to the *Sforno,* the term **חָסִיד** ("pious individual") is linked to **חֶסֶד** ("lovingkindness"), but it also conveys meticulous observance of the letter and spirit of the law. The first facet of this term

ב עָלֶיךָ כְּשֶׁלָּךְ; וְהַתְקֵן עַצְמְךָ לִלְמוֹד תּוֹרָה, שֶׁאֵינָהּ
יז יְרֻשָּׁה לָךְ; וְכָל מַעֲשֶׂיךָ יִהְיוּ לְשֵׁם שָׁמָיִם.

[יז] **רַבִּי** שִׁמְעוֹן אוֹמֵר: הֱוֵי זָהִיר בִּקְרִיאַת שְׁמַע וּבִתְפִלָּה; וּכְשֶׁאַתָּה מִתְפַּלֵּל, אַל תַּעַשׂ תְּפִלָּתְךָ קֶבַע, אֶלָּא רַחֲמִים וְתַחֲנוּנִים לִפְנֵי הַמָּקוֹם, שֶׁנֶּאֱמַר: „כִּי חַנּוּן וְרַחוּם הוּא אֶרֶךְ אַפַּיִם וְרַב חֶסֶד וְנִחָם עַל הָרָעָה"; וְאַל תְּהִי רָשָׁע בִּפְנֵי עַצְמֶךָ.

פירוש לרבי עובדיה ספורנו

טובתו: התקן עצמך ללמוד תורה יותר מההכנה אשר לך בטבע, שאינה ירושה לך, שלא יקרה לך בה כמו שיקרה ליורש שיקנה ממון בזולת השתדלות, כי אמנם בזה לא יספיק מעט השתדלות. ובהשיגך תלמוד תורה תשיג החסידות, לא זולת זה, כאמרם ז"ל „לא עם הארץ חסיד". וכל מעשיך יהיו לשם שמים, תהיה הכוונה לעשות רצון יוצרך ללכת בדרכיו שהוא חסיד בכל מעשיו:

ב:יז. הנה מעלת יראת חטא ששבח הרב תעלה בידך בזהירות על קריאת שמע

SFORNO'S COMMENTARY

וְהַתְקֵן עַצְמְךָ לִלְמוֹד תּוֹרָה, שֶׁאֵינָהּ יְרֻשָּׁה לָךְ — *(b) Apply yourself to study Torah, for it is not yours by inheritance.* Also, "apply yourself to study Torah" more than you are naturally inclined to do, for "it is not yours by inheritance." What is true of an heir, i.e. that he acquires wealth without any effort, will not happen to you in [Torah study]. For in [Torah study], little effort is insufficient.

And when you will acquire Torah knowledge, you will also attain the attribute of "piety." Otherwise, you will not [attain "piety"], for the Sages said, וְלֹא עַם הָאָרֶץ חָסִיד, *"An unlearned person cannot be scrupulously pious"* (Mishnah 6).

וְכָל מַעֲשֶׂיךָ יִהְיוּ לְשֵׁם שָׁמָיִם — *(c) Let all your deeds be for the sake of Hashem.* "Let all your deeds be for the sake of Heaven" means to always intend to fulfill the will of your Creator, and to walk in His ways, for He is חָסִיד בְּכָל מַעֲשָׂיו, *"Pious in all His ways" (Psalms* 145:17).

2:17

הֱוֵי זָהִיר בִּקְרִיאַת שְׁמַע וּבִתְפִלָּה; . . . אַל תַּעַשׂ תְּפִלָּתְךָ קֶבַע, אֶלָּא רַחֲמִים וְתַחֲנוּנִים לִפְנֵי הַמָּקוֹם — *(a) Be meticulous in reading the* ***Shema*** *and in prayer; (b) . . . do not*

NOTES

constant awareness of our obligation to emulate Hashem, we will mirror His attribute of being חָסִיד בְּכָל מַעֲשָׂיו "Pious [חָסִיד], in all His ways."

2:17

הֱוֵי זָהִיר בִּקְרִיאַת שְׁמַע וּבִתְפִלָּה; . . . אַל תַּעַשׂ תְּפִלָּתְךָ קֶבַע . . . וְאַל תְּהִי רָשָׁע בִּפְנֵי עַצְמֶךָ — *(a)*

can be acquired by developing the same sense of concern for other people's possessions as one feels for his own. The latter aspect of חָסִיד can be attained through Torah study, for only Torah knowledge can teach a person the way to *mitzvah* observance. Finally, Rabbi Yose suggests that by

yourself to study Torah, for it is not yours by inheritance; and (c) let all your deeds be for the sake of Heaven.

17. *Rabbi Shimon says: (a) Be meticulous in reading the Shema and in prayer; (b) when you pray, do not make your prayer a set routine, but rather [beg for] compassion and supplication before the Omnipresent, as it is said: "For He is gracious and compassionate, slow to anger, abounding in kindness, and relentful of punishment"; and (c) do not judge yourself to be a wicked person.*

פירוש לרבי עובדיה ספורנו

ותפלה המזכירים גדולת המלך הקדוש שצוה להזהר מן החטא, ובזה שלא תהיה תפלתך קבע כמסיר משא מעליו אבל תהיה רחמים ותחנונים, כי בזה תרגיש שאתה צריך להשיג לחיי עד מלפניו כל משאלותיך ותירא מחטא לו. ואל תהי רשע בפני עצמך כמו שעשה אלישע אחר, שבשביל שחשב שאין לו תקנה לא רצה לחזור בו, אבל ראוי שאם תחטא תחשוב שיש תקנה ותשוב בהיותו מתנחם על הרעה:

SFORNO'S COMMENTARY

make your prayer a set routine, but rather [beg for] compassion and supplication before the Ominpresent. You will attain the virtue of "fear of sin," which the Master praised, by,

"Being meticulous in reading the *Shema* and in prayer," for they remind us of the greatness of the Holy King, Who commanded us to avoid sin and also by, "Not making your prayer a set routine," as though you were unloading a burden from yourself. Rather, let your prayers be [in a spirit of] compassion and supplication, for in this manner you will realize that all your requests can be fulfilled only by Him, and [consequently] you will be afraid to sin against Him.

וְאַל תְּהִי רָשָׁע בִּפְנֵי עַצְמֶךָ — *And (c) do not judge yourself to be a wicked person.* "And do not judge yourself to be a wicked person," as did Elisha (*Acher*), who refused to repent because he thought he was beyond redemption. Rather, if you do sin, you should realize that rectification is possible, and repent in a state of remorse over the evil [you have committed].

NOTES

Be meticulous in reading the Shema and in prayer; (b) . . . do not make your prayer a set routine . . . and (c) do not judge yourself to be a wicked person. Rabbi Shimon was praised by his master as being a man who truly feared sin, for he was ever mindful of the Almighty, Who had cautioned man-kind to reject evil. To reach this level of Godly awareness, one must use the tools of prayer. This includes accepting upon oneself the yoke of Heaven through the careful reading of *Shema,* and refining the nature of one's prayers through proper כַּוָּנָה, *intent.* Only in this manner will a person deter himself from committing sin.

However, in view of mankind's frailties,

[יח] **רַבִּי** אֶלְעָזָר אוֹמֵר: הֱוֵי שָׁקוּד לִלְמוֹד תּוֹרָה, וְדַע מַה שֶּׁתָּשִׁיב לְאֶפִּיקוֹרוֹס; וְדַע לִפְנֵי מִי אַתָּה עָמֵל; וְנֶאֱמָן הוּא בַּעַל מְלַאכְתְּךָ, שֶׁיְּשַׁלֶּם לְךָ שְׂכַר פְּעֻלָּתֶךָ.

[יט] **רַבִּי** טַרְפוֹן אוֹמֵר: הַיּוֹם קָצָר, וְהַמְּלָאכָה מְרֻבָּה, וְהַפּוֹעֲלִים עֲצֵלִים, וְהַשָּׂכָר הַרְבֵּה, וּבַעַל הַבַּיִת דּוֹחֵק.

פירוש לרבי עובדיה ספורנו

ב:יח. הנה בשקידת תלמוד תורה בלבד ולא בזולת זה תמצא בה תשובה מספקת לכופרים, כאמרו „אם תבקשנה ככסף וכמטמונים תחפשנה או תבין יראת יי ודעת קדושים תמצא", ובזה תהיה מעין מתגבר על כל חולק כמו ששבח הרב. ודע לפני מי אתה עמל, שראוי שתרבה עמל בזה לכבודו. ודע שנאמן הוא בעל מלאכתך שישלם, אף על פי שאין ראוי שתכוין אתה לזה אלא לעשות רצונו:

SFORNO'S COMMENTARY

2:18

הֱוֵי שָׁקוּד לִלְמוֹד תּוֹרָה, וְדַע מַה שֶּׁתָּשִׁיב לְאֶפִּיקוֹרוֹס — *(a) Be diligent in the study of Torah and know what to answer a heretic.* Only through diligent Torah study, and in no other manner, will you find a convincing answer to heretics, as it is written, אִם תְּבַקְשֶׁנָּה כַכָּסֶף וְכַמַּטְמֹנִים תַּחְפְּשֶׂנָּה. אָז תָּבִין יִרְאַת ה׳ וְדַעַת אֱלֹהִים תִּמְצָא *If you seek her [i.e., Torah] like silver and search for her as for hidden treasures, then you shall understand the fear of Hashem, and find the knowledge of God* (*Proverbs* 2:4-5). In this way you will become מַעְיָן הַמִּתְגַּבֵּר, "a spring flowing stronger and stronger" against all those who differ, as the teacher said in his praise.

וְדַע לִפְנֵי מִי אַתָּה עָמֵל; וְנֶאֱמָן הוּא בַּעַל מְלַאכְתְּךָ, שֶׁיְּשַׁלֶּם לְךָ שְׂכַר פְּעֻלָּתֶךָ — *(b) Know before Whom you toil; and (c) know that your Employer can be relied upon to*

NOTES

a person may, in spite of all his good intentions, stumble and sin. When this occurs, he must not despair and feel that all is lost, for *teshuvah* is always possible. The very worst thing a person can do is consider himself a רָשָׁע, a wicked person. In this manner, the *Sforno* masterfully links three seemingly disparate statements into a unified whole.

2:18

הֱוֵי שָׁקוּד לִלְמוֹד תּוֹרָה, וְדַע מַה שֶּׁתָּשִׁיב לְאֶפִּיקוֹרוֹס — *Be diligent in the study of Torah and know what to answer a heretic.* The first statement of Rabbi Elazar emphasizes that diligent Torah study is the only way to plumb the depths of Torah wisdom and become a flowing, never-ceasing spring of Torah knowledge. Only in this manner can a person attain the ultimate understanding of Torah and knowledge of God, and thereby arm himself with convincing answers with which to refute the questions of heretics.

וְדַע לִפְנֵי מִי אַתָּה עָמֵל — *Know before Whom you toil.* The *Sforno* interprets Rabbi Elazar's second lesson as emphasizing the need for proper intent and pure motivation

18. *Rabbi Elazar says: (a) Be diligent in the study of Torah and know what to answer a heretic; (b) know before Whom you toil; and (c) know that your Employer can be relied upon to pay you the wage of your labor.*

19. *Rabbi Tarfon says: The day is short, the task is abundant, the laborers are lazy, the wage is great, and the Master of the house is insistent.*

פירוש לרבי עובדיה ספורנו

ב:יט. אמר ראוי לתמוה על עצלות רב בני האדם וכמעט כלם, כאמרו „הכל סר יחדו נאלחו", שאף על פי שלא יעסקו בתורה ובמצות מאהבה ומיראה כראוי היה להם לעסוק בתורה בשביל השכר שהוא הרבה, שאדם אוכל פירותיה בעולם הזה והקרן קיימת לעולם הבא בלי ספק, כאמרו „כי הוא חייכם", ולהשיג ידיעה בה יצטרך זמן רב, והנה חיי האדם קצרים בערך אל המלאכה שהיא ארוכה מארץ מדה, ובעל

SFORNO'S COMMENTARY

pay you the wage of your labor. "And know before Whom you toil," for it is proper that you increase your toil in His honor. And "know that your Employer can be relied upon to pay you the wage of your labor," although it is certainly not proper that this be your motivating factor, but rather, that you fulfill His will.

2:19

הַיּוֹם קָצָר, וְהַמְּלָאכָה מְרֻבָּה, וְהַפּוֹעֲלִים עֲצֵלִים, וְהַשָּׂכָר הַרְבֵּה, וּבַעַל הַבַּיִת דּוֹחֵק — *The day is short, the task is abundant, the laborers are lazy, the wage is great, and the Master of the house is insistent.* [The Tanna] said: One must wonder at the indolence of most — if not all — men, as it is written, הַכֹּל סָר, יַחְדָּו נֶאֱלָחוּ, *They have all gone astray, together become depraved* (*Psalms* 14:3). For even though they do not occupy themselves with Torah study and *mitzvos* out of love and reverence [of God], as is fitting, nonetheless, they should at least study Torah for the great reward, for "one enjoys its fruit in this world, and the principle remains in the World to Come" (*Pe'ah,* Mishnah 1:1), as it is written, כִּי הוּא חַיֵּיכֶם *For it [i.e., Torah] is your life* (*Deuteronomy* 32:47).

Now to attain Torah knowledge requires much time, and man's life span is short in ratio to "the task," which is אֲרֻכָּה מֵאֶרֶץ מִדָּהּ, *longer than the earth*

NOTES

on the part of the scholar who seeks Torah knowledge, for only in this manner will he be granted enlightenment and understanding of Torah. A Torah scholar must never be driven by personal vanity, nor motivated by a desire to attain fame and honor. Instead, he must do everything for the sake of Heaven.

2:19

הַיּוֹם קָצָר, וְהַמְּלָאכָה מְרֻבָּה, וְהַפּוֹעֲלִים עֲצֵלִים, וְהַשָּׂכָר הַרְבֵּה, וּבַעַל הַבַּיִת דּוֹחֵק — *The day is short, the task is abundant, the laborers are lazy, the wage is great, and the Master of the house is insistent.* As the *Sforno* explains, Rabbi Tarfon expresses amazement over

ב
כ

[כ] הוּא הָיָה אוֹמֵר: לֹא עָלֶיךָ הַמְּלָאכָה לִגְמוֹר, וְלֹא אַתָּה בֶן חוֹרִין לְהִבָּטֵל מִמֶּנָּה. אִם לָמַדְתָּ תוֹרָה הַרְבֵּה, נוֹתְנִים לְךָ שָׂכָר הַרְבֵּה; וְנֶאֱמָן הוּא בַּעַל מְלַאכְתְּךָ, שֶׁיְּשַׁלֶּם לְךָ שְׂכַר פְּעֻלָּתֶךָ. וְדַע שֶׁמַּתַּן שְׂכָרָן שֶׁל צַדִּיקִים לֶעָתִיד לָבֹא.

פירוש לרבי עובדיה ספורנו

הבית דוחק, ששם בטבע האדם ביצירתו שיתאוה לדעת בלי ספק, והיה משתדל בזה לולי תאות יצר הרע אל המנוחה ותענוגות בני האדם, כאמרם ז״ל „רבונו של עולם רצוננו לעשות רצונך ומי מעכב שאור שבעיסה״ וכולי:

ב:כ. ואין התנצלות לאומר שיאמר שאין ראוי לעמול בידיעת התורה מפני שאין להשיגה בזמן קצר, כי אמנם כל חלק ממנה שישיג האדם הוא נחשב ומכוון אצל בעל הבית אף על פי שלא תגמור המלאכה. וגם כן מי שלמד את כלה

SFORNO'S COMMENTARY

is its measure (*Job* 11:9). In addition, "the Master of the house is insistent," for He has doubtless implanted in the nature of man a yearning for knowledge. Were it not for the evil inclination for leisure and physical pleasure, man would make an effort to attain this [knowledge], as our Sages said, רִבּוֹנוֹ שֶׁל עוֹלָם, רְצוֹנֵנוּ לַעֲשׂוֹת רְצוֹנְךָ, וּמִי מְעַכֵּב, שְׂאוֹר שֶׁבָּעִסָּה, *Master of the Universe, our desire is to fulfill Your will, but what prevents us? The leaven in the dough* (*Berachos* 11a).

2:20

לֹא עָלֶיךָ הַמְּלָאכָה לִגְמוֹר — *You are not required to complete the task.* There is no excuse for the person who asserts that it is not worthy to toil for the sake of Torah knowledge since it cannot be attained in a short time. Any portion of Torah that a person masters is important and significant to the "Master of the House," even if one does not "complete the task."

NOTES

mankind's indolence: Despite the fact that Man was created with an innate desire to know his Creator, and the time granted him to attain this knowledge is so short, he nevertheless squanders time which is his most precious gift.

Rabbi Tarfon believes that the average man realizes that the knowledge of God can be attained only through the study of Torah and the observance of *mitzvos.* Given the fact that the reward for the pursuit of Torah is so great, one would think that man would dedicate his every available moment to this pursuit.

However, Rabbi Tarfon is also most understanding of man's frailties. He realizes that the evil inclination, which our Sages characterize as the "leaven in the dough," is extremely powerful, to the degree that man finds it difficult to turn a deaf ear to its enticements. That is why Rabbi Tarfon finds it necessary to remind us of

2
20

20. *He used to say: You are not required to complete the task, yet you are not free to withdraw from it. If you have studied much Torah, they will give you great reward; and your Employer can be relied upon to pay you the wage for your labor, but be aware that the reward of the righteous will be given in the World to Come.*

פירוש לרבי עובדיה ספורנו

וחשב שגמר את כל המלאכה אינו בן חורין ליבטל ממנה, שאם תוסיף לעסוק בה תוסיף שלמות תמיד וירבה שכרה שתמצא חן יותר בעיני המלך, כאמרם ז״ל ,,אינו דומה שונה פרקו מאה פעמים לשונה פרקו מאה ואחת״. ונאמן הוא שישלם, אף על פי שאינו ראוי שתכוין אתה לזה אבל ראוי שתעשה מאהבה, מכל מקום הוא מעצמו נאמן, שאינו מקפח שכר כל בריה:

SFORNO'S COMMENTARY

וְלֹא אַתָּה בֶן חוֹרִין לְהִבָּטֵל מִמֶּנָּה — *Yet you are not free to withdraw from it.* And even a person who *has* studied all of it and thinks that he has "completed the entire task," [in truth,] he is "not free to withdraw from it." For a person who continues to occupy himself with Torah continually adds to his perfection and earns greater reward, for he finds more favor in the eyes of the King. As our Sages said, אֵינוֹ דוֹמֶה שׁוֹנֶה פִּרְקוֹ מֵאָה פְּעָמִים לְשׁוֹנֶה פִּרְקוֹ מֵאָה וְאַחַת, *You cannot compare one who repeats his chapter [of Torah study] one hundred times to him who repeats it one hundred and one times* (*Chagigah* 9b).

וְנֶאֱמָן הוּא בַּעַל מְלַאכְתְּךָ, שֶׁיְּשַׁלֶּם לְךָ שְׂכַר פְּעֻלָּתֶךָ — *And your Employer can be relied upon to pay you the wage of your labor.* "And He can be relied upon to pay your wage," even though it is improper that this be your intention. Rather it is fitting that you [serve Him] out of love. Nevertheless, He can be relied upon [to reward you], for אֵינוֹ מְקַפֵּחַ שְׂכַר כָּל בְּרִיָּה, *He does not deprive any creature of its reward* (*Pesachim* 118a).

NOTES

these seemingly obvious truths, and to admonish us for overlooking them. At the same time, though, he expresses sympathy for, and understanding of, man's shortcomings.

2:20

לֹא עָלֶיךָ הַמְּלָאכָה לִגְמוֹר, וְלֹא אַתָּה בֶן חוֹרִין לְהִבָּטֵל מִמֶּנָּה — *You are not required to complete the task, yet your are not free to withdraw from it.* According to the *Sforno,* Rabbi Tarfon teaches that although it is next to impossible for a person to master the entire Torah, a student should not be discouraged from mastering however much of it that he can, because he will receive a great reward for his accomplishments. At the same time, he warns against feeling satisfied with one's accomplishments in Torah, for it has no limits, and one can never say that one has "finished" studying it.

רַבִּי חֲנַנְיָא בֶּן עֲקַשְׁיָא אוֹמֵר: רָצָה הַקָּדוֹשׁ בָּרוּךְ הוּא לְזַכּוֹת אֶת יִשְׂרָאֵל, לְפִיכָךְ הִרְבָּה לָהֶם תּוֹרָה וּמִצְוֹת, שֶׁנֶּאֱמַר: „יהוה חָפֵץ לְמַעַן צִדְקוֹ, יַגְדִּיל תּוֹרָה וְיַאְדִּיר.״

Rabbi Chanania ben Akashia says: The Holy One, Blessed is He, wished to confer merit upon Israel; therefore He gave them Torah and mitzvos in abundance, as it is said: "HASHEM desired, for the sake of its [Israel's] righteousness, that the Torah be made great and glorious."

פרק ג

Chapter Three

כָּל יִשְׂרָאֵל יֵשׁ לָהֶם חֵלֶק לָעוֹלָם הַבָּא, שֶׁנֶּאֱמַר: „וְעַמֵּךְ כֻּלָּם צַדִּיקִים, לְעוֹלָם יִירְשׁוּ אָרֶץ, נֵצֶר מַטָּעַי, מַעֲשֵׂה יָדַי לְהִתְפָּאֵר."

All Israel has a share in the World to Come, as it is said: "And your people are all righteous; they shall inherit the land forever; they are the branch of My planting, My handiwork, in which to take pride."

[א] **עֲקַבְיָא** בֶּן מַהֲלַלְאֵל אוֹמֵר: הִסְתַּכֵּל בִּשְׁלֹשָׁה דְבָרִים וְאֵין אַתָּה בָא לִידֵי עֲבֵרָה: דַּע מֵאַיִן בָּאתָ, וּלְאָן אַתָּה הוֹלֵךְ, וְלִפְנֵי מִי אַתָּה עָתִיד לִתֵּן דִּין וְחֶשְׁבּוֹן. מֵאַיִן בָּאתָ? מִטִּפָּה סְרוּחָה. וּלְאָן אַתָּה הוֹלֵךְ? לִמְקוֹם עָפָר, רִמָּה וְתוֹלֵעָה. וְלִפְנֵי מִי אַתָּה עָתִיד לִתֵּן דִּין וְחֶשְׁבּוֹן? לִפְנֵי מֶלֶךְ מַלְכֵי הַמְּלָכִים, הַקָּדוֹשׁ בָּרוּךְ הוּא.

[ב] **רַבִּי** חֲנִינָא סְגַן הַכֹּהֲנִים אוֹמֵר: הֱוֵי מִתְפַּלֵּל בִּשְׁלוֹמָהּ שֶׁל מַלְכוּת,

פירוש לרבי עובדיה ספורנו

ג:א. ראוי שתתבונן בתחלת מציאותך וסופו אם כפי החלק הגשמי ואם כפי החלק השכלי. והנה מציאות החלק הגשמי תחלתו וסופו דבר נפסד ונמאס ולכן אין ראוי להרבות השתדלות בענינו, אמנם מציאות החלק השכלי הנה ייטב וירע ענינו כפי השתדלותך בו אשר יצא משפטו מלפני המלך הקדוש, ולכן ראוי להשתדל בהצלחתו שיזכה בה בדינו ולהשמר מכל מונע ממנה, ובזה ההתבוננות אי אתה בא לידי עברה, כי אמנם לא ירבה השתדלותך בהשגת התאוות הגשמיות הנפסדות אבל

SFORNO'S COMMENTARY

3:1

הִסְתַּכֵּל . . . וְאֵין אַתָּה בָא לִידֵי עֲבֵרָה: דַּע מֵאַיִן בָּאתָ, וּלְאָן אַתָּה הוֹלֵךְ . . . — *Consider . . . and you will not come into the grip of sin: Know whence you came, whither you go . . .* It is proper that you contemplate the origin of your being and its culmination, be it regarding the physical aspect [of man], or the intellectual one. Now, behold, the physical part [of man], both its beginning and end, is loathsome and perishable. Therefore, it is not fitting to exert one's energies in its pursuit.

The intellectual element, however, can be good and beneficial or, conversely, evil, according to man's endeavors in this realm, as it is judged

NOTES

3:1

דַּע מֵאַיִן בָּאתָ, וּלְאָן אַתָּה הוֹלֵךְ, וְלִפְנֵי מִי אַתָּה עָתִיד לִתֵּן דִּין וְחֶשְׁבּוֹן — *Know whence you came, whither you go, and before Whom you will give justification and reckoning.* The *Sforno*'s commentary on this Mishnah addresses a question which is also discussed by many other commentators: Why does Akavia repeat his three rhetorical questions? Ostensibly, he should have simply provided the answers. Why did he see it necessary to repeat the questions in the second part of the Mishnah?

The *Sforno* explains that Akavia discusses two different aspects of man's nature — the physical and the spiritual. Every person has a dual nature and possesses two disparate temperaments. Thus, there are two ways of approaching the question, "Whence does he come?":

One answer is that man was created in the "image of God," and he will eventually

1. Akavia ben Mahalalel said: *Consider three things and you will not come into the grip of sin: Know whence you came, whither you go, and before Whom you will give justification and reckoning. "Whence you came?" — from a putrid drop; "whither you go?" — to a place of dust, worms, and maggots; "and before Whom you will give justification and reckoning?" — before the King Who reigns over kings, the Holy One, Blessed is He.*

2. Rabbi *Chanina, the deputy Kohen Gadol [High Priest], says: Pray for the welfare of the govern-*

פירוש לרבי עובדיה ספורנו

תשתדל בהצלחת החלק השכלי הנצחי למען יזכה ביום פקדתו לפני מלך מלכי המלכים:

ג:ב. אף על פי שהמלך לפעמים בלתי כשר כמו שקרה ברב מלכי בית שני והוא אולי גוזל וחומס מכל מקום ראוי להתפלל

SFORNO'S COMMENTARY

by the Holy King. Therefore, one must make efforts to succeed in his attempts in the intellectual realm, and use caution to avoid that which may prevent him from its attainment, so that he may be found meritorious when judged [from on High].

As a result of this contemplation, "you will not come into the grip of sin," for you will not pursue the gratification of your physical desires. Instead, you will attempt to succeed in [refining and improving your] intellectual abilities which are permanent, so that you will [merit to] be found worthy on the day of your reckoning before the King of kings.

3:2

הֱוֵי מִתְפַּלֵּל בִּשְׁלוֹמָהּ שֶׁל מַלְכוּת, שֶׁאִלְמָלֵא מוֹרָאָהּ . . . — *Pray for the welfare of the government, because if people did not fear it . . .* Although a king may at times be unworthy — as was often the case in the Second Temple era — to

NOTES

return to His Father in Heaven, as the Torah teaches us, בָּנִים אַתֶּם לַה׳ אֱלֹהֵיכֶם, *You are children of HASHEM, your God* (*Deuteronomy* 14:1). However, this answer is not given by Akavia, for he addresses the physical aspect of man. However, it *is* alluded to in the first part of the Mishnah, where the three questions are treated as rhetorical and are therefore left unanswered.

In the second part of the Mishnah, however, the three questions are addressed on the pragmatic level. From this perspective, man's origin is far from being pure and noble, for he is conceived from a "putrid drop," and eventually, he shall return to the dust whence he came, and give an accounting to the Supreme Judge.

To contemplate upon the first aspect of man is a challenge to one's nobler character, while reflecting upon the second counters his evil inclination and helps to deter him from sin.

3:2

הֱוֵי מִתְפַּלֵּל בִּשְׁלוֹמָהּ שֶׁל מַלְכוּת, שֶׁאִלְמָלֵא מוֹרָאָהּ . . . — *Pray for the welfare of the government, because if people did not fear it . . .* There are

שֶׁאִלְמָלֵא מוֹרָאָהּ, אִישׁ אֶת רֵעֵהוּ חַיִּים בְּלָעוֹ. ג
ג
[ג] **רַבִּי** חֲנִינָא בֶּן תְּרַדְיוֹן אוֹמֵר: שְׁנַיִם שֶׁיּוֹשְׁבִין וְאֵין בֵּינֵיהֶם דִּבְרֵי תוֹרָה, הֲרֵי זֶה מוֹשַׁב לֵצִים, שֶׁנֶּאֱמַר: ,,וּבְמוֹשַׁב לֵצִים לֹא יָשָׁב.״ אֲבָל שְׁנַיִם שֶׁיּוֹשְׁבִין וְיֵשׁ בֵּינֵיהֶם דִּבְרֵי תוֹרָה, שְׁכִינָה בֵּינֵיהֶם, שֶׁנֶּאֱמַר: ,,אָז נִדְבְּרוּ יִרְאֵי יהוה אִישׁ אֶל רֵעֵהוּ, וַיַּקְשֵׁב יהוה וַיִּשְׁמָע, וַיִּכָּתֵב סֵפֶר זִכָּרוֹן לְפָנָיו, לְיִרְאֵי יהוה וּלְחֹשְׁבֵי שְׁמוֹ.״ אֵין לִי אֶלָּא שְׁנַיִם; מִנַּיִן שֶׁאֲפִילוּ אֶחָד שֶׁיּוֹשֵׁב וְעוֹסֵק

פירוש לרבי עובדיה ספורנו

בשלומו, כי אז יטיל מוראו ולא יסכים שיגזלו העם זה את זה ובזה מסיר החמס מבין המון העם:

ג:ג. שיושבין אע״פ שאין בספורם דברי ליצנות כיון שאין בכל דבורם דברי תורה נחשב למושב לצים שכל ענינו הבל ודבר נפסד, והביא ראיה על זה ממה שכתוב ,,ובמושב לצים לא ישב כי אם בתורת יי

SFORNO'S COMMENTARY

the extent that he may rob and plunder [his subjects], nonetheless it is fitting to pray for his welfare. For then he will instill fear of his authority [on them], and he will not consent that the people steal from one another. In this manner, he eliminates violence among the masses.

3:3

שְׁנַיִם שֶׁיּוֹשְׁבִין וְאֵין בֵּינֵיהֶם דִּבְרֵי תוֹרָה, הֲרֵי זֶה מוֹשַׁב לֵצִים — *If two sit together and there are no words of Torah between them, it is a session of scorners.* Even though no words of scorn are exchanged, still, since their interchange is entirely devoid of Torah, it is considered a "session of scorners," for its nature is empty and meaningless. He brings a proof to this thesis from the verse in *Psalms* 1:1, where it is written, "[The praises of man are that he

NOTES

scholars who believe that the *Sforno*'s reference to "kings in the Second Temple era" is a euphemism for rulers who reigned in his day. However, since freedom of expression in the Middle Ages was not overly tolerated, he tactfully used the euphemistic phrase "kings in the Second Temple era."

This instruction of Chanina is in keeping with the *Sforno*'s attitude regarding respect for authority, especially in the Diaspora, which he espouses in his commentary on the Torah. For example, in his commentary on *Exodus* 22:27, he states, "The evil which befalls the king will in most cases cause great evil and harm to the community as well." And in his commentary regarding Avimelech (*Genesis* 26:10), he states, "When the leader is punished, great harm befalls those who find protection under his wing." The *Sforno* echoes those sentiments here by asserting that any government,

ment, because if people did not fear it, a person would swallow his fellow alive.

3. *Rabbi Chanina ben Tradyon says: If two sit together and there are no words of Torah between them, it is a session of scorners, as it is said: "In the session of scorners he does not sit." But if two sit together and words of Torah are between them, the Divine Presence is between them, as it is said: "Then those who fear* HASHEM *spoke to one another, and* HASHEM *listened and heard, and a book of remembrance was written before Him for those who fear* HASHEM *and give thought to His Name." From this verse we would know this only about two people; how do we know that if even one person sits and occupies himself*

פירוש לרבי עובדיה ספורנו

חפצו", כלומר שכל מושב הוא מושב לצים זולתי מה שיהיה בו דבור בתורת יי. אבל שנים שיושבים ויש ביניהם דברי תורה, אף על פי שאין עקר ספורם בזה – שכינה ביניהם. ובהגידו את הנמשך לכל אחד משני ההפכים הודיע גודל הענין וערכו כדי לעורר לטוב גם את ההמון ואם כן אפילו אחד שיושב ועוסק בתורה, כי אמנם

SFORNO'S COMMENTARY

walked not in the counsel of the wicked, and stood not in the path of the sinful,] and sat not in the session of scorners. But his desire is in the Torah of Hashem. . ." That is to say, that every "session" is considered a "session of scorners" unless words of God's Torah are spoken.

אֲבָל שְׁנַיִם שֶׁיּוֹשְׁבִין וְיֵשׁ בֵּינֵיהֶם דִּבְרֵי תוֹרָה, שְׁכִינָה בֵּינֵיהֶם — *But if two sit together and words of Torah are between them, the Divine Presence is between them.* "But if two sit together and words of Torah are between them," even though the main topic of their conversation is not Torah, nonetheless, "the Divine Presence is between them."

Through this instruction regarding the extremes resulting from these disparate behaviors, the Tanna teaches us the importance and worth of such behavior in order to inspire the masses also, to follow the right way.

NOTES

even an evil one, is preferable to anarchy.

3:3

שְׁנַיִם שֶׁיּוֹשְׁבִין וְאֵין בֵּינֵיהֶם דִּבְרֵי תוֹרָה . . . מוֹשַׁב . . . לֵצִים — *If two sit together and there are no words of Torah between them . . . a session of scorners . . .* The *Sforno* asserts that a מוֹשַׁב, or "session," cannot be neutral — if in its course words of Torah are not discussed, it automatically becomes "a session of scorners." Conversely, even if the purpose of the session is secular, words of Torah transform its character and remove from it the label of לֵצָנוּת, *scorn.*

ג בַּתּוֹרָה, שֶׁהַקָּדוֹשׁ בָּרוּךְ הוּא קוֹבֵעַ לוֹ שָׂכָר?
ד שֶׁנֶּאֱמַר: „יֵשֵׁב בָּדָד וְיִדֹּם, כִּי נָטַל עָלָיו.״

[ד] **רַבִּי** שִׁמְעוֹן אוֹמֵר: שְׁלשָׁה שֶׁאָכְלוּ עַל שֻׁלְחָן אֶחָד וְלֹא אָמְרוּ עָלָיו דִּבְרֵי תוֹרָה, כְּאִלּוּ אָכְלוּ מִזִּבְחֵי מֵתִים, שֶׁנֶּאֱמַר: „כִּי כָּל שֻׁלְחָנוֹת מָלְאוּ קִיא צֹאָה, בְּלִי מָקוֹם.״ אֲבָל שְׁלשָׁה שֶׁאָכְלוּ עַל שֻׁלְחָן אֶחָד וְאָמְרוּ עָלָיו דִּבְרֵי תוֹרָה, כְּאִלּוּ אָכְלוּ מִשֻּׁלְחָנוֹ שֶׁל מָקוֹם, שֶׁנֶּאֱמַר: „וַיְדַבֵּר אֵלַי, זֶה הַשֻּׁלְחָן אֲשֶׁר לִפְנֵי יהוה.״

פירוש לרבי עובדיה ספורנו

ליחידי לא יקרה דבור בתורה זולתי כשיעסוק בה, והביא ראיה על שכרו ממה שכתוב למעלה „טוב לגבר כי ישא עול״:

ג:ד. זבחי מתים, מאכלים אשר כל ענינים לקיום חיים נפסדים. וראוי להתבונן בהבדל אשר בין שלחן שתכליתו זה בלבד ובין

SFORNO'S COMMENTARY

שֶׁאֲפִילוּ אֶחָד שֶׁיּוֹשֵׁב וְעוֹסֵק בַּתּוֹרָה, שֶׁהקב״ה קוֹבֵעַ לוֹ שָׂכָר — *If even one person sits and occupies himself with Torah, the Holy One, Blessed is He, determines a reward for him.* Hence, [the Tanna says] "even if one person sits and *occupies* himself with Torah," for one person cannot converse in Torah. Rather, he must study it [i.e., *occupy* himself with it]. Still, he is rewarded, and the Tanna proves this from that which is written in the verse previous [to the one quoted in the Mishnah]: טוֹב לַגֶּבֶר כִּי יִשָּׂא עֹל, *It is good for a man that he bear the yoke . . .* (*Lamentations* 3:27).

3:4

שְׁלשָׁה שֶׁאָכְלוּ עַל שֻׁלְחָן אֶחָד וְלֹא אָמְרוּ עָלָיו דִּבְרֵי תוֹרָה, כְּאִלּוּ אָכְלוּ מִזִּבְחֵי מֵתִים . . . אֲבָל . . . שֶׁאָכְלוּ . . . וְאָמְרוּ עָלָיו דִּבְרֵי תוֹרָה, כְּאִלּוּ אָכְלוּ מִשֻּׁלְחָנוֹ שֶׁל מָקוֹם — *If three have eaten at the same table and have not spoken words of Torah there, it is as if they have eaten of offerings to the dead idols . . . but . . . if (they) have eaten . . . and have spoken words of Torah there, it is as if they have eaten from the*

NOTES

אֶחָד . . . וְעוֹסֵק בַּתּוֹרָה . . . לוֹ שָׂכָר — *One person . . . engages in Torah . . . a reward for him.*

The proof brought by the Tanna from *Lamentations* 3:28 is unclear unless, as the *Sforno* points out, one reads it in context with the previous verse, 3:27. Only then does it become understandable. It teaches that if a person assumes the yoke of Torah and makes it the guiding force in his life, then, even though he studies alone, he will be rewarded.

3 *with Torah, the Holy One, Blessed is He, determines*
4 *a reward for him? For it is said: 'Let one sit in solitude and be still, for he will have received [a reward] for it.' "*

4. *Rabbi Shimon said: If three have eaten at the same table and have not spoken words of Torah there, it is as if they have eaten of offerings to the dead idols, as it is said: "For all tables are full of vomit and filth, without the Omnipresent."*[4] *But if three have eaten at the same table and have spoken words of Torah there, it is as if they have eaten from the table of the Omnipresent, as it is said: "And he said to me, 'This is the table that is before* HASHEM.' "

פירוש לרבי עובדיה ספורנו

שלחן האוכלים משלחנו של הקדוש ברוך הוא והם הכהנים האוכלים משלחן גבוה, והוא המזבח, שכל ענין אכילתם בקדש הוא לעזרת שלמות נצחי אשר בערכו ראוי שיקרא השלחן אשר תכליתו נפסד מלא קיא וצואה, כדבר הנביא באמרו ,,ובשכר תעו, כהן ונביא ... כי כל שלחנות מלאו קיא", כלומר שקרה להם טעות בתורה

SFORNO'S COMMENTARY

table of the Omnipresent. Food prepared and consumed exclusively to sustain physical life, which is transitory and perishable, is called **זִבְחֵי מֵתִים**, *offerings to the dead idols.* Now, it is proper to consider the difference between such a table, whose purpose is as mentioned above, and the table of the Holy One, Blessed is He [i.e., the altar], which is the table on High, from which the priests eat. For their food consumption is marked by sanctity, and the goal is to reach eternal perfection and completeness. Compared to this, the table serving the purpose of physical pleasure alone is called **מָלֵא קִיא צֹאָה**, *full of vomit and filth* (*Isaiah* 28:7-8), as the prophet states: **וּבַשֵּׁכָר תָּעוּ, כֹּהֵן וְנָבִיא ... כִּי כָּל שֻׁלְחָנוֹת מָלְאוּ קִיא צֹאָה**, *And through strong drink the priest and prophet are confused. . .all the tables are full of vomit and filth*; meaning,

NOTES

3:4

שְׁלֹשָׁה שֶׁאָכְלוּ עַל שֻׁלְחָן אֶחָד וְלֹא אָמְרוּ דִּבְרֵי תוֹרָה, כְּאִלּוּ אָכְלוּ מִזִּבְחֵי מֵתִים ... אֲבָל ... שֶׁאָכְלוּ ... וְאָמְרוּ עָלָיו דִּבְרֵי תוֹרָה, כְּאִלּוּ אָכְלוּ מִשֻּׁלְחָנוֹ שֶׁל מָקוֹם — *If three have eaten at the same table and have not spoken words of Torah there, it is as if they have eaten of offerings to the dead idols . . . but if (they) have eaten . . . and have spoken words of Torah there, it is as if they have eaten from the table of the Omnipresent.* Our Sages have taught us that the mundane act of consuming food — although it is an action common to man and all living creatures — can be elevated and sanctified by bringing it as an offering to the Almighty, for then it is eaten by the

ג
ה־ו

[ה] **רַבִּי** חֲנִינָא בֶּן חֲכִינַאי אוֹמֵר: הַנֵּעוֹר בַּלַּיְלָה, וְהַמְּהַלֵּךְ בַּדֶּרֶךְ יְחִידִי, וּמְפַנֶּה לִבּוֹ לְבַטָּלָה — הֲרֵי זֶה מִתְחַיֵּב בְּנַפְשׁוֹ.

[ו] **רַבִּי** נְחוּנְיָא בֶּן הַקָּנָה אוֹמֵר: כָּל הַמְקַבֵּל עָלָיו עֹל תּוֹרָה, מַעֲבִירִין מִמֶּנּוּ עֹל

פירוש לרבי עובדיה ספורנו

לכהן ובנבואה לנביא בהיות כל ענין שלחנותם לתענוגים נפסדים בלבד. והביא ראיה על היות אוכלין שלחן אשר על הפך זה כאוכלים משלחנו של הקדוש ברוך הוא ממה שקרא הנביא את השלחן בשם מזבח כאשר יהיה לפני יי. והנה כבר קדם ששנים שיושבים ויש ביניהם דברי תורה שכינה ביניהם:

ג:ה. אחר שסדר המחבר מאמרים מורים מיני זריזות בשבתך בביתך, היינו בבית

SFORNO'S COMMENTARY

that when the table is used only for vain and passing pleasure, the priests err in Torah and the prophets' prophetic power is impaired.

The Tanna contrasts this kind of table with the one which is לִפְנֵי ה׳ — "before Hashem"; such a table is akin to an altar, and it is as though one is eating from the table of the Holy One, Blessed is He.

And the Tanna has already taught [in the previous Mishnah], "if two sit together and words of Torah are between them, the Divine Presence is between them."

3:5

הַנֵּעוֹר בַּלַּיְלָה, וְהַמְּהַלֵּךְ בַּדֶּרֶךְ יְחִידִי, וּמְפַנֶּה לִבּוֹ לְבַטָּלָה –הֲרֵי זֶה מִתְחַיֵּב בְּנַפְשׁוֹ — *One who stays awake at night, or one who travels alone on the road, and turns his heart to idleness — indeed, he bears guilt for his soul.* After the author

NOTES

Kohanim (priests) in purity and a spirit of holiness. Even an Israelite may partake of certain sacrifices within the confines of the Temple. When he eats from the offering in the presence of Hashem, he transforms the mundane act of consuming food into an exercise in spirituality, thereby transcending the physical aspect of this act.

When three people eat even non-sacrificial food together in this spirit and share words of Torah, they, too, transform their table into an altar. However, when they fail to transcend the physical and eat purely for pleasure, the table is debased and the meal resembles an "offering to the dead idols."

The *Sforno*'s comment at the conclusion of this commentary explains why Rabbi Shimon speaks of three people, but does not make mention of two, as did Rabbi Chanina in the previous Mishnah. He answers that since it has already been established that two people who exchange words of Torah are considered equivalent to three who do so, Rabbi Shimon did not see it necessary to repeat this point in our Mishnah.

3:5

הַנֵּעוֹר בַּלַּיְלָה, וְהַמְּהַלֵּךְ בַּדֶּרֶךְ יְחִידִי, וּמְפַנֶּה לִבּוֹ לְבַטָּלָה – הֲרֵי זֶה מִתְחַיֵּב בְּנַפְשׁוֹ — *One who stays awake at night, or one who travels*

5. *Rabbi Chanina ben Chachinai says: One who stays awake at night, or one who travels alone on the road, and turns his heart to idleness — indeed, he bears guilt for his soul.*

6. *Rabbi Nechunia ben Hakanah says: If someone takes upon himself the yoke of Torah — the yoke of government and the yoke of worldly*

פירוש לרבי עובדיה ספורנו

מדרשך ובמסכת שלחנך, הזכיר עתה מיני זריזות בלכתך בדרך ובשכבך. אמר אם כן זה החכם, שהנעור בלילה וכן המהלך בדרך כשהוא יחידי ואין עמו מי שישיאהו לדברים בטלים וכן המפנה לבו מעסקי חיי שעה, ויהיה אחד מאלו עתות הפנאי לבטלה – הרי זה מתחייב בנפשו, כי אמנם כל אחד מאלו העתים הפנויים מטרדות הזמן בזה האופן הוא עת לעשות ליי ולהביט אל פעלו ולהתבונן בם להחיות את נפשו, ובהתרשלו אז מתחייב בנפשו בלי ספק:

SFORNO'S COMMENTARY

discussed various actions representing areas of זְרִיזוּת — alertness and diligence — required of men, בְּשִׁבְתְּךָ בְּבֵיתֶךָ, *while you sit in your home* — that is, in your study room and around your table — he now directs our attention to the type of זְרִיזוּת required בְּלֶכְתְּךָ בַדֶּרֶךְ וּבְשָׁכְבְּךָ, *while you walk on the way, when you retire.*

Now, this wise sage tells us that one "who stays awake at night" and one "who travels alone on the road," and is therefore not distracted by anyone who would divert him to idle things (לְבַטָּלָה), is one who can turn away his heart from mundane matters, and is [therefore] at liberty to contemplate. But if these free moments are squandered for naught, then he "bears guilt for his soul," for these moments which are free from the demands and duties of everyday life, are עֵת לַעֲשׂוֹת לַה׳, *a time to do for Hashem* (*Psalms* 119:126), to consider God's works and His Torah, and to contemplate upon how to revive one's soul. If, however, he is lax and fails to use these moments, then indeed, "he bears guilt for his soul."

NOTES

alone on the road, and turns his heart to idleness — indeed, he bears guilt for his soul. The *Sforno* explains the sequence of these *mishnayos*. Mishnah 3 and 4 speak of proper conduct in the framework of one's own home, as in the words of the *Shema*, בְּשִׁבְתְּךָ בְּבֵיתֶךָ, *while you sit in your home.* Now, we turn our attention to the following phrase, וּבְלֶכְתְּךָ בַדֶּרֶךְ וּבְשָׁכְבְּךָ וּבְקוּמֶךָ, *While you walk on the way, when you retire, and when you arise.* Since these are times which can lend themselves to contemplation, one should grasp the opportunity and utilize those uninterrupted moments productively.

Failing to do so is to miss the moment and squander the time which one has been granted. Consequently, he is guilty of the most severe kind of waste — namely, failure to expand his mind and nurture his soul.

ג
ז
מַלְכוּת וְעֹל דֶּרֶךְ אֶרֶץ; וְכָל הַפּוֹרֵק מִמֶּנּוּ עֹל תּוֹרָה, נוֹתְנִין עָלָיו עֹל מַלְכוּת וְעֹל דֶּרֶךְ אֶרֶץ.

[ז] **רַבִּי** חֲלַפְתָּא בֶּן דּוֹסָא אִישׁ כְּפַר חֲנַנְיָא אוֹמֵר: עֲשָׂרָה שֶׁיּוֹשְׁבִין וְעוֹסְקִין בַּתּוֹרָה, שְׁכִינָה שְׁרוּיָה בֵינֵיהֶם, שֶׁנֶּאֱמַר: „אֱלֹהִים נִצָּב בַּעֲדַת אֵל." וּמִנַּיִן אֲפִילוּ חֲמִשָּׁה? שֶׁנֶּאֱמַר: „וַאֲגֻדָּתוֹ עַל אֶרֶץ יְסָדָהּ." וּמִנַּיִן אֲפִילוּ שְׁלֹשָׁה? שֶׁנֶּאֱמַר:

פירוש לרבי עובדיה ספורנו

ג:ו. הנה עול דרך ארץ הוא טורח הנהגת עצמו וביתו בפרנסה ובהשמר מנזקי המקרים. אמר שכשיפרק האדם ממנו עול תורה אחר שקבל אותו, כמו מי ששנה ופירש – נותנים עול מלכות, כאומרו „תחת אשר לא עבדת ... ועבדת את אויבך" ועול דרך ארץ, כאמרו אחר כן „ברעב ובצמא ובערום" וכולי:

SFORNO'S COMMENTARY

3:6

וְכָל הַפּוֹרֵק מִמֶּנּוּ עֹל תּוֹרָה, נוֹתְנִין עָלָיו עֹל מַלְכוּת וְעֹל דֶּרֶךְ אֶרֶץ — *But if someone throws off the yoke of Torah from himself — the yoke of government and the yoke of worldly responsibilities are placed upon him.* The "yoke of worldly responsibilities" refers to the bothersome preoccupation with one's personal needs and responsibilities, and securing protection from life's vicissitudes. He teaches us that when one who has accepted the yoke of Torah casts it off — i.e. שָׁנָה וּפָרַשׁ, *one who has studied and left* — he will be burdened with "the yoke of government," as it says, תַּחַת אֲשֶׁר לֹא עָבַדְתָּ. . .וְעָבַדְתָּ אֶת אוֹיְבֶיךָ, *Because you did not serve Hashem. . ..you will serve your enemies* (*Deuteronomy* 28:47-48).

"And the yoke of worldly responsibilities" will also be his, as it says, בְּרָעָב וּבְצָמָא וּבְעֵירֹם, *in hunger, and in thirst, and in nakedness* (ibid. v. 48).

NOTES

3:6

וְכָל הַפּוֹרֵק מִמֶּנּוּ עֹל תּוֹרָה, נוֹתְנִין עָלָיו עֹל מַלְכוּת וְעֹל דֶּרֶךְ אֶרֶץ — *But if someone throws off the yoke of Torah from himself — the yoke of government and the yoke of worldly responsibilities are placed upon him.* The *Sforno* interprets this Mishnah as referring to one who studied Torah and rejected it. Since such an individual cast off and rejected the yoke of Torah, another yoke must per force come in its place, for there can be no vacuum. The verse cited by the *Sforno* from *Deuteronomy* is excellent proof for this thesis, for the verse implies that when one refuses to serve Hashem, he will ultimately serve others. A neutral state cannot exist — he will either serve Hashem or others, for he must subjugate himself to some power.

The second verse quoted by the *Sforno* conveys that had he been loyal to Hashem, he would have been blessed with plenitude. But because he was not loyal to Him, he will now be forced to toil and labor just to clothe and feed himself. This is what is meant by the yoke of worldly responsibility (דֶּרֶךְ אֶרֶץ).

responsibilities are removed from him. But if someone throws off the yoke of Torah from himself — the yoke of government and the yoke of worldly responsibilities are placed upon him.

7. *Rabbi Chalafta ben Dosa of Kfar Chanania says: If ten people sit together and engage in Torah study, the Divine Presence dwells among them, as if it said: "God stands in the assembly of God." How do we know this even of five? For it is said: "He has established His bundle upon earth." How do we know this even of three? For it is said:*

פירוש לרבי עובדיה ספורנו

ג:ז. ועוסקים בתורה. למעלה היה המאמר באנשים מספרים בעסקיהם ויש בתוך דבריהם דברי תורה, ואמר ששכינה ביניהם, אבל בזה דבר על העוסקים בה ואמר שהשכינה שרויה שם. וכבר אמרו בגמרא דתרי כתיבין מילייהו בספר הזכרונות אבל חד לא כתיבן מיליה בספר זכרונות. ושלשה אפילו עוסקים בדין הוו להו עוסקים בתורה,

SFORNO'S COMMENTARY

3:7

עֲשָׂרָה שֶׁיּוֹשְׁבִין וְעוֹסְקִין בַּתּוֹרָה, שְׁכִינָה שְׁרוּיָה בֵּינֵיהֶם . . . וּמִנַּיִן אֲפִילוּ שְׁלֹשָׁה . . . אֲפִילוּ שְׁנַיִם — *If ten people sit together and engage in Torah study, the Divine Presence dwells among them . . . How do we know this even of three . . . even of two*? "And engage in Torah." Above [in Mishnah 3, the Tanna] refers to people who discuss their [mundane] affairs and intersperse words of Torah in their discussion. He tells us that "the Divine Presence *is* between them."

Here, however, [Rabbi Chalafta] speaks of those who engage in Torah. [About them] he says, "the Divine Presence *dwells* among them."

The Talmud teaches us that תְּרֵי כְּתִיבִין מִילַּיְיהוּ בְּסֵפֶר הַזִּכְרוֹנוֹת, אֲבָל חַד לֹא כְּתִיבָן מִילֵּיהּ בְּסֵפֶר הַזִּכְרוֹנוֹת, "If two are engaged in the study of Torah, it is recorded in the Book of Remembrance; however, if only one, it is not

NOTES

3:7

עֲשָׂרָה שֶׁיּוֹשְׁבִין וְעוֹסְקִין בַּתּוֹרָה, שְׁכִינָה שְׁרוּיָה בֵּינֵיהֶם . . . וּמִנַּיִן אֲפִילוּ שְׁלֹשָׁה? — *If ten people sit together and engage in Torah study, the Divine Presence dwells among them . . . How do we know this even of three?* This Mishnah is in some ways similar to Mishnah 3. The *Sforno,* however, points out that there are a number of variations. Rabbi Chanina in Mishnah 3 uses the expression וְיֵשׁ בֵּינֵיהֶם דִּבְרֵי תוֹרָה, "words of Torah are between them," whereas in our Mishnah, Rabbi Chalafta uses the phrase עוֹסְקִין בַּתּוֹרָה, "engage in Torah study," in his initial statement regarding ten people. Also, in Mishnah 3, the reward for speaking words of Torah is phrased as שְׁכִינָה בֵּינֵיהֶם, "the Divine Presence *is* between them" (a term in *Sforno's* commentary referring to שְׁכִינָה שְׁרוּיָה בֵּינֵיהֶם), while our Mishnah states

„בְּקֶרֶב אֱלֹהִים יִשְׁפֹּט." וּמִנַּיִן אֲפִילוּ שְׁנַיִם? שֶׁנֶּאֱמַר: „אָז נִדְבְּרוּ יִרְאֵי יהוה אִישׁ אֶל רֵעֵהוּ וַיַּקְשֵׁב יהוה וַיִּשְׁמָע." וּמִנַּיִן אֲפִילוּ אֶחָד? שֶׁנֶּאֱמַר: „בְּכָל הַמָּקוֹם אֲשֶׁר אַזְכִּיר אֶת שְׁמִי, אָבוֹא אֵלֶיךָ וּבֵרַכְתִּיךָ."

[ח] **רַבִּי** אֶלְעָזָר אִישׁ בַּרְתּוֹתָא אוֹמֵר: תֶּן לוֹ מִשֶּׁלּוֹ, שֶׁאַתָּה וְשֶׁלְּךָ שֶׁלּוֹ; וְכֵן בְּדָוִד

פירוש לרבי עובדיה ספורנו

דדינה נמי היינו תורה. ובעשרה קדמה שכינה ואתיא, תלתא עד דיתבי. אמנם מנין החמשה שלא נזכר בגמרא נראה שהשוהו למנין העשרה, בזמן שהיה קבוצם לכתחלה לעסוק בתורה, ולכן קראם אגודתו. ועל האחד הביא ראיה למעלה על שכרו שגדול שכרו בהיותו עוסק בתורה משכר אותן שיש ביניהן דברי תורה, ובזה

SFORNO'S COMMENTARY

recorded" (*Berachos* 6b). As for three, though they are engaged in deciding the law and dispensing justice, it is still considered that they are engaged in Torah — דְּדִינָא נַמִּי הַיְינוּ תוֹרָה, "for the law process is also equal to Torah."

As for a group of ten, we are taught, וּבְעֲשָׂרָה קָדְמָה שְׁכִינָה וְאַתְיָא, תְּלָתָא עַד דְּיָתְבֵי, "Ten who convene to engage in Torah, the Divine Presence precedes them; if they are three, the Divine Presence joins them once they have convened."

וּמִנַּיִן אֲפִילוּ חֲמִשָּׁה — *How do we know this even of five?* The number five [mentioned here in the Mishnah] is not cited in the Talmud [as a distinct unit]. However, it may be that Rabbi Chalafta equated them with ten, if their gathering from the outset was for the purpose of engaging in Torah. That is why they are designated as an אֲגֻדָּה, *a bundle* [see the *Bartenura* on this Mishnah].

NOTES

שְׁכִינָה שְׁרוּיָה בֵּינֵיהֶם, "the Divine Presence *dwells* among them."

The *Sforno* explains that Rabbi Chanina in Mishnah 3 refers to individuals who converse about mundane matters, but weave words of Torah into their conversation. Rabbi Chalafta, on the other hand, speaks of individuals who gather together for the express purpose of studying Torah or convening a דִּין תּוֹרָה, *court of Jewish law.* This explains why our Mishnah, unlike Mishnah 3, mentions groups of ten and three — these are the numbers of sages required to convene a Jewish court of law.

וּמִנַּיִן אֲפִילוּ חֲמִשָּׁה — *How do we know this even of five?* The *Sforno,* however, is puzzled by the number five, for it is the only number appearing in our Mishnah which is not mentioned in the Talmud (*Berachos* 6). He speculates that the Mishnah teaches that even five sages — which is one half of ten — merit to have the Divine Presence dwell among them when they gather together for the express purpose of studying Torah.

The *Tiferes Yisrael* commentary on this Mishnah suggests that the number five is included by the Tanna because five judges sit on the court which makes the measurement, from the murder victim to the closest city, to determine who is obligated to bring

"In the midst of judges He shall judge." How do we know this even of two? For it is said: "Then those who fear HASHEM spoke to one another, and HASHEM listened and heard." How do we know this even of one? For it is said: "In every place where I cause My Name to be mentioned, I will come to you and bless you."

8. *Rabbi Elazar of Bartosa says: Give Him from His Own, for you and your possessions are His.*

פירוש לרבי עובדיה ספורנו

הביא ראיה על היות שכינה שרויה עמו בהיותו עוסק בה ממה שאמר ,,אבוא אליך״:

ג:ח. אף על פי שנאמר ,,מה יי אלקיך שואל מעמך״ אינו שואל שתתן לו משלך באופן שתוכל למאן בדין, שאתה ושלך שלו ובדין הוא שואל, ואם תמאן תהיה עושק את שלו, והוא דיין ובעל דין:

SFORNO'S COMMENTARY

וּמִנַּיִן אֲפִילוּ אֶחָד — *How do we know this even of one?* As for one "who engages in Torah," the Tanna in Mishnah 3 brought proof [from the verse in *Lamentations*] that his reward is greater than that of two who sit together "and words of Torah are between them." The Tanna of our Mishnah adds that the Divine Presence is with him when he is occupied with Torah, as it is written, אָבוֹא אֵלֶיךָ, *I will come to you* (*Exodus* 20:21).

3:8

תֶּן לוֹ מִשֶּׁלוֹ, שֶׁאַתָּה וְשֶׁלְּךָ שֶׁלוֹ — *Give Him from His Own, for you and your possessions are His.* Although it is written מָה ה׳ אֱלֹהֶיךָ שׁוֹאֵל מֵעִמָּךְ, *What does Hashem, your God, ask of you. . .?* (*Deuteronomy* 10:12), He is not asking that you give Him that which belongs to you, that you should think you have the right to legally refuse Him, for "you and your possessions are His." Therefore, He is entitled to ask anything of you, and if you should refuse, you would be guilty of withholding what is His. And [consider this]: He is the Judge and He is the Plaintiff!

NOTES

the עֶגְלָה עֲרוּפָה (*the axed calf*). Another case when the court had five members, according to Rabbi Yehudah in the Mishnah in *Sanhedrin* 1:3, was for the purpose of סְמִיכַת זְקֵנִים, the placing of the hands on the bullock which is brought as an atonement for a mistaken ruling issued by the *Sanhedrin.* The *Sforno,* however, gives his own answer for the inclusion of the number 5 in our Mishnah.

וּמִנַּיִן אֲפִילוּ אֶחָד — *How do we know this even of one?* As for one person who studies Torah, it would appear from Mishnah 3 that he does not merit to have the Divine Presence in his midst, for that reward seems to be reserved specifically for two people who "have words of Torah between them." However, in this Mishnah, Rabbi Chalafta adds a new dimension to a single person's reward — namely, that he, too, shall merit to be in the proximity of the Divine Presence.

3:8

תֶּן לוֹ מִשֶּׁלוֹ, שֶׁאַתָּה וְשֶׁלְּךָ שֶׁלוֹ — *Give Him from His Own, for you and your possessions are His.* The *Sforno* points out that, ostensibly, Rabbi Elazar's statement can be refuted

ג הוּא אוֹמֵר: „כִּי מִמְּךָ הַכֹּל, וּמִיָּדְךָ נָתַנּוּ לָךְ.״

ט־י [ט] **רַבִּי** יַעֲקֹב אוֹמֵר: הַמְּהַלֵּךְ בַּדֶּרֶךְ וְשׁוֹנֶה, וּמַפְסִיק מִמִּשְׁנָתוֹ, וְאוֹמֵר: „מַה נָּאֶה אִילָן זֶה! וּמַה נָּאֶה נִיר זֶה!״ — מַעֲלֶה עָלָיו הַכָּתוּב כְּאִלּוּ מִתְחַיֵּב בְּנַפְשׁוֹ.

[י] **רַבִּי** דוֹסְתָּאִי בַּר יַנַּאי מִשּׁוּם רַבִּי מֵאִיר אוֹמֵר: כָּל הַשּׁוֹכֵחַ דָּבָר אֶחָד מִמִּשְׁנָתוֹ, מַעֲלֶה עָלָיו הַכָּתוּב כְּאִלּוּ מִתְחַיֵּב בְּנַפְשׁוֹ, שֶׁנֶּאֱמַר: „רַק הִשָּׁמֶר לְךָ, וּשְׁמֹר נַפְשְׁךָ מְאֹד, פֶּן תִּשְׁכַּח אֶת הַדְּבָרִים אֲשֶׁר רָאוּ עֵינֶיךָ.״ יָכוֹל אֲפִילוּ תָּקְפָה עָלָיו מִשְׁנָתוֹ? תַּלְמוּד לוֹמַר: „וּפֶן יָסוּרוּ מִלְּבָבְךָ כֹּל יְמֵי חַיֶּיךָ.״ הָא אֵינוֹ מִתְחַיֵּב בְּנַפְשׁוֹ עַד שֶׁיֵּשֵׁב וִיסִירֵם מִלִּבּוֹ.

פירוש לרבי עובדיה ספורנו

ג:ט־י. הנה המפסיק במשנתו ומשיא עצמו לדברי חול, וכן העומד ומסיר דברי תורה מלבו — שניהם בכלל „פן יסורו מלבבך״, ועל שניהם נאמר „ושמור נפשך מאד״ וזה רצו שניהם באמרם מעלה עליו הכתוב כאלו מתחייב בנפשו:

SFORNO'S COMMENTARY

3:9-10

הַמְּהַלֵּךְ בַּדֶּרֶךְ וְשׁוֹנֶה, וּמַפְסִיק מִמִּשְׁנָתוֹ . . . כְּאִלּוּ מִתְחַיֵּב בְּנַפְשׁוֹ . . . אֵינוֹ מִתְחַיֵּב בְּנַפְשׁוֹ עַד שֶׁיֵּשֵׁב וִיסִירֵם מִלִּבּוֹ — *One who walks on the road while reviewing [a Torah lesson] but interrupts his review .. it is as if he bears guilt for his soul . . . one does not bear guilt for his soul unless he sits [idly] and [through lack of concentration and review] removes them from his consciousness.* Behold, one

NOTES

from the verse in *Deuteronomy*, for if Hashem requests something of man, it would appear that *man* is its owner, not God. This seems to contradict Rabbi Elazar's contention that, "you and your possessions are His."

The *Sforno* resolves this difficulty by explaining that Hashem's request of man to revere Him does not leave man the option to refuse. Man cannot deny God, for He has the legal right, as well as the power, to force compliance. It is comparable to a person who gives another an item for safekeeping, and then asks him to return it — his is not a request, but a demand. So too, the ability of man to revere the Almighty has been granted to him by Hashem Himself!

3:9-10

הַמְּהַלֵּךְ בַּדֶּרֶךְ וְשׁוֹנֶה, וּמַפְסִיק מִמִּשְׁנָתוֹ . . . כְּאִלּוּ מִתְחַיֵּב בְּנַפְשׁוֹ . . . אֵינוֹ מִתְחַיֵּב בְּנַפְשׁוֹ עַד שֶׁיֵּשֵׁב וִיסִירֵם מִלִּבּוֹ — *One who walks on the road while reviewing [a Torah lesson] but interrupts his review . . . as if he bears guilt for his*

And so has David said, "For everything is from You, and from Your Own we have given You."

9. *Rabbi Yaakov said: One who walks on the road while reviewing [a Torah lesson] but interrupts his review and exclaims, "How beautiful is this tree! How beautiful is this plowed field!" — Scripture considers it as if he bears guilt for his soul.*

10. *Rabbi Dostai bar Yannai says in the name of Rabbi Meir: Whoever forgets anything of his Torah learning, Scripture considers it as if he bears guilt for his soul, for it is said: "But beware and guard your soul exceedingly lest you forget the things your eyes have seen." Does this apply even if [he forgot because] his studies were too difficult for him? [This is not so, for] Scripture says, "And lest they be removed from your heart all the days of your life." Thus, one does not bear guilt for his soul unless he sits [idly] and [through lack of concentration and review] removes them from his consciousness.*

SFORNO'S COMMENTARY

who interrupts his study [of Torah] and diverts his attention to secular matters, and also he who removes the words of Torah from his heart, both of these are included in the admonition, וּפֶן יָסוּרוּ מִלְּבָבְךָ, *and lest they be removed from your heart,* and regarding both it is written וּשְׁמֹר נַפְשְׁךָ מְאֹד, *and greatly beware for your soul* (*Deuteronomy* 4:9). This is what both of these sages [Rabbi Shimon and Rabbi Dostai] meant when they said, "Scripture considers it as if he bears guilt for his soul."

NOTES

soul . . . one does not bear guilt for his soul unless he sits [idly] and [through lack of concentration and review] removes them from his consciousness. According to the *Sforno,* Rabbi Yaakov's reference to "one who walks on the road while reviewing [a Torah lesson] but interrupts his review" is a metaphor for those who interrupt their Torah study in order to pursue secular studies. Torah is the way of life — the "road" we are meant to follow — while the wisdom of the world is represented by the beautiful trees and pleasant, bountiful fields.

The *Sforno* explains why the expression "he bears guilt for his soul" is used by both Rabbi Yaakov and Rabbi Dostai: This teaches that a person who interrupts his Torah studies in order to pursue secular knowledge is equivalent to one who lets his Torah fade from his memory. And even though only Rabbi Dostai actually cites the verse from *Deuteronomy,* the *Sforno* is of the opinion that Rabbi Yaakov bases his statement upon the same verse. For whether a person substitutes secular study for Torah study, or neglects his Torah

[יא] **רַבִּי** חֲנִינָא בֶּן דּוֹסָא אוֹמֵר: כֹּל שֶׁיִּרְאַת חֶטְאוֹ קוֹדֶמֶת לְחָכְמָתוֹ, חָכְמָתוֹ מִתְקַיֶּמֶת; וְכֹל שֶׁחָכְמָתוֹ קוֹדֶמֶת לְיִרְאַת חֶטְאוֹ, אֵין חָכְמָתוֹ מִתְקַיֶּמֶת.

[יב] **הוּא** הָיָה אוֹמֵר: כֹּל שֶׁמַּעֲשָׂיו מְרֻבִּין מֵחָכְמָתוֹ, חָכְמָתוֹ מִתְקַיֶּמֶת; וְכֹל שֶׁחָכְמָתוֹ מְרֻבָּה מִמַּעֲשָׂיו, אֵין חָכְמָתוֹ מִתְקַיֶּמֶת.

פירוש לרבי עובדיה ספורנו

ג:יא. הנה באמרו יראת חטא אמר על ההזהר מהרע לבריות, והחכמה אמר על החכמה המדינית, והמעשים אמר על מה שיעשה האדם להיטיב לזולתו. אמר אם כן שכשיתנהג האדם בחכמה המדינית בצדקה ומשפט ובהזהר מן החמס, וזה מפני יראת חטאו – זה הוא מפני שהכיר גודל בוראו ושזה רצונו ושראוי לעשות כל זה לכבודו, ולכן תתקיים חכמתו, כי לא תהיה לעולם שום סברא מנגדת לזאת שתוכל לבטלה:

ג:יב. אמנם אם לא תהיה יראת החטא אלא בשביל חכמתו המדינית, שנזהר מהרע לבריות כדי שלא לקלקל המדינות – אין חכמתו מתקיימת, כי לפעמים יגדל אצלו ענין התענוג או התועלת הפרטי הנמשך

SFORNO'S COMMENTARY

3:11-12

כֹּל שֶׁיִּרְאַת חֶטְאוֹ קוֹדֶמֶת לְחָכְמָתוֹ, חָכְמָתוֹ מִתְקַיֶּמֶת . . . — *Anyone whose fear of sin takes priority over his wisdom, his wisdom will endure . . .* "Fear of sin" is that which deters one from harming others; "wisdom" refers to social and communal conduct, while "good deeds" refers to actions performed by men for the benefit of others. The Tanna therefore states that when man conducts himself with "wisdom," i.e., with social responsibility, righteousness and justice — and he is careful not to rob or be violent due to his "fear of sin," which in turn is due to his recognition of the greatness of his Creator, and that this is His will, and he therefore accepts this heavenly will for the glory of God — if this be so, his wisdom will endure, for there will never be any rational reason to nullify his desire to obey God's will.

NOTES

studies and consequently forgets what he has learned, the root of the sin is the same — through his actions, he removes the word of God from his consciousness. Thus, even though the sin of abandoning one's Torah studies to pursue secular knowledge is a more active sin than allowing one's Torah knowledge to fade away, a person who commits either sin "bears guilt for his soul" to the same degree.

3:11-12

כֹּל שֶׁיִּרְאַת חֶטְאוֹ קוֹדֶמֶת לְחָכְמָתוֹ, חָכְמָתוֹ מִתְקַיֶּמֶת — *Anyone whose fear of sin takes priority over his wisdom, his wisdom will endure . . . .* The *Sforno* — who defines "wisdom" as man's understanding of the need to establish a stable social order, and "deeds" as the actions performed by man to benefit society — explains the teaching of Rabbi Chanina ben Dosa in a most logical manner:

11. *Rabbi Chanina ben Dosa says: Anyone whose fear of sin takes priority over his wisdom, his wisdom will endure; but anyone whose wisdom takes priority over his fear of sin, his wisdom will not endure.*

12. *He used to say: Anyone whose good deeds exceed his wisdom, his wisdom will endure; but anyone whose wisdom exceeds his good deeds, his wisdom will not endure.*

פירוש לרבי עובדיה ספורנו

אליו בפרטות יותר מענין המדינות. ולאות ולסימן מובהק על זה אמר שכל מי שמעשיו מרובים מחכמתו, שיעשה המעשה הטוב אפילו במקום שאין שם צורך לתקון המדיני כלל – אין זה אלא להדמות ליוצרו וללכת בדרכיו אחר שהכיר מעלתו, וזה אות שחכמתו המדינית גם כן תהיה מזה הטעם, ולכן תהיה חכמתו מתקימת, שלא ימצא סברא נכוחה מנגדת לזאת. אמנם כשיקרה הפך זה – הנה יהיה הדבר בהפך:

SFORNO'S COMMENTARY

However, if his conduct is not motivated by "fear of sin," but by a sense of social and civic responsibility, which deters him from harming others only because such behavior would be detrimental to the social structure and stability; then, "his wisdom will not endure," for at times, his pleasure and personal needs will outweigh his social concerns.

And to prove this point, Rabbi Chanina goes on to say, "Anyone whose good deeds exceed his wisdom . . .". A person like this will act properly even in the absence of a compelling social need. This person recognizes the greatness of his Creator, and seeks to emulate Him. His actions demonstrate that his social wisdom and responsibilities are motivated by this desire. It is for this reason that his wisdom endures, for no circumstance will prevent him from pursuing his ideal. However, if the reverse is true, then the result will also be the opposite.

NOTES

If the motivating force driving man to conduct himself in a civil and responsible manner is fear of God, then he will behave in a responsible manner. However, if this element of יִרְאַת חֵטְא is lacking, then he will ultimately compromise his ethical beliefs in order to fulfill his personal desires and selfish needs.

כֹּל שֶׁמַּעֲשָׂיו מְרֻבִּין מֵחָכְמָתוֹ, חָכְמָתוֹ מִתְקַיֶּמֶת . . . — *Anyone whose good deeds exceed his wisdom, his wisdom will endure* . . . The *Sforno* elaborates on this theme by interpreting Mishnah 12 as Rabbi Chanina's proof for this thesis. If man's deeds for the good of society are motivated by his desire to emulate God, then it will be reflected in his civic, social actions and endeavors, and will therefore be lasting. But if his civility and responsible behavior is only motivated by his desire to preserve the social order, then his behavior can be affected by selfish desires and personal considerations which are anti-ethical. In time, he will compromise his morals, and they will gradually erode and crumble. This is what is meant by "his wisdom will not endure."

[יג] **הוּא** הָיָה אוֹמֵר: כֹּל שֶׁרְוּחַ הַבְּרִיּוֹת נוֹחָה הֵימֶנּוּ, רְוּחַ הַמָּקוֹם נוֹחָה הֵימֶנּוּ; וְכֹל שֶׁאֵין רְוּחַ הַבְּרִיּוֹת נוֹחָה הֵימֶנּוּ, אֵין רְוּחַ הַמָּקוֹם נוֹחָה הֵימֶנּוּ.

[יד] **רַבִּי** דוֹסָא בֶּן הַרְכִּינַס אוֹמֵר: שֵׁנָה שֶׁל שַׁחֲרִית, וְיַיִן שֶׁל צָהֳרַיִם, וְשִׂיחַת הַיְלָדִים, וִישִׁיבַת בָּתֵּי כְנֵסִיּוֹת שֶׁל עַמֵּי הָאָרֶץ – מוֹצִיאִין אֶת הָאָדָם מִן הָעוֹלָם.

[טו] **רַבִּי** אֶלְעָזָר הַמּוֹדָעִי אוֹמֵר: הַמְּחַלֵּל אֶת הַקֳּדָשִׁים, וְהַמְּבַזֶּה אֶת הַמּוֹעֲדוֹת, וְהַמַּלְבִּין פְּנֵי חֲבֵרוֹ בָּרַבִּים, וְהַמֵּפֵר בְּרִיתוֹ שֶׁל אַבְרָהָם אָבִינוּ, וְהַמְּגַלֶּה פָנִים בַּתּוֹרָה שֶׁלֹּא כַהֲלָכָה,

פירוש לרבי עובדיה ספורנו

ג:יג. הנה כשיזהר האדם מהרע לזולתו כשיוכל על זה, אף על פי שימשך מזה איזה תועלת אליו בפרטות, הנה לא יקרה ברוב אלא כשתהיה כוונתו בזה לכבוד קונו, וזה אות מבואר שרוח האל יתברך נוחה הימינו. וכשיהיה הפך זה – אין ספק שענינו בהפך:

SFORNO'S COMMENTARY

3:13

כֹּל שֶׁרוּחַ הַבְּרִיּוֹת נוֹחָה הֵימֶנּוּ, רוּחַ הַמָּקוֹם נוֹחָה הֵימֶנּוּ — *If the spirit of one's fellows is pleased with him, the spirit of the Omnipresent is pleased with him.* Behold, when a person refrains from harming his fellow man, even though he is able to do so, and such action may benefit him personally, the reason for this behavior in most cases is due to his desire to honor his Maker. This in turn is a sign that "the spirit of the Omnipresent is pleased with him." If the opposite is true, then doubtless the situation [i.e., his motivation and action] is also the reverse [i.e., and "the spirit of the Omnipresent is not pleased with him"].

NOTES

3:13

כֹּל שֶׁרוּחַ הַבְּרִיּוֹת נוֹחָה הֵימֶנּוּ, רוּחַ הַמָּקוֹם נוֹחָה הֵימֶנּוּ — *If the spirit of one's fellows is pleased with him, the spirit of the Omnipresent is pleased with him.* As the *Sforno* explains, Rabbi Chanina's teachings in the previous Mishnah are brought to a logical conclusion here, in Mishnah 13. Man's motivations are of the utmost importance, for they affect and color his behavior as he interacts with others. A God-fearing person who wishes to fulfill the will of the Almighty and seeks to please Him will find favor in the eyes of Hashem and man. Thus, although we cannot peer into the inner recesses of a man's heart, the opinions of others and their assessment of him are indicators of the sincerity and honesty of his deeds.

13. *He used to say: If the spirit of one's fellows is pleased with him, the spirit of the Omnipresent is pleased with him; but if the spirit of one's fellows is not pleased with him, the spirit of the Omnipresent is not pleased with him.*

14. *Rabbi Dosa ben Harkinas said: Late morning sleep, midday wine, children's chatter, and sitting in the assemblies of the ignorant remove a man from the world.*

15. *Rabbi Elazar the Moda'ite said: One who desecrates sacred things, who disgraces the Festivals, who humiliates his fellow in public, who nullifies the covenant of our forefather Abraham, or who perverts the Torah contrary to the halachah —*

פירוש לרבי עובדיה ספורנו

ג:יד. מונעים את האדם מהשיג חיי עולם וגם כן מהשיג חיי שעה, וזה לרב מה שנמשך מהם מאבוד הזמן בלתי שירגיש האדם בו:

ג:טו. אמר שהעובר על אחת מאלה שהזכיר אין לו חלק לעולם הבא, כי אמנם כל אחת מהן בכלל „כי דבר יי בזה" שנאמר עליו

SFORNO'S COMMENTARY

3:14

שֵׁנָה שֶׁל שַׁחֲרִית וכו׳ מוֹצִיאִין אֶת הָאָדָם מִן הָעוֹלָם — *Late morning sleep etc. remove a man from the world.* This conduct prevents man from attaining eternal life, and also deters him even from attaining life in this world. Now, this is the consequence of the waste of time which results from these practices, of which man is unaware.

3:15

הַמְחַלֵּל אֶת הַקֳּדָשִׁים וכו׳ . . . אע״פ שֶׁיֵּשׁ בְּיָדוֹ תוֹרָה וּמַעֲשִׂים טוֹבִים – אֵין לוֹ חֵלֶק לָעוֹלָם הַבָּא — *One who desecrates sacred things etc. — though he may have Torah and good deeds, he has no share in the World to Come.* The Tanna states that if one is guilty of any one of these transgressions, "he has no share in the

NOTES

3:14

מוֹצִיאִין אֶת הָאָדָם מִן הָעוֹלָם — *Remove a man from the world.* The *Sforno* interprets the phrase "removes a man from the world" as referring to both this world and the World to Come. The four things listed in the Mishnah cause a man to lose both "worlds" by squandering his precious time, thus preventing him from succeeding in his worldly pursuits, and inhibiting his ability to earn a share in the World to Come.

3:15

וְהַמְגַלֶּה פָנִים בַּתּוֹרָה שֶׁלֹּא כַהֲלָכָה, אע״פ שֶׁיֵּשׁ בְּיָדוֹ תּוֹרָה וּמַעֲשִׂים טוֹבִים – אֵין לוֹ חֵלֶק לָעוֹלָם הַבָּא — *Or who perverts the Torah contrary to the*

אַף עַל פִּי שֶׁיֵּשׁ בְּיָדוֹ תּוֹרָה וּמַעֲשִׂים טוֹבִים — אֵין לוֹ חֵלֶק לָעוֹלָם הַבָּא.

[טז] **רַבִּי** יִשְׁמָעֵאל אוֹמֵר: הֱוֵי קַל לְרֹאשׁ, וְנוֹחַ לְתִשְׁחֹרֶת, וֶהֱוֵי מְקַבֵּל אֶת כָּל הָאָדָם בְּשִׂמְחָה.

[יז] **רַבִּי** עֲקִיבָא אוֹמֵר: שְׂחוֹק וְקַלּוּת רֹאשׁ מַרְגִּילִין אֶת הָאָדָם לְעֶרְוָה. מַסּוֹרֶת סְיָג לַתּוֹרָה; מַעְשְׂרוֹת סְיָג לָעֹשֶׁר; נְדָרִים סְיָג

פירוש לרבי עובדיה ספורנו

„הכרת תכרת", וכבר פרשו ז"ל הכרת בעולם הזה תכרת בעולם הבא. ואמר אף על פי שיש בידו תורה ומעשים טובים, כי אמנם מעשיו הם בלי ספק בלתי מכוונים לרצון קונם ותורתו אינה אלא מן השפה ולחוץ:

ג:טז. הוי קל לראש, כענין אל תתהדר לפני מלך, כל שכן לפני המלך הקדוש, כענין דוד

SFORNO'S COMMENTARY

World to Come," because each of these actions is included in the Biblical phrase, כִּי דְבַר ה׳ בָּזָה, *For he scorned the word of Hashem* (*Numbers* 15:31). Regarding this person it has been written, הִכָּרֵת תִּכָּרֵת, *he shall surely be cut off* (ibid.), and the Sages comment: "Cut off" refers to this world, "surely cut off" refers to the World to Come (*Sanhedrin* 64b).

And when our Tanna adds, "though he may have Torah and good deeds," he implies that even his good deeds are doubtless not motivated by the desire to fulfill God's will, nor is his Torah sincere, for it is "from the lips outward."

3:16

הֱוֵי קַל לְרֹאשׁ, וְנוֹחַ לְתִשְׁחֹרֶת, וֶהֱוֵי מְקַבֵּל אֶת כָּל הָאָדָם בְּשִׂמְחָה — *Be yielding to a superior, pleasant to the young, and receive every person cheerfully.* "Be

NOTES

halachah — though he may have Torah and good deeds, he has no share in the World to Come. Our Sages have taught us that if a Torah scholar who performs *mitzvos* is insincere, and the words of study and prayer which are upon his lips do not emanate from his heart, then "even though he has Torah and good deeds" to his credit, they are rejected by the Almighty.

Two major figures in Scripture exemplified this type of behavior: Achitofel and Doeg. In reference to Doeg, the Talmud (*Sanhedrin* 106b) cites the verse, מַה לְּךָ לְסַפֵּר חֻקָּי וַתִּשָּׂא בְרִיתִי עֲלֵי פִיךָ, *To what purpose do you recount My decrees, while bearing My Covenant upon your lips* (*Psalms* 50:16). In another psalm, Doeg and Achitofel are characterized as דִּבְרֵי כָזָב, *speakers of deception* (ibid., 5:7).

3:16

הֱוֵי קַל לְרֹאשׁ, וְנוֹחַ לְתִשְׁחֹרֶת, וֶהֱוֵי מְקַבֵּל אֶת כָּל הָאָדָם בְּשִׂמְחָה — *Be yielding to a superior, pleasant to the young, and receive every person cheerfully.* In a person's relationship with others, he must strike a delicate

though he may have Torah and good deeds, he has no share in the World to Come.

16. *Rabbi Yishmael said: Be yielding to a superior, pleasant to the young, and receive every person cheerfully.*

17. *Rabbi Akiva said: Mockery and levity accustom a man to immorality. The transmitted Oral Torah is a protective fence around the Torah; tithes are a protective fence for wealth; vows are a protective*

פירוש לרבי עובדיה ספורנו

באמרו ,,ונקלותי עוד מזאת." ונוח לתשחורת, לפני צעירים לימים הוי נוח ומתכבד לתועלתם, שלא יגיסו דעתם בך כדי שיקבלו ממך. והוי מקבל את כל האדם בשמחה, שלא תתכבד עליהם באופן שייראו מגשת אליך אבל תקבלם בסבר פנים יפות באופן שתקרבם לעבודת האל, כענין שספרו על הלל שנתעטף וישב לפני השואל ואמר שאל בני שאל, ובמדתו זאת הקריב גרים לחסות תחת כנפי שכינה ורבים השיב מעון:

ג:יז. הזכיר דרכי שמירה וקיום לזהירות

SFORNO'S COMMENTARY

yielding to a superior." Similar to, אַל תִּתְהַדַּר לִפְנֵי מֶלֶךְ, *Do not give yourself airs in the presence of the king* (*Proverbs* 25:6). How much more so vis-a-vis the Holy King, as we find by David when he said, וּנְקַלֹּתִי עוֹד מִזֹּאת, *And yet I will be more lightly esteemed than this* (*II Samuel* 6:22).

"[Be] pleasant to the young." In relationship with the young, act pleasantly so as to be respected by them, for their own benefit, that they not act arrogantly with you, so that they will be prepared to accept your guidance and instruction.

"And receive every person cheerfully." However, do not be overbearing with them lest they be afraid to approach you; rather receive them with a pleasant demeanor, thereby drawing them close to the service of God, as we are told regarding Hillel, who wrapped himself in his *tallis* and sat in front of the one who inquired and said, שְׁאַל בְּנִי, שְׁאַל, "Ask, my son, ask" (*Shabbos* 31a). Through this behavior, he brought proselytes under the wings of the שְׁכִינָה (Divine Presence) and "turned many away from iniquity" [see *Malachi* 2:6].

NOTES

balance between cordiality and humbleness. The former trait should be practiced in his relationship with those who are younger in years and lesser in wisdom, while the latter trait should be applied in his behavior towards those who are older and superior in wisdom.

The *Sforno* cites verses from Scriptures, as well as an episode from the Talmud regarding Hillel, to elucidate the teachings of Rabbi Ishmael. One must not be overbearing with one's juniors, but also careful not to become too familiar with them, lest one lose their respect. Conversely, one must take great pains to show respect to one's superiors and elders.

ג לַפְּרִישׁוּת; סְיָג לַחָכְמָה שְׁתִיקָה.

יח [יח] **הוּא** הָיָה אוֹמֵר: חָבִיב אָדָם שֶׁנִּבְרָא בְצֶלֶם; חִבָּה יְתֵרָה נוֹדַעַת לוֹ שֶׁנִּבְרָא

פירוש לרבי עובדיה ספורנו

ולזריזות ואמר שראוי להשמר משחוק וקלות ראש כדי להזהר מן הערוה, ולקיום העיון והמעשה והעושר אשר הוא כלי להם אמר שראוי להזדרז במסורות לשמירת התורה, כאמרם ז״ל „עשה סימניות לתורה״, ובמעשרות לשמירה העושר, כאמרם ז״ל „מלח ממון חסר״, וכבר באר הנביא ואמר ובחנוני נא בזאת. וכמו כן אמר שהנדרים הם סייג לשמור הפרישות, כענין „נשבעתי ואקימה לשמור משפטי

SFORNO'S COMMENTARY

3:17

שְׂחוֹק וְקַלּוּת רֹאשׁ מַרְגִּילִין . . . לְעֶרְוָה. מַסּוֹרֶת סְיָג לַתּוֹרָה; מַעְשְׂרוֹת סְיָג לָעֹשֶׁר — *Mockery and levity accustom . . . to immorality. The transmitted Oral Torah is a protective fence around the Torah; tithes are a protective fence for wealth.* [Rabbi Akiva] lists cautionary ways to ensure זְהִירוּת, *watchfulness,* and זְרִיזוּת, *zeal.* He first states that it is proper to guard against "mockery and levity" so as to protect one from immorality. And to ensure the endurance of man's intellectual/philosophical powers and his good deeds as well as his wealth, which is a necessary vessel for them, he teaches us that we must zealously guard Torah by being careful of transmission [tradition], as our Sages say עֲשֵׂה סִימָנִיּוֹת לַתּוֹרָה, "make marks [mnemonic devices] in the Torah" (*Shabbos* 115b). Through tithes a person preserves his wealth, as our Sages say מֶלַח מָמוֹן חַסֵּר, "To preserve your wealth, diminish it" (*Kesuvos* 66b). And as the prophet explains and exhorts us, in God's Name, וּבְחָנוּנִי נָא בָּזֹאת, *And put Me to the test with that* (*Malachi* 3:10).

NOTES

3:17

מַסּוֹרֶת סְיָג לַתּוֹרָה; מַעְשְׂרוֹת סְיָג לָעֹשֶׁר; נְדָרִים סְיָג לַפְּרִישׁוּת; סְיָג לַחָכְמָה שְׁתִיקָה — *The transmitted Oral Torah is a protective fence around the Torah; tithes are a protective fence for wealth; vows are a protective fence for abstinence; a protective fence for wisdom is silence.* The *Sforno* explains the common theme of Rabbi Akiva's four cautionary teachings, or "protective fences": It is not sufficient for a person to merely recognize the significance of Torah, the value of wealth, the necessity to distance oneself from sin, and the importance of wisdom. But these valuable treasures must be guarded, be it through oral transmission, tithes, vows, or silence. Otherwise, these material, intellectual, and spiritual assets will be endangered.

At the beginning of his commentary on this and the next Mishnah, the *Sforno* speaks of two character traits which he discussed in his introduction: זְהִירוּת, *watchfulness,* and זְרִיזוּת, *zeal* or *alacrity.*

These terms are defined, developed, and explained by Rabbi Moshe Chaim Luzzatto, the famous 18th-century ethical philosopher, in his classic work *Mesillas Yesharim.* There, he explains that זְהִירוּת pertains to exercising great caution in the observance of negative commandments by scrutinizing one's actions to determine whether they are proper and good. The second principle, זְרִיזוּת, pertains to enhancing one's obser-

3
18

fence for abstinence; a protective fence for wisdom is silence.

18. *He used to say: Beloved is man, for he was created in God's image; it is indicative of a greater love that it was made known to him that he was created*

פירוש לרבי עובדיה ספורנו

צדקך." ואמר שהשמירה מן השכחה מן הטעות בכל חכמה תהיה בשתיקה מכל דבור מותר ומשיחה בטלה המשיאה מן ההתבוננות בחכמה אל דמיונות כוזבות:

ג:יח. אמר הנה ראוי לאדם לשים לבו אל דברי זהירות וזריזות שאמרתי לכבוד קונו

SFORNO'S COMMENTARY

נְדָרִים סְיָג לַפְּרִישׁוּת; סְיָג לַחָכְמָה שְׁתִיקָה — *Vows are a protective fence for abstinence; a protective fence for wisdom is silence.* The Tanna also teaches us that vows are a protective fence around a person, ensuring distancing oneself from [transgression], as the verse in *Psalms* states, נִשְׁבַּעְתִּי וָאֲקַיֵּמָה לִשְׁמֹר מִשְׁפְּטֵי צִדְקֶךָ, *I have sworn and I will fulfill it, to keep Your righteous judgments* (*Psalms* 119:106).

[Rabbi Akiva] also teaches us that the way to protect oneself from forgetfulness and error, in the pursuit of wisdom, is "silence" — abstaining from unnecessary words and idle talk, for these divert a person's application and attention to wisdom, bringing him to false and erroneous thoughts.

3:18

חָבִיב אָדָם שֶׁנִּבְרָא בְצֶלֶם; חִבָּה יְתֵרָה נוֹדַעַת לוֹ — *Beloved is man, for he was created in God's image; it is indicative of a greater love that it was made known to him.* Rabbi Akiva tells us that it is proper for man to consider and pay close attention to the principles of זְהִירוּת, *watchfulness,* and זְרִיזוּת, *zeal,* for

NOTES

vance of positive commandments by exhibiting alacrity in the pursuit and fulfillment of *mitzvos.*

The *Sforno* explains that Rabbi Akiva sets the tone for this Mishnah by first cautioning against "mockery and levity," for this kind of behavior hinders זְהִירוּת and זְרִיזוּת. The absence of these two positive traits will induce a person to pay scant attention to the finer goals set forth in this Mishnah — namely, the pursuit of Torah knowledge, material well-being, voluntary abstinence, and wisdom.

Regarding the importance of סִימָנִיּוֹת, making "marks" in the Torah, which the *Sforno* cites as an example of tradition, the Sages ascribed great importance to this practice in *Shabbos* 104, where the Talmud states "make marks in the Torah so as to acquire it." Similarly, in *Eruvin* 54, the Sages teach us that Torah cannot be acquired without "marks." This is based on their reading of the verse שִׂימָהּ בְּפִיהֶם (*Deuteronomy* 31:19), *place it in their mouths,* amended to read סִימָנָהּ instead of שִׂימָהּ; do not read "place it in their mouths" but "mark it for them," as a means of instruction, which alludes to traditional teachings.

3:18

חָבִיב אָדָם שֶׁנִּבְרָא בְצֶלֶם . . . חֲבִיבִין יִשְׂרָאֵל שֶׁנִּקְרְאוּ בָנִים לַמָּקוֹם; . . . חֲבִיבִין יִשְׂרָאֵל, שֶׁנִּתַּן לָהֶם כְּלִי חֶמְדָּה — *Beloved is man, for he was created in God's image . . . Beloved are the*

ג בְּצֶלֶם, שֶׁנֶּאֱמַר: „כִּי בְּצֶלֶם אֱלֹהִים עָשָׂה אֶת
יט הָאָדָם.” חֲבִיבִין יִשְׂרָאֵל, שֶׁנִּקְרְאוּ בָנִים לַמָּקוֹם;
חִבָּה יְתֵרָה נוֹדַעַת לָהֶם שֶׁנִּקְרְאוּ בָנִים לַמָּקוֹם,
שֶׁנֶּאֱמַר: „בָּנִים אַתֶּם לַיהוה אֱלֹהֵיכֶם.” חֲבִיבִין
יִשְׂרָאֵל, שֶׁנִּתַּן לָהֶם כְּלִי חֶמְדָּה; חִבָּה יְתֵרָה נוֹדַעַת
לָהֶם, שֶׁנִּתַּן לָהֶם כְּלִי חֶמְדָּה, שֶׁבּוֹ נִבְרָא הָעוֹלָם,
שֶׁנֶּאֱמַר: „כִּי לֶקַח טוֹב נָתַתִּי לָכֶם, תּוֹרָתִי אַל
תַּעֲזֹבוּ.”

[יט] **הַכֹּל** צָפוּי, וְהָרְשׁוּת נְתוּנָה. וּבְטוּב הָעוֹלָם

פירוש לרבי עובדיה ספורנו

בהיותו חביב לפניו שנברא בצלם. ועם זה הוזהר בשמירת זה הצלם, כאמרו לבני נח „ואך את דמכם לנפשותיכם אדרוש” וגומר „כי בצלם אלדים עשה את האדם”. ויותר ראוי זה בין המין האנושי לישראל שנקראו בנים ולכן הם חייבים בכבוד אביהם שבשמים יותר משאר בני אדם שהם לא בניו, כל שכן מאחר שהוזהרו על שמירת

SFORNO'S COMMENTARY

the honor and glory of one's Maker, of which I have spoken, being that mankind is beloved by Him and was created in His image, and is also cautioned to protect this image, as God said to the children of Noah, וְאַךְ אֶת דִּמְכֶם לְנַפְשֹׁתֵיכֶם אֶדְרֹשׁ. . .כִּי בְּצֶלֶם אֱלֹהִים עָשָׂה אֶת הָאָדָם, *However, your blood which belongs to your souls, I will demand . . . for in the image of God He made man* (*Genesis* 9:5-6).

חֲבִיבִין יִשְׂרָאֵל, שֶׁנִּקְרְאוּ בָנִים לַמָּקוֹם; חִבָּה יְתֵרָה נוֹדַעַת לָהֶם — *Beloved are the people Israel, for they are described as children of the Omnipresent; it is indicative of a greater love that it was made known to them . . .* And this is even more proper for Israel, who are called בָּנִים, *children.* Therefore, they are obligated to honor their Heavenly Father more so than the rest of mankind, who are not His children. This is especially true in light of the fact that they have been admonished to protect this special status through their conduct and behavior, as it is written, בָּנִים אַתֶּם לַה' אֱלֹהֵיכֶם לֹא תִתְגֹּדְדוּ, *You are children to Hashem, your God, you shall not cut yourself* (*Deuteronomy* 14:1).

NOTES

people Israel, for they are described as children of the Omnipresent . . . Beloved are the people Israel, for a cherished utensil was given to them. In his commentary on *Shemos* 19:5, the *Sforno* writes: "Although the entire human race is precious to God, nonetheless, Israel is considered 'a treasure among all nations.' " As proof, he quotes Rabbi Akiva's statement in this Mishnah.

With this same concept, he also elucidates Rabbi Akiva's teaching in this Mishnah: Mankind was created in Hashem's image, and as such, is superior to all other

3 *in God's image, as it is said: "For in the image of God He*
19 *made man." Beloved are the people Israel, for they are described as children of the Omnipresent; it is indicative of a greater love that it was made known to them that they are described as children of the Omnipresent, as it is said: "You are children to* HASHEM, *Your God." Beloved are the people Israel, for a cherished utensil was given to them; it is indicative of a greater love that it was made known to them that they were given a cherished utensil, with which the universe was created, as it is said: "For I have given you a good teaching; do not forsake My Torah."*

19. E*verything is foreseen, yet the freedom of choice is given. The world is judged with*

פירוש לרבי עובדיה ספורנו

מעלתם זאת כאמרו „בנים אתם לייי אלקיכם לא תתגודדו״. ובין האומה הישראלית יותר ראוי זה לתופשי התורה שנתן להם כלי חמדה שבו נברא העולם, כאמרו „יי בחכמה יסד ארץ כונן שמים בתבונה״, והוזהרו על שמירת זה הכל כאמרו „תורתי אל תעזובו״:

ג:יט. הנה אין התנצלות לחוטא שיאמר

SFORNO'S COMMENTARY

שֶׁנִּתַּן לָהֶם כְּלִי חֶמְדָּה; חִבָּה יְתֵרָה נוֹדַעַת לָהֶם . . . — *. . . for a cherished utensil was given to them; it is indicative of a greater love that it was made known to them* . . . And among the people of Israel, this is especially fitting for Torah scholars, to whom "the cherished utensil with which the world was created [i.e., the Torah] was given," as the verse says, ה׳ בְּחָכְמָה יָסַד אָרֶץ כּוֹנֵן שָׁמַיִם בִּתְבוּנָה, *With wisdom* [i.e., the Torah] *Hashem founded the earth, He established the heavens with understanding* (*Proverbs* 3:19). And they have been cautioned to guard this vessel, as it says, תּוֹרָתִי אַל תַּעֲזֹבוּ, *Do not forsake My Torah* (ibid., 4:2).

3:19

הַכֹּל צָפוּי, וְהָרְשׁוּת נְתוּנָה. וּבְטוֹב הָעוֹלָם נָדוֹן — *Everything is foreseen, yet the freedom of choice is given. The world is judged with goodness.* Behold, there

NOTES

living creatures. Israel, as God's children, was granted special status among the nations, which it is bound to guard for all eternity. Those among the children of Israel who understand and appreciate the importance of Torah, which was the blueprint of the world, as the Sages said, "God looked into the Torah and created the world," have an even greater responsibility to preserve the unique character and status of Israel.

3:19

הַכֹּל צָפוּי, וְהָרְשׁוּת נְתוּנָה . . . — *Everything is foreseen, yet the freedom of choice is given* . . . The classic commentators explain

נָדוֹן, וְהַכֹּל לְפִי רוֹב הַמַּעֲשֶׂה.

פירוש לרבי עובדיה ספורנו

שהוא מוכרח לחטוא מפני ידיעת האל הקודמת לחטאו אשר לא יפול בה כזב בשום אופן, כי אמנם הוא יודע בחירת האדם העתיד ושהיא בלתי מוכרחת, כמו שנדע אנחנו בהווים ידיעה בלתי מסופקת ועם זה בלתי מכרחת, כי אמנם כל העתיד הוא לפני ידיעתו יתברך במדרגת ההווה מבלי אין גם לאותו העתיד שום מציאות כי אם ממציאותו. ואמר ובטוב העולם נדון, כאמרם ז״ל „ורב חסד מטה כלפי חסד מעביר ראשון ראשון״, וכל זה הערה לחוטא שיזכה בתשובה על נקלה בהיות הדיין מטה כלפי חסד. ואמר והכל כפי רב המעשה, שכל ענין

SFORNO'S COMMENTARY

is no excuse for the sinner who may say, "I am compelled to sin, since God has foreknowledge and knows I will sin, and there can be no falsehood before Him." [This is not so,] for although He knows beforehand what man will choose in the future, nonetheless, there is no compulsion, in the same manner as we have certain knowledge of what is taking place in the present, and yet we [through our knowledge] are not the compelling cause of that event. To God, the future is no different, in His knowledge, than the present. For there is no reality of future acts (מְצִיאוּת) and events except through His reality.

And the Tanna continues, "The world is judged with goodness," as our Sages say, וְרַב חֶסֶד מַטֶּה כְּלַפֵּי חֶסֶד מַעֲבִיר רִאשׁוֹן רִאשׁוֹן , "He that abounds in kindness inclines [the scales] toward kindness, putting aside [iniquity] one by one" (*Rosh Hashanah* 17a). This is meant as encouragement to the sinner: He will not find it difficult to repent, since the Heavenly Judge tilts the scale toward benevolence.

וְהַכֹּל לְפִי רוֹב הַמַּעֲשֶׂה — *And everything depends on the abundance of good deeds.* "And everything depends on the abundance of good deeds," for reward and punishment do not depend upon one's mastery of the

NOTES

these cryptic words of Rabbi Akiva in a variety of ways. *Rashi* interprets the phrase הַכֹּל צָפוּי, "everything is foreseen," to mean that what a person does in private cannot be concealed from God, for He is all knowing.

The *Rambam* in his commentary on this Mishnah interprets the full phrase "everything is foreseen, yet the freedom of choice is given" to mean that although God has foreknowledge of man's actions and everything is revealed to Him, nevertheless, this foreknowledge does not determine man's actions nor interfere with his בְּחִירָה חָפְשִׁית, *free choice.* Although the concept of man's freedom of choice and God's omniscience seem mutually exclusive, the *Rambam* (*Mishnah Torah, Yesodei HaTorah* Ch. 2, *Hilchos Teshuvah* 5:5) reconciles this apparent contradiction as follows: God's knowledge is not external to Himself, but rather, He and His knowledge are one. As such, God's knowledge does not determine the actions of man. However, the *Rambam* himself admits that this contradiction cannot be fully explained by logic alone, and

3 *goodness, and everything depends on the abundance*
19 *of good deeds.*

פירוש לרבי עובדיה ספורנו

הגמול והעונש אינו תלוי בחלק העיוני הנקנה אבל בחלק המעשי, וזה כי אמנם חיות השכל האנושי הכחיי יקנהו האדם בהוציאו את שכלו הכחיי מן הכח אל הפעל, כי בהיותו משכיל בפעל יהיה בעל חיות שכלי בפעל אשר הוא נצחי נכבד מכל שאר מיני חיים, ויחזק זה החיות ויחלש כפי מדרגת העיון הקנוי. אמנם אישור זה החיות השכלי והצלחתו ושמחתו וכבודו או הפך כל זה יהיה כפי רוב המעשה הטוב הרצוי לפני האדון יי יתברך, כי בו ידמה השכל הבחיריי לבוראו המטיב לזולת כאשר באר באמרו בצלמנו כדמותינו:

SFORNO'S COMMENTARY

philosophical/intellectual area of Torah, but upon the practical realm of actual deeds. This is because man's intellectual powers are realized only when translated into action, for it is only then that they acquire a life of their own which is everlasting, and in this manner, man's superiority above all living creatures is actualized.

Now, the significance and vitality of one's actions depends upon the level of one's intellectual capacities, but this, in turn, is confirmed only through one's deeds, for they grant man success, joy and honor, or, the reverse. All this is determined according to "the abundance of good deeds" which are acceptable to the Master — Hashem the blessed One — for in this manner will man's conscious choice emulate his Creator Who is good to His creation and all His creatures, as stated in the expression בְּצַלְמֵנוּ כִּדְמוּתֵנוּ, *in Our image, after Our likeness* (*Genesis* 1:26).

NOTES

that one must accept on faith that God's foreknowledge and man's freedom are able to coexist.

The *Raavad* criticizes the *Rambam* for introducing this entire matter, since he himself admits that it cannot be fully resolved. He then attempts to give his own explanation, differentiating between גְּזֵרָה, a Godly *decree,* and יְדִיעָה, Divine *knowledge.*

The *Sforno,* in his commentary on this Mishnah, presents a reasonable and relatively simple explanation based on the element of time. The Divine clock is always set to the present, and there is no past or future from Hashem's perspective. Hence, God's *foreknowledge* is a misnomer, for He is but observing man's actions, which are freely chosen as they occur. Obviously, such Divine "observation" does not determine man's actions.

וְהַכֹּל לְפִי רוֹב הַמַּעֲשֶׂה — *And everything depends on the abundance of good deeds.* The *Sforno*'s commentary on the last part of the Mishnah, regarding "the abundance of one's deeds," mirrors his commentary on the Torah on the verse, "in Our image, after Our likeness," which he quotes here. In *Genesis,* he explains that man's power of reason, his intellect, is called "image," while "likeness" refers to man's actions, which result from man's choice. In this manner, man emulates God, and not the angels, for they have no such freedom. Hence, reward and punishment depend totally upon man's deeds, and not upon his comprehension or intellectual abilities.

ג [כ] **הוּא** הָיָה אוֹמֵר: הַכֹּל נָתוּן בָּעֵרָבוֹן,
כ וּמְצוּדָה פְּרוּסָה עַל כָּל הַחַיִּים.
הֶחָנוּת פְּתוּחָה, וְהַחֶנְוָנִי מַקִּיף, וְהַפִּנְקָס פָּתוּחַ,
וְהַיָּד כּוֹתֶבֶת, וְכָל הָרוֹצֶה לִלְווֹת יָבֹא וְיִלְוֶה.
וְהַגַּבָּאִים מַחֲזִירִין תָּדִיר בְּכָל יוֹם וְנִפְרָעִין מִן
הָאָדָם, מִדַּעְתּוֹ וְשֶׁלֹּא מִדַּעְתּוֹ, וְיֵשׁ לָהֶם עַל מַה
שֶׁיִּסְמֹכוּ. וְהַדִּין דִּין אֱמֶת, וְהַכֹּל מְתֻקָּן לִסְעוּדָה.

פירוש לרבי עובדיה ספורנו

ג:כ. אמר אף על פי שהרשות נתונה – היא אמנם נתונה בערבון, לא לנצח אלא לזמן קצוב, באופן שתשוב על כל פנים הנפש החוטאת או הזוכה אל האלקים אשר נתנה ליתן דין וחשבון, ומצודה פרושה על כל החיים – בחיי עולם או בחיי שעה, שלא ימלט גם אחד מהענש הראוי לו בשני מיני החיים, אף על פי שבבחירתו ימלט ממקרי הזמן או מקצתם כאמרו שומר נפשו ירחק מהם, מכל מקום

SFORNO'S COMMENTARY

3:20

הַכֹּל נָתוּן בָּעֵרָבוֹן, וּמְצוּדָה פְּרוּסָה עַל כָּל הַחַיִּים — *Everything is given on collateral and a net is spread over all the living.* Although "freedom of choice" is given to man [see previous Mishnah], it is given only on collateral — i.e., not forever, but for a limited, set period of time, following which the soul, be it a sinful or meritorious one, will be returned to the Almighty Who gave it, for judgment and accounting.

"And a net is spread over all the living," be it eternal life or transitory life, for none can escape the punishment befitting him in either life, even though one can, through his choice, protect himself from all or some of the vicissitudes of life, as it says: שׁוֹמֵר נַפְשׁוֹ יִרְחַק מֵהֶם, *He that guards his soul, let him distance himself from them* (*Proverbs* 22:5). Nonetheless, he cannot avoid punishment.

וְהַחֶנְוָנִי מַקִּיף . . . — *The Merchant extends credit.* "The Merchant extends credit," when He grants men His Divine image *in potentia* to perfect it and transform it into reality. He does not demand payment of the laggard, but continues to extend credit to him until the day of his death.

NOTES

3:20

הַכֹּל נָתוּן בָּעֵרָבוֹן, וּמְצוּדָה פְּרוּסָה . . . וְהַגַּבָּאִים מַחֲזִירִין תָּדִיר . . . וְהַדִּין דִּין אֱמֶת — *Everything is given on collateral and a net is spread over . . . The collectors make their rounds constantly . . . the judgment is a truthful judgment.* The *Sforno* elucidates these concluding teachings of Rabbi Akiva, which caution us that the Almighty holds man accountable for all his actions. For although He is patient, nonetheless, reward and punishment await us in the World to Come. There are reminders in this world as well, and one should be sensitive to these "collectors," which remind us to repent and mend our ways.

3
20

20. *He used to say: Everything is given on collateral and a net is spread over all the living. The shop is open; the Merchant extends credit; the ledger is open; the hand writes; and whoever wishes to borrow, let him come and borrow. The collectors make their rounds constantly, every day, and collect payment from the person whether he realizes it or not. They have proof to rely upon; the judgment is a truthful judgment; and everything is prepared for the [final festive] banquet.*

פירוש לרבי עובדיה ספורנו

לא ימלט מן העונשים. החנוני מקיף – כשהוא נותן את צלמו הכוחיית להשלימה ולהוציאה אל הפעל הוא בלתי נפרע על זה מן המתרשל אבל מקיף עד יום המות, וכל הרוצה ללוות ולהתחייב למלך בחטאו או בחטאים – בא ולוה, ואינו נפרע מיד, אבל הגבאים מחזירים תמיד להפרע מן האדם, בין מדעתו שיכיר זה וישוב, בין שלא ירגיש כזה, ויש להם על מה שיסמכו בגבייתם, שלא ימנעו מן הגבייה מבלי אין מה לגבות ממנו אבל יגבו עשיר בשורו ועני בשיו או בגופו כפי המשפט האלקי, והדין דין אמת, שומר היחס לעני ולעשיר, כי יחס השה דרך משל לעני כיחס השור

SFORNO'S COMMENTARY

וְכָל הָרוֹצֶה לִלְווֹת יָבֹא . . . וְהַגַּבָּאִים מַחֲזִירִין תָּדִיר . . . — *And whoever wishes to borrow, let him come . . . The collectors make their rounds constantly . . .* "And whoever wishes to borrow," and thereby obligate himself to the King through his sins, may do so, and the Almighty will not exact payment immediately. However, "the collectors make their rounds constantly" . . . to collect from the person, "whether he realizes it" — i.e., he recognizes what is happening and repents — "or not" — i.e. he remains oblivious and desensitized.

וְיֵשׁ לָהֶם עַל מַה שֶׁיִּסְמֹכוּ — *They have proof to rely upon.* And "they have proof to rely upon" when collecting, for they will not refrain from collecting even if the person does not have the means by which to pay. For they will collect עָשִׁיר בְּשׁוֹרוֹ וְעָנִי בְשֵׂיוֹ, "from the rich man his ox, and from the poor man, his sheep" (*Pesachim* 118a). Or, [failing that, they will collect] from his physical being, all according to heavenly justice.

וְהַדִּין דִּין אֱמֶת, וְהַכֹּל מְתֻקָּן לִסְעוּדָה — *The judgment is a truthful judgment; and everything is prepared for the [final festive] banquet.* And "the judgment is a truthful judgment," meaning that He is always mindful of the relative ability

NOTES

The age-old question as to why the righteous suffer in this world while the wicked prosper is explained by our Tanna as being the epitome of justice: Ultimately, hardship in this world will benefit the *tzaddik,* for it ensures that his full measure of eternal reward in the World to Come shall not be diminished by his sins. Conversely, by compensating the wicked for their good deeds in this world, their punishment in the World to Come will be absolute.

ג
כא

[כא] **רַבִּי** אֶלְעָזָר בֶּן עֲזַרְיָה אוֹמֵר: אִם אֵין תּוֹרָה, אֵין דֶּרֶךְ אֶרֶץ; אִם אֵין דֶּרֶךְ אֶרֶץ, אֵין תּוֹרָה. אִם אֵין חָכְמָה, אֵין יִרְאָה; אִם אֵין יִרְאָה, אֵין חָכְמָה. אִם אֵין דַּעַת, אֵין בִּינָה; אִם אֵין בִּינָה, אֵין דַּעַת. אִם אֵין

פירוש לרבי עובדיה ספורנו

לעשיר, והכל מתוקן לסעודה – וכל זה הדין והגבייה בעולם הזה מתוקן לאותה הסעודה שבאר הנביא, כאמרו „ועשה יי לכל העמים משתה שמנים משתה שמרים שמנים ממוחים שמרים מזוקקים", כי אמנם יפרע מן הצדיקים עד כחוט השערה כדי שבשמחתם לא יתערב דבר של פורענות לחיי עולם, וכן מטיב לרשעים בעולם הזה כדי שלא יתערב דבר שלגמול בפורענותם לחיי עולם, כאמרו „ומשלם לשונאיו אל פניו להאבידו" וכאמרו „להשמדם עדי עד":

ג:כא. אם אין תורה, והוא החלק העיוני – אין אותו מין דרך ארץ המכוון ממנה, והוא

SFORNO'S COMMENTARY

of the poor and the rich to pay. To the poor man, a lamb is as important as an ox is to the rich man.

"And everything is prepared for the [final festive] banquet." And this judgment and "collection" in this world is in preparation for the banquet of which the Prophet spoke when he said, וְעָשָׂה ה׳ צְבָאוֹת לְכָל הָעַמִּים בָּהָר הַזֶּה מִשְׁתֵּה שְׁמָנִים מִשְׁתֵּה שְׁמָרִים שְׁמָנִים מְמֻחָיִם שְׁמָרִים מְזֻקָּקִים, *And on this mountain, the Lord of Hosts will make for all the peoples, a feast of fat things, a feast of wines on the lees, of fat things full of marrow of wines on the lees well refined* (*Isaiah* 25:6). For indeed, He will judge the pious and righteous in this world, even for a minor transgression of a hair's breadth, so that their joy not be impaired by any retribution in the World to Come. Similarly, He will reward the wicked in this world, so that their punishment in the World to Come will be complete, and not reduced or mitigated, by consideration for any good deeds on their part, as it is written: וּמְשַׁלֵּם לְשֹׂנְאָיו אֶל פָּנָיו לְהַאֲבִידוֹ, *And He repays His enemies in his lifetime, to make him perish* (*Deuteronomy* 7:10). And as it is written: לְהִשָּׁמְדָם עֲדֵי עַד, *To destroy them for all eternity* (*Psalms* 92:8).

3:21

אִם אֵין תּוֹרָה, אֵין דֶּרֶךְ אֶרֶץ — *If there is no Torah, there is no positive social behavior . . .* "If there is no Torah" — i.e., the intellectual aspect of Torah —

NOTES

3:21

אִם אֵין תּוֹרָה, אֵין דֶּרֶךְ אֶרֶץ . . . אִם אֵין חָכְמָה, אֵין יִרְאָה . . . — *If there is no Torah, there is no positive social behavior . . . If there is no wisdom, there is no fear of God . . .* The

Sforno interprets the words, תּוֹרָה, דֶּרֶךְ אֶרֶץ, and חָכְמָה as referring to specific aspects of these terms. In the context of this Mishnah, תּוֹרָה refers to the חֵלֶק הָעִיּוּנִי, the philosophical-intellectual parts, דֶּרֶךְ אֶרֶץ refers to

21. *Rabbi Elazar ben Azariah says: If there is no Torah, there is no positive social behavior; if there is no positive social behavior, there is no Torah. If there is no wisdom, there is no fear of God; if there is no fear of God, there is no wisdom. If there is no knowledge, there is no understanding; if there is no understanding, there is no knowledge. If there is no*

פירוש לרבי עובדיה ספורנו

ההיטיב לזולתו לכבוד בוראו ולהדמות אליו כרצונו, וכן כשאין אותו המין מדרך ארץ – התבאר שאין שם תורה. וכן אם אין חכמה מדינית לישא וליתן באמונה באופן שתהיה רוח הבריות נוחה הימנו – זהו מפני שאין שם יראת האל יתברך, וכן אם אין יראת האל באמת, והיא ההווה כשיכיר האדם גדלו יתברך – אין שם חכמה מדינית הראויה לעבודתו, ולא יתנהג בה החכם זולתי כאשר יחשוב שתהיה עם תועלתו הפרטי. אם אין בינה, והיא אותה פעולת השכל אשר בה יפשיט הצורות מן החומר – אין דעת, הנה אז לא ישכילם כלל, וכן אם אין דעת מושכל אצלנו – הנה זה קרה לנו מפני שלא יגענו בבינה להפשיט הצורות מחומר ולשים אותם

SFORNO'S COMMENTARY

then, there will be an absence of the type of "positive social behavior" which results from it — namely, the willingness to do good unto others for the sake of honoring one's Creator and emulating Him, in accordance with His will. Similarly, if this kind of "positive social behavior" is not present, it demonstrates that there is no Torah.

אִם אֵין חָכְמָה, אֵין יִרְאָה; אִם אֵין יִרְאָה, אֵין חָכְמָה — *If there is no wisdom, there is no fear of God; if there is no fear of God, there is no wisdom.* So too, if there is no social "wisdom" — i.e., the type of ethical behavior which compels people to conduct their affairs with integrity and honesty, in such a manner that the spirit of one's fellows is pleased with him — it is because there is no fear of God. And if there is no genuine "fear of God," which only comes about when a man recognizes His greatness, then there can be no social "wisdom" worthy to foster His service, and even the wise will not contribute to society unless it be for their personal benefit.

אִם אֵין בִּינָה, אֵין דָּעַת — *If there is no understanding, there is no knowledge.* "If there is no understanding" — meaning, man's intellectual, theoretical thought process, removed from practical application — then there can be no pure "knowledge." And if there is an absence of such knowledge, then it is due to one's failure to toil and fully exert one's powers of understanding and

NOTES

man's ethical, moral conduct, and חָכְמָה, to man's social wisdom.

"Fear of God," or יִרְאָה, does not mean fear of Divine retribution, but rather the awe and reverence evoked by man's recognition of God's greatness, while בִּינָה, "understanding," refers to man's power of reasoning, which refines his knowledge.

ג קֶמַח, אֵין תּוֹרָה; אִם אֵין תּוֹרָה, אֵין קֶמַח.
כב [כב] **הוּא** הָיָה אוֹמֵר: כֹּל שֶׁחָכְמָתוֹ מְרֻבָּה מִמַּעֲשָׂיו, לְמָה הוּא דוֹמֶה? לְאִילָן שֶׁעֲנָפָיו מְרֻבִּין וְשָׁרָשָׁיו מוּעָטִין, וְהָרוּחַ בָּאָה וְעוֹקַרְתּוֹ וְהוֹפַכְתּוֹ עַל פָּנָיו, שֶׁנֶּאֱמַר: „וְהָיָה כְּעַרְעָר בָּעֲרָבָה, וְלֹא יִרְאֶה כִּי יָבוֹא טוֹב, וְשָׁכַן חֲרֵרִים בַּמִּדְבָּר, אֶרֶץ מְלֵחָה וְלֹא תֵשֵׁב." אֲבָל כֹּל שֶׁמַּעֲשָׂיו מְרֻבִּין מֵחָכְמָתוֹ, לְמָה הוּא דוֹמֶה? לְאִילָן שֶׁעֲנָפָיו מוּעָטִין וְשָׁרָשָׁיו מְרֻבִּין, שֶׁאֲפִילוּ כָּל הָרוּחוֹת שֶׁבָּעוֹלָם בָּאוֹת וְנוֹשְׁבוֹת

פירוש לרבי עובדיה ספורנו

מושכל בפעל, כאמרם ז"ל „יגעתי ולא מצאתי אל תאמן, לא יגעתי ומצאתי אל תאמן". אם אין קמח – לא יוכל האדם לעסוק בתורה, וראוי להשתדל השתדלות מה בהשגת הצריך ממנה, וכן אם אין תורה הנה אין קמח, אשר תכלית מציאותו למאכל אדם באמת, וזה בהיותו מיוחד אז למאכל בהמה דומה לאדם:

ג:כב. אמר שכל מי שהוא משתדל יותר בענין החכמה המדינית ממה שיתנהג

SFORNO'S COMMENTARY

apply it to the practical and the real, as our Sages say: יָגַעְתִּי וְלֹא מָצָאתִי אַל תַּאֲמֵן, לֹא יָגַעְתִּי וּמָצָאתִי אַל תַּאֲמֵן — "Do not believe one who says, 'I labored and did not find,' nor one who says, 'I did not labor and found' " (*Megillah* 6b).

אִם אֵין קֶמַח, אֵין תּוֹרָה; אִם אֵין תּוֹרָה, אֵין קֶמַח — *If there is no flour, there is no Torah; if there is no Torah, there is no flour.* "If there is no flour," then a person cannot occupy himself with Torah; therefore, it is fitting that one pursue those activities which are necessary in order to earn a livelihood.

Similarly, "if there is no Torah," then, "there is no flour." For [flour] is a food inherently meant for man's consumption, when he is distinguished [from the animals], but [when there is no Torah], flour becomes like animal fodder to a man.

NOTES

אִם אֵין תּוֹרָה, אֵין קֶמַח — *If there is no Torah, there is no flour.* The *Sforno*'s commentary on "flour and Torah" is based on the Talmud, *Pesachim* 118, which portrays Adam's fear when he was told that he would have to till the earth and bring forth his bread by the sweat of his brow, that he and the animals would "eat from the same trough." God reassures him that man will remain superior to the animals even in this area, for man will transform wheat into flour and bake bread, a much more sophisticated and refined way of consuming food. This is what the *Sforno* means when he interprets the words of Elazar ben Azariah: If there is Torah in man's life, his flour and bread — i.e. his manner of preparation and eating — will be far different than that of animals and beasts.

flour, there is no Torah; if there is no Torah, there is no flour.

22. *He used to say: Anyone whose wisdom exceeds his good deeds, to what is he likened? — to a tree whose branches are numerous but whose roots are few; then the wind comes and uproots it and turns it upside down; as it is said: "And he shall be like an isolated tree in an arid land and shall not see when good comes; he shall dwell on parched soil in the wilderness, on a salted land, uninhabited." But one whose good deeds exceed his wisdom, to what is he likened? — to a tree whose branches are few but whose roots are numerous; even if all the winds in the world were to come and blow*

פירוש לרבי עובדיה ספורנו

בשאר מצות התורה אשר המכוון בהם העיון וכבוד האל יתברך וקדשיו, הנה התבאר שאין חכמתו זאת מיוקרת על מה שידע ויכיר מהאל יתברך ולכבודו אבל היא מכוונת לתועלת עצמו לחיי שעה, כמו שבאר הנביא באמרו „ושם בשר זרועו ומן יי יסור לבו", כי זה אמנם כמעט סבה נוגעת לפרטות עצמו מנגדת להנהגת אותה

SFORNO'S COMMENTARY

3:22

כֹּל שֶׁחָכְמָתוֹ מְרֻבָּה מִמַּעֲשָׂיו . . . וְהָרוּחַ בָּאָה וְעוֹקַרְתּוֹ . . . — *Anyone whose wisdom exceeds his good deeds . . . the wind comes and uproots it . . .* He who dedicates more effort to the area of social wisdom than to other areas of Torah commandments, whose purpose is intellectual analysis, and the honor of God and His holy Ones — this reveals that his wisdom is not primarily directed toward attaining knowledge and recognition of Hashem, and glorifying Him. Rather, his primary intent and purpose is directed toward fulfilling his personal goals and accomplishments in this transitory life, as the Prophet says: וְשָׂם בָּשָׂר זְרֹעוֹ וּמִן ה' יָסוּר לִבּוֹ, *And makes flesh his arm, and whose heart departs from Hashem* (*Jeremiah* 17:5).

This motivation for personal benefit, as opposed to the pursuit of altruistic wisdom, is abhorrent [in God's eyes], and will ultimately be nullified.

NOTES

3:22

כֹּל שֶׁחָכְמָתוֹ מְרֻבָּה מִמַּעֲשָׂיו . . . דוֹמֶה לְאִילָן . . . וְשָׁרָשָׁיו מוּעָטִין . . . כֹּל שֶׁמַּעֲשָׂיו מְרֻבִּין מֵחָכְמָתוֹ . . . דוֹמֶה לְאִילָן . . . וְשָׁרָשָׁיו מְרֻבִּין — *Anyone whose wisdom exceeds his good deeds . . . is . . . likened — to a tree . . . whose roots are few . . . one whose good deeds exceed his wisdom . . . is . . . likened — to a tree . . . whose roots are numerous.* The Tanna quotes liberally from *Jeremiah,* Chapter 17, and the *Sforno,* in his commentary, skillfully weaves together verses 5 through 8 in that chapter and explains their logical sequence. Jeremiah states, אָרוּר הַגֶּבֶר אֲשֶׁר יִבְטַח בָּאָדָם, *cursed is the man who places his trust in man* (v. 5). One who is motivated by

ג בּוֹ, אֵין מְזִיזִין אוֹתוֹ מִמְּקוֹמוֹ, שֶׁנֶּאֱמַר: „וְהָיָה כְּעֵץ
כג שָׁתוּל עַל מַיִם, וְעַל יוּבַל יְשַׁלַּח שָׁרָשָׁיו, וְלֹא
יִרְאֶה כִּי יָבֹא חֹם, וְהָיָה עָלֵהוּ רַעֲנָן, וּבִשְׁנַת בַּצֹּרֶת
לֹא יִדְאָג, וְלֹא יָמִישׁ מֵעֲשׂוֹת פֶּרִי."

[כג] **רַבִּי** אֱלְעָזָר (בֶּן) חִסְמָא אוֹמֵר: קִנִּין
וּפִתְחֵי נִדָּה הֵן הֵן גּוּפֵי הֲלָכוֹת;
תְּקוּפוֹת וְגִמַטְרִיָּאוֹת — פַּרְפְּרָאוֹת לַחָכְמָה.

פירוש לרבי עובדיה ספורנו

החכמה – תהיה אז החכמה נמאסת אצלו ותבטל, אבל מי שמעשיו המכוונים לכבוד יתברך בלבד הם מרובים מפרטי השתדלותו בחכמה המדינית והנהגתה, הנה מעשיו אלה מיוסדים על שרשי ידיעה אשר בה הכיר בוראו וידע שראוי לעשות האפשר לכבודו ולנחת רוח לפניו, ובזה לא יחרף לבבו מימיו, כאמרו והיה יי מבטחו וגומר ולא ימיש מעשות פרי:

ג:כג. כבר אמרו ז"ל בביאור מה שנאמר

SFORNO'S COMMENTARY

אֲבָל כֹּל שֶׁמַּעֲשָׂיו מְרֻבִּין מֵחָכְמָתוֹ . . . כָּל הָרוּחוֹת שֶׁבָּעוֹלָם . . . אֵין מְזִיזִין . . . — *But one whose good deeds exceed his wisdom . . . all the winds in the world . . . could not budge it. . .* However, he whose deeds are meant only to bring honor to God, and they are more numerous than his efforts to attain social wisdom and its implementation — then this person's deeds are rooted in the knowledge and recognition of the Almighty, and he knows that one must do whatever is possible to bring honor to God and be pleasing in His sight. In this manner his heart will always be refreshed with the waters of Torah, as it is written: וְהָיָה ה׳ מִבְטַחוֹ . . . וְלֹא יָמִישׁ מֵעֲשׂוֹת פֶּרִי, *Then Hashem will be his security. . .he shall not cease from yielding fruit* (ibid. 17:7-8).

3:23

קִנִּין וּפִתְחֵי נִדָּה הֵן הֵן גּוּפֵי הֲלָכוֹת; תְּקוּפוֹת וְגִמַטְרִיָּאוֹת - פַּרְפְּרָאוֹת לַחָכְמָה — *The laws [and calculations] of bird-offerings, and the laws regarding the beginning of menstrual cycles — these are the essential laws; astronomy and mathematics are like the seasonings of wisdom.* Our Sages, commenting on the verse

NOTES

The *Sforno* explains that such a person is motivated by a desire to bring honor to the Almighty in all his deeds, and fulfills God's will without personal interests.

his own personal honor and prestige — such a man is compared to a tree with weak roots, whose permanence is doubtful and whose future is bleak. The prophet then states, בָּרוּךְ הַגֶּבֶר אֲשֶׁר יִבְטַח בַּה׳, *Blessed is the man who places his trust in Hashem* (v. 7). Elazar ben Azariah compares such a person to a tree with strong roots that shall not be uprooted and will always bear fruit.

3:23

קִנִּין וּפִתְחֵי נִדָּה הֵן הֵן גּוּפֵי הֲלָכוֹת; תְּקוּפוֹת וְגִמַטְרִיָּאוֹת - פַּרְפְּרָאוֹת לַחָכְמָה — *The law [and calculations] of bird-offerings, and the*

3
23

against it, they could not budge it from its place; as it is said: 'And he shall be like a tree planted by waters, toward the stream spreading its roots, and it shall not notice the heat's arrival, and its foliage shall be fresh; in the year of drought it shall not worry, nor shall it cease yielding fruit.'

23. *Rabbi Eliezer ben Chisma said: The laws [and calculations] of bird-offerings, and the laws regarding the beginning of menstrual cycles — these are the essential laws; astronomy and mathematics are like the seasonings of wisdom.*

פירוש לרבי עובדיה ספורנו

„כי היא חכמתכם ובינתכם לעיני העמים", איזוהי חכמה שהיא לעיני העמים? הוי אומר זה חשוב תקופת ומזלות". והנה זה החכם שאמרו עליו שהיה יודע לשער כמה טיפין יש בים, כדאיתא בהוריות וכולי, וזה לרב חכמתו במספר, הגיד מעלת חכמת התכונה בידיעת מקומות הכוכבים ותנועותיהם, ואמר כי הנה חשבונות של מספר קינין ושל פתחי נדה הנחשבים קשי ההשגה הם אמנם גופי הלכות, אמנם חשבונות של תקופות וכן מלאכת המספר הנקרא גיאומיטריא הם פרפראות בלבד

SFORNO'S COMMENTARY

in *Deuteronomy* 4:6, כִּי הוּא חָכְמַתְכֶם וּבִינַתְכֶם לְעֵינֵי הָעַמִּים, *For it is your wisdom and discernment in the eyes of the peoples,* state: אֵיזוֹ חָכְמָה וּבִינָה שֶׁהִיא לְעֵינֵי הָעַמִּים? הֱוֵי אוֹמֵר, זֶה חִישּׁוּב תְּקוּפוֹת וּמַזָּלוֹת — "What is considered 'wisdom and discernment' in the eyes of nations; it is the calculation of cycles and constellations" (*Shabbos* 75a).

Now, this Sage, [Elazar ben Chisma] — who we are told knew how to estimate the number of drops of water found in the sea, as recorded in Tractate *Horayos* [10a], for he possessed great mathematical wisdom, extols the superior degree of the wisdom of astronomy, which can establish the position and movement of the stars. However, he tells us that the calculations in Tractate *Kinin* ("the law [and calculations] of bird-offerings") and those related to the laws regarding the onset of menstrual cycles, which are difficult to grasp, are nevertheless "essential laws," while calculations of

NOTES

laws regarding the beginning of menstrual cycles — these are the essential laws; astronomy and mathematics are like the seasonings of wisdom. Most commentators interpret the statement of Elazar ben Chimsa as extolling the paramount importance and primacy of *Halachah,* including laws which are not currently applicable, such as the *halachos* regarding the sacrificial birds offered in the Temple, or laws which are somewhat indelicate, such as those concerning a woman's menstrual cycle.

The *Kessef Mishnah* (*Yesodei HaTorah* 4:13) makes the following comment regarding our Mishnah: "Although astronomy and geometry deal with superior

רַבִּי חֲנַנְיָא בֶּן עֲקַשְׁיָא אוֹמֵר: רָצָה הַקָּדוֹשׁ בָּרוּךְ הוּא לְזַכּוֹת אֶת יִשְׂרָאֵל, לְפִיכָךְ הִרְבָּה לָהֶם תּוֹרָה וּמִצְוֹת, שֶׁנֶּאֱמַר: „יהוה חָפֵץ לְמַעַן צִדְקוֹ, יַגְדִּיל תּוֹרָה וְיַאְדִּיר.״

פירוש לרבי עובדיה ספורנו

לחכמת התכונה, ובזה תחשב מעלת חכמת התכונה בהיות אלו החכמות החשובות

SFORNO'S COMMENTARY

astronomical cycles and the mathematical discipline called geometry are merely "seasonings" [i.e., peripheral] to the "wisdom" of astronomy. In light of this, consider the magnificence of the "wisdom" of astronomy, being that

NOTES

and sophisticated subject matter, whereas bird-offerings and *niddah* questions are on the surface mundane and repulsive, nevertheless, the former are but 'seasonings of wisdom,' whereas the latter represent the essentials of Torah."

The *Sforno,* however, explains the Mishnah differently. Rabbi Elazar ben Chisma, who was a renowned Torah sage, astronomer and mathematician, stresses the

Rabbi Chanania ben Akashia says: The Holy One, Blessed is He, wished to confer merit upon Israel; therefore He gave them Torah and mitzvos in abundance, as it is said: "HASHEM desired, for the sake of its [Israel's] righteousness, that the Torah be made great and glorious."

פירוש לרבי עובדיה ספורנו

כפרפראות לה, ובזה העיר אזן כל שומע להרבות השתדלות להשיגה:

SFORNO'S COMMENTARY

these important calculations and disciplines are but "like seasonings" in comparison. With this he is drawing our attention to the study of astronomy and urging us to make a great effort to master it.

NOTES

importance of the *halachos* regarding bird-offerings and *niddah,* which are essential laws. And, while extolling the knowledge of cycles and geometry, he tells us that one should realize that they are secondary to the greater wisdom of astronomy, which in the field of science represents the ultimate wisdom. Hence, even Torah scholars should study it and attempt to master it.

פרק ד

Chapter Four

כָּל יִשְׂרָאֵל יֵשׁ לָהֶם חֵלֶק לָעוֹלָם הַבָּא, שֶׁנֶּאֱמַר: „וְעַמֵּךְ כֻּלָּם צַדִּיקִים, לְעוֹלָם יִירְשׁוּ אָרֶץ, נֵצֶר מַטָּעַי, מַעֲשֵׂה יָדַי לְהִתְפָּאֵר.״

All Israel has a share in the World to Come, as it is said: "And your people are all righteous; they shall inherit the land forever; they are the branch of My planting, My handiwork, in which to take pride."

ד א [א] **בֶּן זוֹמָא** אוֹמֵר: אֵיזֶהוּ חָכָם? הַלּוֹמֵד מִכָּל אָדָם, שֶׁנֶּאֱמַר: „מִכָּל מְלַמְּדַי הִשְׂכַּלְתִּי.״ אֵיזֶהוּ גִבּוֹר? הַכּוֹבֵשׁ אֶת יִצְרוֹ, שֶׁנֶּאֱמַר: „טוֹב אֶרֶךְ אַפַּיִם מִגִּבּוֹר, וּמֹשֵׁל בְּרוּחוֹ מִלֹּכֵד עִיר.״ אֵיזֶהוּ עָשִׁיר? הַשָּׂמֵחַ בְּחֶלְקוֹ,

פירוש לרבי עובדיה ספורנו

ד:א. הנה כוונת זה הפרק להדריך האדם ולהורות לפניו אופן להשיג מדת זהירות וזריזות. והעולה ממנו, שזה אמנם יושג כאשר תהיה כוונת האדם בכל מעשיו לכבוד קונו, כי אז יזדרז לעשות מה שימשך ממנו כבוד לאל יתברך וישמר מכל שיהיה הפך זה. ובהיות שכבר אמר הנביא „אל יתהלל החכם בחכמתו ואל יתהלל הגבור בגבורתו ואל יתהלל עשיר בעשרו כי אם בזאת יתהלל המתהלל השכל וידוע אותי״, כלומר שבזה האופן ראוי שיתהלל החכם והגבור והעשיר – בשתקדם לו ידיעה אשר בה ישכיל וידע את גודל האל יתברך וטובו, ומזה ימשך שישתמש בחכמתו וגבורתו ועושרו לכבוד האל יתברך לא זולת זה, אמר בן זומא שאותו החכם אשר בו דבר

SFORNO'S COMMENTARY

4:1

אֵיזֶהוּ חָכָם? הַלּוֹמֵד מִכָּל אָדָם — *Who is wise? He who learns from every person.* The intent of this chapter is to guide and instruct man to attain the attributes of זְהִירוּת (watchfulness) and זְרִיזוּת (zeal). These virtues can be realized when man's purpose, in all his deeds, is to honor his Maker. For then, he will zealously act in such a way as to bring honor to God, the blessed One, and will carefully desist from actions which will yield negative results [such as desecrating God's Name].

Now, the Prophet said, אַל יִתְהַלֵּל חָכָם בְּחָכְמָתוֹ, וְאַל יִתְהַלֵּל הַגִּבּוֹר בִּגְבוּרָתוֹ, אַל יִתְהַלֵּל עָשִׁיר בְּעָשְׁרוֹ: כִּי אִם בְּזֹאת יִתְהַלֵּל הַמִּתְהַלֵּל הַשְׂכֵּל וְיָדֹעַ אוֹתִי, *Let not the wise man glory in his wisdom; let not the strong man glory in his strength; let not the rich man glory in his riches. But let him that glories, glory in this: that he understands and knows Me* (*Jeremiah* 9:22-23). This means that the wise, the strong, and the rich should only glory [in these traits] if they are preceded by and predicated upon the knowledge and understanding of God's greatness, for this will cause him to utilize his wisdom, might, and riches, exclusively in honor of the Almighty, Blessed is He.

NOTES

4:1

אֵיזֶהוּ חָכָם? . . . גִּבּוֹר? . . . עָשִׁיר? . . . — *Who is wise? . . . strong? . . . rich? . . .* The *Sforno* links Ben Zoma's teachings regarding wisdom, strength, and wealth, to the words of Jeremiah the Prophet. Both Ben Zoma and Jeremiah emphasize that the usual meaning of each of these terms — wisdom, strength, and wealth — would be overly superficial and quite insignificant. The Prophet, according to the *Sforno*, teaches us that these gifts are blessings only if they are informed by the knowledge of God and an understanding of what He expects man to use them for.

Ben Zoma now elaborates on the

1. **B**en Zoma says: *Who is wise? He who learns from every person, as it is said: "From all my teachers I grew wise." Who is strong? He who subdues his personal inclination, as it is said: "He who is slow to anger is better than the strong man, and a master of his passions is better than a conqueror of a city." Who is rich? He who is happy with his lot,*

פירוש לרבי עובדיה ספורנו

הנביא הוא החכם במדיניות, אשר רב ענינם מיוסד על הנסיון, וזה לא יושג אלא כשילמד מכל אדם למען יעלה בידו נסיונות רבים; ואיזהו גבור אשר בו דבר הנביא – הוא הכובש את יצרו, והביא ראיה שהכובש יצרו נקרא גבור ממה שכתב „טוב ארך אפים מגבור", וזה כי אמנם לא יאות היחס בין שנים ברב ובמעט זולתי בהיותם תחת סוג אחד, אמר אם כן שמי שהוא ארך אפים הוא מעביר על מדותיו יותר מן הגבור הכובש את יצרו לשעה; ואיזהו אותו העשיר שאמר הנביא – הוא השמח בחלקו, ולא יאבד כל זמנו בהשגת הקנינים המדומים, והביא ראיה שזה יקרא עשיר ממה שאמר

SFORNO'S COMMENTARY

Ben Zoma explains that the "wise man" of whom the Prophet speaks refers to a person who is wise in the ways of the world, and has attained the kind of wisdom that comes mostly from experience. This wisdom can only be acquired when one "learns from every person," for then one accumulates wisdom through the various experiences of numerous individuals.

אֵיזֶהוּ גִבּוֹר? הַכּוֹבֵשׁ אֶת יִצְרוֹ — *Who is strong? He who subdues his personal inclination.* And to whom did the Prophet refer when he said, "Who is strong"? To "he who subdues his personal inclination." He proves this from the verse, טוֹב אֶרֶךְ אַפַּיִם מִגִּבּוֹר, *He who is slow to anger is better than the strong man* (*Proverbs* 16:32) — superiority can only be measured when one compares two things which belong in the same category. Hence, the Tanna says that "he who is slow to anger" is forbearing (מַעֲבִיר עַל מִדּוֹתָיו), and as such, is greater than a strong man, who subdues his personal inclination for only a brief period.

אֵיזֶהוּ עָשִׁיר? הַשָּׂמֵחַ בְּחֶלְקוֹ — *Who is rich? He who is happy with his lot.* And to whom did the Prophet refer when he said, "Who is rich"? To "he who is happy with his lot," and does not waste all of his time attaining illusory possessions. As proof, Ben Zoma quotes the verse in *Psalms* 128:2,

NOTES

Prophet's teaching. As he understands it, "wisdom" refers to worldly wisdom, which one acquires in time through personal interaction, life's experiences, and exposure to varied circumstances and people. "Strength" is to be understood as internal moral strength and self-control, while "wealth" is not to be measured quantitatively, but qualitatively. Ben Zoma teaches that a person who understands and appreciates these three blessings for what they truly are will have honor bestowed upon him.

ד
ב

שֶׁנֶּאֱמַר: „יְגִיעַ כַּפֶּיךָ כִּי תֹאכֵל אַשְׁרֶיךָ וְטוֹב לָךְ.” „אַשְׁרֶיךָ” – בָּעוֹלָם הַזֶּה, „וְטוֹב לָךְ” – לָעוֹלָם הַבָּא. אֵיזֶהוּ מְכֻבָּד? הַמְּכַבֵּד אֶת הַבְּרִיּוֹת, שֶׁנֶּאֱמַר: „כִּי מְכַבְּדַי אֲכַבֵּד, וּבֹזַי יֵקָלּוּ.”

[ב] **בֶּן** עַזַּאי אוֹמֵר: הֱוֵי רָץ לְמִצְוָה קַלָּה, וּבוֹרֵחַ מִן הָעֲבֵרָה; שֶׁמִּצְוָה גוֹרֶרֶת מִצְוָה, וַעֲבֵרָה גוֹרֶרֶת עֲבֵרָה, שֶׁשְּׂכַר מִצְוָה מִצְוָה, וּשְׂכַר עֲבֵרָה עֲבֵרָה.

פירוש לרבי עובדיה ספורנו

„יגיע כפיך כי תאכל אשריך”, כלומר שכשיספיק לך יגיע כפיך ולא תבקש יותר מזה הנך מאושר בעולם הזה כמו שיאושר בו העשיר אצל ההמון. ובהיות שכוונת הצדיק הראוי שיתהלל בכל אלה ותכליתו בהתהללו הוא שיכובד בעיני הבריות והשתדלו להיות כמוהו לכבוד קונו, אמר בן זומא שזה אמנם ישיג האדם כשיכבד את הבריות ולא יתגאה עליהם בהתהללו, ותהיה כל תהלתו בכבוד קונו בענין כך תהלתו תמיד, וזה יכובד בלי ספק, כאמרו „כי מכבדי אכבד”:

SFORNO'S COMMENTARY

יְגִיעַ כַּפֶּיךָ כִּי תֹאכֵל אַשְׁרֶיךָ, *When you eat of the labor of your hands, you are happy. . .* — meaning, that when the labor of your hands suffices for all your needs, and you do not seek more, then you will be happy in this world to the same degree that the rich man is happy in comparison to the masses.

אֵיזֶהוּ מְכֻבָּד? הַמְּכַבֵּד אֶת הַבְּרִיּוֹת — *Who is honored? He who honors others.* Since the intent and purpose of the righteous individual who is worthy to be praised for all these qualities is to gain the respect of the people so that they will ultimately try to emulate him, and thereby bring honor to God, Ben Zoma tells us that this can only be accomplished when one "honors others," and does not become arrogant and vain as a result of his praise. Rather, one's praise should be entirely for the honor of Hashem, as it is written, בְּךָ תְהִלָּתִי תָמִיד, *I continually praise You* (*Psalms* 71:6). One who does this will ultimately be honored, as it is written, כִּי מְכַבְּדַי אֲכַבֵּד, *those who honor Me, I will honor* (*I Samuel* 2:30).

NOTES

4:2

שֶׁמִּצְוָה גוֹרֶרֶת מִצְוָה, וַעֲבֵרָה . . . שֶׁשְּׂכַר מִצְוָה . . . — *For one mitzvah leads to another mitzvah, and one sin . . .; for the reward of a mitzvah . . .* At first glance, the Mishnah seems redundant. Ben Azzai tells us that one *mitzvah* leads to a second *mitzvah*, and one sin to another. Why, then, does he have to tell us, "the reward of a *mitzvah* is a *mitzvah*"? The *Sforno* explains that since there is no actual reward for a *mitzvah* in this world, being that Divine reward is reserved for the World to Come, nevertheless, there is some reward — namely, the opportunity to perform other *mitzvos*. Every act creates a habit, and man becomes adept at doing

and it is said: "When you eat of the labor of your hands, you are happy and all is well with you." "You are happy' — in this world; "and all is well with you" — in the World to Come. Who is honored? He who honors others, as it is said: "For those who honor Me I will honor, and those who scorn Me shall be degraded."

2. *Ben Azzai says: Run to perform even a "minor" mitzvah, and flee from sin; for one mitzvah leads to another mitzvah, and one sin leads to another sin; for the reward of a mitzvah is a mitzvah, and the reward of a sin is a sin.*

פירוש לרבי עובדיה ספורנו

ד:ב. אמר, אף על פי שלפעמים תהיה המצוה או העבירה ממנין הקלות אשר הן מצד עצמן אינן ראויות לריצה ובריחה, הנה הן ראויות לזה מפני הנמשך אחריהן, וזה מפני שמצוה גוררת מצוה אחרת וכן עבירה גוררת עבירה אחרת. וסבת זאת הגרירה היא ששכר מצוה בעולם הזה אינו אלא שיתן האל יתברך לשומר מצוה איזו הכנה למצוה אחרת, כמו שדרשו בסמיכות שלוח הקן למצות מעקה וציצית וזולתם

SFORNO'S COMMENTARY

4:2

הֱוֵי רָץ לְמִצְוָה קַלָּה . . . שֶׁמִּצְוָה . . . וַעֲבֵרָה . . . עֲבֵרָה — *Run to perform even a "minor" mitzvah . . . for one mitzvah . . . and one sin . . .* Although certain *mitzvos* and sins are considered to be "minor" [inconsequential], and thus are not worthy to be pursued or fled from, nonetheless they are important because of what results from them. For "one *mitzvah* leads to another *mitzvah*," and "one sin leads to another sin." The reasoning behind this rule is that there is no immediate reward for a *mitzvah* in this world. Therefore, the Almighty prepares the way to fulfill other *mitzvos,* to the person who observes *mitzvos*, as we find regarding שִׁלּוּחַ הַקֵּן, the *mitzvah* of sending away the mother bird before taking the young — by fulfilling this *mitzvah*, one shall merit the *mitzvah* of building a parapet to his roof, and the *mitzvah* of making *tzitzis* [in *Parashas Ki Seitzei* (22:6-8,12), these two *mitzvos* are mentioned immediately after שִׁלּוּחַ הַקֵּן].

NOTES

what he practices all the time. Hence, a *mitzvah* does not exist in a vacuum, isolated and solitary, but rather, brings other *mitzvos* in its wake. This is the greatest reward, not in the sense of payment, but in creating and developing man's character. The same is also true, unfortunately, of transgressions.

The verse quoted by the *Sforno* from the Book of *Exodus* is also quoted by him in his commentary on the Book of *Numbers,* on the verse וַיָּחֶל הָעָם לִזְנוֹת אֶל בְּנוֹת מוֹאָב, *and the people began to commit harlotry with the daughters of Moab* (*Numbers* 25:1), which is followed by the account of the Israelites prostrating themselves before the gods of Moab. There, he comments: "At first they

[ג] **הוּא** הָיָה אוֹמֵר: אַל תְּהִי בָז לְכָל אָדָם, וְאַל תְּהִי מַפְלִיג לְכָל דָּבָר, שֶׁאֵין לְךָ אָדָם שֶׁאֵין לוֹ שָׁעָה, וְאֵין לְךָ דָּבָר שֶׁאֵין לוֹ מָקוֹם.

[ד] **רַבִּי** לְוִיטַס אִישׁ יַבְנֶה אוֹמֵר: מְאֹד מְאֹד הֱוֵי שְׁפַל רוּחַ, שֶׁתִּקְוַת אֱנוֹשׁ רִמָּה.

פירוש לרבי עובדיה ספורנו

המורה שבקיום מצות שלוח הקן יזכה האדם להכנת קיום המצות הסמוכות לה, וכן שכר ותענוג העבירה בעולם הזה מוכן אל עבירה אחרת, כענין „ואכלת מזבחו ולקחת מבנותיו . . . והזנו את בניך״:

ד:ג. לכל אדם, אפילו לאותם בני אדם שלא ידעת ולא יאות לך לכבדם, עם היותך מכבד את הבריות אל תהי בז. ואל תהי מפליג וחושב לנמנע את האיפשרי עם היותו רחוק, כי לפעמים יצא לפעל, ולכן

SFORNO'S COMMENTARY

This teaches us that by fulfilling the *mitzvah* of sending away the mother bird, one will merit to fulfill the *mitzvos* mentioned immediately thereafter [in the *parashah*).

By the same token, the consequence of a sin and the pleasure derived from it in this world prepares the way to other sins, as it is written: וְאָכַלְתָּ מִזִּבְחוֹ וְלָקַחְתָּ מִבְּנֹתָיו . . . וְהִזְנוּ אֶת בָּנֶיךָ, *And you eat from his slaughter, and you take their daughters . . . and entice your sons to stray* (*Exodus* 34:15-16).

4:3

אַל תְּהִי בָז . . . וְאַל תְּהִי מַפְלִיג . . . — *Do not be scornful . . . and do not be disdainful . . .* The phrase לְכָל אָדָם, "of any person," refers even to those whom you do not know, and even those who are not deserving of honor. Thus, you must honor every person [as we are taught in Mishnah 1 of this *Perek,* by Ben Zoma], and "not be scornful" of anyone.

And "do not be disdainful of anything" by considering it as impossible or farfetched, for at times it can come to pass. That is why I told you to "flee

NOTES

did not worship idols, for their sole intent was to commit harlotry," but as Ben Azzai cautions us, "one sin leads to another sin," and from harlotry to idolatry is but a short step.

4:3

אַל תְּהִי בָז . . ., וְאַל תְּהִי מַפְלִיג . . . — *Do not be scornful . . . and do not be disdainful . . .* If every person is worthy to be honored, as Ben Zoma taught in Mishnah 1 of this chapter, why did Ben Azzai deem it necessary to warn us not to "be scornful of any person"? The *Sforno* explains that Ben Azzai warns us that even though some people may be unworthy of honor, we must be careful not to insult them.

According to the *Sforno*, Ben Azzai's cautionary statement in the previous Mishnah to "flee from sin" is linked to the second part of our Mishnah, where he tells us not to "be disdainful of anything" — that is, not to consider anything impossible. This concept was demonstrated by King Solomon, who erroneously relied on his wisdom and power, and convinced himself that the

3. *He used to say: Do not be scornful of any person and do not be disdainful of anything, for you have no person without his hour and no thing without its place.*

4. *Rabbi Levitas of Yavneh says: Be exceedingly humble in spirit, for the anticipated end of mortal man is worms.*

פירוש לרבי עובדיה ספורנו

יפה אמרתי שתהיה בורח מן העבירה ולא תחשוב לנמנע שתכשל בה ובנמשך ממנה, כענין שלמה באמרו אני ארבה ולא אסור, והנה סר, וגרם הפסד מלכות לבניו וקלקול וגלות לישראל:

ד:ד. הנה שפל רוח הוא מי שאינו נכסף לעלות אל מיני הכבוד בעולם הזה, על הפך רוח גבוהה שייחסו לבלעם אשר בשבילה אמר לו בלק היודע גאותו „כי כבד אכבדך", ואמר „האמנם לא אוכל כבדך",

SFORNO'S COMMENTARY

from sin" [Mishnah 2], and not delude yourself into thinking that you will never stumble and transgress in a particular area.

We see this from what happened to Solomon, who said, אֲנִי אַרְבֶּה וְלֹא אָסוּר, *"I will increase [women] and not be led astray"* (*Sanhedrin* 21); he *did* stray [from God's way], thereby causing harm and irreparable damage to the kingship of his children, to all his people and ultimately this led to Israel's exile.

4:4

מְאֹד מְאֹד הֱוֵי שְׁפַל רוּחַ, שֶׁתִּקְוַת אֱנוֹשׁ רִמָּה — *Be exceedingly humble in spirit, for the anticipated end of mortal man is worms.* Behold, the term שְׁפַל רוּחַ, "humble in spirit," refers to one who has no longing for any kind of honor in this world. This is the opposite of one who has a רוּחַ גְּבוֹהָה, "an arrogant spirit," the trait which is attributed to Balaam (see below, 5:18). That is why Balak, who recognized Balaam's pride and arrogance, said כִּי כַבֵּד אֲכַבֶּדְךָ, *I will surely honor you* (*Numbers* 22:17), and הַאֻמְנָם לֹא אוּכַל כַּבְּדֶךָ , *am I unable*

NOTES

Torah law which prohibits a Jewish king from taking numerous wives did not apply to him. In other words, he felt, "It can't happen to me"! But as Ben Azzai points out, it certainly can, and did!

4:4

מְאֹד מְאֹד הֱוֵי שְׁפַל רוּחַ — *Be exceedingly humble in spirit.* The *Sforno* explains that humility is to be understood as the antithesis of the pursuit of honor. He proves this from the Mishnah in Chapter 5, where our Sages contrast the personality of Abraham with that of Balaam. The former is characterized as being "of humble spirit," as opposed to the latter, who is said to have possessed an "arrogant spirit," for he sought honor, as the *Sforno* proves from the verses in *Parashas Balak.*

Interestingly, the *Sforno* finds it necessary to caution us not to eschew the concept of pride and self-assurance completely, for at times it can be utilized and channeled positively, as did King Yehoshafat. He also explains the reason why Rabbi Levitas concludes his remarks by comparing the

[ה] רַבִּי יוֹחָנָן בֶּן בְּרוֹקָא אוֹמֵר: כָּל הַמְּחַלֵּל שֵׁם שָׁמַיִם בַּסֵּתֶר, נִפְרָעִין מִמֶּנּוּ בְּגָלוּי. אֶחָד שׁוֹגֵג וְאֶחָד מֵזִיד בְּחִלּוּל הַשֵּׁם.

[ו] רַבִּי יִשְׁמָעֵאל בַּר רַבִּי יוֹסֵי אוֹמֵר: הַלּוֹמֵד עַל מְנָת לְלַמֵּד, מַסְפִּיקִין בְּיָדוֹ לִלְמוֹד

פירוש לרבי עובדיה ספורנו

„אמרתי כבד אכבדך" וכולי. ועל זה הדרך ייחס הכתוב ליהושפט גובה לב לטוב, באמרו „ויגבה לבו בדרכי ה׳", וזה בהיותו נכסף ומשתדל תמיד להוסיף מעלה בחכמה וחסידות. ואמר מאד מאד, כלומר לא בלבד אזהירך שלא תשתדל להשיג מיני הכבוד הרחוקים מהשיג, אבל אומר שלא יפנה לבך להשיג אפילו מיני הכבוד קלי ההשגה. ונתן טעם לזה באמרו שתקות אנוש רמה, כי אמנם מעלת השררה והכבוד שישתדל ויקוה האדם בגובה רוחו להשיגם בעולם הזה הם רמה ותולעה, שהיא דבר בעצמו בזוי מאד ובלתי מתקיים זמן נחשב, כאמרם ז״ל כל בריה שאין בה עצם אינה

SFORNO'S COMMENTARY

to give you honor (ibid. v. 37), and אָמַרְתִּי כַּבֵּד אֲכַבֶּדְךָ, *I said I would honor you* (ibid. 24:11).

Scripture attributes a prideful spirit also to Yehoshafat, but in a positive light, as it says, וַיִּגְבַּהּ לִבּוֹ בְּדַרְכֵי ה׳, *and his heart was lifted up in the ways of Hashem* (*II Chronicles* 17:6) — meaning, that he constantly longed for and attempted to increase and elevate his level of wisdom and piety.

The Tanna adds the words מְאֹד מְאֹד, "exceedingly," by which he means to say, "Not only do I caution you against trying to attain honors which are too difficult to attain, but also that you must not even be tempted by honors which are easily obtained." The reason is that "the anticipated end of mortal man is worms" — meaning, that the elevated position and glory gained by men in this world is akin to maggots and worms, which are intrinsically despicable and have no meaningful existence, as our Sages tell us, כָּל בְּרִיָּה שֶׁאֵין בָּהּ עֶצֶם אֵינָהּ מִתְקַיֶּמֶת שְׁנֵים עָשָׂר חֹדֶשׁ, *"Every creature which has no bone structure does not live twelve months"* (*Chullin* 58a).

NOTES

end of man to that of worms — the Tanna wishes to impress upon us the nature of honor, which is not only fleeting, but also insubstantial, similar to the existence and nature of worms.

The repetition of the word מְאֹד, *very,* to denote "exceedingly," is interpreted by the *Sforno* as referring to all kinds of honor, regardless of whether they be easy or difficult to attain, for they are of little importance and of even less significance.

4:5

כָּל הַמְחַלֵּל שֵׁם שָׁמַיִם בַּסֵּתֶר, נִפְרָעִין מִמֶּנּוּ בְּגָלוּי — *Whoever desecrates the Name of Heaven in secret, they will exact punishment from him in public.* The *Sforno* refers us to the painful episode of David and Batsheva, the wife of Uriah, to illustrate Rabbi Yochanan ben Beroka's teaching.

Our Rabbis teach us (*Shabbos* 56) that David was technically not guilty of adultery, for every soldier would write a divorce

5. Rabbi Yochanan ben Beroka says: *Whoever desecrates the Name of Heaven in secret, they will exact punishment from him in public; unintentional or intentional, both are alike regarding desecration of the Name.*

6. Rabbi Yishmael bar Rabbi Yose says: *One who studies Torah in order to teach is given the means*

פירוש לרבי עובדיה ספורנו

מתקיימת שנים עשר חדש:

ד:ה. הזהיר על כבוד האל יתברך שיצטרך האדם להזהר בו מאד, כי אמנם אפילו על השוגג ממנו נפרעים מן החוטא בגלוי – לא להגדיל יותר מהראוי לו, אבל להועיל לרבים להודיעם גודל ענינו, כמו שקרה לדוד שנאמר לו „כי אתה עשית בסתר ואני אעשה נגד כל ישראל ונגד השמש", אף על פי שבענין חלול השם היה שוגג בלי ספק כי חשב שלא יודע ושלא יתחלל שם שמים על ידו כלל:

ד:ו. אמר שהלמד על מנת ללמד, אף על פי

SFORNO'S COMMENTARY

4:5

כָּל הַמְחַלֵּל שֵׁם שָׁמַיִם בַּסֵּתֶר, נִפְרָעִין מִמֶּנּוּ בְּגָלוּי — *Whoever desecrates the Name of Heaven in secret, they will exact punishment from him in public.* Whoever desecrates the Name of Heaven in secret, whether he does it "unintentionally or intentionally," is regarded as having committed חִלּוּל הַשֵּׁם, "desecration of the Name." The Tanna warns us to be extremely cautious in protecting God's honor, for even if one unintentionally desecrates God's Name "in secret, they will exact punishment from him in public" — not because Heaven wants to magnify his punishment beyond his due, but to impress upon others the severity of this transgression.

We see this idea illustrated in the episode of David [and Batsheva], where he was told [by Nathan the Prophet]: כִּי אַתָּה עָשִׂיתָ בַסָּתֶר וַאֲנִי אֶעֱשֶׂה אֶת הַדָּבָר הַזֶּה נֶגֶד כָּל יִשְׂרָאֵל וְנֶגֶד הַשָּׁמֶשׁ, *For you did it secretly, but I will do this thing before all Israel and before the sun* (*II Samuel* 12:12) — even though the חִלּוּל הַשֵּׁם (desecration of God's Name) was unintentional [on the part of David], for he was confident that no one would know, and that God's Name would not be desecrated.

4:6

הַלּוֹמֵד עַל מְנָת לְלַמֵּד . . . — *One who studies Torah in order to teach . . .* The

NOTES

contract before going to the front, and if he was killed, as was Batsheva's husband, Uriah, the divorce would take effect retroactively. Nevertheless, David was morally culpable and held accountable by Hashem. Although there was no חִלּוּל הַשֵּׁם, since *halachically* he did not commit a transgression, and the act was done privately, nonetheless, the punishment from on High was destined to become public, as the verse quoted by the *Sforno* states. This constitutes a clear proof from Scripture to the dictum of our Tanna.

4:6

הַלּוֹמֵד עַל מְנָת לְלַמֵּד . . . וְהַלּוֹמֵד עַל מְנָת לַעֲשׂוֹת . . . — *One who studies Torah in order to*

ד וּלְלַמֵּד; וְהַלּוֹמֵד עַל מְנָת לַעֲשׂוֹת, מַסְפִּיקִין בְּיָדוֹ
ז לִלְמוֹד וּלְלַמֵּד, לִשְׁמוֹר וְלַעֲשׂוֹת.

[ז] רַבִּי צָדוֹק אוֹמֵר: אַל תִּפְרוֹשׁ מִן הַצִּבּוּר; וְאַל תַּעַשׂ עַצְמְךָ כְּעוֹרְכֵי הַדַּיָּנִין; וְאַל תַּעֲשֶׂהָ עֲטָרָה לְהִתְגַּדֶּל בָּהּ, וְלֹא קַרְדֹּם לַחְפָּר בָּהּ. וְכָךְ הָיָה הִלֵּל אוֹמֵר: וְדִאִשְׁתַּמֵּשׁ בְּתָגָא חֲלָף.

פירוש לרבי עובדיה ספורנו

שיהיה התכלית גרוע כי אמנם ענינו לכבוד או לתועלת בחיי שעה, מכל מקום מספיקים אותו שיוכל ללמוד וללמד, שמתוך שלא לשמה בא לשמה. אמנם הלמד על מנת לעשות, שתכלית זה בלי ספק לעשות רצון קונו – מסייעים ללמוד וללמד לאחרים ולשמור עצמו מעון ולעשות מצות בוראו:

ד:ז. אין ספק שהמשתמש בקדש לצרכי חול מחלל את הקדש וראוי למיתה, כאמרו

SFORNO'S COMMENTARY

Tanna is saying that even though "one who studies Torah in order to teach" may be improperly motivated, for his objective may be to gain honor for himself, or to attain a worldly goal of transitory success, he is nevertheless "given the means [from heaven] to study and to teach." For מִתּוֹךְ שֶׁלֹּא לִשְׁמָהּ בָּא לִשְׁמָהּ, *"he who performs a mitzvah for ulterior motives will eventually do so for its own sake"* (*Pesachim* 50b).

However, וְהַלּוֹמֵד עַל מְנָת לַעֲשׂוֹת, *One who studies in order to practice* — i.e., one whose objective is purely to fulfill the will of his Maker — will be helped [from on High] to "study and to teach" others, and "to observe" and guard himself against sin, and also "to practice" the *mitzvos* of his Creator.

4:7

וְאַל תַּעֲשֶׂהָ עֲטָרָה לְהִתְגַּדֶּל בָּהּ, וְלֹא קַרְדֹּם . . . וְדִאִשְׁתַּמֵּשׁ בְּתָגָא חֲלָף — *Do not make the Torah a crown for self-glorification, nor a spade . . . He who exploits the crown . . . shall fade away.* Without a doubt, he who uses קֹדֶשׁ [a holy object

NOTES

teach . . .; and one who studies in order to practice. . . The person "who studies in order to practice" is superior to the one "who studies Torah in order to teach." As the *Sforno* explains, the latter may be motivated by personal ambition and selfish goals, whereas the former is motivated purely by an altruistic desire to observe God's commandments. As such, he is assisted from on High, and "given the means" not only to attain his goal of Torah observance, but also "to study and to teach."

4:7

וְאַל תַּעֲשֶׂהָ עֲטָרָה לְהִתְגַּדֵּל בָּהּ, וְלֹא קַרְדֹּם . . . וְדִאִשְׁתַּמֵּשׁ בְּתָגָא חֲלָף — *Do not make the Torah a crown for self-glorification, nor a spade . . . He who exploits the crown . . . shall fade away.* Strictly speaking, one is not permitted to profit from teaching Torah or giving instruction regarding the performance of *mitzvos*. However, the Talmud in *Kesubos* (105b-106a), permits a scholar to accept payment as שְׂכַר בַּטָּלָה — i.e., compensation for his time, which he could have

to study and to teach; and one who studies in order to practice is given the means to study and to teach, to observe and to practice.

7. *Rabbi Tzadok says: Do not separate yourself from the community; [when serving as a judge] do not act as a lawyer; do not make the Torah a crown for self-glorification, nor a spade with which to dig. So too Hillel used to say: He who exploits the crown [of Torah for personal benefit] shall fade away.*

פירוש לרבי עובדיה ספורנו

„ומתו בו כי יחללוהו". ובהיות דברי תורה קדש קדשים הנה העושה אותם מלאכת חול ותכליתה לחפור בהם אוכל לחיי שעה בלבד או להשיג כבוד בחיי שעה, כמו העטרה והקורדום אשר התבאר מהם שזה תכליתם, על הרוב הנה זה מחלל את הקדש, ועל זה הזהיר זה החכם ואמר שעל כיוצא בזה בלבד אמר הלל ודאשתמש בתגא חלף. אמנם המשתדל להשיג בהם חיי שעה ותכליתו מכוון בזה להוסיף לקח עיון ומעשה לעצמו או לזולתו אין זה אלא כמשתמש בבלי קדש לעבוד עבודת קדש

SFORNO'S COMMENTARY

or item] for non-sacred purposes desecrates the holy and deserves to die, as it is written, וּמֵתוּ בוֹ כִּי יְחַלְּלֻהוּ, *and die because of it, for they will have desecrated it* (*Leviticus* 22:9). Now, being that Torah is considered to be "holy of holies" [קֹדֶשׁ קָדָשִׁים], one who uses it for a non-sacred purpose such as earning a livelihood, as if it were "a spade," or for attaining transitory honor, as if it were "a crown," is guilty of desecrating the holy. Our Tanna cautions against such a practice. This is what Hillel meant when he said, "He who exploits the crown [of Torah for personal benefit] shall fade away."

However, when a person utilizes his Torah knowledge to sustain himself in this transitory world, his goal being to add to his knowledge and understanding, and to be able to perform more good deeds, either on behalf of himself or in order to teach others, then it is considered as though he used a holy item for a legitimate, sacred purpose.

NOTES

utilized to work and earn a livelihood.

According to the *Sforno*, Rabbi Tzadok and Hillel caution us not to earn our livelihood by means of the Torah, lest we be guilty of using קֹדֶשׁ (a holy object) for a non-sacred purpose, since we would be utilizing Torah for personal gain.

The *Sforno* refers us to the abovementioned Gemara, which is the source of the *Rambam*'s ruling that those who issued judicial decisions, and those who instructed the priests in the laws of ritual slaughter and קְמִיצָה (the removal of a handful of flour from the *minchah* offering), received their wages from the Temple treasury (*Hilchos Shekalim* Chapter 4).

This is not in conflict with the teaching of Hillel or Rabbi Tzadok, for these teachers and judges had no other source of income, and indeed, the gifts of *terumah* and *maaser,* given to the *Kohanim* and Levites, were commanded by the Torah so as to free them from mundane occupations, that they might devote themselves completely to the

ד הָא לָמַדְתָּ: כָּל הַנֶּהֱנֶה מִדִּבְרֵי תוֹרָה, נוֹטֵל חַיָּיו מִן
ח הָעוֹלָם.

[ח] **רַבִּי** יוֹסֵי אוֹמֵר: כָּל הַמְּכַבֵּד אֶת הַתּוֹרָה, גּוּפוֹ מְכֻבָּד עַל הַבְּרִיּוֹת; וְכָל הַמְּחַלֵּל אֶת הַתּוֹרָה, גּוּפוֹ מְחֻלָּל עַל הַבְּרִיּוֹת.

פירוש לרבי עובדיה ספורנו

וזה אמנם יתאמת כאשר יתבטל האדם בטלה דמוכח ללמד לזולתו או לדונו כדמוכח פרק בתרא דכתובות, ועל זה הדרך אמרו ז״ל שגוזרי גזירות בירושלם ומלמדי הלכות שחיטה וקמיצה לכהנים היו נוטלין שכרן מתרומת הלשכה, ועל זה הדרך צוה הוא יתברך לתת מתנות תרומות ומעשרות, כאמרו „לתת מנת הכהנים והלויים למען יחזקו בתורת יי״. וכל זה ביאר התנא באמרו הא למדת שכל הנהנה מדברי תורה נוטל חייו מן העולם, כי אמנם המתפרנס בדברי תורה

SFORNO'S COMMENTARY

This is proven to be so if the person ceases from all other activities in order to instruct or judge others, as is mentioned in the concluding chapter of Tractate *Kesubos*. And it is regarding this that our Sages tell us: גּוֹזְרֵי גְזֵרוֹת בִּירוּשָׁלַיִם וּמְלַמְּדֵי הִלְכוֹת שְׁחִיטָה וּקְמִיצָה לַכֹּהֲנִים הָיוּ נוֹטְלִין שְׂכָרָן מִתְּרוּמַת הַלִּשְׁכָּה, *"The judges of civil law in Jerusalem, and those who taught the priests ritual slaughtering and how to take a handful from the meal offering, drew their wages from the Temple's coffers"* (*Kesubos* 105a).

And it is regarding this that the Almighty, Blessed is He, commanded Israel to give priestly gifts, offerings, and tithes to the priests and Levites, as it is written: לָתֵת מְנָת הַכֹּהֲנִים וְהַלְוִיִּם לְמַעַן יֶחֶזְקוּ בְּתוֹרַת ה׳, *To give the portion of the priests and Levites, that they might adhere firmly to the Torah* of Hashem" (*II Chronicles* 31:4).

כָּל הַנֶּהֱנֶה מִדִּבְרֵי תוֹרָה, נוֹטֵל חַיָּיו מִן הָעוֹלָם — *Whoever derives personal benefit from the words of Torah removes his life from the world.* This is what the Tanna is teaching us when he says, "From this you learn that whoever

NOTES

Temple service and the teaching of Torah. The verse from *II Chronicles,* quoted by the *Sforno* here, is also quoted by him in Chapter 1, Mishnah 13. It qualifies the prohibition against using one's Torah knowledge for personal status or aggrandizement.

כָּל הַנֶּהֱנֶה מִדִּבְרֵי תוֹרָה, נוֹטֵל חַיָּיו מִן הָעוֹלָם — *Whoever derives personal benefit from the words of Torah removes his life from the world.* The *Sforno* makes a subtle comment on the phrase כָּל הַנֶּהֱנֶה, "whoever derives personal benefit," used by Rabbi Tzadok. This the *Sforno* says, can apply only to one who uses Torah to feed his ego, not his physical needs. It applies only to one who derives personal benefit from Torah, but not to a person who utilizes his Torah knowledge to make a living or to teach others how to perform *mitzvos*, for as our Sages teach us, the concept of הֲנָאָה, *pleasure,* cannot be attached to a *mitzvah*.

From this you learn that whoever derives personal benefit from the words of Torah removes his life from the world.

8. R*abbi Yose says: Whoever honors the Torah is himself honored by people; and whoever disgraces the Torah is himself disgraced by people.*

פירוש לרבי עובדיה ספורנו

ללמוד או ללמד או לדבר מצוה אין זה נהנה כלל, שכבר אמרו מצות לא ליהנות ניתנו:

ד:ח. הנה המכבד את התורה הוא מכבד מי שנתנה ומקרב אחרים לעבדו שכם אחד, והפך זה יקרה למי שיחלל את התורה, כאמרו „את יי הוא מגדף", „כי דבר יי בזה", ולזה ראוי שהמכבד את התורה יכובד והפכו יחולל, כאמרו יתברך „כי מכבדי אכבד ובוזי יקלו":

SFORNO'S COMMENTARY

derives personal benefit from the words of Torah removes his life from the world." For when a person makes his livelihood from Torah in order to study or teach, or for the purpose of a *mitzvah*, he does not derive הֲנָאָה, *pleasure,* since we have been told, מִצְווֹת לָאו לֵיהָנוֹת נִתְּנוּ, *"Mitzvos were not given for [our] enjoyment"* (*Eruvin* 31).

4:8

כָּל הַמְכַבֵּד אֶת הַתּוֹרָה . . . וְכָל הַמְחַלֵּל אֶת הַתּוֹרָה . . . — *Whoever honors the Torah . . . and whoever disgraces the Torah . . .* "Whoever honors the Torah" honors the One Who gave the Torah. In this manner, he draws others close to serve God שְׁכֶם אֶחָד, "with one consent" [an expression derived from *Tzefaniah* 3:9].

Conversely, "whoever disgraces the Torah" causes defection from God among Israel, as it is said: אֶת ה׳ הוּא מְגַדֵּף . . . כִּי דְבַר ה׳ בָּזָה, *That person dishonors Hashem . . . he has despised the word of Hashem* (*Numbers* 15:30,31). Therefore, it is proper that he who honors Torah receive honor, and conversely, [he who desecrates Torah] be defamed, as the verse tells us: כִּי מְכַבְּדַי אֲכַבֵּד וּבֹזַי יֵקָלּוּ, *For those who honor Me I will honor, and those who scorn Me shall be degraded* (*I Samuel* 2:30).

NOTES

4:8

כָּל הַמְכַבֵּד אֶת הַתּוֹרָה, . . . וְכָל הַמְחַלֵּל אֶת הַתּוֹרָה . . . — *Whoever honors the Torah . . . and whoever disgraces . . .* In this Mishnah, Rabbi Yose expands the scope of Ben Zoma's teaching "Who is honored? He who honors others" (Mishnah 4:1), which is based on the verse in the Book of *Samuel*. According to Rabbi Yose, this maxim can also be applied to Torah and the Almighty.

The *Sforno* explains that Rabbi Yose is applying the principle of "measure for measure" (מִדָּה כְּנֶגֶד מִדָּה): If one honors Hashem and His Torah, he is worthy to be honored as well. Indeed, the *Sforno* quotes the same verse from the Book of *Samuel* as was cited by Ben Zoma as proof for his teaching in Mishnah 1.

[ט] **רַבִּי** יִשְׁמָעֵאל בְּנוֹ אוֹמֵר: הַחוֹשֵׂךְ עַצְמוֹ מִן הַדִּין, פּוֹרֵק מִמֶּנּוּ אֵיבָה וְגָזֵל וּשְׁבוּעַת שָׁוְא. וְהַגַּס לִבּוֹ בְּהוֹרָאָה שׁוֹטֶה, רָשָׁע וְגַס רוּחַ.

[י] **הוּא** הָיָה אוֹמֵר: אַל תְּהִי דָן יְחִידִי, שֶׁאֵין דָּן יְחִידִי אֶלָּא אֶחָד. וְאַל תֹּאמַר: „קַבְּלוּ דַעְתִּי!" שֶׁהֵן רַשָּׁאִין וְלֹא אָתָּה.

פירוש לרבי עובדיה ספורנו

ד:ט. החושך עצמו כאשר יאות לו זה, והוא כשיוכל לבצוע או בהיותו בלתי מיוחד לדיין לרבים, כי אמנם אז חושך ממנו איבת המתחייב בדין, וגזל הקורה בדין מרומה, ושבועת שוא אשר עושה מוטל על המשביע אם יטעון שקר או על הנשבע אם ישבע לשקר. שוטה, שהוא בלתי חושש לנזק הנמשך מן האיבה, והוא גם כן רשע, שאינו מקפיד אם תצא מתחת ידו תקלת גזל או שבועת שוא, והוא גם כן גס רוח, כי הוא בלי ספק לא נכנס לכל זה אלא כדי להתכבד בפסק דינו:

SFORNO'S COMMENTARY

4:9

הַחוֹשֵׂךְ עַצְמוֹ מִן הַדִּין, פּוֹרֵק . . . — *One who withdraws from judgment removes from himself . . .* [The Mishnah refers to] "one who withdraws from judgment" when it is fitting that he do so — namely, when he can arrange a compromise between the litigants, or when he is not empowered to serve as a qualified judge. In this manner, he will "remove from himself hatred" of the one who is found guilty, avoid the "robbery" which results from the miscarriage of justice, and prevent "an unnecessary oath," which is the responsibility of the one who imposes the oath, through a false claim, or of the one who swears falsely.

וְהַגַּס לִבּוֹ . . . שׁוֹטֶה, רָשָׁע וְגַס רוּחַ — *But one who is too self-confident . . . is a fool, wicked, and arrogant of spirit.* [One who fails to do this is considered] "a

NOTES

4:9

הַחוֹשֵׂךְ עַצְמוֹ מִן הַדִּין, פּוֹרֵק . . . וְהַגַּס לִבּוֹ . . . — *One who withdraws from judgment removes from himself . . . one who is too self-confident . . .* The *Sforno* gives two reasons for a judge to withdraw — either because there are more competent judges available, or because a compromise can be reached. *Rabbi Yonah,* in his commentary on *Avos,* offers the first reason, while *Rashi* offers the second.

The *Sforno* explains the careful choice of phrases used by Rabbi Yishmael, as well as the logical sequence of the Mishnah. "Hatred" refers to the litigant who has lost the case; "robbery," if there is an erroneous ruling; "an unnecessary oath" refers to one that has been imposed without justification, or sworn to falsely. In either case, since the judge was involved, he has a share in the transgression. The terms "fool," "wicked," and "arrogant of spirit" refer exclusively to the judge, as the *Sforno* explains.

9. *Rabbi Yishmael his son says: One who withdraws from judgment removes from himself hatred, robbery, and [the responsibility for] an unnecessary oath; but one who is too self-confident in handing down legal decisions is a fool, wicked and arrogant of spirit.*

10. *He used to say: Do not act as judge alone, for none judges alone except One; and do not say, "Accept my view," for they are permitted to, but not you.*

פירוש לרבי עובדיה ספורנו

ד:י. ומאחר שענין הדין רב הסכנה כאשר אמרתי, ראוי לך שאף על פי שתוכל לדון יחידי בהיותך מומחה טוב לך שלא תדון יחידי אלא עם שנים אחרים ונשאו אתך, שאין דן יחידי אלא אחד, שהוא דן בלתי העדאת עדים ובלתי טענות בעלי דינין שיטעוהו, אבל הוא עד ודיין ובעל דין, אבל שאר דיינים הצריכים בדיניהם לשמוע

SFORNO'S COMMENTARY

fool" because he shows no concern for the damage that will result from the hatred he engenders. He is also considered "wicked," for he shows no concern over his role in instigating robbery or imposing an unnecessary oath. He is also "arrogant of spirit," for without a doubt, he only became involved in this case in order to gain repute and prestige for himself through his legal decision.

4:10

אַל תְּהִי דָן יְחִידִי . . . וְאַל תֹּאמַר: ,,קַבְּלוּ דַעְתִּי'' . . . — *Do not act as a judge alone . . . and do not say, "Accept my view" . . .* As I have said above [in the previous Mishnah], dispensing law and justice is fraught with danger. Therefore, it is fitting that even if you are a מוּמְחֶה [an expert master judge], and as such, technically permitted to judge alone, it is preferable that you not do so. Rather, sit in a court with two others, so that you will have the opportunity to discuss the case with them. For "none judges alone except One" [i.e., the Almighty]. He does so without the testimony of witnesses and without the claims and counterclaims of the litigants, which are liable to mislead a judge. Rather, the Almighty Himself serves as the Witness, the Judge, and the Plaintiff! But other judges, who must rely on the testimony and

NOTES

4:10

שֶׁאֵין דָן יְחִידִי אֶלָּא אֶחָד — *For none judges alone except One.* The *Sforno* explains why only the Almighty can judge alone, for as the concluding Mishnah in this chapter states, "He is the Judge, He is the Witness, He is the Plaintiff." As such, He has exclusive knowledge of the facts of the case, unlike a corporeal judge, who can be misled by the parties or the witnesses, and therefore requires the participation and counsel of other judges to insure that justice will prevail.

[יא] **רַבִּי** יוֹנָתָן אוֹמֵר: כָּל הַמְקַיֵּם אֶת הַתּוֹרָה מֵעֹנִי, סוֹפוֹ לְקַיְּמָהּ מֵעֹשֶׁר; וְכָל הַמְבַטֵּל אֶת הַתּוֹרָה מֵעֹשֶׁר, סוֹפוֹ לְבַטְּלָהּ מֵעֹנִי.

[יב] **רַבִּי** מֵאִיר אוֹמֵר: הֱוֵי מְמַעֵט בְּעֵסֶק, וַעֲסֹק בַּתּוֹרָה; וֶהֱוֵי שְׁפַל רוּחַ בִּפְנֵי כָל אָדָם; וְאִם בָּטַלְתָּ מִן הַתּוֹרָה, יֶשׁ לְךָ בְּטֵלִים הַרְבֵּה כְּנֶגְדֶּךָ; וְאִם עָמַלְתָּ בַּתּוֹרָה, יֶשׁ לוֹ שָׂכָר הַרְבֵּה לִתֵּן לָךְ.

פירוש לרבי עובדיה ספורנו

דברי עדים ובעלי דינים יקרה בדינם טעות ומרמה לפעמים. ואל תאמר לדיינים חבריך קבלו דעתי אף על פי שאתה גדול מהם, שהן רשאין לפסוק הדין במצות התורה, שכבר אמרה „אחרי רבים להטות״:

ד:יא. סופו לקיימה מעושר כאמרו „למען ענותך ולמען נסותך להיטיבך באחריתך״, כי בזה שקיימו ישראל את התורה מעוני נעשו ראוים לקיימה מעושר כפי המשפט האלהי שהיא מדה כנגד מדה. וכן כל

SFORNO'S COMMENTARY

statements of witnesses and litigants, are liable to make mistakes, and at times be deceived.

And do not say to your colleagues on the bench, "accept my view" even though you are superior to them, "for they are permitted to" reach a decision according to the Torah law which states אַחֲרֵי רַבִּים לְהַטֹּת, *Follow the [opinion of the] majority* (*Exodus* 23:2).

4:11

כָּל הַמְקַיֵּם אֶת הַתּוֹרָה מֵעֹנִי, סוֹפוֹ . . . מֵעֹשֶׁר . . . הַמְבַטֵּל אֶת הַתּוֹרָה . . . — *Whoever fulfills the Torah despite poverty will ultimately . . . in wealth . . . whoever neglects the Torah . . .* "[Whoever fulfills the Torah despite poverty] will ultimately fulfill it in wealth," as it is written (*Deuteronomy* 8:16), לְמַעַן עַנֹּתְךָ וּלְמַעַן נַסֹּתֶךָ לְהֵיטִבְךָ בְּאַחֲרִיתֶךָ, *In order to afflict you, and in order to test you, to do good for you in your end.* Meaning, that because Israel fulfilled the Torah in poverty, they were deemed worthy to do so in wealth, in keeping with Divine judgment, which is מִדָּה כְּנֶגֶד מִדָּה (measure for measure). Conversely, he who neglects and nullifies Torah when he is wealthy will ultimately do so in poverty, as it is written, תַּחַת אֲשֶׁר לֹא עָבַדְתָּ אֶת ה׳ . . . מֵרֹב כֹּל וְעָבַדְתָּ אֶת אֹיְבֶיךָ . . . וּבְחֹסֶר כֹּל, *Because you did not serve Hashem . . . when everything was*

NOTES

4:12

הֱוֵי מְמַעֵט בְּעֵסֶק, וַעֲסֹק בַּתּוֹרָה; וֶהֱוֵי שְׁפַל רוּחַ — *Reduce your business activities and engage in Torah study. Be of humble spirit.* A person who is honored for his knowledge of Torah must demonstrate through his behavior and demeanor that he is not using his mastery of Torah for the purpose of gain-

11. *Rabbi Yonasan says: Whoever fulfills the Torah despite poverty will ultimately fulfill it in wealth; but whoever neglects the Torah because of wealth will ultimately neglect it in poverty.*

12. *Rabbi Meir says: Reduce your business activities and engage in Torah study. Be of humble spirit before every person. If you should neglect the [study of] Torah, you will come upon many excuses to neglect it; but if you labor in the Torah, God has ample reward to give you.*

פירוש לרבי עובדיה ספורנו

המבטל מעושר סופו לבטלה מעוני, כאומרו „תחת אשר לא עבדת את השם ... מרוב כל – ועבדת את אויבך ... בחוסר כל״:

ד:יב. הוי ממעט בעסק, שבזה האופן יהיה לך זמן לעסוק בתורה ותודיע חשיבותה אצלך, ובזה תכבד את התורה ואת מי שנתנה, כאמרו „סלסלה ותרוממך״. והוי שפל רוח בפני כל האדם, שיכירו שאין כוונתך בעוסקך בתורה להשיג מיני הכבוד. ואמר אם בטלת מן התורה, כלומר וגם צריך שתמעט בשאר עסקך שאם בטלת מן

SFORNO'S COMMENTARY

abundant . . . so you shall serve your enemies . . . without anything (ibid. 28:47-48).

4:12

הֱוֵי מְמַעֵט בְּעֵסֶק, וַעֲסֹק בַּתּוֹרָה — *Reduce your business activities and engage in Torah study.* "Reduce your business activities," for in this manner you will have time to occupy yourself with Torah study. You will also demonstrate its importance and priority in your view, and thereby honor Torah and He who gave it, as it is written: סַלְסְלֶהָ וּתְרוֹמְמֶךָּ, *Exalt her, and she shall elevate you* (*Proverbs* 4:8).

וֶהֱוֵי שְׁפַל רוּחַ — *Be of humble spirit . . .* And "be of humble spirit before every person," for then they will recognize that your intent in studying Torah is not motivated by a desire to attain honor for yourself.

בָּטַלְתָּ מִן הַתּוֹרָה . . . בְּטֵלִים הַרְבֵּה . . . עָמַלְתָּ בַּתּוֹרָה . . . שָׂכָר הַרְבֵּה — *Neglect the [study of] Torah . . . many excuses to neglect . . . labor in the Torah . . . ample reward.* And "if you should neglect the [study of] Torah" because of your

NOTES

ing recognition, respect, and honor. Otherwise, it might seem as though he were abusing Torah, rather than pursuing it to gain knowledge of G-d's will and wisdom. That is why Rabbi Meir combines his admonition to reduce one's business pursuits and devote more time to Torah with the admonition to be humble in spirit.

עָמַלְתָּ בַּתּוֹרָה . . . שָׂכָר הַרְבֵּה . . . לָךְ — *Labor in the Torah . . . ample reward to . . . you.* The *Sforno* applies the verse in the Book of

[יג] **רַבִּי** אֱלִיעֶזֶר בֶּן יַעֲקֹב אוֹמֵר: הָעוֹשֶׂה מִצְוָה אַחַת קוֹנֶה לּוֹ פְּרַקְלִיט אֶחָד; וְהָעוֹבֵר עֲבֵרָה אַחַת, קוֹנֶה לּוֹ קַטֵּיגוֹר אֶחָד. תְּשׁוּבָה וּמַעֲשִׂים טוֹבִים כִּתְרִיס בִּפְנֵי הַפֻּרְעָנוּת.

[יד] **רַבִּי** יוֹחָנָן הַסַּנְדְּלָר אוֹמֵר: כָּל כְּנֵסִיָּה שֶׁהִיא לְשֵׁם שָׁמַיִם, סוֹפָהּ לְהִתְקַיֵּם; וְשֶׁאֵינָהּ לְשֵׁם שָׁמַיִם, אֵין סוֹפָהּ לְהִתְקַיֵּם.

פירוש לרבי עובדיה ספורנו

התורה בשביל עסקך לא בלבד יקרה לך בטול בשביל אותם העסקים, אבל יקרה גם כן ששאר מונעים זולתם יבטלוך. ואם עסקת בתורה ותמעט עסקי חיי שעה יש שכר הרבה ליתן לך באותו המעט עסק, שתרויח בו הרבה לחיי שעה ותשיג חיי עולם, כאמרו „לא ימוש ספר התורה הזה מפיך" כולי „כי אז תצליח את דרכיך" לחיי שעה „ואז תשכיל" ותשיג חיי עולם:
ד:יג. כתריס בפני הפורענות, אף על פי

SFORNO'S COMMENTARY

business activities, this neglect will be compounded by many other demands that will deter you from Torah study. Therefore, you are admonished to reduce these activities.

"But if you labor in the Torah" and reduce your transitory pursuits, "God has ample reward to give you," which will be realized from the little labor expended by you. For you will enjoy great gain, both in this world and the World to Come, as it is written, לֹא יָמוּשׁ סֵפֶר הַתּוֹרָה הַזֶּה מִפִּיךָ . . . כִּי אָז תַּצְלִיחַ אֶת דְּרָכֶךָ, *This Book of Torah shall not depart out of your mouth . . . for then your way will be prosperous* (*Joshua* 1:8), referring to transitory life, and אָז תַּשְׂכִּיל, *then you shall succeed,* referring to the attainment of eternal life.

4:13

תְּשׁוּבָה וּמַעֲשִׂים טוֹבִים כִּתְרִיס בִּפְנֵי הַפֻּרְעָנוּת — *Repentance and good deeds are like a shield against retribution.* "[Repentance and good deeds] are like a shield

NOTES

Joshua to Rabbi Meir's assurance that a little labor will go a long way, providing one's intent is to spend more time in Torah study. He interprets the verse to mean that God promised Joshua prosperity in this world and success in the World to Come on condition that Israel would continue to apply themselves to the study of Torah after entering *Eretz Yisrael.* For when they would settle in the land, they would no longer live in a miraculous fashion, as they did in the Wilderness, where they were free to study Torah. It was therefore important for the Almighty to caution Joshua and Israel to limit their time in pursuit of the material, so as to continue their diligent study of Torah, which was their sole occupation when they were אוֹכְלֵי מָן, sustained by manna from Heaven.

Now, as they begin a new life as a nation in *Eretz Yisrael,* they will have to live a normal, natural existence. Hence, they must be cautioned not to abandon their intellectual and spiritual growth as a people.

13. Rabbi *Eliezer ben Yaakov says: He who fulfills even a single mitzvah gains himself a single advocate, and he who commits even a single transgression gains himself a single accuser. Repentance and good deeds are like a shield against retribution.*

14. Rabbi *Yochanan the Sandler says: Every assembly that is dedicated to the sake of Heaven will have an enduring effect, but one that is not for the sake of Heaven will not have an enduring effect.*

פירוש לרבי עובדיה ספורנו

שלא יהיה המעשה הטוב אלא מיראת עונש, מכל מקום הוא כתריס מגין מן הפורענות שהיה ראוי לבא, כמו שקרה בענין נינוה אף על פי שהחזיקו בעבודה זרה, וכאמרו „שובו שובו מדרכיכם הרעים ולמה תמותו בית ישראל" – בזה הורה הנביא שימלטו מן העונש אף על פי שלא תהיה התשובה אלא מיראת העונש:

ד:יד. כאשר ראה זה החכם בימיו מיני כתות של פרושים וצבועים וצדוקים ומהם

SFORNO'S COMMENTARY

against retribution" — even when your good deeds are motivated by fear of Divine punishment, nonetheless, they serve as a shield, protecting you "against retribution." This is similar to the event which transpired in the city of Ninveh [i.e., that it was spared destruction] despite the fact that its inhabitants retained their idolatrous beliefs. As the verse says, שׁוּבוּ שׁוּבוּ מִדַּרְכֵיכֶם הָרָעִים וְלָמָּה תָמוּתוּ בֵּית יִשְׂרָאֵל, *Turn, turn from your evil ways, for why should you die, House of Israel?* (*Ezekiel* 33:11). The Prophet teaches us that a person may escape punishment even if his repentance is motivated by fear of heavenly retribution.

4:14

כָּל כְּנֵסִיָּה . . . וְשֶׁאֵינָהּ לְשֵׁם שָׁמַיִם, אֵין סוֹפָהּ לְהִתְקַיֵּם — *Every assembly . . . that is not for the sake of Heaven will not have an enduring effect.* When this sage

NOTES

4:13

הָעוֹשֶׂה מִצְוָה . . . קוֹנֶה . . . פְּרַקְלִיט . . . תְּשׁוּבָה . . . כִּתְרִיס — *He who fulfills a . . . mitzvah gains . . . [an] advocate . . . Repentance [is] . . . like a shield.* The *Sforno* differentiates between a person who performs a *mitzvah* and one who repents for his sins. He explains that Rabbi Eliezer teaches us that a *mitzvah* is pro-active and creates a heavenly advocate, who will actively plead on the person's behalf before the Heavenly Court.

On the other hand, he who repents will not gain an active advocate. Nevertheless, his repentance will protect him from heavenly punishment in the same manner as a shield deflects arrows, spears, and other dangerous missiles.

He brings proof from the story of Ninveh, recorded in the Book of *Jonah.* Although the inhabitants of that city responded to the Prophet's warning of impending disaster and rectified their ways, they did not reject their idols and fully accept God, nor commit themselves to His teachings. Even so, God revoked the evil decree against the city. Thus, we see that their repentance shielded them from destruction even though it was not completely sincere and pure.

[טו] **רַבִּי** אֶלְעָזָר בֶּן שַׁמּוּעַ אוֹמֵר: יְהִי כְבוֹד תַּלְמִידְךָ חָבִיב עָלֶיךָ כְּשֶׁלָּךְ; וּכְבוֹד חֲבֵרְךָ כְּמוֹרָא רַבָּךְ; וּמוֹרָא רַבָּךְ כְּמוֹרָא שָׁמָיִם.

[טז] **רַבִּי** יְהוּדָה אוֹמֵר: הֱוֵי זָהִיר בְּתַלְמוּד, שֶׁשִּׁגְגַת תַּלְמוּד עוֹלָה זָדוֹן.

פירוש לרבי עובדיה ספורנו

פרוש נוקפי ופרוש שכמי וזולתם שספרו ובארו ז״ל ולא היה כח ביד חכמי הדור לבטלם והיו מצטערים על זה, אמר שאין להצטער מאד על זה, כי אמנם הכתות הנעשות שלא לשם שמים תכלינה מאליהן, כאמרם ז״ל הנח להם לרשעים והם כלים מאליהם:

ד:טו. הנה מכלל כבוד האל יתברך הוא שנכבד קדשיו וקדושיו כאמרו „והדרת פני זקן ויראת מאלהיך״, ולכן הזהיר זה החכם

SFORNO'S COMMENTARY

took note of the diverse groups of Pharisees, hypocrites and Sadducees — among them פָּרוּשׁ נוֹקְפִי וּפָרוּשׁ שִׁכְמִי (insincere and sanctimonious Pharisees, as related by our Sages in *Mesechta Sotah* 22b) — and the Sages of that generation were powerless and could not combat them, which caused them great mental anguish and suffering, he comforted them and urged them not to be overly troubled. He assured them that these groups, whose actions were not "dedicated to the sake of Heaven," would ultimately disintegrate of their own accord, as our Sages tell us, הַנַּח לָהֶם לָרְשָׁעִים וְהֵם כָּלִים מֵאֲלֵיהֶם, *"Leave the wicked alone, and they will expire of their own accord"* (*Gittin* 7a).

4:15

יְהִי כְבוֹד תַּלְמִידְךָ . . . וּמוֹרָא רַבָּךְ כְּמוֹרָא שָׁמַיִם — *Let the honor of your student . . . and the reverence for your teacher as the reverence of Heaven.* Behold, included in the honor of God, Blessed is He, is the obligation to honor His sacred things and holy ones, as it is written, וְהָדַרְתָּ פְּנֵי זָקֵן וְיָרֵאתָ מֵאֱלֹהֶיךָ, *And you shall honor the presence of a sage and you shall revere your God* (*Leviticus* 19:32).

NOTES

4:14

כָּל כְּנֵסִיָּה . . . וְשֶׁאֵינָהּ לְשֵׁם שָׁמַיִם, אֵין סוֹפָהּ לְהִתְקַיֵּם — *Every assembly . . . that is not for the sake of Heaven, will not have an enduring effect.* The *Sforno* is of the opinion that the teaching of Rabbi Yochanan the Sandler in this Mishnah refers specifically to a certain historic period when not only the Sadducees and other sectarian groups distorted the truth of Torah, but even the Pharisees were infiltrated with insincere and hypocritical elements who created havoc within their beleaguered camp (*Sotah* 22b).

Rabbi Yochanan reassures us that when a group assembles to take common action, but their intention "is not for the sake of Heaven," their agenda will not succeed, and it will ultimately disintegrate and collapse. Indeed, as this sage had predicted, that is precisely what came to pass.

4:15

יְהִי כְבוֹד תַּלְמִידְךָ . . . חֲבֵרְךָ . . . רַבָּךְ . . . — *Let the honor of your student . . . your colleague . . . your teacher . . .* There is a tendency to inflate one's own importance and deprecate

15. *Rabbi Elazar ben Shamua says: Let the honor of your student be as dear to you as your own; the honor of your colleague as the reverence for your teacher; and the reverence for your teacher as the reverence of Heaven.*

16. *Rabbi Yehudah says: Be meticulous in study, for a careless misinterpretation is considered tantamount to willful transgression.*

פירוש לרבי עובדיה ספורנו

שנכבד תופשי התורה על דרך מעלין בקדש, וזה שיהיה אצלך כבוד התלמיד השפל ממך שוה לכבודך, וכבוד חברך השוה אליך יהיה אצלך במדרגת מורא רבך שהוא גדול ממך, ומורא רבך יהיה אצלך במדרגת מורא שמים שאין מדרגה במדרגות:

ד:טז. ששגגת מה שלא למדת מחמת התרשלות עולה זדון להענישך על שהיית מזיד להתרשל, כאמרו „ואת פעל יי לא יביטו ... ולכן גלה עמי מבלי דעת":

SFORNO'S COMMENTARY

Therefore, this sage cautions us to honor Torah scholars on an ascending scale, in keeping with מַעֲלִין בַּקּוֹדֶשׁ, *"we ascend in matters of sanctity"* (*Berachos* 28a). Thus, "let the honor of your student," who is inferior to you, "be as dear to you as your own"; "the honor of your colleague," who is equal to you, should be on the level of your "reverence for your teacher," who is superior to you; and your "reverence for your teacher" should be equal to your awe and "reverence of Heaven," of which there is nothing more elevated.

4:16

הֱוֵי זָהִיר בְּתַלְמוּד, שֶׁשִּׁגְגַת תַּלְמוּד . . . — *Be meticulous in study, for a careless misinterpretation . . .* That which you failed to learn due to carelessness is regarded as a "willful transgression," for you were willful in your indolence, as it is written: וְאֵת פֹּעַל ה׳ לֹא יַבִּיטוּ . . . לָכֵן גָּלָה עַמִּי מִבְּלִי דָעַת, *But they regard not the work of Hashem . . .therefore, My people are gone into captivity, for want of knowledge* (*Isaiah* 5:12-13).

NOTES

the worth of others. To correct this imbalance, we should elevate each person one level higher, and thus reach parity. The *Sforno* reads this idea into the words of Rabbi Elazar ben Shamua. He urges his disciples to honor everyone a level higher than their perceived status, be it one's student, colleague or teacher.

4:16

הֱוֵי זָהִיר בְּתַלְמוּד, שֶׁשִּׁגְגַת תַּלְמוּד . . . — *Be meticulous in study, for a careless misinterpretation. . .* In *halachah,* a distinction is drawn between שׁוֹגֵג, an *inadvertent* act, and מֵזִיד, a *willful* one. Morally, however, it is not only the action and result that is judged, but also the circumstances (including indolence) which brought it about. Failure to learn is not a willful positive act, but rather a negative action. But what was the cause for this failing? The *Sforno* explains the statement of Rabbi Yehudah as follows: One's careless misinterpretation may have been inadvertent, but it was caused by his

[יז] **רַבִּי** שִׁמְעוֹן אוֹמֵר: שְׁלֹשָׁה כְתָרִים הֵם: כֶּתֶר תּוֹרָה, וְכֶתֶר כְּהֻנָּה, וְכֶתֶר מַלְכוּת; וְכֶתֶר שֵׁם טוֹב עוֹלֶה עַל גַּבֵּיהֶן.

[יח] **רַבִּי** נְהוֹרָאִי אוֹמֵר: הֱוֵי גוֹלֶה לִמְקוֹם תּוֹרָה וְאַל תֹּאמַר שֶׁהִיא תָבוֹא אַחֲרֶיךָ,

פירוש לרבי עובדיה ספורנו

ד:יז. שלשה כתרים הם שהושמו בישראל מפי עליון, אמנם הם כתרים לזוכים בהם כאשר יהיה כתר שם טוב עולה על גביהם ולא באופן אחר, ואין צריך לומר כשיהיה הפך זה, כי אמנם בבעל תורה כשתהיה רוח הבריות נוחה הימנו אמרו ז״ל מה הבריות אומרות עליו ראיתם פלוני שלמד תורה כמה מתוקנים דרכיו כולי עליו נאמר „ישראל אשר בך אתפאר״, ואז תהיה לו התורה לכתר ונזר הקדש, והפך זה תהיה התורה לבר בי רב דסנו שומעניה, כמו שאמרו ז״ל מה הבריות אומרות עליו

SFORNO'S COMMENTARY

4:17

שְׁלֹשָׁה כְתָרִים . . . וְכֶתֶר שֵׁם טוֹב עוֹלֶה . . . — *Three crowns . . . but the crown of a good name surpasses . . .* "Three crowns" were granted to Israel from on High. However, these "crowns" may only be worn by those who merit to wear them, providing they have "the crown of a good name" but not in any other manner, and certainly not if it is to the contrary.

For, indeed, the Sages said about a Torah scholar whose ways are pleasing to the people: מַה הַבְּרִיּוֹת אוֹמְרוֹת עָלָיו, רְאִיתֶם פְּלוֹנִי שֶׁלָּמַד תּוֹרָה, כַּמָּה מְתוּקָּנִים דְּרָכָיו . . . , עָלָיו נֶאֱמַר, „יִשְׂרָאֵל אֲשֶׁר בְּךָ אֶתְפָּאָר, *"What do people say concerning him? [They say,] 'Do you see how fine are the ways of this man who studied Torah? Of him the verse says, 'Israel, in whom I will be glorified' "* (*Yoma* 86a; *Isaiah* 49:3). It is then that the Torah is a crown and a sacred diadem.

The reverse, however, is true of a Torah student and scholar who has a bad reputation, as our Sages state: מַה הַבְּרִיּוֹת אוֹמְרוֹת עָלָיו, רְאִיתֶם פְּלוֹנִי שֶׁלָּמַד תּוֹרָה

NOTES

failure to apply himself to Torah study, and that was done knowingly. The proof from the verse in *Isaiah* is also a most telling one. "The want of knowledge" is due to a failure to study and pursue knowledge, which may seem to be a negative act, but nevertheless, the Prophet cautions us that one will be punished for this indolence.

4:17

שְׁלֹשָׁה כְתָרִים . . . וְכֶתֶר שֵׁם טוֹב עוֹלֶה . . . — *Three crowns . . . but the crown of a good name surpasses . . .* The commentary of the *Sforno,* which links the crowns of Torah, priesthood, and royalty with the "crown of a good name" — i.e., that each of these crowns must be accompanied by a good name — is similar to the interpretation of the *Bartenura.*

The proof that "the crown of Torah" must be accompanied by "the crown of a good name" is found in Tractate *Yoma* (86a), and is self-explanatory.

As for "the crown of priesthood," his proof is from the sons of Eli, who are called בְּנֵי בְלִיָּעַל and were guilty of unseemly

17. *Rabbi Shimon says: There are three crowns — the crown of Torah, the crown of priesthood, and the crown of kingship; but the crown of a good name surpasses them all.*

18. *Rabbi Nehorai says: Exile yourself to a place of Torah — and do not say that it will come after*

פירוש לרבי עובדיה ספורנו

ראיתם פלוני שלמד תורה כמה מכוערים דרכיו כולי עליו הכתוב אומר „באמור להם עם יי אלה ומארצו יצאו״, וכן הענין בכתר כהנה, כמו שקרה לבני עלי וכאמרו „ואמאסך מכהן לי״, וכן בכתר מלכות, כמו שקרה ליורם שהרג את אחיו וגם משרי ישראל, „ולא עשו לו ... שרפה כשרפת אבותיו ויקברוהו בעיר דוד ולא בקברות המלכים״:

ד:יח. הוי גולה, כשתצטרך לגלות ממקומך לבקש פרנסתך או לסבה אחרת בחר לגלות למקום תורה, ואל תאמר שאתה

SFORNO'S COMMENTARY

כַּמָּה מְכוֹעָרִים דְּרָכָיו – עָלָיו הַכָּתוּב אוֹמֵר, „בֶּאֱמֹר לָהֶם עַם ה׳ אֵלֶּה וּמֵאַרְצוֹ יָצָאוּ״, *"What do people say concerning him? [They say,] 'See how corrupt are the deeds of this person who studied Torah!' Of him the verse says, 'These are the people of Hashem and are gone forth from the land' "* (*Yoma* 86a; *Ezekiel* 36:20).

The same can be said of the "crown of priesthood," as is evident from the sons of Eli, about whom the Prophet says: וְאֶמְאָסְךָ מִכַּהֵן לִי , *I will reject you, that you will not be a priest to Me* (*Hosea* 4:6).

The same can be said of the "crown of kingship," as we find in the case of Yehoram, who killed his brothers and the princes of Israel (see *II Chronicles* 21:4). As a consequence, the verse says, ... וְלֹא עָשׂוּ לוֹ ... שְׂרֵפָה כִּשְׂרֵפַת אֲבֹתָיו וַיִּקְבְּרֻהוּ בְּעִיר דָּוִיד וְלֹא בְּקִבְרוֹת הַמְּלָכִים, *and they made no burning for him as they did for his fathers . . .and they buried him in the City of David but not in the tombs of the kings* (*II Chronicles* 21:19-20).

4:18

הֱוֵי גוֹלֶה לִמְקוֹם תּוֹרָה, וְאַל תֹּאמַר . . . שֶׁחֲבֵרֶיךָ יְקַיְּמוּהָ — *Exile yourself to a place of Torah — and do not not say . . . for it is your colleagues who will cause it to remain.* "Exile yourself to a place of Torah." Meaning, that when you are compelled to move away from your community in order to earn a livelihood, or for some other reason, choose a place of Torah. "Do not say" that you will

NOTES

behavior, as recorded in the Book of *Samuel* (2:12).

The need for a king to conduct himself in a proper manner is proven by the *Sforno* from the life and death of Yehoram, son of Yehoshafat, king of Judah, who killed his brothers. He was not accorded the royal honors at his funeral, which normally consisted of burning the royal bed and certain personal belongings, to indicate that no other person was worthy to use them. This practice, as well as the privilege of being buried in the tombs of the kings, was denied Yehoram.

שֶׁחֲבֵרֶיךָ יְקַיְּמוּהָ בְּיָדֶךָ. וְאֶל בִּינָתְךָ אַל תִּשָּׁעֵן.

[יט] **רַבִּי** יַנַּאי אוֹמֵר: אֵין בְּיָדֵינוּ לֹא מִשַּׁלְוַת הָרְשָׁעִים וְאַף לֹא מִיִּסּוּרֵי הַצַּדִּיקִים.

פירוש לרבי עובדיה ספורנו

תרביץ תורה במקום שאינה שם ותעמיד תלמידים הרבה, שאף על פי שהתלמידים ירבו הבנה ופלפול – הנה חבריך השוים לך בקבלה יקימוה בידך, ולא יוכלו על זה התלמידים, ואל בינתך אל תשען שתתקים בידך בלתי חברים, כי לפעמים יקרה כמו שקרה לזה החכם בעצמו ששכח תלמודו או קצת והשיבוהו חבריו לאיתנו, כמבואר בשבת פרק חבית:

ד:יט. הנה באמרו שלות הרשעים אמר זה

SFORNO'S COMMENTARY

disseminate Torah in your new community which is presently devoid of it, and that you will cultivate new disciples. Because even though it may be true that a large number of students will *increase and sharpen* your understanding of Torah, nonetheless, they cannot "cause it to remain with you" to the same degree as your "colleagues," who are equal to you in erudition.

וְאֶל בִּינָתְךָ אַל תִּשָּׁעֵן — *And do not rely on your own understanding.* That is, do not assume that your understanding will endure even without intellectual interchange with colleagues, for it may happen, as it did indeed with this Sage [Rabbi Nehorai], that you may forget all or some of your Torah. In his case, the ones who retrieved it for him were his colleagues, as related in Tractate *Shabbos* 147b.

NOTES

4:18

שֶׁחֲבֵרֶיךָ יְקַיְּמוּהָ בְּיָדֶךָ — *For it is your colleague who will cause it to remain with you.* The *Sforno* interprets the phrase שֶׁחֲבֵרֶיךָ יְקַיְּמוּהָ בְּיָדֶךָ — "for it is your colleagues who will cause it to remain with you" — as meaning that only they can ensure the retention of your Torah knowledge. As for your students, although they may stimulate your innovative talents, they cannot preserve your original store of knowledge.

This interpretation differs from that of the *Bartenura,* who explains that Rabbi Nehorai teaches us that the transmission of a teacher's instruction through another cannot be fully understood or appreciated unless one hears it directly from the teacher. Alternatively, he interprets this statement to mean that only your colleagues can clarify Torah through their intellectual interchange with you, but you alone cannot grasp the true meaning of Torah, regardless of how bright and sharp you may be. This explains the concluding statement, "and do not rely on your own understanding."

The *Sforno* points out that Nehorai was another name for Rabbi Elazar ben Arach, who went to the Galilee and was enticed into leading a life of luxury and pleasure, as a result of which he forgot all of his Torah knowledge (see Tractate *Shabbos* 147b). However, his colleagues prayed on his behalf, and he regained his knowledge. This is the meaning of the phrase "for it is your colleagues who will cause it to remain with you." He did, however, learn a lesson from this experience — therefore, he emphasizes the importance of moving only to a place where Torah study is practiced.

4 19 *you — for it is your colleagues who will cause it to remain with you; "and do not rely on your own understanding."*

19. *Rabbi Yannai says: It is not in our power to explain either the tranquility of the wicked or the suffering of the righteous.*

פירוש לרבי עובדיה ספורנו

על אותו המין מהשלוה שלא ישיגוה זולתי הרשעים הגמורים בלבד, כאמרו ,,ושלות כסילים תאבדם", וכאמרו ,,שלו כל בוגדי בגד", ולא ישיגוה אפילו הצדיקים הגמורים עם היותם זוכים לשתי שלחנות, כאמרם ז"ל בבראשית רבה בקש יעקב לישב בשלוה קפץ עליו שטנו של יוסף אמר המקטרג לא דיין לצדיקים מה שמתוקן להם לחיי העולם הבא אלא שמבקשין לישב בשלוה בעולם הזה.

SFORNO'S COMMENTARY

4:19

אֵין בְּיָדֵינוּ לֹא מִשַּׁלְוַת הָרְשָׁעִים וְאַף לֹא מִיִּסּוּרֵי הַצַּדִּיקִים — *It is not in our power to explain either the tranquility of the wicked or the suffering of the righteous.* Behold when the Tanna says, "the tranquility of the wicked," he refers to the kind of tranquility that only the totally wicked can attain, as it is written, וְשַׁלְוַת כְּסִילִים תְּאַבְּדֵם, *and the tranquility of fools shall destroy them* (*Proverbs* 1:32); and it is written, שָׁלוּ כָּל בֹּגְדֵי בָגֶד, *those who deal treacherously are tranquil* (*Jeremiah* 12:1).

Now, this kind of tranquility cannot be realized even by the perfectly righteous, although they may merit "two tables" [in this world and the World to Come], as the Sages said: בִּקֵּשׁ יַעֲקֹב לֵישֵׁב בְּשַׁלְוָה קָפַץ עָלָיו שָׂטָנוֹ שֶׁל יוֹסֵף. אָמַר הַמְקַטְרֵג, לֹא דַיָּן לַצַּדִּיקִים מַה שֶּׁמְּתוּקָּן לָהֶם חַיֵּי עוה"ב, אֶלָּא שֶׁמְּבַקְּשִׁין לֵישֵׁב בְּשַׁלְוָה בָּעוֹלָם הַזֶּה *"Jacob desired to live in tranquility, but the Satan came and disrupted his plan through Joseph. The Accuser said: Is it not sufficient that the righteous have reward stored for them in the World to Come, that they seek to live at ease in This World as well!"* (*Bereishis Rabbah* 84:3).

NOTES

4:19

אֵין בְּיָדֵינוּ לֹא מִשַּׁלְוַת הָרְשָׁעִים וְאַף לֹא מִיִּסּוּרֵי הַצַּדִּיקִים — *It is not in our power to explain either the tranquility of the wicked or the suffering of the righteous.*

In this lengthy commentary, the *Sforno* offers a unique interpretation of Rabbi Yannai's terse statement regarding the lot of the righteous and the fate of the wicked in this world, an enigma which has puzzled wise men for thousands of years: Why do the wicked prosper while the righteous suffer?

He first defines the terms "tranquility" and "suffering," as applied by Rabbi Yannai to the wicked and the righteous. The kind of tranquility he speaks of here is that which only the wicked can experience, for as he explains later in his commentary, it is denied to the righteous. This does not mean that the *tzaddik* cannot enjoy a degree of calm and serenity in his life, but it is not the שַׁלְוָה, the "tranquility," of which Rabbi Yannai speaks, for that is reserved exclusively for the wicked.

אמנם כי כל זה נראה הפך ייעודי התורה הטובים והפך אמרם ז״ל מי שני להו לצדיקי דעכלו תרי עלמי, וכן אותו המין מיסורים המיוחס לצדיקים בלבד והן ייסורים שלאהבה נראה מאברהם ז״ל שיחולו על האדם בלי חטא קודם, כאמרם ז״ל ראה אדם יסורין באין עליו יפשפש במעשיו פשפש ולא מצא יתלה בבטול תורה פשפש ולא מצא אינן אלא יסורים שלאהבה. וכבר בארו הם ז״ל שלא יהיה זה המין מיסורים באדם אלא כשיהיו חביבים עליו, כאמרם ז״ל יכול אפילו שלא לדעת תלמוד לומר ,,ויי חפץ דכאו החלי אם תשים אשם נפשו״ מה אשם לדעת אף יסורים לדעת.

However, all this seems to run contrary to the beneficial assurances of the Torah, and also seemingly contradicts the teaching of our Sages, who rhetorically asked, אַטוּ צַדִּיקִים אִי אָכְלֵי תְּרֵי עָלְמֵי מִי סָנֵי לְהוּ, *"If the righteous could enjoy both worlds, would they find it distasteful?"* (*Horayos* 10b).

Also, the kind of suffering which is the lot only of the righteous, namely יִסּוּרִין שֶׁל אַהֲבָה, "suffering of love," which befell Abraham, can befall a person even though he has not sinned, as our Sages of blessed memory teach us: רָאָה אָדָם יִסּוּרִין בָּאִין עָלָיו יְפַשְׁפֵּשׁ בְּמַעֲשָׂיו. פִּשְׁפֵּשׁ וְלֹא מָצָא יִתְלֶה בְּבִיטּוּל תּוֹרָה. פִּשְׁפֵּשׁ וְלֹא מָצָא אֵינָן אֶלָּא יִסּוּרִין שֶׁל אַהֲבָה, *"If a man sees that suffering is visited upon him, let him examine his conduct; if he examines and finds nothing objectionable, let him attribute it to the neglect of Torah; if he does not find this to be the cause, let him be sure they are chastenings of love"* (*Berachos* 5a).

Our Sages also explained that this category of suffering will befall a person only if he cherishes them and they are beloved and acceptable to him, as our Sages state: יָכוֹל אֲפִילוּ שֶׁלֹּא לְדַעַת? תַּלְמוּד לוֹמַר,וַה׳ חָפֵץ דַּכְּאוֹ הֶחֱלִי אִם תָּשִׂים אָשָׁם נַפְשׁוֹ.׳ מַה אָשָׁם לְדַעַת, אַף יִסּוּרִין לְדַעַת, *"Is this true even if it is against one's will? Therefore it is written: 'It pleased Hashem to crush him with illness, [to see] if his soul would accept it as a guilt offering'* (*Isaiah* 53:10) — *just as a guilt offering must be brought willingly, so too, suffering must be endured willingly"* (*Berachos* 5a).

NOTES

Even that tranquility is not one which the Torah fully explains. Following Adam's sin and his departure from *Gan Eden,* man has not been able to enjoy it fully, nor has it existed since the Great Flood. Only in Messianic times will the righteous once again experience this absolute tranquility.

As for "the suffering of the righteous," this refers to those יִסּוּרִים which are visited upon him because he wants and accepts them, so as to purge himself and expiate his sins.

The *Sforno's* mention of Rabbi Elazar the son of Rabbi Shimon (see p. 127) refers to an episode related in the Talmud (*Bava Metzia* 84b). Rabbi Elazar was appointed as a marshal by the government, and in that capacity ordered the arrest of a certain laundryman, who was subsequently executed. Rabbi Elazar agonized over his involvement, even though he was legally and morally justified in his action, and accepted Divine suffering as expiation for his sin. This is another example of a righteous person's acceptance of suffering which he can control, i.e., he can bring it upon himself as atonement, but also has the power to stop it when he so chooses. The צַדִּיק desires their chastisements but also controls them, which is why he can

וכבר ספרו על רבי חנינא ורבי יוחנן שאמרו למדוכאים ביסורים חביבים עליך ייסורים, וכשהשיב המשיב לא הם ולא שכרם יהב ליה ידיה ואוקמיה, וסרו מעליו אז הייסורים. ובהיות כי ישומו ישרים על כל אלה, כי אמנם יראה מזה שהאל יתברך חפץ בצער גופות חסידיו בלי חטא קודם, על הפך אמרו „כי לא ענה מלבו ויגה בני איש״, ועל הפך אמרם ז״ל אין יסורים בלא עון. ועוד, שאם בזה יחפוץ האל יתברך איך ימאן אותם הצדיק נגד רצון קונו, ואיך יקרה שיסורו מעליו כאשר לא יחפוץ בם: ולהתיר כל כל אלה הספקות אמר זה החכם אין בידינו כולי, כלומר אין אצלנו בייעודי התורה לטוב שום דבר משלות הרשעים, וכן בייעודי התורה לרע אין בידינו שום

SFORNO'S COMMENTARY

The Talmud relates that both Rabbi Chanina and Rabbi Yochanan would ask those who were crushed by suffering, חֲבִיבִים עָלֶיךָ יִסּוּרִים, "Do you cherish your affliction?" When the individual would answer לֹא הֵם וְלֹא שְׂכָרָם, "neither they nor their reward," they would extend a hand and stand him up, and the suffering would cease.

But *upright men are astonished by this* [an expression based on *Job* 17:18], for all this would seem to imply that God, Blessed is He, desires that His pious ones suffer physical pain even if they have not sinned. Also, this would seem to contradict the verse: כִּי לֹא עִנָּה מִלִּבּוֹ וַיַּגֶּה בְּנֵי אִישׁ, *For He does not willingly afflict or aggrieve the children of men* (*Lamentations* 3:33) and also contradicts the teaching of our Sages, who said, אֵין יִסּוּרִין בְּלִי עָוֹן, *"there is no affliction without transgression"* (*Shabbos* 55a). And besides, if this is God's will, how could a *tzaddik* (righteous person) reject his suffering? Would this not be contrary to the will of his Maker? And how can it happen that his affliction would suddenly cease if he does not willingly accept it?

To resolve all of these difficulties, this wise man [Rabbi Yannai] states, אֵין בְּיָדֵינוּ, "it is not in our power to explain either the tranquility of the wicked or the suffering of the righteous." He means, that in all the benevolent assurances stated in the Torah, there is no mention of "the tranquility of the wicked." Similarly, in all the maledictions stated in the Torah, no mention is

NOTES

remove them if he finds them unbearable. This explains the episodes recorded in the Talmud, where the righteous were given the option to accept or reject suffering.

The main thesis of Rabbi Yannai, as expounded by the *Sforno,* is that the suffering of the *tzaddik* is not a punishment from the Almighty, nor is the prosperity of the wicked a reward or gift from on High. On the contrary, the latter is, as King David says in *Psalms,* for the purpose of increasing and intensifying their ultimate punishment in the World to Come.

Therefore, the expression "it is not in our power" means that the Torah has not revealed these ideas to man, and all theories offered are speculative on our part, having puzzled even the Prophets. The main thrust of the *Sforno*'s commentary is that neither the tranquility enjoyed by the wicked nor the suffering experienced by the righteous can be characterized as reward and punishment taught to us by Moses, the Prophets, and tradition which is indeed a fundamental principle of our faith. Rather, they are meant to serve other purposes and, Rabbi Yannai states, as a caveat that there is no certainty even to these explanations, for it is "not in our power" to fully understand the ways of the Almighty.

דבר מייסורי הצדיקים. כי אמנם שלות הרשעים, והיא ההתפרנס שלא בצער, כמו שקרה לאנשי דור המבול שאמרו ז״ל שהטעימן הקדוש ברוך הוא מעין העולם הבא – לא השיג אותה שום צדיק אחר חטאו של אדם הראשון שנגזר עליו בזעת אפך תאכל לחם, ועם כל ייעודי התורה הטובים לא ייעד שיתפרנס הצדיק שלא בצער, אבל אמר „ואספת דגנך״, ומדברי הנביאים ומדברי רז״ל נראה שלא ישיג שום צדיק זה המין מהשלוה עד כי יבוא שילה, שכתוב בו „יהי פסת בר בארץ״ ובארו ז״ל בזה שעתידה ארץ ישראל שתוציא גלוסקאות וכלי מילת, כלומר שישוב אז ענין ישראל לכמו שהיה ענין אדם הראשון קודם חטאו, עד שאמרו שכל מי שעברו עליו ארבעים יום בלא יסורין בעולם הזה קבל עולמו. וכמו כן אמר זה החכם שאין אצלנו מייעודי התורה לרע שום דבר מורה שיבואו יסורים על האדם בלתי עון קודם. ומזה יתחייב שלא היה דבר מזה המין משלות הרשעים לגמול המיועד בתורה, וכן ייסורי הצדיקים מזה לא יהיה המין לענש המיועד בה, אבל תהיה שלות הרשעים להפילם מאגרא רמא לבירא עמיקתא, וייסורי הצדיקים מזה המין שהם

made of "the suffering of the righteous." For indeed, the tranquility of the wicked, which means that they have sustenance without pain — as was the experience of the Generation of the Flood, of whom our Sages say, שֶׁהִטְעִימָן הקב״ה מֵעֵין עוֹלָם הַבָּא, *"The Almighty, Blessed is He, granted them a taste of the World to Come"* (*Sanhedrin* 108b). for seven days before the rains began — was never attained by any righteous individual after Adam's sin, upon whom it was decreed, בְּזֵעַת אַפֶּיךָ תֹּאכַל לֶחֶם, *by the sweat of your brow shall you eat bread* (*Genesis* 3:19).

Despite all the benevolent assurances stated in the Torah, it was never destined that the righteous be sustained without pain. Rather, it is written וְאָסַפְתָּ דְגָנֶךָ, *and you will gather in your grain* (*Deuteronomy* 11:14). From prophetic writings and the teachings of our Sages, it is apparent that no righteous person will ever attain this kind of tranquility until Messianic times, as it is written, יְהִי פִסַּת בַּר בָּאָרֶץ , *There will be an abundance of grain in the land* (*Psalms* 72:16), and as our Rabbis explained, עֲתִידָה אֶרֶץ יִשְׂרָאֵל שֶׁתּוֹצִיא גְלוּסְקָאוֹת וּכְלֵי מֵילַת, *"Eretz Yisrael is destined to bring forth cakes and robes of fine wool"* (*Shabbos* 30), meaning that Israel and Eretz Yisrael will at that time revert to the condition of Adam before the sin. This is also what the Sages meant when they said, כָּל מִי שֶׁעָבְרוּ עָלָיו אַרְבָּעִים יוֹם בְּלִי יְסוּרִין בָּעוֹלָם הַזֶּה קִבֵּל עוֹלָמוֹ, *"He who experiences no suffering for forty days in this world has already received his reward of restful tranquility destined for him in the World to Come"* (*Eruvin* 16) .

Now, this sage [Rabbi Yannai] tells us that, as for evil visited upon man, the Torah does not indicate that painful suffering can come to man without prior sin. By the same token, it follows that the kind of tranquility enjoyed by the wicked is not the recompense foretold by the Torah, nor are the sufferings of the righteous the punishment ordained by the Torah. Rather, the tranquility and prosperity of the wicked is for the purpose of elevating

יסורים שלאהבה לא יהיו כלל זולתי מה שירצה הצדיק להביא עליו כרצונו, וזה יקרה כשתבוא ליד הצדיק איזו מצוה שאם עשאה מקבל עליה שכר ואם לא עשאה אינו מקבל עליה פורענות כענין נחום כשלא מהר לפרנס העני קודם שיפרק מן החמור, כי אז כשיצטער הצדיק על זה עד שיענוש הוא עצמו את גופו על ש[לא] נשתדל ויקבל עליו יסורים על זה, הנה הוא בלי ספק כאלו עשה אותה המצוה והוסיף למצוא בה חן בעיני האל יתברך, ולכן על פיו יצאו ועל פיו יבואו אותן היסורים, כמו שספרו ז״ל על רבי אלעזר ברבי שמעון וזולתו. ובזה גם כן התיר זה החכם אותו הספק הנופל על דברי ירמיהו וחבקוק שצעקו על משפט צדיק ורע לו רשע וטוב לו, והנה משה רבינו באר זה, כאמרו „ומשלם לשונאיו אל פניו להאבידו״, וכאמרו „אשר לא ישא פנים ולא יקח שחד״. והתיר זה החכם את זה הספק באמרו אין בידינו, כי אמנם בכל מה שבידינו מייעודי התורה לטוב או לרע שהם

him to a "high roof" so that his fall into the "deep pit" be all the more intense and dramatic.

As for the sufferings of the righteous, which can be characterized as "chastisements of love," these can only come to pass when the righteous person wants them to be visited upon him. This in turn may occur when the *tzaddik* was presented with the opportunity to perform a *mitzvah*, which, had he performed it, would have entitled him to reward, but does not make him liable for punishment when he fails to perform it, as we find in the episode of Nachum (*Taanis* 21a). He did not hasten to feed the poor man before he unloaded his mule [and felt deeply distressed because he had been negligent]. When the righteous one is deeply pained (by such an act of omission) to the extent that he accepts Divine punishment upon himself, and willingly accepts painful suffering upon himself (as a penance), then it is doubtless considered as though he did perform the *mitzvah* and he thereby finds increased favor in the eyes of the Almighty, the Blessed One. It is in such a case that the *tzaddik* can control his suffering, commanding it to be visited on him or to depart, as the Talmud relates regarding Rabbi Elazar the son of Rabbi Shimon, and others as well (*Bava Metzia* 84b).

With this, our wise Tanna [Rabbi Yannai] also resolves the doubts and questions raised by Jeremiah [Chap. 12] and Habakuk [Chap. 1], who lamented and cried out against the injustice of צַדִּיק וְרַע לוֹ רָשָׁע וְטוֹב לוֹ, "the righteous who experiences adversity and the wicked who prosper." Now, Moses, our master and teacher, explained this phenomenon when he said, וּמְשַׁלֵּם לְשֹׂנְאָיו אֶל פָּנָיו לְהַאֲבִידוֹ, *And He repays His enemies in his lifetime to make him perish* (*Deuteronomy* 7:10), and when he said, אֲשֶׁר לֹא יִשָּׂא פָנִים וְלֹא יִקַּח שֹׁחַד, *Who does not show favor and Who does not accept a bribe* (ibid. 10:17).

Now, our Tanna resolves these doubts by stating . . . אֵין בְּיָדֵינוּ, "it is not in our power to explain either the tranquility of the wicked or the suffering of the righteous" — meaning, all that is in our range of knowledge regarding

[כ] **רַבִּי** מַתְיָא בֶּן חָרָשׁ אוֹמֵר: הֱוֵי מַקְדִּים
בִּשְׁלוֹם כָּל אָדָם, וֶהֱוֵי זָנָב לָאֲרָיוֹת,
וְאַל תְּהִי רֹאשׁ לְשׁוּעָלִים.

———— פירוש לרבי עובדיה ספורנו ————

מִינֵי הַכָּנָה אוֹ מִינֵי גְמוּל וְעֹנֶשׁ לַצַּדִּיקִים
וְלָרְשָׁעִים בָּעוֹלָם הַזֶּה וּבָעוֹלָם הַבָּא אֵין
בָּהֶם שׁוּם דְּבַר מִשְׁלֹות הָרְשָׁעִים וְלֹא
מִיִּסּוּרִים שֶׁלְּאַהֲבָה, וּמִזֶּה יִתְחַיֵּב שֶׁאֵין
אֶחָד מֵהֶם גְּמוּל אוֹ עֹנֶשׁ מֵאֵת הָאֵל יִתְבָּרֵךְ
אֲבָל שַׁלְוַת הָרְשָׁעִים הִיא לְהַגְדִּיל עֹנֶשׁ
לָהֶם וּלְהֻמָּם וּלְאַבְּדָם יוֹתֵר, כְּאָמְרוֹ ,,אַךְ

בַּחֲלָקוֹת תָּשִׁית לָמוֹ הִפַּלְתָּם לְמַשּׁוּאוֹת",
כִּי בְּהַרְגִּישָׁם מַפַּלְתָּם מִגֹּבַהּ מַעֲלָתָם יְהִי
צַעֲרָם גָּדוֹל בָּזֶה, וְכֵן יִסּוּרֵי הַצַּדִּיקִים
אֵינָן עֹנֶשׁ לָהֶם מֵאֵת הָאֵל יִתְבָּרֵךְ אֲבָל
יַחְפֹּץ בָּם אֵיזֶה צַדִּיק לְמַעַן יִצְטַעֵר עַל דְּבַר
מִצְוָה שֶׁאָבַד מִמֶּנּוּ לְמַעַן תָּשׁוּב נַפְשׁוֹ
בְּהִצְטַעֲרָהּ עַל זֶה בְּמַדְרֵגַת טוֹב כְּאִלּוּ

———— SFORNO'S COMMENTARY ————

the designation, mission and purpose of Torah, be it for good or evil, which are either preparation (for life and death) or reward and punishment for the righteous and the wicked in this world and the World to Come — in all the teachings of Torah there is no mention of the tranquility of the wicked or the chastenings of love of the righteous. Hence, we see that neither of these puzzling anomalies is to be regarded as reward or punishment from on High. Rather, the "tranquility of the wicked" is for the purpose of magnifying their punishment and to increase their destruction, as it is written, אַךְ בַּחֲלָקוֹת תָּשִׁית לָמוֹ, הִפַּלְתָּם לְמַשּׁוּאוֹת, *Only on slippery places do You place them, You throw them down into destruction* (Psalms 73:18), for when they are conscious of their fall from an exalted level of greatness, their pain will be very great.

So, too, "the sufferings of the righteous" — they are not a punishment from the Almighty, Blessed is He. Rather, a *tzaddik* may desire them to suffer pain for having failed to perform a particular *mitzvah*. This chastisement will restore his soul to an improved level and credit to him the *mitzvah*, as though he had performed it. And if we find that the Prophets [i.e. Jeremiah and Habakuk] were deeply troubled and pained by the "tranquility of the wicked," it was not because they were pained by the good fortune of the wicked as a distortion of justice — but because they

———— NOTES ————

4:20

הֱוֵי מַקְדִּים בִּשְׁלוֹם כָּל אָדָם — *Initiate a greeting to every person.* The Sforno links the beginning and end of our Mishnah, as is his wont, for he feels that there must be continuity in the words of a Tanna.

It would seem that there is no connection between the opening remarks of Rabbi

Masya, "Initiate a greeting to every person" and the balance of the Mishnah, "be a tail to lions rather than a head to foxes." The Sforno explains: the Tanna is urging us to initiate a greeting to every person, even if we have no association with them, and even if they belong to that stratum of society which is compared to foxes, i.e.,

4 20 **20.** *Rabbi Masya ben Charash says: Initiate a greeting to every person; and be a tail to lions rather than a head to foxes.*

פירוש לרבי עובדיה ספורנו

עשתה אותה מצוה. אמנם הצטערו הנביאים על זה המין מהשלוה הקורה לרשעים, לא כמצטערים על טובת הרשעים ועוות הדין, אבל הצטערו מפני ההיזק הקורה מזה לצדיקים ברב גאות הרשעים ותקפם בה, כאמרו „בבלע רשע צדיק ממנו":

ד:כ. גם בשלום אותם בני אדם שלא תתחבר עמהם אפילו להיות להם לראש או לזנב אל תחדל מלקדם בשלומם על דרך ענוה וחבה. אמנם הוי זנב לאריות, כי בחברתם תוסיף על מעלתך ותהיה ארי, כענין „הולך את חכמים יחכם" ואל תהי ראש לשועלים, כי אז תשתמש במעלתך להאיר להם ולא תוסיף ואולי תמעיט, כענין „ורועה כסילים ירוע":

SFORNO'S COMMENTARY

were concerned by the damage and harm caused to the righteous by the arrogance of the wicked and their power, as it is said: בְּבַלַּע רָשָׁע צַדִּיק מִמֶּנּוּ, *When the wicked devour the man who is more righteous than he* (*Habakuk* 1:13).

4:20

הֱוֵי מַקְדִּים בִּשְׁלוֹם כָּל אָדָם — *Initiate a greeting to every person.* When you meet individuals with whom you would not associate, be it as their "head" or their "tail" [i.e., their leader or their follower], nevertheless, do not desist from "initiating a greeting" to them, as a gesture of humility.

וֶהֱוֵי זָנָב . . . וְאַל תְּהִי רֹאשׁ . . . — *And be a tail . . . rather than a head . . .* You should be willing to be a "tail to lions," for by associating with them you will increase your worth and also become a "lion," as it is written, הוֹלֵךְ אֶת חֲכָמִים יֶחְכָּם, *He that walks with wise men shall be wise* (*Proverbs* 13:20).

But do not be "a head to foxes," for though you will use your talents to bring illumination to them, but you will not grow, and perhaps you will even retrogress, as it is written, וְרֹעֶה כְסִילִים יֵרוֹעַ, *a companion of fools suffers harm* (ibid.).

NOTES

inferior and unsavory individuals. Nonetheless, he tells us not to shun and ignore them, but to be cordial, and even to take the initiative in greeting them.

וֶהֱוֵי זָנָב . . ., וְאַל תְּהִי רֹאשׁ . . . — *And be a tail . . . rather than a head . . .* The *Sforno*'s commentary on the second teaching of Rabbi Masya is most instructive and incisive: A person must be willing to play a secondary role in the company of superiors, for it will have a positive and salutary effect upon him. On the other hand, he should avoid the company of unsavory, inferior people, for even though one may rationalize that by associating with them he will have a positive influence upon them, this is not so, for he will lose more than he will gain.

[כא] **רַבִּי** יַעֲקֹב אוֹמֵר: הָעוֹלָם הַזֶּה דּוֹמֶה לִפְרוֹזְדוֹר בִּפְנֵי הָעוֹלָם הַבָּא, הַתְקֵן עַצְמְךָ בַּפְּרוֹזְדוֹר, כְּדֵי שֶׁתִּכָּנֵס לַטְּרַקְלִין.

[כב] **הוּא** הָיָה אוֹמֵר: יָפָה שָׁעָה אַחַת בִּתְשׁוּבָה וּמַעֲשִׂים טוֹבִים בָּעוֹלָם הַזֶּה מִכֹּל חַיֵּי הָעוֹלָם הַבָּא; וְיָפָה שָׁעָה אַחַת שֶׁל קוֹרַת רוּחַ בָּעוֹלָם הַבָּא מִכֹּל חַיֵּי הָעוֹלָם הַזֶּה.

[כג] **רַבִּי** שִׁמְעוֹן בֶּן אֶלְעָזָר אוֹמֵר: אַל תְּרַצֶּה אֶת חֲבֵרְךָ בִּשְׁעַת כַּעְסוֹ; וְאַל תְּנַחֲמֵהוּ בְּשָׁעָה שֶׁמֵּתוֹ מֻטָּל לְפָנָיו; וְאַל תִּשְׁאַל לוֹ בִּשְׁעַת נִדְרוֹ; וְאַל תִּשְׁתַּדֵּל לִרְאוֹתוֹ בִּשְׁעַת קַלְקָלָתוֹ.

פירוש לרבי עובדיה ספורנו

ד:כא. דומה לפרוזדור, שאין העמידה שם מכוונת בעצמה כלל אבל היא להשיג בה אופן להכנס ולמצוא חן שהוא התכלית המכוון, ומי שלא ישיג זה היתה עמידתו שם לריק, וכן הענין בחיי שעה, שמי שלא ישיג בם חיי עולם הנה חיי שעה היו לו לריק:

ד:כב. אף על פי שאמרתי שחיי העולם הזה אינם מכוונים בעצמן כלל — אין ראוי

SFORNO'S COMMENTARY

4:21

הָעוֹלָם הַזֶּה דּוֹמֶה לִפְרוֹזְדוֹר בִּפְנֵי הָעוֹלָם הַבָּא — *This world is like a lobby before the World to Come.* "This world is like a lobby" means that man's presence there does not serve a purpose unto itself, but is for the purpose of preparing himself to enter the palace and find favor there [in the eyes of the King]. Indeed, that is the ultimate goal. He who does not grasp this truth will have spent his time there in vain, and so it is in this transitory life (חַיֵּי שָׁעָה). He who does not attain eternal life here (on earth) has lived in vain.

4:22

יָפָה שָׁעָה אַחַת . . . — *Better one hour . . .* Although I have said that this transitory, temporal existence does not serve a purpose unto itself [but is a

NOTES

4:21,22

הָעוֹלָם הַזֶּה דּוֹמֶה לִפְרוֹזְדוֹר בִּפְנֵי הָעוֹלָם הַבָּא . . . יָפָה שָׁעָה אַחַת . . . — *This world is like a lobby before the World to Come . . . Better one hour . . .* The *Sforno* links Rabbi Yaakov's two statements into a single, unified teaching. Since this world is of little significance unto itself, serving only as a preparatory stage for the World to Come, one may make the mistake of completely negating the importance of this world. He may even consciously attempt to shorten his stay in

21. Rabbi Yaakov says: *This world is like a lobby before the World to Come; prepare yourself in the lobby so that you may enter the banquet hall.*

22. He used to say: *Better one hour of repentance and good deeds in This World than the entire life of the World to Come; and better one hour of spiritual bliss in the World to Come than the entire life of This World.*

23. Rabbi Shimon ben Elazar says: *Do not appease your fellow in the time of his anger; do not console him while his dead lies before him; do not question him about his vow at the time he makes it; and do not attempt to see him at the time of his degradation.*

פירוש לרבי עובדיה ספורנו

לצדיק למאוס בם ולקצר ימיו, אבל ראוי לו להשתדל להאריכם כפי האיפשר, כי אמנם בהם יוכל לקנות אישור לחיי העולם הבא אשר לא יקנהו אחרי כן, אבל אמרתי שאינם מכוונים בעצמם כי גם שהיה בהם כל הצלחה איפשרית בעולם הזה – אין אותה ההצלחה נחשבת בערך אל חיי העולם הבא:

ד:כג. אף על פי שראוי לצדיק להשתדל בתקון חבירו כאמרו ואהבת לרעך כמוך,

SFORNO'S COMMENTARY

preparatory stage for attaining eternal life], nevertheless, it is not fitting for a righteous person to reject it and attempt to shorten his days. Rather, it is fitting that he attempt to lengthen them as much as possible, for through them, he can acquire the right to his share in the World to Come, something which he cannot do later on. However, I *did* say that this temporal existence is not man's ultimate goal, for even if one attains the greatest possible success in this world, it is of no significance in comparison to the life of the World to Come.

4:23

אַל תְּרַצֶּה אֶת חֲבֵרְךָ בִּשְׁעַת כַּעְסוֹ . . . — *Do not appease your fellow in the time of his anger . . .* Although it is fitting that a *tzaddik* (righteous person) attempt to assist his fellow man, as it is written, **וְאָהַבְתָּ לְרֵעֲךָ כָּמוֹךָ**, *love your*

NOTES

"the lobby" so as to enter "the banquet hall" with no further delay!

To counter this erroneous view, Rabbi Yaakov teaches us that what can be accomplished in this world cannot be accomplished in the World to Come. For although it is true that the World to Come is the ultimate goal, and that true fulfillment and joy can only be experienced there, nonetheless, one must realize that this goal can only be reached by man through his actions in this transitory world.

[כד] **שְׁמוּאֵל** הַקָּטָן אוֹמֵר: „בִּנְפֹל אוֹיִבְךָ אַל תִּשְׂמָח, וּבִכָּשְׁלוֹ אַל יָגֵל לִבֶּךָ. פֶּן יִרְאֶה יהוה וְרַע בְּעֵינָיו, וְהֵשִׁיב מֵעָלָיו אַפּוֹ."

[כה] **אֱלִישָׁע** בֶּן אֲבוּיָה אוֹמֵר: הַלּוֹמֵד יֶלֶד, לְמָה הוּא דוֹמֶה? לִדְיוֹ כְתוּבָה עַל נְיָר חָדָשׁ. וְהַלּוֹמֵד זָקֵן, לְמָה הוּא דוֹמֶה? לִדְיוֹ כְתוּבָה עַל נְיָר מָחוּק.

פירוש לרבי עובדיה ספורנו

הנה אין ראוי שתשתדל בכמו אלה באלה הזמנים, כי אמנם ההתפעלות בהם הוא טבעי לא רצוני, ואינו בבחירתו שיקבל ממך אז, ובכן לא תשיג המכוון ואולי תוסיף קלקול:

ד:כד. כבר אמרו גדולה שנאה ששונאים עמי הארץ את תלמיד חכם משנאת אומות העולם לישראל. ובראות זה החכם שקצת חכמי דורו שהקפידו על זה היו שמחים בתקלת עמי הארץ עד שאמר רבי עקיבא

SFORNO'S COMMENTARY

neighbor as yourself (*Leviticus* 19:18), nonetheless, it is not proper to do so under these trying circumstances, for at such times, it is difficult for a person to remain in control of his emotions. He does not even have the ability to consciously choose to accept your words, and hence, you will not be able to accomplish your goal, and may even exacerbate the situation.

4:24

בִּנְפֹל אוֹיִבְךָ אַל תִּשְׂמָח . . . — *When your enemy falls . . . be not glad . . .* Our Sages said: גְּדוֹלָה שִׂנְאָה שֶׁשּׂוֹנְאִים עַמֵּי הָאָרֶץ אֶת תַּלְמִיד חָכָם מִשִּׂנְאַת אוה״ע לְיִשְׂרָאֵל, *"Greater is the hatred of the unlettered ignoramuses for Torah scholars than that of the nations of the world for Israel"* (*Pesachim* 49b). When this sage (Shmuel) observed that certain scholars of his time were extremely upset by

NOTES

4:24

בִּנְפֹל אוֹיִבְךָ אַל תִּשְׂמָח . . . — *When your enemy falls be not glad . . .* In *Mesechta Pesachim* (49b), we are told that Rabbi Akiva said, "When I was an עַם הָאָרֶץ, an *ignoramus,* I used to say: If only I could be given the opportunity to bite a scholar as would a donkey." In the version quoted by the *Sforno,* the statement is reversed. Rabbi Akiva states, "If only I had the opportunity, I would bite an ignoramus like a donkey!" The *Sforno* uses this statement of Rabbi Akiva to illustrate the animosity which prevailed in his day between Torah scholars and עַמֵּי הָאָרֶץ (lit. "people of the land"), the unlettered and uneducated folk.

As the *Sforno* sees it, Shmuel HaKattan chastises these intolerant and intemperate scholars, quoting the verse in *Proverbs* 24 to prove his point. He urges them to hate the sin, not the sinner.

24. *Shmuel HaKattan says: "When your enemy falls be not glad, and when he stumbles let your heart not be joyous. Lest* HASHEM *see and it displease Him, and He will turn His wrath from him [to you]".*

25. *Elisha ben Avuyah says: One who studies Torah as a child, to what can he be likened? — to ink written on fresh paper. And one who studies Torah as an old man, to what can he be likened? — to ink written on smudged paper.*

פירוש לרבי עובדיה ספורנו

מי יתן לי עם הארץ ואנשכנו כחמור, אמר זה החכם שאין ראוי לשמוח במפלתם כלל, אבל ראוי לדאג על רשעם שגרם המפלה, כמדת בוראנו שאמר „כי לא אחפוץ במות המת":

ד:כה. כי אמנם בילד יהיה הכח הזוכר יותר חזק ובכח המדמה שלו לא עברו דמיונות רבות מטרידות מהבין האמת, והפך כל זה בזקן:

SFORNO'S COMMENTARY

this animosity, and that they rejoiced whenever such ignoramuses stumbled and fell — as Rabbi Akiva said, מִי יִתֵּן לִי עַם הָאָרֶץ וַאֲנַשְּׁכֶנּוּ כַּחֲמוֹר, *"If only I had the opportunity, I would bite an ignoramus like a donkey"* (ibid.) — he said that it is not proper to rejoice over their downfall. Rather, one should be concerned regarding their wickedness which caused their downfall, and thereby emulate our Creator, Who said, כִּי לֹא אֶחְפֹּץ בְּמוֹת הַמֵּת, *I do not want the death [of the wicked]* (*Ezekiel* 18:32).

4:25

הַלּוֹמֵד יֶלֶד . . . נְיָר חָדָשׁ . . . — *One who studies Torah as a child . . . fresh paper . . .* A young person's memory is strong, and his power of imagination has not yet been clouded by a multitude of events and experiences which affect one's capacity to grasp the truth. The reverse is true of an older person.

NOTES

4:25

הַלּוֹמֵד יֶלֶד . . . נְיָר חָדָשׁ . . . — *One who studies Torah as a child . . . fresh paper.* The *Sforno* expounds upon the words of Elisha ben Avuyah, who extolled the ability of a young mind to absorb knowledge. He explains that a young person is not burdened with preconceptions, and therefore is open to new ideas and concepts. He is also able, if he is blessed with a good mind, to grasp knowledge quickly and remember it, unlike an older person, who is more prone to forget.

[כו] **רַבִּי** יוֹסֵי בַּר יְהוּדָה אִישׁ כְּפַר הַבַּבְלִי אוֹמֵר: הַלּוֹמֵד מִן הַקְּטַנִּים, לְמָה הוּא דוֹמֶה? לְאוֹכֵל עֲנָבִים קֵהוֹת, וְשׁוֹתֶה יַיִן מִגִּתּוֹ. וְהַלּוֹמֵד מִן הַזְּקֵנִים, לְמָה הוּא דוֹמֶה? לְאוֹכֵל עֲנָבִים בְּשׁוּלוֹת, וְשׁוֹתֶה יַיִן יָשָׁן.

[כז] **רַבִּי** מֵאִיר אוֹמֵר: אַל תִּסְתַּכֵּל בַּקַּנְקַן, אֶלָּא בְמַה שֶׁיֵּשׁ בּוֹ; יֵשׁ קַנְקַן חָדָשׁ מָלֵא יָשָׁן, וְיָשָׁן שֶׁאֲפִילּוּ חָדָשׁ אֵין בּוֹ.

[כח] **רַבִּי** אֶלְעָזָר הַקַּפָּר אוֹמֵר: הַקִּנְאָה וְהַתַּאֲוָה וְהַכָּבוֹד מוֹצִיאִין אֶת הָאָדָם מִן הָעוֹלָם.

פירוש לרבי עובדיה ספורנו

ד:כו־כז. ענבים כהות ויין מגיתו שלא הגיעו לשלמותם, וזה גם כן יקרה בלמוד הקטנים שלא השיגו עיון שלם נקי מטעות, והפך זה יקרה בלמוד הזקנים. אמר שמה שגנה רבי יוסי הלמוד מן הקטנים ושבח הלמוד מן הזקנים – לא אמר זה על הצעירים לימים והזקנים הבאים בימים, אבל אמר קטנים על הצעירים בהשגה אף על פי שיהיו זקנים

SFORNO'S COMMENTARY

4:26-27

הַלּוֹמֵד מִן הַקְּטַנִּים . . . מִן הַזְּקֵנִים . . . — *One who learns Torah from the young . . . from the old . . .* "Unripe grapes" and "unfermented wine," which have not yet reached completeness and perfection. This is also true of learning from the young, who have not as yet grasped the full depth of Torah, nor cleansed and purified it of error. The reverse is true of learning from the old.

אַל תִּסְתַּכֵּל בַּקַּנְקַן . . . — *Do not look at the vessel . . .* The Tanna in the next Mishnah [i.e., Rabbi Meir] teaches us that Rabbi Yose's criticism of learning from the young, and his praise of learning from the old, does not refer to

NOTES

4:26-27

הַלּוֹמֵד מִן הַזְּקֵנִים . . . דוֹמֶה לְאוֹכֵל עֲנָבִים בְּשׁוּלוֹת . . . — *One who learns Torah from the old . . . likened to one who eats ripe grapes.* In the previous Mishnah, the intellectual virtues of the young student, as opposed to the older student, are described by Elisha ben Avuyah. In this Mishnah, Rabbi Yose turns his attention to the role of the teacher. He points out to the student the advantage of learning Torah under a senior, veteran mentor, whom he likens to "vintage wine." For as the *Sforno* explains, that teacher has removed the dregs, strained out the impurities, and mastered the profound teachings of Torah.

26. Rabbi Yose bar Yehudah of Kfar HaBavli says: *One who learns Torah from the young, to what can he be likened? — to one who eats unripe grapes or drinks unfermented wine from his vat. But one who learns Torah from the old, to what can he be likened? — to one who eats ripe grapes or drinks aged wine.*

27. *Rabbi Meir says: Do not look at the vessel, but what is in it; there is a new vessel filled with old wine and an old vessel that does not even contain new wine.*

28. *Rabbi Elazar HaKappar says: Jealousy, lust, and glory remove a man from the world.*

פירוש לרבי עובדיה ספורנו

לימים, ואמר זקנים על אותם שיקנו חכמה עם היותם צעירים לימים:

ד:כח. כי אמנם התכלית המכוון בכל אחד מאלה הוא דבר בלתי מוגבל ואין עמהם עת לעשות לײ, אבל מטרידים את האדם תמיד מהשיג חיי עולם:

SFORNO'S COMMENTARY

those who are young or old in years. Rather, "the young" refers to those who are intellectually immature despite their advanced age, while the expression "the old" refers to those have acquired wisdom, even though they may be young in years.

4:28

הַקִּנְאָה וְהַתַּאֲוָה וְהַכָּבוֹד מוֹצִיאִין . . . — *Jealousy, lust, and glory remove . . .* The intended goal and purpose of each of these (three) traits are boundless, and are not governed or controlled by the dictum of *Psalms* (119:126), **עֵת לַעֲשׂוֹת לַה׳**, *It is a time to act for Hashem.* Rather, they constantly trouble and prevent man from attaining eternal life.

NOTES

אַל תִּסְתַּכֵּל בַּקַּנְקַן. . . — *Do not look at the vessel . . .* Rabbi Meir, whom the *Sforno* refers to as "the Tanna in the next Mishnah," does not disagree with Rabbi Yose, but comes to clarify and qualify his teachings by defining the terms "young" and "old." He cautions us that it is not years, but the accumulation and assimilation of Torah wisdom, that is the determining factor in establishing the excellence of the teacher.

4:28

הַקִּנְאָה וְהַתַּאֲוָה וְהַכָּבוֹד מוֹצִיאִין . . . — *Jealousy, lust, and glory remove . . .* The *Sforno* quotes the verse from *Psalms* 119, which is interpreted by Rava, in Tractate *Berachos* 63a, as meaning that there are times when it is permissible to transgress a law of the Torah in order to act for Hashem. Some examples are Elijah offering sacrifices on an altar outside the Temple, and Rabbi Yehudah HaNasi committing the Oral Law

ד כט [כט] **הוּא** הָיָה אוֹמֵר: הַיִּלּוֹדִים לָמוּת, וְהַמֵּתִים לִחְיוֹת, וְהַחַיִּים לִדּוֹן — לֵידַע לְהוֹדִיעַ וּלְהִוָּדַע שֶׁהוּא אֵל, הוּא הַיּוֹצֵר, הוּא הַבּוֹרֵא, הוּא הַמֵּבִין, הוּא הַדַּיָּן, הוּא הָעֵד, הוּא בַּעַל דִּין, הוּא עָתִיד לָדוּן. בָּרוּךְ הוּא, שֶׁאֵין לְפָנָיו לֹא עַוְלָה, וְלֹא שִׁכְחָה, וְלֹא מַשּׂוֹא פָנִים, וְלֹא מִקַּח שֹׁחַד; שֶׁהַכֹּל שֶׁלּוֹ. וְדַע, שֶׁהַכֹּל לְפִי הַחֶשְׁבּוֹן.

פירוש לרבי עובדיה ספורנו

ד:כט. הנה סוף הילודים למות וסוף המתים להחיות ולהתחדש מהם נמצאות חדשות, כאמרו „ואל עפרם ישובון, תשלח רוחך יבראון ותחדש פני אדמה״. והנה זה האופן מן המציאות אשר אין לו קיום זולתי בחזרת חלילה היה פועל בטל לגמרי לולי היה המכוון בכל החיים הילודים והמחודשים מהם שיהיו עתידים לידון, שישפוט בם ממציאם כפי מה שישיג מהם מה שכיון בהמציאו אותם או הפכו. והיתה הכוונה בילודים בהכרח שיתבוננו וידעו, וזה כי אמנם פעל הידיעה שנרגיש בהם הוא

SFORNO'S COMMENTARY

4:29

וְהַמֵּתִים לִחְיוֹת . . . לֵידַע לְהוֹדִיעַ וּלְהִוָּדַע שֶׁהוּא אֵל . . . — *The dead will live again . . . that they know, make known, and become aware that He is God . . .* Behold, the "newborn (are destined) to die" and ultimately "the dead will live again," and renewed beings will emerge from them, as it is written: וְאֶל עֲפָרָם יְשׁוּבוּן תְּשַׁלַּח רוּחֲךָ יִבָּרֵאוּן וּתְחַדֵּשׁ פְּנֵי אֲדָמָה, *And to their dust they will return. When You send forth Your breath, they are created and You renew the surface of the earth* (*Psalms* 104:29-30).

This manner of existence, which cannot be preserved unless there is a constantly revolving cycle, would be meaningless unless the purpose of all those born and those renewed is to be judged by their Creator, Who will determine whether or not they have fulfilled the purpose for which they were given existence. Now, the purpose of newborn people must perforce be to contemplate and know [God], for the outcome of knowledge is to appreciate this, which is the most exalted of every possible outcome

NOTES

to writing. At any rate, this verse teaches us that even the laws of Hashem's Torah can be modified under special circumstances. Not so these three weaknesses of man, for his pursuit of honor, lustful appetites, and jealous spirit are very difficult to channel constructively. Although our Sages teach us that jealousy and honor do have their place — jealousy among Torah scholars increases wisdom, and honoring others is commendable — nonetheless, these exceptions do not prevent Rabbi Elazar from issuing a blanket condemnation of these traits, which are so harmful to man's peace of mind and jeopardize his eternal life.

29. *He used to say: The newborn will die; the dead will live again; the living will be judged — in order that they know, make known, and become aware that He is God, He is the Fashioner, He is the Creator, He is the Discerner, He is the Judge, He is the Witness, He is the Plaintiff, He will judge. Blessed is He, before Whom there is no iniquity, no forgetfulness, no favoritism, and no acceptance of bribery, for everything is His. Know that everything is according to the reckoning.*

פירוש לרבי עובדיה ספורנו

הנכבד מכל מיני פעלותם. והכוונה בחזרת חלילה היתה להודיע מציאותו לשפלים מכח תנועת ההויה וההפסד החוזר חלילה, כי היא המחייבת את המתבונן לעלות בחקירתן אל מציאות פועל ראשון והמכוון בדין האלדי בעולם הזה עד שלא יספיק המשפט באלה לחיי עולם הוא כדי להודיע לנשארים. אמנם באמרם לידע, רצוני שכיון הממציא בזה שידעו שהוא אל יכול בתכלית בהכירם יכלתו על הבריאה שאין כמוהו במיני היכולת, כי אמנם בהיות המכוון מהם שידעו הנה זה המין מן הידיעה הוא הנכבד מכל מיני הידיעות. וכשאמרתי להודיע, רצוני שכיון הממציא שבזה ידעו

SFORNO'S COMMENTARY

of knowledge. The purpose of constant return in a cycle is to make known His existence to lowly men, through the constant cycle of existence and deterioration, for this will obligate the one who contemplates to advance through his speculation and study to recognize the existence of a First Cause. The objective of Divine justice in this world, to the extent that justice in the eternal world does not suffice, is to teach this truth to the living.

Now, when I say לֵידַע, "in order that they know," I mean to say that the intent of the Creator is for man to know that He is God and that He is Omnipotent; to recognize His absolute power to control Creation, and to acknowledge that there is none like Him in any realm of the ability to act. For the purpose of all [existence] is that man should realize that this aspect of knowledge is the most exalted of all aspects of knowledge.

And when I said לְהוֹדִיעַ, "to make known," my intention was that He Who is the cause of all existence intended that lowly beings should acknowledge

NOTES

4:29

. . . וְהַמֵּתִים לִחְיוֹת . . . לֵידַע לְהוֹדִיעַ וּלְהִוָּדַע שֶׁהוּא אֵל . . . — *The dead will live again . . . that they know, make known, and become aware that He is God . . .* The verse in *Psalms* 104, quoted by the *Sforno,* is interpreted by *Radak* as alluding to the resurrection of the dead (תְּחִיַּת הַמֵּתִים), when the original physical beings will be renewed and brought back to life. This is proven by the verse, *You send forth Your breath, they are created . . . anew,* bringing back the old, decayed bodies from the grave *to the surface of the earth,* there to be renewed. So our Sages teach us, in Tractate *Sanhedrin* 91a. *Bartenura* and others

ד וְאַל יַבְטִיחֲךָ יִצְרְךָ שֶׁהַשְּׁאוֹל בֵּית מָנוֹס לָךְ –
כט שֶׁעַל כָּרְחֲךָ אַתָּה נוֹצָר; וְעַל כָּרְחֲךָ אַתָּה נוֹלָד;
וְעַל כָּרְחֲךָ אַתָּה חַי; וְעַל כָּרְחֲךָ אַתָּה מֵת; וְעַל
כָּרְחֲךָ אַתָּה עָתִיד לִתֵּן דִּין וְחֶשְׁבּוֹן לִפְנֵי מֶלֶךְ
מַלְכֵי הַמְּלָכִים, הַקָּדוֹשׁ בָּרוּךְ הוּא.

פירוש לרבי עובדיה ספורנו

השפלים שהוא היוצר שסדר טבע מציאות יש מיש בחזרת חלילה בעלותם בחקירתם אל מציאות פועל ראשון מכוין אל תכלית, ומזה יעלו אל הידיעה שאמרנו שהוא אל בורא. ובאמרו להודע, רצוני לומר שיודיע לנשארים שהוא המכוין אל כל מעשיהם ומשגיח, וזה יבינו בעשותו דין גם בעולם הזה, ויבינו כן שהוא דיין בראותם משפטיו בעולם הזה, ושהוא גם כן בעל דין, כי מאחר שיבינו שהוא סדר את כל אלה יתחייב שישמח על העוזר לכוונתו ויקפיד על המנגד אליה ומקלקל אותה. ומכל זה יתחייב שהוא עתיד לדון לחיי עולם, כי אמנם מדת הדין בעולם הזה בלתי שלמה כמבואר מענין צדיק ורע לו רשע וטוב לו, וזה החסרון נמנע בחק האל יתברך שאין

SFORNO'S COMMENTARY

that He is the Creator Who ordered nature (after the initial Creation), in such a manner that what exists evolves from what exists through a continuous cycle, by comprehending through their speculative analysis the existence of a First Cause Who plans His desired conclusion. Thereby they will attain the knowledge of which we spoke: that "He is God, the Creator."

And when I stated לְהִוָּדַע, "[that they] become aware," I mean to say that it should become known to others that God directs and watches over everyone's deeds. This they will understand when God applies the law in this world as well, and from this they will discern that "He is the Witness" Who is aware of all their deeds, whether they be done in private or in public, even when there are no witnesses. It also follows that "He is the Judge," when they observe His justice in this world. And "He is the Plaintiff," for once they understand that He arranged and ordered all this, it follows that He is happy with whoever helps Him to attain His goal, and will hold accountable whoever opposes His intent and disrupts it.

And from all this it follows that "He will judge" in the eternal life, because the attribute of justice in this world is perforce imperfect and incomplete, as

NOTES

agree that our Tanna is speaking of resurrection.

The *Sforno,* however, interprets this verse differently. He is of the opinion that it refers to the recurrent, unceasing cycle of nature, as discussed by the *Rambam* in *Mishneh Torah, Yesodei HaTorah* (4:4), where he states, "All entities are constantly returning to their elemental state in a cycle." The question then is: What is the purpose of man's existence, and of this constant recurrence? He explains that Rabbi Elazar teaches us that each person was created for the purpose of "knowing" God, and living one's life in keeping with his unique mission, as the only living

4
29 *And let not your evil inclination promise you that the grave will be an escape for you — for against your will you were created; against your will you were born; against your will you live; against your will you die, and against your will you are destined to give an account before the King Who rules over kings, the Holy One, Blessed is He.*

פירוש לרבי עובדיה ספורנו

לפניו לא עולה ולא שכחה ולא משוא פנים ההווים באדם מצד התפעלות, ולא יקרא זה אליו יתברך הבלתי משתנה. ולא יקח שחד שאין מצוה מכבה עבירה, והטעם בזה הוא שהכל שלו, ולפיכך כשקיימת איזו מצוה לא נתת לו דבר משלך בזה באופן שיהיה ראוי למחוק כנגד מה שהתחייבת לו בחטאך, שהכל שלו אתה ושלך שלו ולכן היית מחוייב לעשות רצונו. ודע שאף על פי שקיימת מצות רבות ולמדת תורה הרבה ראוי לך להשתדל להוסיף, שהרי הכל בא לפי חשבון וכל מה שתוסיף להטיב תוסיף לנפש הנצחי טוב חיי עולם ואישורם. ואל יבטיחך יצרך שיש בשאול

SFORNO'S COMMENTARY

it is clear from the matter of צַדִּיק וְרַע לוֹ, רָשָׁע וְטוֹב לוֹ, "the righteous facing adversity while the wicked prosper." And this deficiency cannot be according to the statutes of God, Blessed is He, because, "before Him there is no iniquity, no forgetfulness, no favoritism." These failings are found only among man, due to his changeable nature, but never with the Almighty, Who is unchanging.

"He does not accept bribery" — meaning, that the performance of a *mitzvah* cannot cancel a transgression. The reason for this is that "everything is His." Hence, when you perform a *mitzvah*, you give Him nothing that is truly yours, that He should cancel the consequences of your sin, for all is His, "you and all that is yours are His" (see above, 3:8). Therefore, you are obligated to fulfill His will.

Know also that even if you have fulfilled many *mitzvos* and studied much Torah, it is fitting that you attempt to increase both, for "everything is according to the reckoning." Thus, the more good you do, the more you will add goodness and bliss of eternal life to your eternal, immortal soul.

"And let not your evil inclination promise you" that in the grave there is a

NOTES

creature created in the image of God. Regarding this, man will be judged.

The *Sforno* then proceeds to explain the balance of Rabbi Elazar's teaching:

God is all-knowing, and as such, serves as Plaintiff, Witness, and Judge, when man stands before the bar of Heavenly justice. God's judgment is fair, but the reckoning is a demanding one, for justice must be executed. Hence, a person's *mitzvos* cannot cancel out his transgressions, even though he will be rewarded for these *mitzvos.* And let not man be deluded into thinking that death and burial is the last chapter, for every person must give an accounting to the King of kings.

רַבִּי חֲנַנְיָא בֶּן עֲקַשְׁיָא אוֹמֵר: רָצָה הַקָּדוֹשׁ בָּרוּךְ הוּא לְזַכּוֹת אֶת יִשְׂרָאֵל, לְפִיכָךְ הִרְבָּה לָהֶם תּוֹרָה וּמִצְוֹת, שֶׁנֶּאֱמַר: „יהוה חָפֵץ לְמַעַן צִדְקוֹ, יַגְדִּיל תּוֹרָה וְיַאְדִּיר.״

פירוש לרבי עובדיה ספורנו

בית מנוס מכל עונש, כמחשבת האומרים שאין אחר הפסד הגוף השארות שום נושא שיפול בו גמול ועונש, שאם היה זה אמת הנה זה הממציא אשר ראוי שיאהב פעלו אחר שהשתדל להמציאו היה ממציא אותך על אופן מאושר וטוב בחיי שעה, והנה אנו רואים הפך זה, שעל כרחך אתה חי, שהרבה פעמים יקרה לאדם שיהיה

SFORNO'S COMMENTARY

place of refuge from all punishment, as is the belief of those who say that after the demise and deterioration of the body, there is nothing left of man to be rewarded or punished. For if this were true, then the One Who gave man existence, and certainly loves His handiwork, would have granted him existence in such a manner that would be blissful and good in his temporal life. But behold, we see that the opposite is true, for "against your will you live" (עַל כָּרְחֲךָ אַתָּה חַי) — often, man's state is such that he abhors and rejects life, and continues living against his will. On the other hand, it may

Rabbi Chanania ben Akashia says: The Holy One, Blessed is He, wished to confer merit upon Israel; therefore He gave them Torah and mitzvos in abundance, as it is said: "HASHEM desired, for the sake of its [Israel's] righteousness, that the Torah be made great and glorious."

פירוש לרבי עובדיה ספורנו

ענינו באופן שימאס בחייו והוא חי על כרחו, ולפעמים יקרה שיהיו חייו טובים בתכלית האפשר להם ויחפוץ בם האדם מאד ומכל מקום יקרה המות על כרחו, וכן אופן היצירה והלידה אין לאדם בהם בלתי צער וענין רע, ומכל זה יתחייב על כרחך שאתה עתיד ליתן דין וחשבון כי אמנם לא תשלם כוונת הפועל וצדקתו בזולת זה:

SFORNO'S COMMENTARY

happen that one's life is as good as it can possibly be, and one will desire it very much — and yet death will occur against his will (וְעַל כָּרְחֲךָ אַתָּה מֵת). And similarly, the manner of creation and birth is usually accompanied with pain and difficulty.

From all the above it follows that "against your will you are destined to give an account" (וְעַל כָּרְחֲךָ אַתָּה עָתִיד לִתֵּן דִּין וְחֶשְׁבּוֹן), for otherwise the intent of the Doer of Righteousness would not be fulfilled and completed.

פרק ה
Chapter Five

כָּל יִשְׂרָאֵל יֵשׁ לָהֶם חֵלֶק לָעוֹלָם הַבָּא, שֶׁנֶּאֱמַר: „וְעַמֵּךְ כֻּלָּם צַדִּיקִים, לְעוֹלָם יִירְשׁוּ אָרֶץ, נֵצֶר מַטָּעַי, מַעֲשֵׂה יָדַי לְהִתְפָּאֵר.״

All Israel has a share in the World to Come, as it is said: "And your people are all righteous; they shall inherit the land forever; they are the branch of My planting, My handiwork, in which to take pride."

[א] **בַּעֲשָׂרָה** מַאֲמָרוֹת נִבְרָא הָעוֹלָם. וּמַה תַּלְמוּד לוֹמַר? וַהֲלֹא בְמַאֲמָר אֶחָד יָכוֹל לְהִבָּרְאוֹת? אֶלָּא לְהִפָּרַע מִן הָרְשָׁעִים, שֶׁמְּאַבְּדִין אֶת הָעוֹלָם שֶׁנִּבְרָא בַּעֲשָׂרָה מַאֲמָרוֹת, וְלִתֵּן שָׂכָר טוֹב לַצַּדִּיקִים, שֶׁמְּקַיְּמִין אֶת הָעוֹלָם שֶׁנִּבְרָא בַּעֲשָׂרָה מַאֲמָרוֹת.

[ב] **עֲשָׂרָה** דוֹרוֹת מֵאָדָם וְעַד נֹחַ, לְהוֹדִיעַ כַּמָּה אֶרֶךְ אַפַּיִם לְפָנָיו; שֶׁכָּל

פירוש לרבי עובדיה ספורנו

ה:א. הנה בזה הפרק הורה המחבר גודל ענין העיון והמעשה, והביא ראיה על זה ממה שהשתדלה התורה להודיענו שנברא העולם בעשרה מאמרות. כי אמנם לא היתה הכונה ללמד שלא היה הממציא יכול להמציאו באופן אחר, כי הנה כח הבריאה הממציא בלתי נושא ובלתי זמן לא ילאה בהמצאת נושאים רבים מאד כמו שלא ילאה בהמצאת נושא אחד בלבד, מאחר שלא יפול בה תנועה ולא זמן ולא נושא מוכן באופן שבהתרבות הנושאים תפול תלאה, אבל היתה הכונה להודיע שכדי להמציא נמצא כדמותו בצלמו היה בהכרח על צד היותר טוב לעשות כל סדר העשרה

SFORNO'S COMMENTARY

5:1

בַּעֲשָׂרָה מַאֲמָרוֹת נִבְרָא הָעוֹלָם — *With ten utterances the world was created.* In this chapter, the author teaches us the importance of the analytical aspects [of Torah] and their implementation through deeds [see introduction]. He brings proof [to this thesis] from the fact that the Torah tells us that "With ten utterances the world was created."

The purpose of teaching us this is not to say that the Creator could not create the world in any other manner, for the power of creation from nothingness (יֵשׁ מֵאַיִן) beginning without matter, where no movement or time was involved, is unaffected by the number of utterances — there is no added fatigue or weariness engendered by ten statements in comparison to one. The intent, therefore, is to tell us that in order to bring into existence a being [i.e., man] *in His form and image* (*Genesis* 1:26) who would meet the

NOTES

5:1

בַּעֲשָׂרָה מַאֲמָרוֹת נִבְרָא הָעוֹלָם — *With ten utterances the world was created.* The *Tosafos Yom Tov,* in his commentary on this Mishnah, speaks of creation יֵשׁ מֵאַיִן, *ex nihilo* (something from absolute nothingness), as does the *Sforno* in his commentary. However, *Tosafos Yom Tov* uses this concept as proof that Creation could have been accomplished with a single utterance. If, however, there was primordial matter, as some philosophers believed, the nature of that matter may have been such, that it was impossible to create everything with but a single utterance. The *Sforno,* on the other hand, utilizes this concept of יֵשׁ מֵאַיִן to

1. *With ten utterances the world was created. What does this come to teach us? Indeed, could it not have been created with one utterance? This was to exact punishment from the wicked who destroy the world that was created with ten utterances, and to bestow goodly reward upon the righteous who sustain the world that was created by ten utterances.*

2. *There were ten generations from Adam to Noah — to show the degree of His patience; for all*

פירוש לרבי עובדיה ספורנו

מאמרות אשר בהם נתהוו הנמצאות זה מזה, ומזה יתחייב שמי שיעזור לכונתו זאת שהיה מציאותה בכל כך השתדלות יהיה ראוי לשכר טוב אצל הממציא, ומי שיעשה הפך יהיה ראוי לפורענות רב:

ה:ב. ובזה הודיע דרכי טובו למען יאהבהו כל משכיל וישמח לעשות רצונו ועם זה לא יתבלבל בראותו רשע מאריך ברעתו

SFORNO'S COMMENTARY

standard of טוֹב, that which is "good" [the yardstick of all creation], it was perforce necessary to do so through ten progressive utterances through which all of Creation came into existence [culminating with the creation of Adam]. From this, it follows that whoever assists God in reaching this goal, mindful that there was great effort in attaining it, is worthy of significant reward from the Almighty. Conversely, he who prevents the attainment of this goal of perfecting [the world and man] incurs great punishment.

5:2

עֲשָׂרָה דוֹרוֹת . . . וְקִבֵּל שְׂכַר כֻּלָּם — *There were ten generations . . . and He received the reward of them all.* And thus He informed us of His goodness, so that every intelligent person will love Him and rejoice in doing His will, and not be misled or confused when he sees the wicked permitted to continue in

NOTES

explain that since neither matter, or movement, or time existed at the time of Creation, the number of utterances which were used is immaterial. He therefore explains that the reason Hashem used ten utterances to create the world was in order to proceed incrementally from the simple, to the complex, and finally, to the "crown of creation" — i.e., man. This was done to instruct man, and impress upon him, that the end purpose of Creation was to create, here on earth, one being who is fashioned in the Divine Image. This, in turn, teaches the human being his unique, great responsibility, to perfect himself and to imitate Hashem, in keeping with God's intent. How great, therefore, will be man's reward when he fulfills his mission, thereby becoming a partner with Hashem in the work of Creation. Conversely, his punishment will be severe if he thwarts God's plan to attain the goal set for him by God.

5:2

עֲשָׂרָה דוֹרוֹת . . . וְקִבֵּל שְׂכַר כֻּלָּם — *There were ten generations . . . and He received the reward of them all.* All the commentators accept the literal translation of this Mishnah,

ה
ג־ד

הַדּוֹרוֹת הָיוּ מַכְעִיסִין וּבָאִין, עַד שֶׁהֵבִיא עֲלֵיהֶם אֶת מֵי הַמַּבּוּל. עֲשָׂרָה דוֹרוֹת מִנֹּחַ וְעַד אַבְרָהָם, לְהוֹדִיעַ כַּמָּה אֶרֶךְ אַפַּיִם לְפָנָיו; שֶׁכָּל הַדּוֹרוֹת הָיוּ מַכְעִיסִין וּבָאִין, עַד שֶׁבָּא אַבְרָהָם אָבִינוּ וְקִבֵּל שְׂכַר כֻּלָּם.

[ג] **עֲשָׂרָה** נִסְיוֹנוֹת נִתְנַסָּה אַבְרָהָם אָבִינוּ וְעָמַד בְּכֻלָּם, לְהוֹדִיעַ כַּמָּה חִבָּתוֹ שֶׁל אַבְרָהָם אָבִינוּ.

[ד] **עֲשָׂרָה** נִסִּים נַעֲשׂוּ לַאֲבוֹתֵינוּ בְּמִצְרַיִם וַעֲשָׂרָה עַל הַיָּם. עֶשֶׂר מַכּוֹת

פירוש לרבי עובדיה ספורנו

כי זה מצד דרכי טובו בארך אפים: וקבל הוא יתברך שכר ותועלת נחת רוח לפניו כל כך שאלו היה כל אחד מהדורות עושה חלק מעשרה מאותו נחת רוח לא היה אובד. וקרא זה הנחת רוח שכר אליו יתברך, על דרך „כי חלק יי עמו" ועל דרך „הבו לי שכרי, וישקלו את שכרי שלשים כסף" שבארו ז"ל על צדיקי הדור:

SFORNO'S COMMENTARY

their wicked ways, for this is allowed by God because of His kindness and forbearance.

The expression, "and received the reward of them all," refers to the Almighty's spiritual contentment (נַחַת רוּחַ). Had each of these generations [from Noah to Abraham] but given one-tenth of נַחַת [contentment to God], they would not have been lost.

This נַחַת רוּחַ (spiritual contentment) is regarded as God's "reward," as it were, by our Tanna, as we find in the verse, כִּי חֵלֶק ה׳ עַמּוֹ, *For HASHEM's portion is His people* (*Deuteronomy* 32:9). Similarly, the verse says, הָבוּ שְׂכָרִי . . . וַיִּשְׁקְלוּ אֶת שְׂכָרִי שְׁלֹשִׁים כָּסֶף, *Give me my hire . . . so they weighed for my hire thirty pieces of silver* (*Zechariah* 11:12), which our Sages say refers to the righteous ones of that generation (*Chullin* 92a).

NOTES

that the phrase, "and received the reward of all," refers to Abraham. The *Sforno,* however, asserts that וְקִבֵּל שְׂכַר refers to God! Building his thesis on verses in *Deuteronomy, Zechariah,* and the Talmud (*Mesechta Chullin* 92a), he explains that God's שָׂכָר, "hire" or "reward," are the righteous men in each generation. According to the Midrash, Abraham had been promised by the Almighty that each generation would have at least thirty *tzaddikim.*

This assurance is alluded to in the verse כֹּה יִהְיֶה זַרְעֶךָ, *so shall your offspring be* (*Genesis* 15:5) — the Hebrew letters of יִהְיֶה have a numerical value of thirty. The thirty pieces of silver mentioned in the prophecy

those generations angered Him increasingly, until He brought upon them the waters of the Flood. There were ten generations from Noah to Abraham — to show the degree of His patience; for all those generations angered Him increasingly, until our forefather Abraham came, and He received the reward of them all.

3. *Our forefather Abraham was tested with ten trials, and he withstood them all — to show the degree of our forefather Abraham's love for God.*

4. *Ten miracles were performed for our ancestors in Egypt and ten at the Sea. Ten plagues did the*

פירוש לרבי עובדיה ספורנו

ה:ג. להודיע כמה חבב את יוצרו להרבות לקרוא בשמו ולהכניס רבים תחת כנפיו אף על פי שהיה מרובה בנסיונות, ושזה ראוי שיעשו כל בני בריתו, כאמרו „הביטו אל אברהם אביכם":

ה:ד. וכנגד עשרה נסיונות שעמד בהם

SFORNO'S COMMENTARY

5:3

עֲשָׂרָה נִסְיוֹנוֹת . . . חִבָּתוֹ שֶׁל אַבְרָהָם — . . .*Ten trials . . . to show the degree of Abraham's love.* [Abraham] demonstrated the degree of his love for his Creator by constantly proclaiming His Name and bringing many under His wings even though he was tested with many trials. This is to teach his children that they should do likewise, as it is written, הַבִּיטוּ אֶל אַבְרָהָם אֲבִיכֶם, *Look to Abraham your father* (*Isaiah* 51:2).

5:4

עֲשָׂרָה נִסִּים . . . לַאֲבוֹתֵינוּ . . . עֲשָׂרָה נִסְיוֹנוֹת נִסּוּ . . . אֶת הקב״ה — *Ten miracles . . . for our ancestors . . . with ten trials did test . . . the Holy One, Blessed is He.* As recompense for Abraham's ability to withstand the ten trials, the Almighty,

NOTES

of Zechariah are a metaphor for these thirty righteous men, as the Talmud explains. God's only reward — His שָׂכָר — is afforded Him by the pious righteous ones in each generation, who represent His "portion," as the Children of Israel are called in *Deuteronomy* 32:9. Since the ten generations from Noah to Abraham failed to produce such men, God, as it were, was deprived of His hire until Abraham came and compensated for all those generations. God then received His reward through this righteous one, namely our father Abraham, who was equal to all the righteous ones of these generations.

5:3-4

עֲשָׂרָה נִסְיוֹנוֹת . . . אַבְרָהָם . . . עֲשָׂרָה נִסִּים . . . לַאֲבוֹתֵינוּ . . . עֲשָׂרָה נִסְיוֹנוֹת נִסּוּ . . . אֶת הקב״ה — *Abraham . . . (tested) with ten trials . . . ten miracles . . . for our ancestors . . .. with ten trials did . . . test the Holy One, Blessed is He.* The *Sforno* skillfully links these two Mishnahs together. God was most generous in His reward to Abraham for withstanding the

ה הֵבִיא הַקָּדוֹשׁ בָּרוּךְ הוּא עַל הַמִּצְרִים בְּמִצְרַיִם
ה וְעֶשֶׂר עַל הַיָּם. עֲשָׂרָה נִסְיוֹנוֹת נִסּוּ אֲבוֹתֵינוּ אֶת
הַקָּדוֹשׁ בָּרוּךְ הוּא בַּמִּדְבָּר, שֶׁנֶּאֱמַר: „וַיְנַסּוּ אֹתִי זֶה
עֶשֶׂר פְּעָמִים, וְלֹא שָׁמְעוּ בְּקוֹלִי.״

[ה] **עֲשָׂרָה** נִסִּים נַעֲשׂוּ לַאֲבוֹתֵינוּ בְּבֵית הַמִּקְדָּשׁ: לֹא הִפִּילָה אִשָּׁה מֵרֵיחַ בְּשַׂר הַקֹּדֶשׁ; וְלֹא הִסְרִיחַ בְּשַׂר הַקֹּדֶשׁ מֵעוֹלָם; וְלֹא נִרְאָה זְבוּב בְּבֵית הַמִּטְבְּחַיִם; וְלֹא אִירַע קֶרִי לְכֹהֵן גָּדוֹל בְּיוֹם הַכִּפּוּרִים; וְלֹא כִבּוּ הַגְּשָׁמִים אֵשׁ שֶׁל עֲצֵי הַמַּעֲרָכָה; וְלֹא נִצְּחָה הָרוּחַ אֶת עַמּוּד הֶעָשָׁן; וְלֹא נִמְצָא פְסוּל בָּעֹמֶר, וּבִשְׁתֵּי הַלֶּחֶם, וּבְלֶחֶם הַפָּנִים; עוֹמְדִים צְפוּפִים, וּמִשְׁתַּחֲוִים רְוָחִים; וְלֹא הִזִּיק נָחָשׁ וְעַקְרָב בִּירוּשָׁלַיִם מֵעוֹלָם; וְלֹא אָמַר אָדָם לַחֲבֵרוֹ: „צַר לִי הַמָּקוֹם שֶׁאָלִין בִּירוּשָׁלַיִם.״

פירוש לרבי עובדיה ספורנו

אברהם אבינו עשה האל יתברך חסד עם בניו בעשרה נסים פעמים, ובהפך זה עשו כפויי טובה בנסותם ובהצותם על יי. וכל אלה ספרה תורת קדשו ללמד אורח חיים למעלה למשכיל ולמען יסור משאול מטה:

SFORNO'S COMMENTARY

Blessed is He, showed kindness to his children by performing ten miracles on their behalf on two different occasions [in Egypt, and at the Sea of Reeds]. Conversely, they, the Children of Israel, demonstrated their ingratitude by testing and angering God. All this is told to us in His holy Torah in order to teach us "the way of life for the wise, which leads upward" and to deter one מִשְּׁאוֹל מָטָּה, *from She'ol [the deep] which is beneath* (*Proverbs* 15:24).

5:5

עֲשָׂרָה נִסִּים נַעֲשׂוּ לַאֲבוֹתֵינוּ בְּבֵית הַמִּקְדָּשׁ — *Ten miracles were performed for our*

NOTES

difficult trials he faced, for while Abraham underwent only ten trials, God performed twenty miracles on behalf of his descendants — ten in Egypt, and ten at the Sea of Reeds. Unfortunately, the Children of Israel repayed Him with ingratitude and tested the Almighty ten times in the Wilderness.

The phraseology, used by the *Sforno* at the conclusion of his commentary on Mishnah 4, is a paraphrase of the verse in *Proverbs* 15:24, where King Solomon teaches us that there are two paths which man can travel in his lifetime: One is the path of eternal life, of elevating the soul and leading it back to its source. The second is the path which leads to the nether world.

Holy One, Blessed is He, bring upon the Egyptians in Egypt and ten at the Sea. With ten trials did our ancestors test the Holy One, Blessed is He, in the Wilderness, as it is said: "They have tested Me these ten times and did not heed My voice."

5. *Ten miracles were performed for our ancestors in the Holy Temple: No woman miscarried because of the aroma of the sacrificial meat; the sacrificial meat never became putrid; no fly was seen in the place where the meat was butchered; no seminal emission occurred to the High Priest on Yom Kippur; the rains did not extinguish the fire on the Altar-pyre; the wind did not disperse the vertical column of smoke from the Altar; no disqualification was found in the Omer, or in the Two Loaves, or in the Showbread; the people stood crowded together, yet prostrated themselves in ample space; neither serpent nor scorpion ever caused injury in Jerusalem; nor did any man say to his fellow, "The space is insufficient for me to stay overnight in Jerusalem."*

פירוש לרבי עובדיה ספורנו

ה:ה. הנה אלה נסים נעשו גם במקדש שני אף על פי שלא היה ענין ישראל אז בכל אופן שלם ולבן לא נכון עמו, והגיד שעם כל זה לא חדל החסד האלהי מעשות עמהם נסים מנגדים לטבע בעיר קדשו בעוד בית מקדשו בתוכה:

SFORNO'S COMMENTARY

ancestors in the Holy Temple. Behold, these miracles were performed during the Second Temple period as well, even though the status of Israel was imperfect at that time, וְלִבָּם לֹא נָכוֹן עִמּוֹ, *and their heart was not constant with Him* (*Psalms* 78:37). The Tanna tells us that, nevertheless, God's kindness was not removed from us — as long as His holy Temple stood in His holy city, He continued to perform miracles which defied the laws of nature.

NOTES

5:5

עֲשָׂרָה נִסִּים נַעֲשׂוּ לַאֲבוֹתֵינוּ בְּבֵית הַמִּקְדָּשׁ — *Ten miracles were performed for our ancestors in the Holy Temple.* The *Sforno,* in his commentary on *Psalms* (78:37) which he quotes here, says that sometimes people profess repentance for having committed a sin, but they do not make a sincere resolution to never again repeat it. He states that this was true of the Jewish people during the period of the Second Temple. As a consequence, they did not merit to have the Holy Ark with its cover and *cherubim,* the *Urim V'Tumim,* the holy spirit, or the heavenly fire which would descend upon the altar, as we are told in *Yoma* (21b). Nonetheless, the ten miracles enumerated in this Mishnah *did* take place in that era, a fact which demonstrates the loving kindness of Hashem, as well as the power of the Holy Temple in the Holy City, to suspend the laws of nature.

[ו] **עֲשָׂרָה** דְבָרִים נִבְרְאוּ בְּעֶרֶב שַׁבָּת בֵּין הַשְּׁמָשׁוֹת, וְאֵלּוּ הֵן; פִּי הָאָרֶץ, וּפִי הַבְּאֵר, פִּי הָאָתוֹן, וְהַקֶּשֶׁת, וְהַמָּן, וְהַמַּטֶּה, וְהַשָּׁמִיר, הַכְּתָב, וְהַמִּכְתָּב, וְהַלּוּחוֹת. וְיֵשׁ אוֹמְרִים: אַף הַמַּזִּיקִין, וּקְבוּרָתוֹ שֶׁל מֹשֶׁה, וְאֵילוֹ שֶׁל אַבְרָהָם אָבִינוּ. וְיֵשׁ אוֹמְרִים; אַף צְבַת בִּצְבַת עֲשׂוּיָה.

[ז] **שִׁבְעָה** דְבָרִים בְּגֹלֶם, וְשִׁבְעָה בְּחָכָם.

פירוש לרבי עובדיה ספורנו

ה:ו. אמר שאלו נבראו בין השמשות, כי אמנם אף על פי שעשה האל יתברך אותות ומופתים רבים משנים את טבעי הדברים כמו נגעי מצרים ונסי ים סוף וזולתם, מכל מקום לא חדש שום נמצא אחרי ששת ימי בראשית, כאמרו „ויכל אלקים ביום השביעי. . . וישבות", וכאמרו „אין כל חדש תחת השמש". ולכן על אלה העשרה שהם נמצאות שלא נזכרו במעשה בראשית אמר שחודשו אז בלי ספק, והטעם מפני מה לא נזכרו עם שאר מעשה בראשית הוא מפני שלא היה אפשר להגיד לנו זמן חדושם, כי

SFORNO'S COMMENTARY

5:6

עֲשָׂרָה דְבָרִים נִבְרְאוּ בְּעֶרֶב שַׁבָּת בֵּין הַשְּׁמָשׁוֹת — *Ten things were created on Sabbath eve, at twilight.* The Tanna tells us that these ten phenomena were created at twilight, for although God, Blessed is He, does many signs and wonders, causing changes in the nature of things, such as the plagues in Egypt, the miracles at the Sea of Reeds, and other similar supernatural acts, nonetheless, He did not create any new species or natural phenomena after the six days of Creation, as it says, וַיְכַל אֱלֹהִים בַּיּוֹם הַשְּׁבִיעִי . . . וַיִּשְׁבֹּת, *On the seventh day God completed His work . . . and He abstained* (*Genesis* 2:2), and as the verse says, וְאֵין כָּל חָדָשׁ תַּחַת הַשָּׁמֶשׁ, *There is nothing new under the sun* (*Ecclesiastes* 1:9).

Therefore, these ten things, which existed, and yet are not recorded in the acts of Creation, doubtless were called into being at that time [i.e., at twilight on Sabbath eve, at the close of Creation]. Now, the reason they are not mentioned in the story of Creation with all other things is because they were

NOTES

5:6

עֲשָׂרָה דְבָרִים נִבְרְאוּ בְּעֶרֶב שַׁבָּת בֵּין הַשְּׁמָשׁוֹת — *Ten things were created on Sabbath eve, at twilight.* Miracles do occur, as the Tanna tells us in Mishnahs 4 and 5, but the ten things listed in this Mishnah are not supernatural, for they are part of God's Creation. Why, then, are they not included in the story of Creation, as recorded in *Parashas Bereishis*?

The *Sforno* answers that the Torah only records what was created on a specific day. Hence, since these ten things came into being at twilight, an indistinct hour between day and night, the Torah chooses not to record them.

6. *Ten things were created on Sabbath eve, at twilight. They are: The mouth of the earth; the mouth of the well; the mouth of the donkey; the rainbow [which was Noah's sign that there would be no future floods]; the manna; the staff; the shamir worm; the script; the inscription; and the Tablets. Some say also destructive spirits, Moses' grave, and the ram of our forefather Abraham. And some say also tongs, which are made with tongs.*

7. *Seven traits characterize an uncultivated person and seven a learned one. A learned person does*

פירוש לרבי עובדיה ספורנו

אמנם היה בזמן אמצעי בין שני ימים בלתי ראוי להתיחס אל שום אחר מהם:

ה:ז. אחר שהגיד גודל העיון והמעשה וחין ערכו לפני האל יתברך, ודרכי טובו יתברך ודרכי מורדי אור ודרכי עבדיו אשר מצאו חן לפניו בעיון במעשה – הזהיר על דברים מועילים בהשגת החלק העיוני, והם דרכי החכם ולהשמר מדרכי הגולם המונעים

SFORNO'S COMMENTARY

not created on a specific day, for it occurred at a time between two days [i.e., twilight], and therefore could not be attributed to any particular day.

5:7

שִׁבְעָה דְבָרִים בְּגֹלֶם, וְשִׁבְעָה בְּחָכָם — *Seven traits characterize an uncultivated person and seven a learned one.* After teaching us the importance of the theoretical part of Torah, and of its practical part as well, [see Mishnah 1 in this chapter], and their "impressive worth" [a term based on *Job* 41:5] to God, Blessed is He, as well as His ways of goodness; also after telling us the conduct of those who rebelled against the light (of God), and conversely the ways of His servants who pursue the analytical and practical aspects of Torah, thereby finding favor in His eyes — after all this — the Tanna cautions us regarding those things which are useful in comprehending the theoretical part of Torah, these being the ways of the wise person. He then urges us not to follow the ways of the uncultivated person (גֹּלֶם) for his ways

NOTES

5:7

שִׁבְעָה דְבָרִים בְּגֹלֶם, וְשִׁבְעָה בְּחָכָם — *Seven traits characterize an uncultivated person and seven a learned one.* The expression, "Those who rebel against the light of God," refers to the ten generations from Adam to Noah and from Noah to Abraham, who angered the Almighty through their behavior and evil deeds. This was also true of the Children of Israel in the Wilderness, who tested God ten times. The term "light" used by the *Sforno* is one used frequently in *Tanach* and in our *tefillah* (prayers) as well, as a descriptive word for the illumination and radiance emanating from Hashem. It is also a metaphor for Torah. Some examples

ה חָכָם אֵינוֹ מְדַבֵּר לִפְנֵי מִי שֶׁגָּדוֹל מִמֶּנּוּ בְּחָכְמָה
ז וּבְמִנְיָן; וְאֵינוֹ נִכְנָס לְתוֹךְ דִּבְרֵי חֲבֵרוֹ; וְאֵינוֹ נִבְהָל

פירוש לרבי עובדיה ספורנו

מהשיג המכוון. והתחיל במספר דרכי הגולם כי אותם או רובם הורה משה רבינו בספר איוב המיוחס לו, ומרוע ענינם נודע טוב הפכם. אמנם ביאר דרכי החכם הנכבדים, ומחלופם יתבאר הפכם. ואמר, כי מדרכי החכם הוא שאינו מדבר לפני מי שגדול ממנו בחכמה, כענין אליהוא שלא דבר בפני זקנים ממנו בחשבו שהיו גדולים ממנו בחכמה, כאמרו „אמרתי ימים ידברו ורב שנים יודיעו חכמה״, „בישישים חכמה״

SFORNO'S COMMENTARY

deter a person from attaining the intended goal of mankind.

Now, the Tanna begins by enumerating the ways of the *golem*, for these are ways taught to us by our teacher Moses in the Book of *Job,* which is attributed to him by our Sages [*Bava Basra* 14b]. And from these negative, wicked character traits, one can infer the virtue of their opposites. However, he begins by explaining the noble ways of the wise person, and from these explanations, one can understand the opposite traits [which characterize the *golem*].

(1) He says, "A learned person does not begin speaking before one who is greater than he in wisdom," as we find in the case of Elihu, who did not speak before those older than him, for he believed that they were superior to him in wisdom, as it is written: אָמַרְתִּי יָמִים יְדַבֵּרוּ וְרֹב שָׁנִים יֹדִיעוּ חָכְמָה, *I had thought, "Let days have their say, let years dispense wisdom"* (*Job* 32:7), and בִּישִׁישִׁים חָכְמָה, *Wisdom resides with the elderly* (ibid. 12:12).

NOTES

are: בְּאוֹרְךָ נִרְאֶה אוֹר, *By Your light shall we see light* (*Psalms* 36:10), and כִּי נֵר מִצְוָה וְתוֹרָה אוֹר, *for the mitzvah is a lamp and Torah is light* (*Proverbs* 6:23).

In the *Amidah* we read, בָּרְכֵנוּ . . . בְּאוֹר פָּנֶיךָ, *Bless us .. with the light of Your countenance.* Therefore, those who turn away from God and violate His commandments are characterized as "rebels against light." It is interesting to note that the *Sforno,* in his commentary on the verse in *Psalms* cited above (36:10), interprets the words "by Your light shall we see light" as a prayer uttered by David, when Absalom his son rebelled against him, beseeching Hashem that the people should understand his rebellion "in the light of God," and not be misled. The concept of rebellion is carried over here as well by the *Sforno.*

The sequence and order of this Mishnah present an obvious difficulty. Since the Tanna begins with the seven traits which characterize a *golem* (an uncultivated person), why then does he proceed to enumerate first the character traits of a wise man, rather than those of the *golem*? The *Sforno* resolves this discrepancy by linking the deficient character traits of the *golem* to Job's friends. Since the author of the Book of *Job* was Moses, according to our Sages, it would therefore be proper to begin our Mishnah with the characteristics of the *golem.* Nonetheless, the Tanna prefers to present the positive character traits found in the conduct and behavior of the wise man first, and by inference the student will be able to reach the logical conclusion that the opposite of these traits characterize the *golem.*

The Book of *Job* (*Iyov*) relates the story of a righteous man who is sorely afflicted from Heaven through the death of his

5 7 *not begin speaking before one who is greater than he in wisdom or in years; he does not interrupt the words of his fellow; he does not answer impetuously;*

פירוש לרבי עובדיה ספורנו

וגומר. ואינו נכנס לתוך דברי חברו, כאמרו ,,ואליהוא חכה את איוב בדברים", על הפך רעיו שאמר להם איוב ,,שאוני ואנכי אדבר ואחר דברי תלעיג". ואינו נבהל להשיב בטרם ישמע אל נכון דעת חבירו, על הפך בלדד כאמרו ,,האל יעות משפט", והשיבו איוב שלא הבין כוונתו, באמרו ,,אמנם ידעתי כי כן ומה יצדק אנוש עם אל".

SFORNO'S COMMENTARY

(2) "He does not interrupt the words of his fellow," as it is written, וֶאֱלִיהוּ חִכָּה אֶת אִיּוֹב בִּדְבָרִים, *Elihu bided his time to address Job* (Job 32:14), as opposed to the other friends, to whom Job said, שָׂאוּנִי וְאָנֹכִי אֲדַבֵּר וְאַחַר דַּבְּרִי תַלְעִיג, *Bear with me, that I might speak; after I have had my say, you may deride me* (ibid. 21:3).

(3) "He does not answer impetuously" — i.e., he does not answer before he hears the opinion of his friend, which is the opposite of the behavior of Bildad, who said, הַאֵל יְעַוֵּת מִשְׁפָּט, *Would God pervert justice?* (ibid. 8:3); but Job responds that he has been misunderstood, as he says, אָמְנָם יָדַעְתִּי כִּי כֵן וּמַה יִּצְדַּק אֱנוֹשׁ עִם אֵל, *Truly, I know that it is so; but how can man expect to best God?* (ibid. 9:2).

NOTES

children, the loss of his possessions, and personal pain and suffering. Four friends come to comfort him and share in his troubles. They discuss the ramifications of his tragic fate and attempt to explain why all this has happened to him. Job, in turn, rejects most of their arguments and admonitions. According to one opinion in the Talmud, this book was authored by Moses.

The *Sforno,* in a most unique approach, suggests that the character traits of the wise man and the *golem,* described in our Mishnah, are reflected in the arguments and statements of Job's four friends, i.e., Eliphaz, Bildad, Tzophar, and Elihu. He draws parallels from their statements, as well as from some of Job's responses and Hashem's rebuke, to a number of the traits enumerated in our Mishnah. He carefully matches verses in the Book of *Job* with the descriptive phrases of our Mishnah, depicting the wise man and the uncultivated clod.

In his opinion, the first two statements in our Mishnah — "He does not begin speaking before one who is greater than he," and, "he does not interrupt the words of his fellow" — are reflected in the words of Elihu. The verses he cites as proof are: יָמִים יְדַבֵּרוּ, *Let days have their say* (32:7), and וֶאֱלִיהוּ חִכָּה, *and Elihu bided his time* (32:4). Regarding this second trait, Job's other friends prove themselves to be unwise, the proof being from the need of Job to say to them, *"Bear with me,"* since they have demonstrated a lack of patience in listening to him, and are totally wrapped up in their own opinions. Hence, they are guilty of interrupting their friend even as he speaks to them.

The third trait of the wise man, which is, "He does not answer impetuously," is demonstrated in the reverse by Bildad, when he self-confidently judges and chides Job, saying, *"Would God pervert justice?"* (8:3). This, despite the fact that Job never made such an accusation against the Almighty! Indeed, Job protests that he never made such a claim, stating: יָדַעְתִּי כִּי כֵן וּמַה יִּצְדַּק אֱנוֹשׁ עִם אֵל, *I know that it is so; but how can man expect to best God?* (9:2).

ה לְהָשִׁיב; שׁוֹאֵל כְּעִנְיָן, וּמֵשִׁיב כַּהֲלָכָה; וְאוֹמֵר עַל
ח רִאשׁוֹן רִאשׁוֹן, וְעַל אַחֲרוֹן אַחֲרוֹן; וְעַל מַה שֶׁלֹּא
שָׁמַע אוֹמֵר: „לֹא שָׁמַעְתִּי"; וּמוֹדֶה עַל הָאֱמֶת.
וְחִלּוּפֵיהֶן בְּגֹלֶם.

[ח] **שִׁבְעָה** מִינֵי פֻרְעָנִיּוֹת בָּאִין לָעוֹלָם עַל
שִׁבְעָה גוּפֵי עֲבֵרָה: מִקְּצָתָן

פירוש לרבי עובדיה ספורנו

שואל כענין, על הפך אליפז באמרו „זכור נא מי הוא נקי אבד", שהשיבו איוב ואמר „חטאתי מה אפעל לך נוצר האדם, ומה לא תשא פשעי", שהיה ראוי שתספיק התשובה להיות נקי. ומשיב כהלכה, הפך מה שעשו שלשת רעי איוב שתפש עליהם האל יתברך באמרו „כי לא דברתם אלי נכונה". ומשיב על ראשון ראשון, כענין אליהוא באמרו „הנה אימתי לא תבעתך ... „ אך אמרת באזני ... זך אני בלי פשע

SFORNO'S COMMENTARY

(4) "He questions with relevance to the subject," as opposed to Eliphaz, who said, זְכָר נָא מִי הוּא נָקִי אָבָד, *Do recall, I beg you: Who is innocent who was ever lost* (*Job* 4:7), to which Job responds, ... חָטָאתִי, מָה אֶפְעַל לָךְ, נֹצֵר הָאָדָם, וּמֶה לֹא תִשָּׂא פִשְׁעִי, *I have sinned, can I do ought to You, Watcher of man . . . How is it that You cannot forgive my sin?* (ibid. 7:20-21). Meaning, that it would be fitting that my repentance should be sufficient to cleanse me.

(5) "And he replies accurately," as opposed to the conduct of Job's three companions, who were rebuked by God, the Blessed One, as He states, כִּי לֹא דִבַּרְתֶּם אֵלַי נְכוֹנָה, *For you did not speak appropriately in your defense of Me* (ibid. 42:7). He also "discusses first things first," as did Elihu, who said: הִנֵּה אֵימָתִי לֹא תְבַעֲתֶךָּ . . . אַךְ אָמַרְתָּ בְאָזְנָי . . . זַךְ אֲנִי בְּלִי פָשַׁע . . . הֵן תְּנוּאוֹת עָלַי יִמְצָא, *See, no fear of me need terrorize you . . . but you spoke to my ears . . . I am*

NOTES

As for the trait of, "He questions with relevance to the subject and he replies accurately," the *Sforno* attributes the opposite of this characteristic to Eliphaz, who states, *Who is innocent who was ever lost?*" (4:7), implying that Job is no innocent. This rhetorical question, however, is inappropriate and irrelevant, for as Job says in his refutation of this statement, "True, I have sinned," but does God not accept repentance and forgive all sinners? Why, then, does He not forgive me? Hence, your question is irrelevant, since I do not claim to be innocent. Rather, my claim is that I have repented.

The second part of this trait, וּמֵשִׁיב כַּהֲלָכָה, ". . . and replies accurately," is one that all three have violated, for God ultimately tells them, "You did not speak appropriately." Hence their answers were not accurate, which is called "not in keeping with *halachah,*" and thus is characteristic of a *golem,* not a *chacham.*

Another character trait of the wise man is, "He discusses first things first, and last things last." The *Sforno* submits that Elihu followed this advice, and when he spoke to Job, he carefully reviewed what Job had to say, listed his complaints succinctly and clearly, and then proceeded to answer them one by one, in proper order.

The trait mentioned in the Mishnah regarding a wise man, that "About something

5
8 *he questions with relevance to the subject and he replies accurately; he discusses first things first and last things last; about something he has not heard he says, "I have not heard"; and he acknowledges the truth. And the reverse of these characterize an uncultivated person.*

8. *Seven kinds of punishment come to the world for seven kinds of transgressions. (a) If some*

פירוש לרבי עובדיה ספורנו

... הן תנואות עלי ימצא" כולי. ועל מה שלא שמע אומר לא שמעתי, על הפך צופר באמרו „מי יתן אלוה דבר ויגד לך תעלומות חכמה". ומודה על האמת, על הפך מה שעשו שלשתן כאמרו „ובשלשת רעיו חרה אפו על אשר לא מצאו מענה וירשיעו את איוב":

ה:ח. הזכיר שבעה מיני פורעניות, והם –

SFORNO'S COMMENTARY

blameless without iniquity . . . behold, He seeks to find pretexts against me (*Job* 33:7-10).

(6) "About something he has not heard, he says, 'I have not heard,' " as opposed to Tzophar, who said, מִי יִתֵּן אֱלוֹהַּ דַּבֵּר . . . וְיַגֶּד לְךָ תַּעֲלֻמוֹת חָכְמָה, *Would that God would speak . . . and inform you of the hidden recesses of wisdom* (ibid., 11:5-6).

(7) "And he acknowledges the truth," as opposed to all three of Job's friends, as it is written, וּבִשְׁלֹשֶׁת רֵעָיו חָרָה אַפּוֹ, עַל אֲשֶׁר לֹא מָצְאוּ מַעֲנֶה, וַיַּרְשִׁיעוּ אֶת אִיּוֹב, *And against his three friends, his anger flared, because they were unable to find an appropriate answer, and they pronounced Job guilty* (ibid. 32:3).

5:8

שִׁבְעָה מִינֵי פֻרְעָנִיּוֹת בָּאִין לָעוֹלָם עַל שִׁבְעָה גוּפֵי עֲבֵרָה — *Seven kinds of punishment come to the world for seven kinds of transgressions.* The Tanna lists seven

NOTES

he has not heard, he says, 'I have not heard,' " is violated by Tzophar when he says, *"Would that God would speak . . . and inform you of the hidden recesses of wisdom"* (11:5-6). He is presuming that if God would but speak to Job, He would reveal the reason for his suffering. But how does Tzophar know this? He would be wise to admit that he has no knowledge of what God would say, even were He to speak to Job. In this manner, Tzophar would have demonstrated the wise trait of saying, "I have not heard."

The last trait mentioned by the Tanna, which marks the wise man, is "He acknowledges the truth." Elihu is angered by the fact that the three friends were unable to find answers to explain Job's plight, and yet they pronounced him guilty. They should have at least admitted that they did not have an answer, and acknowledge that they were wrong in judging him to be a wicked man. Had they done so, they would have met the standard of the seventh trait of the *chacham.* The *Sforno* skillfully interprets the teachings of our Tanna, making everything more relevant and understandable by linking the verses in the Book of *Job* to the words of our Mishnah.

5:8

שִׁבְעָה מִינֵי פֻּרְעָנִיּוֹת בָּאִין לָעוֹלָם עַל שִׁבְעָה גוּפֵי עֲבֵרָה — *Seven kinds of punishment*

ה מְעַשְּׂרִין וּמִקְצָתָן אֵינָן מְעַשְּׂרִין, רָעָב שֶׁל בַּצֹּרֶת
ח בָּא, מִקְצָתָן רְעֵבִים וּמִקְצָתָן שְׂבֵעִים; גָּמְרוּ שֶׁלֹּא
לְעַשֵּׂר, רָעָב שֶׁל מְהוּמָה וְשֶׁל בַּצֹּרֶת בָּא; וְשֶׁלֹּא
לִטֹּל אֶת הַחַלָּה, רָעָב שֶׁל כְּלָיָה בָּא; דֶּבֶר בָּא
לָעוֹלָם – עַל מִיתוֹת הָאֲמוּרוֹת בַּתּוֹרָה שֶׁלֹּא
נִמְסְרוּ לְבֵית דִּין, וְעַל פֵּרוֹת שְׁבִיעִית; חֶרֶב בָּאָה
לָעוֹלָם – עַל עִנּוּי הַדִּין, וְעַל עִוּוּת הַדִּין, וְעַל
הַמּוֹרִים בַּתּוֹרָה שֶׁלֹּא כַהֲלָכָה; חַיָּה רָעָה בָּאָה
לָעוֹלָם – עַל שְׁבוּעַת שָׁוְא, וְעַל חִלּוּל הַשֵּׁם;

פירוש לרבי עובדיה ספורנו

שלשה מיני רעב, דבר, וחרב, חיה רעה, וגלות. ושבעה גופי עבירה, והן – החטא במעשר, והחטא בדין, והחטא בחלול השם, והחטא בעבודה זרה, והחטא בגלוי עריות, והחטא בשפיכות דמים, והחטא בשמטת הארץ. ואמר שעל החטא במעשרות כפי רובו ומעוטו יהיו אחד משלשה מיני רעב, על הפך ,,הביאו את כל המעשר . . . והריקותי לכם ברכה עד בלי די'', ושעל חטא בהסיר היכולת מבית דין,

SFORNO'S COMMENTARY

kinds of punishment, which fall into three categories: (1) famine; (2) pestilence and the sword of war; (3) wild beasts and exile. He also mentions seven kinds of transgressions, and these are: (1) sins associated with tithes; (2) sins associated with law and justice; (3) the sin of desecrating God's Name; (4) the sin of idolatry; (5) the sin of immorality; (6) the sin of bloodshed; (7) sins related to the Sabbatical year.

He teaches us that for the transgression in the area of "tithes," depending upon its degree, the punishment will be one of three kinds of famine, the reverse of what the Almighty promises when one tithes properly, which is great blessing, as it is written, הָבִיאוּ אֶת כָּל הַמַּעֲשֵׂר . . . וַהֲרִיקֹתִי לָכֶם בְּרָכָה עַד בְּלִי דָי, *Bring all the tithes . . . and I will pour out for you blessing immeasurable* (*Malachi* 3:10).

For the sin of depriving the court of the power to dispense justice — which

NOTES

come to the world for seven kinds of transgressions. The *Sforno* separates the punishments listed by the Tanna into three major categories, and then proceeds to explain how these punishments fit the seven transgressions enumerated in this Mishnah.

Tithing evokes God's heavenly blessings of well-being for Israel. Hence, the failure to tithe brings in its wake various kinds and degrees of famine, three of which are enumerated by the Tanna.

A just society enjoys God's protection from pestilence and the sword, but the erosion of the legal system — i.e., through intimidation of judges, miscarriage of justice, and justice deferred — results in man's vulnerability, allowing pestilence and the sword to descend upon the community. Since the punishment fits the

5 *people tithe and others do not, a famine caused by lack of*
8 *rain ensues, some go hungry and others are satisfied; (b) if all decided not to tithe, general famine caused by both armed bands and drought ensues; and (c) [if they also decided] not to separate the challah, a famine caused by destructive drought ensues; (d) pestilence comes to the world for the death penalties prescribed by the Torah that were not carried out by the court, and for illegally using the fruits of the Sabbatical year; (e) the sword of war comes to the world for the delay of justice, for the perversion of justice and for interpreting the Torah decision in opposition to the halachah; (f) wild beasts come upon the world for vain oaths and for Desecration of God's Name;*

פירוש לרבי עובדיה ספורנו

שזה יקרה בזרוע המון קרובי החייבים מיתה או אוספי שביעית יקרה הדבר, כענין „ואם העלם יעלימו עם הארץ את עיניהם מן האיש ההוא ושמתי אני את פני באיש ההוא ובמשפחתו", ושעל החטא בעִנוי הדין והוותו וקלקול ההוראה, שכל אלה חטא בתופשי התורה, יבוא ענש החרב כאמרו „חרב נוקמת נקם ברית", ושעל החטא בחלול השם ומכללו שבועת שוא, אשר סבתו מעוט הכרת

SFORNO'S COMMENTARY

often happens due to the violent pressure of the families of those sentenced to death, or those guilty of violating the laws of the Sabbatical year — pestilence occurs, as it is written: וְאִם הַעְלֵם יַעְלִימוּ עַם הָאָרֶץ אֶת עֵינֵיהֶם מִן הָאִישׁ הַהוּא . . . וְשַׂמְתִּי אֲנִי אֶת פָּנַי בָּאִישׁ הַהוּא וּבְמִשְׁפַּחְתּוֹ, *But if the people of the land avert their eyes from that man . . . then I shall set My face upon that man and his family* (*Leviticus* 20:4-5).

And for the sin of delaying justice, perverting justice, and distorting Torah decisions — all these being sins of those "who grasp the Torah" — the punishment of the sword will come, as it says, חֶרֶב נֹקֶמֶת נְקַם בְּרִית, *a sword, avenging the vengeance of a covenant* (ibid. 26:25).

And for the sin of "Desecration of God's Name," including the sin of vain oaths, for both come about due to a diminishment of the recognition

NOTES

crime, and in Divine reckoning "measure for measure" is the norm, when man rejects God and no longer "knows Him," manifested in his desecration of His Name and taking His name in vain, the vehicle of retribution chosen by Hashem will also be those who are devoid of knowledge and understanding — namely, the wild beasts.

Israel's security in the land of Israel is dependent on God's providence and protection, which is removed when the people violate the three cardinal sins of idolatry, murder, and sexual immorality. The failure to observe the Sabbatical year demonstrates that the nation does not recognize God's mastery over, and ownership of, Eretz Yisrael. Hence, they are cast out and exiled from the Almighty's land.

גָּלוּת בָּאָה לָעוֹלָם — עַל עוֹבְדֵי עֲבוֹדָה זָרָה, וְעַל גִּלּוּי עֲרָיוֹת, וְעַל שְׁפִיכוּת דָּמִים, וְעַל שְׁמִטַּת הָאָרֶץ.

[ט] **בְּאַרְבָּעָה** פְרָקִים הַדֶּבֶר מִתְרַבֶּה: בָּרְבִיעִית, וּבַשְּׁבִיעִית, וּבְמוֹצָאֵי שְׁבִיעִית, וּבְמוֹצָאֵי הֶחָג שֶׁבְּכָל שָׁנָה וְשָׁנָה. בָּרְבִיעִית, מִפְּנֵי מַעְשַׂר עָנִי שֶׁבַּשְּׁלִישִׁית; בַּשְּׁבִיעִית, מִפְּנֵי מַעְשַׂר עָנִי שֶׁבַּשִּׁשִּׁית; בְּמוֹצָאֵי שְׁבִיעִית, מִפְּנֵי פֵּרוֹת שְׁבִיעִית; בְּמוֹצָאֵי הֶחָג שֶׁבְּכָל שָׁנָה וְשָׁנָה, מִפְּנֵי גֶּזֶל מַתְּנוֹת עֲנִיִּים.

[י] **אַרְבַּע** מִדּוֹת בָּאָדָם. הָאוֹמֵר: „שֶׁלִּי שֶׁלִּי וְשֶׁלְּךָ שֶׁלָּךְ,״ זוֹ מִדָּה בֵינוֹנִית, וְיֵשׁ

פירוש לרבי עובדיה ספורנו

וידיעת גודל האל יתברך, יהיה העונש על ידי חיה רעה נעדרת הידיעה ולא חלק לה בבינה, ועל החטא בע״ז והחטא בשמטת הארץ, אשר בשניהם צד כפירת ממשלת אלדי הארץ כאמרו „כי לי הארץ כי גרים ותושבים אתם עמדי״, לכן יהיה הענש שיגרש הכופרים בו מארצו ויגלה האומה כענין „לא ישבו בארץ יי״, וכן על חטא גלוי עריות ושפיכות דמים המקלקלת המדינות לגמרי, יהיה הענש גלות כאמרו „ולא תקיא אתכם הארץ״ וכאמרו „כי הדם הוא יחניף את הארץ״:

SFORNO'S COMMENTARY

and knowledge of the greatness of God, the Blessed One, the punishment comes through wild beasts, who also lack knowledge, וְלֹא חָלַק לָהּ בַּבִּינָה, *and have not been granted understanding* (*Job* 39:17).

As for the sin of idolatry and violation of the Sabbatical year, both reflect a denial of God's governance of the earth, as it says, כִּי לִי הָאָרֶץ כִּי גֵרִים וְתוֹשָׁבִים אַתֶּם עִמָּדִי, *For the land is Mine, for you are sojourners and residents with Me* (*Leviticus* 25:23). Therefore, the punishment is that those who deny this will be cast out from His land and go into exile, as it is written, לֹא יֵשְׁבוּ בְּאֶרֶץ ה׳, *They shall not dwell in Hashem's land* (*Hosea* 9:3).

Similarly, for the sin of immorality and bloodshed, which erode and undermine society and the social order, the punishment will be exile, as it says, וְלֹא תָקִיא הָאָרֶץ אֶתְכֶם , *And the land will not disgorge you* (*Leviticus* 18:28); and as it is written, כִּי הַדָּם הוּא יַחֲנִיף אֶת הָאָרֶץ, *For the blood will bring guilt upon the land* (*Numbers* 35:33).

(g) *exile comes to the world for idolatry, for immorality, for bloodshed, and for working the earth during the Sabbatical year.*

9. *At four periods [of the seven-year Sabbatical cycle] pestilence increases — in the fourth year, in the seventh year, in the year following the Sabbatical year, and annually following the Succos festival. In the fourth year, for [neglecting] the tithe of the poor in the third; in the seventh year, for [neglecting] the tithe of the poor in the sixth; in the year following the Sabbatical year, for [violating the laws of] the Sabbatical produce; annually, at the conclusion of the festival of Succos, for robbing the poor of their gifts.*

10. *There are four character types among people: (a) One who says, "My property is mine and yours is yours," is an average character type, but some*

פירוש לרבי עובדיה ספורנו

ה:ט. הדבר מרובה על כל אלה, שבהם יקרה גזל מתנות עניים כאמרו ,,אל תגזול דל וכולי כי יי יריב ריבם וקבע את קובעיהם נפש":

ה:י. הזכיר קצת תכונות טבעיות שצריך שישתדל האדם בתיקונם, כי בתכונות נפשיות מוכנות אל המעשה הטוב תהיה הנפש מוכנת אל האשור הנצחי בהדמותה בזה לבוראה שנאמר עליו ,,טוב יי לכל":

SFORNO'S COMMENTARY

5:9

בְּאַרְבָּעָה פְרָקִים הַדֶּבֶר מִתְרַבֶּה — *At four periods . . . pestilence increases.* "Pestilence increases" as a consequence of "robbing the poor of their gifts," as it is written, אַל תִּגְזָל דָּל . . . כִּי ה׳ יָרִיב רִיבָם וְקָבַע אֶת קֹבְעֵיהֶם נָפֶשׁ, *Do not rob the poor . . . for HASHEM will plead their cause and rob the life of those who rob them* (*Proverbs* 22:22-23).

5:10

אַרְבַּע מִדּוֹת בָּאָדָם — *There are four character types among people.* The Tanna lists a few negative natural traits which a person must attempt to correct, for only through the development of positive spiritual traits, which are directed toward the performance of good deeds will man's spirit be prepared to find eternal approval (in God's eyes), for it is then that one has imitated the ways of His Creator, of whom it is said, טוֹב ה׳ לַכֹּל, *Hashem is good to all* (*Psalms* 145:9).

אוֹמְרִים: זוֹ מִדַּת סְדוֹם; „שֶׁלִּי שֶׁלָּךְ וְשֶׁלְּךָ שֶׁלִּי," עַם הָאָרֶץ; "שֶׁלִּי שֶׁלָּךְ וְשֶׁלְּךָ שֶׁלָּךְ," חָסִיד; „שֶׁלְּךָ שֶׁלִּי וְשֶׁלִּי שֶׁלִּי," רָשָׁע.

[יא] **אַרְבַּע** מִדּוֹת בְּדֵעוֹת: נוֹחַ לִכְעוֹס וְנוֹחַ לִרְצוֹת, יָצָא שְׂכָרוֹ בְּהֶפְסֵדוֹ; קָשֶׁה לִכְעוֹס וְקָשֶׁה לִרְצוֹת, יָצָא הֶפְסֵדוֹ בִּשְׂכָרוֹ; קָשֶׁה לִכְעוֹס וְנוֹחַ לִרְצוֹת, חָסִיד; נוֹחַ לִכְעוֹס וְקָשֶׁה לִרְצוֹת, רָשָׁע.

[יב] **אַרְבַּע** מִדּוֹת בְּתַלְמִידִים: מָהִיר לִשְׁמוֹעַ וּמָהִיר לְאַבֵּד, יָצָא שְׂכָרוֹ בְּהֶפְסֵדוֹ; קָשֶׁה לִשְׁמוֹעַ וְקָשֶׁה לְאַבֵּד, יָצָא הֶפְסֵדוֹ בִּשְׂכָרוֹ; מָהִיר לִשְׁמוֹעַ וְקָשֶׁה לְאַבֵּד, זֶה חֵלֶק טוֹב; קָשֶׁה לִשְׁמוֹעַ וּמָהִיר לְאַבֵּד, זֶה חֵלֶק רָע.

פירוש לרבי עובדיה ספורנו

ה:יא. אחר שהזכיר התכונות בענין חמדת הממון והפכה הזכיר תכונות בענין החמה והכעס, וקרא הנוטה אל הרע מפסיד ובעל התכונה הרעה רשע בשניהם, כי אמנם עם היות הנטייה אליהם טבעית, הנה תקונם תלוי בבחירה לגמרי:

SFORNO'S COMMENTARY

5:11

אַרְבַּע מִדּוֹת בְּדֵעוֹת — *There are four types of temperament.* After discussing character traits regarding the coveting of money [material possessions] and its opposite, the Tanna now lists traits regarding wrath and anger. The term he uses to describe a person who is *inclined* toward bad traits is **מַפְסִיד**, "he causes 'loss' " — while he who *possesses* bad traits is called a **רָשָׁע** — a wicked person. Both, however, have the option of correcting their attitudes, since these are natural traits which one can choose to rectify.

NOTES

5:10-12

אַרְבַּע מִדּוֹת בָּאָדָם . . . בְּדֵעוֹת . . . בְּתַלְמִידִים — *There are four character types among people . . . temperament . . . students.* The *Sforno* carefully differentiates between various phrases used in these *Mishnahs:* **הֶפְסֵד**, "loss," **רָשָׁע**, "a wicked person," and **חֵלֶק רָע**, "a bad portion."

The first term, **הֶפְסֵד**, is applicable to one who has a *tendency* toward bad traits, whereas the second term, **רָשָׁע**, describes one who possesses bad traits, be it in the area of material possessions, or emotions. However, these failings can be rectified, more readily in the former case, where there is only a tendency, than the

say this is characteristic of Sodom; (b) "Mine is yours, and yours is mine," is an unlearned person; (c) 'Mine is yours and yours is yours," is scrupulously pious; (d) "Yours is mine and mine is mine," is wicked.

11. *There are four types of temperament: (a) One who is angered easily and pacified easily, his gain is offset by his loss; (b) one who is hard to anger and hard to pacify, his loss is offset by his gain; (c) one who is hard to anger and easy to pacify is pious; (d) one who is easily angered and hard to pacify is wicked.*

12. *There are four types of students: (a) One who grasps quickly and forgets quickly, his gain is offset by his loss; (b) one who grasps slowly and forgets slowly, his loss is offset by his gain; (c) one who grasps quickly and forgets slowly, this is a good portion; (d) one who grasps slowly and forgets quickly, this is a bad portion.*

פירוש לרבי עובדיה ספורנו

ה:יב. הזכיר תכונות טבעיות אשר לא תוכל הבחירה לתקנם אבל תוכל להשמר מן ההיזק הנמשך מהן בהשתדלות רב ההתבוננות וההתמדה, ולכן לא אמר על בעל התכונה הרעה בזה שיהיה רשע כי אמנם ענינה בלתי בחיריי, אבל אמר זה חלק רע, כי יצטרך בעל זה החלק אל רב השתדלות להשמר מתכלית היזקו:

SFORNO'S COMMENTARY

5:12

אַרְבַּע מִדּוֹת בְּתַלְמִידִים — *There are four types of students.* These are natural traits which cannot be altered and corrected through man's choice alone. However, one can control and limit the damage resulting from these natural tendencies through diligence and concentration, and by striving to improve and excel. Therefore, he does not call the person who unfortunately is not blessed with intellectual abilities a **רָשָׁע**, "a wicked man," for he does not have any option available. Rather, he terms this condition "a bad portion," because this person was given this trait from heaven, and he will have to try much harder to guard himself from the consequence of his fate.

NOTES

latter [where the person already possesses these character traits]. The term "bad portion" used in Mishnah 12 describes a person's weak intellectual capacities, for which he cannot be faulted. Nonetheless, one can attempt to practice "damage control" and make the best of a "bad portion.'

ה
יג

[יג] **אַרְבַּע** מִדּוֹת בְּנוֹתְנֵי צְדָקָה: הָרוֹצֶה שֶׁיִּתֵּן וְלֹא יִתְּנוּ אֲחֵרִים, עֵינוֹ רָעָה בְּשֶׁל אֲחֵרִים; יִתְּנוּ אֲחֵרִים וְהוּא לֹא יִתֵּן, עֵינוֹ רָעָה בְּשֶׁלּוֹ; יִתֵּן וְיִתְּנוּ אֲחֵרִים, חָסִיד; לֹא יִתֵּן וְלֹא יִתְּנוּ אֲחֵרִים, רָשָׁע.

פירוש לרבי עובדיה ספורנו

ה:יג. הנה עין רעה היא מדת מה שתקשה עליו טובת חברו, וזה לפעמים יהיה בזולת שישנאהו אבל שיחפוץ בשפלות חברו כדי שיהיה נכנע אליו, ועל זה אמר הכתוב בפרשת הצדקה ולא בפרשת שמטת כספים „קרבה שנת השבע . . . ורעה עינך" כלומר שיעלה על דעתך שמאחר שתהיה בקרוב שנת השבע שהתבואה הפקר והיא גם כן שנת שמטת כספים שלא יצטרך העני לפרוע חובות תהיה בשביל זה נתינת הצדקה בעיניך תוספת טובה יתרה לעני. אמר אם כן זה החכם שהרוצה לתת צדקה

SFORNO'S COMMENTARY

5:13

אַרְבַּע מִדּוֹת בְּנוֹתְנֵי צְדָקָה — *There are four types of donors to charity.* Behold, the expression עַיִן רָעָה [lit. "an evil eye"] represents the trait of begrudging — i.e., one who finds it difficult to accept another's good fortune. Now, this is not because he hates him, but because he desires to humble him so that he should be subservient to him.

This explains why the verse [*Deuteronomy* 15:9], קָרְבָה שְׁנַת הַשֶּׁבַע . . . וְרָעָה עֵינְךָ, *The seventh year approaches . . . and your eye be evil* (i.e., look malevolently), is written in the *parashah* [section] of *tzedakah* (charity), rather than in the *parashah* of remission of loans (שְׁמִטַּת כְּסָפִים). For the verse's meaning is thus: One may think that since the seventh [Sabbatical] year is rapidly approaching, when all grain and fruits will become ownerless, and all loans will be canceled, and the poor man will not have to repay his debt, therefore the giving of charity, in the donor's eyes, is viewed as a superfluous supplement.

Therefore, this wise teacher [the Tanna of our Mishnah] states that one who is willing to give charity to a poor person, but is bothered by the fact that

NOTES

5:13

אַרְבַּע מִדּוֹת בְּנוֹתְנֵי צְדָקָה — *There are four types of donors to charity.* The *Sforno* explains the three terms used by the Tanna to describe the four types of donors to charity. He focuses first on the expression עֵינוֹ רָעָה, literally, "he possesses an evil eye," referring to one who begrudges others. Why is this phrase used by the Tanna regarding the first two types? And why is the third one called a חָסִיד, "pious," while the last one is called a רָשָׁע, "wicked"?

Our Sages choose their words very carefully. The *Sforno* calls our attention to the fact that the expression עֵינוֹ רָעָה, "he begrudges" is based on וְרָעָה עֵינְךָ (*Deuteronomy* 15:9). The verse refers to a person who is reluctant to help his fellow Jew because the Sabbatical Year is approaching. Therefore, he feels justified in not giving.

However, this presents a difficulty, for that segment in the Torah deals with *tzedakah*. If so, what is its connection to *Shemittah*? Would it not have been more

13. *There are four types of donors to charity: (a) One who wishes to give himself but wants others not to give, he begrudges others; (b) that others should give but that he should not give, he begrudges himself; (c) that he should give and that others should give is pious; (d) that he should not give and that others should not give is wicked.*

פירוש לרבי עובדיה ספורנו

לעני וקשה בעיניו שאחר שקבל ממנו העני את מתנתו יקבל גם כן מאחרים – אין לדון לכף חובה שיהיה זה מצד אכזריות שיתאכזר על העני, אבל מצד עין רעה שיקשה עליו תוספת טובת העני היתרה בעיניו במה שיקבל מאחרים, וכן כשיתנו אחרים והוא לא יתן אין זה אלא מפני שעינו רעה שיקבל עוד העני טובה בשלו. אמנם כשיחפוץ שיתן הוא ויתנו אחרים ראוי לדונו לכף זכות שאין חפצו בזה בשביל טובת העני בלבד אבל שעם זה חפץ שיזכו אחרים וזו היא מדת אדם חסיד לא צדיק בלבד. אבל מי שלא יתן וקשה בעיניו שיתנו אחרים אין לדון שיהיה זה מפני שיאהב

SFORNO'S COMMENTARY

after the poor man received his gift, he will also receive gifts from others — that person has an "evil eye." Do not, however, condemn this giver and consider him to be a cruel person (אַכְזָר). Rather, he suffers from an "evil eye" — he begrudges the poor man receiving additional charity from others!

Similarly, when others give and he does not, it is also due to his evil eye, for he resents the poor man receiving an additional gift from him, after having already received from others. However, when he wants others to give, in addition to his own giving, he should be judged meritoriously, for his desire is not only that the poor man benefit, but also that others merit [the *mitzvah* of charity]. Hence, he is correctly called a חָסִיד [pious man], and not just a צַדִּיק [righteous man].

However, if one does not give nor can he abide that others give, he should not be judged as being motivated by his concern for them and the

NOTES

reasonable to place these verses in the previous section (15:2), which discusses the cancellation of debts at the end of the Sabbatical year? The *Sforno* explains that the intent of our Tanna is to answer this question: The Torah is concerned lest there be those who normally are willing to give charity, but are reluctant to do so if the recipient has other resources, such as during the Sabbatical year, when he has access to the produce in the fields and orchards, and when his debts are canceled as well. The donor is bothered by the fact that the recipient will overly benefit. This type of giver is one whose nature is a begrudging one, be it as manifested in the first case (יִתֵּן וְלֹא יִתְּנוּ אֲחֵרִים), or the second (יִתְּנוּ אֲחֵרִים וְהוּא לֹא יִתֵּן). However, one who not only gives, but is anxious that others have the opportunity to do so as well, is called a חָסִיד, for a pious saintly person is precisely that — one who is concerned for others, be it for the material benefit of the recipient, or the spiritual benefit of the donor.

The concluding type is rightfully called a רָשָׁע, "a wicked person," for not only does he

[יד] **אַרְבַּע** מִדּוֹת בְּהוֹלְכֵי בֵית הַמִּדְרָשׁ: הוֹלֵךְ וְאֵינוֹ עוֹשֶׂה, שְׂכַר הֲלִיכָה בְּיָדוֹ; עוֹשֶׂה וְאֵינוֹ הוֹלֵךְ, שְׂכַר מַעֲשֶׂה בְּיָדוֹ; הוֹלֵךְ וְעוֹשֶׂה, חָסִיד; לֹא הוֹלֵךְ וְלֹא עוֹשֶׂה, רָשָׁע.

[טו] **אַרְבַּע** מִדּוֹת בְּיוֹשְׁבִים לִפְנֵי חֲכָמִים: סְפוֹג, וּמַשְׁפֵּךְ, מְשַׁמֶּרֶת, וְנָפָה. סְפוֹג, שֶׁהוּא סוֹפֵג אֶת הַכֹּל; וּמַשְׁפֵּךְ, שֶׁמַּכְנִיס בְּזוֹ וּמוֹצִיא בְזוֹ; מְשַׁמֶּרֶת, שֶׁמּוֹצִיאָה אֶת הַיַּיִן וְקוֹלֶטֶת אֶת הַשְּׁמָרִים; וְנָפָה, שֶׁמּוֹצִיאָה אֶת הַקֶּמַח וְקוֹלֶטֶת אֶת הַסֹּלֶת.

פירוש לרבי עובדיה ספורנו

אותם אחרים ויקשה עליו פיזור ממונם, אבל ראוי לדון שזה מפני רשעת אכזריותו על העני והיותו מואס במצות הצדקה:
ה:יד. אמר שבהליכה לבית המדרש יזכה האדם במה שיכבד את התורה ואת מי שנתנה במה שיטרח ללכת ולבקשה במקום הוועד, ובמה שילך ויעשה שיעסוק בה שם עם חבריו עושה חסד בהוסיף חכמה לעצמו ולזולתו, כאמרם ומחברי יותר מרבותי, ולכן קראו חסיד והפך זה רשע:

SFORNO'S COMMENTARY

conservation of their money. Rather, in this case he should be judged as a wicked person (רָשָׁע), who is cruel to the poor and despises and rejects the *mitzvah* of charity.

5:14

אַרְבַּע מִדּוֹת בְּהוֹלְכֵי בֵית הַמִּדְרָשׁ — *There are four types among those who go to the house of study.* The Tanna teaches that by going to the house of study, one gains merits, for he honors the Torah and the One Who gave it, by exerting himself to go and seek it out in the meeting place. By going and doing [i.e., learning], and participating in Torah study there, with his companions, he also performs חֶסֶד (a kindness) by increasing his wisdom, as well as theirs, as our Sages teach us: וּמֵחֲבֵרַי יוֹתֵר מֵרַבּוֹתַי, *"and from my companions more so than from my teachers"* (*Taanis* 7a). Therefore, he is called חָסִיד (a pious individual), while the converse is called a רָשָׁע (wicked).

NOTES

not give himself, but he also impedes others from giving, due to his callous character.

5:15

אַרְבַּע מִדּוֹת בְּיוֹשְׁבִים לִפְנֵי חֲכָמִים — *There are four types among students who sit before the sages.* Not all that the student hears is worth retaining and storing in his storehouse of knowledge. He must be discriminating and discerning. The fourth type of student discussed in our Mishnah is compared to "a sieve," which is used to sift flour. In Mishnaic times, the finest flour remained inside the sieve, while the flour dust fell out

14. *There are four types among those who go to the house of study: (a) One who goes but does not study has the reward for going; (b) one who studies [at home] but does not attend [the house of study] has the reward for accomplishment; (c) one who goes and studies is pious; (d) one who does not go and does not study is wicked.*

15. *There are four types among students who sit before the sages: A sponge, a funnel, a strainer and a sieve: a sponge, which absorbs everything; a funnel, which lets in from one end and lets out from the other; a strainer, which lets the wine flow through and retains the sediment; and a sieve, which allows the flour dust to pass through and retains the fine flour.*

פירוש לרבי עובדיה ספורנו

ה:טו. ספר הכנות טבעיות קצתם מונעות מידיעת האמת כדי שישתדל האדם בתיקונם באופן שיקנה ההכנה הרביעית המבחנת הטוב מן הרע עד שיחיה זוכר החלק הטוב מן המעויין ושמרו וישכח החלק הרע ויסירהו מלבו, על דרך רמון מצא תוכו אכל קלפתו זרק:

SFORNO'S COMMENTARY

5:15

אַרְבַּע מִדּוֹת בְּיוֹשְׁבִים לִפְנֵי חֲכָמִים — *There are four types among students who sit before the sages.* The Tanna discusses a number of natural, intellectual, and individual traits, some of which deter man from grasping true knowledge. He teaches us this so that one will attempt to correct these shortcomings in such a manner that will ultimately permit him to reach the fourth level (i.e., that of a sieve), which examines and selects the good from the bad. He will then retain the quality part of the subject matter studied, and rid himself of the bad sediments and remove them from his heart. This is akin to [the Talmudic description of Rabbi Meir]: רִמּוֹן מָצָא, תּוֹכוֹ אָכַל קְלִיפָּתוֹ זָרָק, *"He found a pomegranate, ate the fruit within it, and threw away the peel"* (*Chagigah* 15b).

NOTES

through the perforations. Likewise, the selective student retains the essential principles of wisdom while discarding the unessential, rather than cluttering up his mind with useless information.

The Talmudic citation of the *Sforno* refers to Rabbi Meir, who was the pupil of *Acher* (Elisha ben Avuyah). This great scholar, unfortunately, departed from the ways of Torah and was ostracized by his colleagues, who forbade students from studying with him. However, despite this ban, Rabbi Meir continued his association with his *rebbi*. To justify Rabbi Meir's actions, the Talmud explains that he had the intellectual and spiritual strength to accept *Acher's* Torah instruction while remaining immune to his heretical beliefs. The former is compared to the fruit of the pomegranate and the latter to the peel.

[טז] **כָּל** אַהֲבָה שֶׁהִיא תְלוּיָה בְדָבָר, בָּטֵל דָּבָר, בְּטֵלָה אַהֲבָה; וְשֶׁאֵינָהּ תְּלוּיָה בְדָבָר, אֵינָהּ בְּטֵלָה לְעוֹלָם. אֵיזוֹ הִיא אַהֲבָה שֶׁהִיא תְלוּיָה בְדָבָר? זוֹ אַהֲבַת אַמְנוֹן וְתָמָר. וְשֶׁאֵינָהּ תְּלוּיָה בְדָבָר? זוֹ אַהֲבַת דָּוִד וִיהוֹנָתָן.

[יז] **כָּל** מַחֲלֹקֶת שֶׁהִיא לְשֵׁם שָׁמַיִם, סוֹפָהּ לְהִתְקַיֵּם; וְשֶׁאֵינָהּ לְשֵׁם שָׁמַיִם, אֵין סוֹפָהּ לְהִתְקַיֵּם. אֵיזוֹ הִיא מַחֲלֹקֶת שֶׁהִיא לְשֵׁם

פירוש לרבי עובדיה ספורנו

ה:טז. הנה האהבה תקרא תלויה בדבר כשמציאותה נתלה בדבר חוץ מן הנאהב, כמו שיקוה האוהב להשיג דבר אשר בלעדיו לא היתה אותה האהבה נמצאת כלל. אמנם האהבה שאינה תלויה בדבר היא שסיבתה היא היות הנאהב ראוי לכך בעיני האוהב בלתי שישגיח בזה אל דבר חוץ מן הנאהב:

SFORNO'S COMMENTARY

5:16

אַהֲבָה . . . תְּלוּיָה בְדָבָר . . . וְשֶׁאֵינָהּ תְּלוּיָה . . . — *Love that depends on a specific cause . . . if it does not depend . . .* Love is considered "dependent upon a specific cause" when it is dependent upon something other than the love of the beloved one. This means that the lover hopes to obtain something (by way of his love), and were it not for this ulterior motive, his love would not exist.

On the other hand, any love "that does not depend upon a specific cause" — meaning, that it is evoked exclusively by the feeling on the part of the lover that his beloved one is worthy of this emotion, and is unrelated to any factor beyond the beloved one — [that is true love which "will never cease"].

NOTES

5:16

אַהֲבָה . . . תְּלוּיָה בְדָבָר . . . וְשֶׁאֵינָהּ תְּלוּיָה . . . — *Love that depends on a specific cause . . . if it does not depend . . .* Amnon's "love" for Tamar was lustful, and as soon as his desire was fulfilled and his appetite appeased, he despised her. For as the commentators point out, he loved himself, and not her. This is what the *Sforno* is referring to when he says that it was dependent "upon something other than the love of the beloved one." Hence, this is a fitting example of תָּלוּי בְּדָבָר, "dependent upon a specific cause."

In contrast, the love of David and Jonathan was altruistic and honest, for Jonathan knew that David was destined to deny him the royal succession, yet his love did not wane. This is what the *Sforno* describes as love unaffected by external considerations and "unrelated to any factors beyond the beloved one."

16. *Any love that depends on a specific cause, when that cause is gone, the love is gone; but if it does not depend on a specific cause, it will never cease. What sort of love depended upon a specific cause? — The love of Amnon for Tamar. And what did not depend upon a specific cause? — The love of David and Jonathan.*

17. *Any dispute that is for the sake of Heaven will have a constructive outcome; but one that is not for the sake of Heaven will not have a constructive outcome. What sort of dispute was for the sake of*

פירוש לרבי עובדיה ספורנו

ה:יז. אמר כשיקרה איזה ויכוח על חלוק דעות בין חכמים ויהיה תכלית הויכוח למצוא האמת לא לניצוח הנה אותו התכלית יצא לפעל ויתקים, כמו שהיה הענין בויכוח הלל עם שמאי שמתוכו התברר האמת, והפך זה קרה בויכוח קרח ועדתו עם משה ואהרן באמרם „ומדוע תתנשאו", שלא היה תכלית זה בקשת האמת אבל היה לנצח ולהשתרר, והנה התכלית המבוקש מהם עלה בתהו.

SFORNO'S COMMENTARY

5:17

כָּל מַחֲלֹקֶת . . . לְשֵׁם שָׁמַיִם . . . וְשֶׁאֵינָהּ . . . — *Any dispute . . . for the sake of Heaven . . . but one that is not . . .* The Tanna says that whenever there is an argument between wise men due to a sincere difference of opinion between them — the purpose of that dispute being to determine the truth, and not merely to emerge triumphant — then that goal will be reached and have permanence. This was true of the debate between Hillel and Shammai, through which the truth was clarified.

The reverse occurred in the controversy between Korach and his followers and Moses and Aaron, when they said **וּמַדּוּעַ תִּתְנַשְּׂאוּ**, "why do you exalt yourselves" (*Numbers* 16:3). For their purpose was not to determine the truth, but to emerge victorious and grasp the leadership. They failed in their goal, and their plot collapsed into nothingness.

NOTES

5:17

כָּל מַחֲלֹקֶת . . . לְשֵׁם שָׁמַיִם . . . וְשֶׁאֵינָהּ . . . — *Any dispute . . . for the sake of Heaven . . . but one that is not . . .* The example given by our Tanna to illustrate a controversy which is "for the sake of Heaven," as opposed to one which is not, becomes clear when we consider the commentary of the *Sforno*. The litmus test is to determine whether the goal of the argument is to find the truth, or to attain self-aggrandizement. Our Sages tell us that the many differences of opinion between Hillel and Shammai did not affect the cordial relationship between them, nor create a split in the community, for each respected the *halachic* decisions of the other.

ה שָׁמַיִם? זוֹ מַחֲלֹקֶת הִלֵּל וְשַׁמַּאי. וְשֶׁאֵינָהּ לְשֵׁם
יז שָׁמַיִם? זוֹ מַחֲלֹקֶת קֹרַח וְכָל עֲדָתוֹ. כָּל הַמְּזַכֶּה אֶת
הָרַבִּים, אֵין חֵטְא בָּא עַל יָדוֹ; וְכָל הַמַּחֲטִיא אֶת
הָרַבִּים, אֵין מַסְפִּיקִין בְּיָדוֹ לַעֲשׂוֹת תְּשׁוּבָה. מֹשֶׁה
זָכָה וְזִכָּה אֶת הָרַבִּים, זְכוּת הָרַבִּים תָּלוּי בּוֹ,
שֶׁנֶּאֱמַר: „צִדְקַת יהוה עָשָׂה, וּמִשְׁפָּטָיו עִם
יִשְׂרָאֵל.״ יָרָבְעָם בֶּן נְבָט חָטָא וְהֶחֱטִיא אֶת הָרַבִּים,
חֵטְא הָרַבִּים תָּלוּי בּוֹ, שֶׁנֶּאֱמַר: „עַל חַטֹּאות
יָרָבְעָם אֲשֶׁר חָטָא, וַאֲשֶׁר הֶחֱטִיא אֶת יִשְׂרָאֵל.״

פירוש לרבי עובדיה ספורנו

אין חטא בא על ידו שלא יזדמן לפניו מכשול עון. והזכיר טעם לזה כי אמנם זכות הרבים תלוי בו, והנה נראה כמו עול שיהיה השתדלותו מטיב לזולתו והוא יפול בענין רע. והמחטיא את הרבים לא יזדמן לפניו דרך שיסייעהו לשוב בתשובה כמו שהוא ראוי לכל שאר הבא לטהר שמסייעין אותו, והזכיר טעם

SFORNO'S COMMENTARY

כָּל הַמְזַכֶּה אֶת הָרַבִּים . . . הַמַּחֲטִיא אֶת הָרַבִּים — *Whoever influences the masses to become meritorious . . . who influences the masses to sin . . .* [The Mishnah says, "Whoever influences the masses to become meritorious] shall not stumble into transgression." The reason is that "the merit of the masses is to his credit" — it would be wrong and unfair that his efforts benefit others while he himself falls into evil ways!

"But one who influences the masses to sin will not be given the means to repent," or be assisted to do so, as is normally the case of one who comes to purify himself, who *does* receive Heavenly assistance. The reason given by

NOTES

כָּל הַמְזַכֶּה אֶת הָרַבִּים . . . הַמַּחֲטִיא אֶת הָרַבִּים . . . — *Whoever influences the masses to become meritorious . . . who influences the masses to sin . . .* The *Sforno* explains the latter portion of the Mishnah from the perspective of fairness and equitable compensation from Heaven. A man who is responsible for influencing the masses to conduct themselves properly, thereby assisting them in adding to their merit, will not be permitted by the Almighty to be ensnared into sin, for this would be extremely unfair. As the Talmud expresses this point in *Yoma* 86, "His pupils would be in *Gan Eden,* and he in *Gehinnom*!" Indeed, the *Bartenura* quotes

In contrast, Korach, in spite of seemingly championing the honor and prestige of his fellow Levites and *Klal Yisrael,* showed his true colors when he complained, "Why do you exalt yourselves," thereby revealing what really irked him, and what his ultimate goal was in challenging Moses and Aaron — namely, to rise to power and usurp their authority!

Had his motives been pure, his claims may have had some validity. But his outrageous, disrespectful question showed that he was not a seeker of truth, but a glorious, vain pretender to the positions held by Moses and Aaron.

5
17 *Heaven? — The dispute between Hillel and Shammai. And which was not for the sake of Heaven? — The dispute of Korach and his entire company. Whoever influences the masses to become meritorious shall not stumble into transgression; but one who influences the masses to sin will not be given the means to repent. Moses was meritorious and influenced the masses to be meritorious, so the merit of the masses was to his credit, as it is said: "He performed the righteousness of* HASHEM *and His laws together with Israel." Jeroboam ben Nebat sinned and caused the masses to sin, so the sin of the masses is charged against him, as it is said: "For the sins of Jeroboam which he committed and which he caused Israel to commit."*

פירוש לרבי עובדיה ספורנו

על זה באמרו שחטא הרבים תלוי בו, והיה נראה כמו עול שיהיה השתדלותו הרע מחייב את אחרים והוא יזכה. מכל מקום לא ימנעהו שום מונע כלל אם יבחר לשוב בתשובה, כמו שקרה למנשה אחר שחטא והחטיא שנאמר עליו, ,,ובהצר לו חלה את פני יי אלדיו ויעתר לו'' וכולי:

SFORNO'S COMMENTARY

the Mishnah is that "the sin of the masses is charged against him" — it would be wrong that his evil efforts bring guilt upon others, while he is found innocent! Nonetheless, if he chooses to repent, he will not be prevented from on High, as we see from the episode of Menashe, who sinned and caused others to sin. Of him it is written: וּכְהָצֵר לוֹ חִלָּה אֶת פְּנֵי ה׳ אֱלֹהָיו . . . וַיֵּעָתֶר לוֹ, *And when he was in affliction, he besought Hashem his God . . . and He received his entreaty* (*II Chronicles* 33:12-13).

NOTES

this saying of our Sages in his commentary on the Mishnah.

On the other hand, if one is responsible for causing many to sin, he will not be assisted from Heaven to repent, for the same reasoning: lest "he be in *Gan Eden* and his pupils in *Gehinnom*!" Again, the *Bartenura* also quotes this saying of our Sages.

The concept of Heaven assisting one to repent is found in *Shabbos* 104a, where it is stated, בָּא לִיטַּהֵר מְסַיְּיעִים אוֹתוֹ, *"He who wishes to purify himself is assisted [from on High]."* However, there is one exception to this rule: One who causes a community of people to sin will not be aided in his quest to repent.

The *Sforno* hastens to add that although he will not be helped, the door to repentance is not sealed shut, for if this sinner is persistent, he *will* find an opening, and his *teshuvah* will be effective. This we find in the case of Menashe, king of Israel, who was guilty of misleading his people into idolatry. He was punished for this grave sin by falling into captivity at the hands of his enemies, yet when he implored God to forgive him, his prayers were accepted by the Almighty despite the objections of the angels.

ה [יח] **כָּל** מִי שֶׁיֵּשׁ בְּיָדוֹ שְׁלֹשָׁה דְבָרִים הַלָּלוּ,
יח הוּא מִתַּלְמִידָיו שֶׁל אַבְרָהָם אָבִינוּ;
וּשְׁלֹשָׁה דְבָרִים אֲחֵרִים, הוּא מִתַּלְמִידָיו שֶׁל בִּלְעָם
הָרָשָׁע. עַיִן טוֹבָה, וְרוּחַ נְמוּכָה, וְנֶפֶשׁ שְׁפָלָה,
תַּלְמִידָיו שֶׁל אַבְרָהָם אָבִינוּ. עַיִן רָעָה, וְרוּחַ
גְּבוֹהָה, וְנֶפֶשׁ רְחָבָה, תַּלְמִידָיו שֶׁל בִּלְעָם הָרָשָׁע.

פירוש לרבי עובדיה ספורנו

ה:יח. עין טובה היא מדת אדם המתעסק בשלו ואינו מסתכל בשל אחרים על צד קנאה, כענין אברהם באמרו „ואם אקח מכל אשר לך״, ורוח נמוכה היא מדת מי שאין עצמו וכבודו גבוה בעיניו באופן שירדוף אחר הכבוד, כמו שנראה באברהם שנאמר בו „וישתחו לעם הארץ לבני חת״ אף על פי שהיה נחשב לנשיא אלקים בתוכם, ונפש שפלה היא מדת מי שאינו מתאוה לתענוגים עוברים גדר ההכרחי, כמו שנראה באברהם באמרו הנה נא ידעתי כי אשה יפת מראה את, ואמרו ז״ל עד

SFORNO'S COMMENTARY

5:18

עַיִן טוֹבָה, וְרוּחַ נְמוּכָה, וְנֶפֶשׁ שְׁפָלָה, תַּלְמִידָיו שֶׁל אַבְרָהָם — *Those who have a good eye, a humble spirit, and a meek soul are among the disciples of . . . Abraham.* The phrase "a good eye" describes a person whose character trait is to be satisfied with what he possesses, and does not cast a jealous eye at the possessions of others. This trait we find in Abraham, who said: וְאִם אֶקַּח מִכָּל אֲשֶׁר לָךְ, *Or if I shall take anything of yours* (*Genesis* 14:23).

"A humble spirit" is the trait of a person who does not have an inflated opinion of himself, nor great concern for his own honor, hence he does not pursue honor. This we also find regarding Abraham, of whom we read, וַיִּשְׁתַּחוּ לְעַם הָאָרֶץ לִבְנֵי חֵת, *And he bowed down to the people of the land, to the children of Heth* (ibid. 23:7), even though he was considered נְשִׂיא אֱלֹהִים , *a prince of God,* in their midst (ibid. 23:6).

"A meek soul" refers to the trait of one who does not desire pleasures beyond the necessities of life, as we find regarding Abraham, who said, הִנֵּה נָא יָדַעְתִּי כִּי אִשָּׁה יְפַת מַרְאֶה אָתְּ, *Behold, I now realize that you are a woman*

NOTES

5:18

עַיִן טוֹבָה, וְרוּחַ נְמוּכָה, וְנֶפֶשׁ שְׁפָלָה, תַּלְמִידָיו שֶׁל אַבְרָהָם — *Those who have a good eye, a humble spirit, and a meek soul are among the disciples of . . . Abraham.* The *Sforno* proves that Abraham possessed these three characteristics — a good eye, a humble spirit, and a meek soul — from a variety of verses in the Torah. His conduct in the aftermath of his military victory against the four kings, and his demeanor in the presence of the children of Heth, when he purchased a grave for his wife, demonstrate the first two character traits of a "good eye" (a lack of greed) and "a humble spirit." His modesty is manifested in his conduct with his own wife Sarah. Our Sages tell us that Abraham was not even aware of how beautiful she was until he saw her reflection in the water on their way down to Egypt.

5
18

18. *Whoever has the following three traits is among the disciples of our forefather Abraham; and [whoever has] three different traits is among the disciples of the wicked Balaam. Those who have a good eye, a humble spirit, and a meek soul are among the disciples of our forefather Abraham. Those who have an evil eye, an arrogant spirit, and a greedy soul are among the disciples of the wicked Balaam.*

פירוש לרבי עובדיה ספורנו

עכשו לא הכיר בה ועכשו על ידי מעשה. והפכם בבלעם שנתן עיניו בממון חברו, כמבואר באומרו „אם יתן לי בלק מלא ביתו כסף וזהב לא אוכל לעבור את פי יי״, כלומר שאם היה יכול על זה היה עובר כדי לקבל הממון שהיה חומד, וכן ממדותיו שהיה רודף אחר הכבוד, כמו שאמר לו בלק שהיה מכיר ענינו „כי כבד אכבדך מאד״,

SFORNO'S COMMENTARY

of beautiful appearance (ibid. 12:11). Our Sages comment: עַד עַכְשָׁיו לֹא הִכִּיר בָּהּ מִתּוֹךְ צְנִיעוּת שֶׁבִּשְׁנֵיהֶם, וְעַכְשָׁיו הִכִּיר בָּהּ ע״י מַעֲשֶׂה, *"Until now he had not been aware [of her beauty] due to both their modesty, but now he became aware of her [beauty] due to an event [he saw her reflection in the river"]* (*Bava Basra* 16a).

עַיִן רָעָה, וְרוּחַ גְּבוֹהָה, וְנֶפֶשׁ רְחָבָה, תַּלְמִידָיו שֶׁל בִּלְעָם — *Those who have an evil eye, an arrogant spirit, and a greedy soul are among the disciples of . . . Balaam.* The reverse [of these three traits] is to be found in Balaam, who was filled with greed for other people's money. As he said, אִם יִתֶּן לִי בָלָק מְלֹא בֵיתוֹ כֶּסֶף וְזָהָב לֹא אוּכַל לַעֲבֹר אֶת פִּי ה׳, *If Balak will give me his houseful of silver and gold, I cannot transgress the word of Hashem* (*Numbers* 22:18) — meaning, that had he been able to do so, he would have done so in order to get the money which he coveted. He also pursued honor, as we see from the assurance of Balak, who recognized Balaam's desires, and therefore said, כִּי כַבֵּד אֲכַבֶּדְךָ מְאֹד, *For*

NOTES

עַיִן רָעָה, וְרוּחַ גְּבוֹהָה, נֶפֶשׁ רְחָבָה, תַּלְמִידָיו שֶׁל בִּלְעָם — *Those who have an evil eye, an arrogant spirit, and a greedy soul are among the disciples of . . . Balaam.* As for Balaam, his greed for wealth, which is called an "evil eye," is demonstrated, as the *Sforno* points out, by his protestation that even if Balak were to give him a houseful of silver and gold to curse Israel, he could not do it without the Almighty's permission. An examination of Balak's initial invitation reveals that only honor was offered to Balaam, and no mention was made of silver and gold. But obviously, in Balaam's mind that would be his greatest motivation to curse the Jews.

Concerning a haughty spirit, this we learn from Balak's offer to honor him, for Balak knew of Balaam's weakness for honor. The trait of a lustful, insatiable spirit is manifested by Balaam's advice to use the daughters of Moab to seduce the Children of Israel and then entice them to serve idols and behave immorally. As the *Sforno* says, and proves from the statement of Rabbi Yochanan to Resh Lakish (who had been a highwayman before he became a *baal teshuvah*), every person reveals his own

ה
יט

מַה בֵּין תַּלְמִידָיו שֶׁל אַבְרָהָם אָבִינוּ לְתַלְמִידָיו שֶׁל בִּלְעָם הָרָשָׁע? תַּלְמִידָיו שֶׁל אַבְרָהָם אָבִינוּ אוֹכְלִין בָּעוֹלָם הַזֶּה, וְנוֹחֲלִין הָעוֹלָם הַבָּא, שֶׁנֶּאֱמַר: „לְהַנְחִיל אֹהֲבַי יֵשׁ, וְאֹצְרֹתֵיהֶם אֲמַלֵּא.״ אֲבָל תַּלְמִידָיו שֶׁל בִּלְעָם הָרָשָׁע יוֹרְשִׁין גֵּיהִנֹּם, וְיוֹרְדִין לִבְאֵר שַׁחַת, שֶׁנֶּאֱמַר: „וְאַתָּה אֱלֹהִים תּוֹרִדֵם לִבְאֵר שַׁחַת, אַנְשֵׁי דָמִים וּמִרְמָה לֹא יֶחֱצוּ יְמֵיהֶם, וַאֲנִי אֶבְטַח בָּךְ.״

[יט] **יְהוּדָה** בֶּן תֵּימָא אוֹמֵר: הֱוֵי עַז כַּנָּמֵר, וְקַל כַּנֶּשֶׁר, רָץ כַּצְּבִי, וְגִבּוֹר כָּאֲרִי לַעֲשׂוֹת רְצוֹן אָבִיךְ שֶׁבַּשָּׁמָיִם. הוּא הָיָה

פירוש לרבי עובדיה ספורנו

וענין היותו מתאוה ובוחר בתענוגים ובתאוות הגשמיות התבאר ממה שיעץ מזימת הנשים, כאמרו „הן הנה היו לבני ישראל בדבר בלעם״, כאמרם ז״ל לסטאה בליסטאותיה ידע. והביא ראיה על ענין תלמידיו של אברהם ממה שנאמר „להנחיל אוהבי יש״, שהם היוצאים בעקבות אברהם אבינו שנאמר עליו „זרע

SFORNO'S COMMENTARY

I shall honor you greatly (ibid. 22:17). As for the trait of "a greedy soul" — i.e., a profound desire and lust for physical pleasures — this we see from his counsel and advice that the Moabite women seduce the Israelites, as we read: הֵנָּה הָיוּ לִבְנֵי יִשְׂרָאֵל בִּדְבַר בִּלְעָם, *They caused the Children of Israel by the word of Balaam*. . . (ibid. 31:16). This is in keeping with the statement [of Rabbi Yochanan to Resh Lakish] (*Bava Metzia* 84a): לִסְטָאָה בְּלִיסְטָאוּתֵי׳ יָדַע, *"A bandit knows banditry."*

תַּלְמִידָיו שֶׁל אַבְרָהָם . . . אוֹכְלִין . . . וְנוֹחֲלִין . . . שֶׁל בִּלְעָם . . . — *The disciples of Abraham . . . enjoy . . . and inherit . . . of Balaam . . .* The Tanna then proves his statement regarding the reward of the disciples of Abraham from the verse (*Proverbs* 8:21): לְהַנְחִיל אֹהֲבַי יֵשׁ, *that I may cause those who love Me to*

NOTES

attitude and tendencies by that which he proposes, for that is a reflection of his own personality.

תַּלְמִידָיו שֶׁל אַבְרָהָם . . . אוֹכְלִין . . . וְנוֹחֲלִין . . . שֶׁל בִּלְעָם . . . — *The disciples of . . . Abraham enjoy . . . and inherit . . . of Balaam . . .* The concluding part of the *Sforno*'s commentary explains the Tanna's proofs regarding the reward in store for the disciples of Abraham, and the punishment in store for the disciples of Balaam. Abraham is called God's "beloved one," and the promise of God to grant יֵשׁ (an everlasting, substantive blessing) to his beloved ones refers to Abraham's followers. The verse quoted by

How are the disciples of our forefather Abraham different from the disciples of the wicked Balaam? The disciples of our forefather Abraham enjoy [the fruits of their good deeds] in this world and inherit the World to Come, as is said: "To cause those who love Me to inherit an everlasting possession [the World to Come], and I will fill their storehouses [in this world]." But the disciples of the wicked Balaam inherit Gehinnom and descend into the well of destruction, as is said: "And You, O God, shall lower them into the well of destruction, men of bloodshed and deceit shall not live out half their days; but as for me, I will trust in You."

19. *Yehudah ben Teima said: Be bold as a leopard, light as an eagle, swift as a deer, and strong as a lion, to carry out the will of your Father in Heaven. He*

פירוש לרבי עובדיה ספורנו

אברהם אוהבי״, ועל תלמידיו של בלעם הביא ראיה ממה שנאמר „אנשי דמים ומרמה״, והם היוצאים בעקבות בלעם ששפך רב דמים במרמת עצתו:

ה:יט. עז כנמר להוכיח החוטאים פעם אחר פעם אף על פי שלא קבלו, וקל

SFORNO'S COMMENTARY

inherit (an everlasting possession [the World to Come]), for they follow in the footsteps of Abraham our father, of whom it is said (*Isaiah* 41:8), **זֶרַע אַבְרָהָם אֹהֲבִי**, *the seed of Abraham, My beloved one [friend].*

And regarding the fate of the disciples of Balaam, he brings proof from the verse (*Psalms* 55:24): **אַנְשֵׁי דָמִים וּמִרְמָה**, *men of bloodshed and deceit,* for they follow in Balaam's footsteps, who was guilty of shedding much blood through his deceitful counsel.

5:19

הֱוֵי עַז כַּנָּמֵר . . . לַעֲשׂוֹת רְצוֹן . . . עַז פָּנִים . . . — *Be bold as a leopard . . . to carry out the will . . . the brazen . . .* One is to be "bold as a leopard" in admonishing sinners, time after time, even though they may refuse to accept the admonition.

NOTES

5:19

הֱוֵי עַז כַּנָּמֵר . . . לַעֲשׂוֹת רְצוֹן . . . — *Be bold as a leopard . . . to carry out the will . . .* Our Sages interpret the verse, הוֹכֵחַ תּוֹכִיחַ אֶת עֲמִיתֶךָ , *you shall surely reprove your fellow* (*Leviticus* 19:17), to mean that if it is necessary, you must do so אֲפִילוּ עַד מֵאָה פְּעָמִים,

our Tanna, from *Psalms* 55, referring to Balaam's disciples, is based on the descriptive phrase, "men of bloodshed and deceit." It reflects the wicked character of their teacher, who was deceitful, and was responsible for the death of 22,000 Israelites in the aftermath of their transgression at Peor.

ה כ אוֹמֵר: עַז פָּנִים לְגֵיהִנֹּם, וּבֹשֶׁת פָּנִים לְגַן עֵדֶן. יְהִי רָצוֹן מִלְּפָנֶיךָ יהוה אֱלֹהֵינוּ וֵאלֹהֵי אֲבוֹתֵינוּ שֶׁיִּבָּנֶה בֵּית הַמִּקְדָּשׁ בִּמְהֵרָה בְיָמֵינוּ וְתֵן חֶלְקֵנוּ בְּתוֹרָתֶךָ.

[כ] **הוּא** הָיָה אוֹמֵר: בֶּן חָמֵשׁ שָׁנִים לַמִּקְרָא, בֶּן עֶשֶׂר שָׁנִים לַמִּשְׁנָה, בֶּן שְׁלֹשׁ עֶשְׂרֵה לַמִּצְוֹת, בֶּן חֲמֵשׁ עֶשְׂרֵה לַגְּמָרָא, בֶּן שְׁמוֹנֶה עֶשְׂרֵה לַחֻפָּה, בֶּן עֶשְׂרִים לִרְדּוֹף, בֶּן שְׁלֹשִׁים לַכֹּחַ, בֶּן אַרְבָּעִים לַבִּינָה, בֶּן חֲמִשִּׁים

פירוש לרבי עובדיה ספורנו

כנשר לעלות אל גרם מעלות המדות והמושכלות, על הפך „ראמות לאויל חכמות", ורץ כצבי למצוה קלה וחמורה, וגבור כארי להתקומם נגד החוטאים בשיש בידך למחות, כענין „ובתקוממיך אתקוטט": עז פנים הוא מי שלא תחת בו גערה אפילו במקום הראוי. ובהיות שראוי להשתמש בעזות לקיים מצות בוראנו ולהשמר ממנו בזולת זה – יהי רצון שתבנה עירך ושם תאיר עינינו בתורתך

SFORNO'S COMMENTARY

"Light as an eagle," to strive to reach the most exalted moral-ethical and intellectual level, as opposed to [the fool depicted by Solomon]: רָאמוֹת לֶאֱוִיל חָכְמוֹת, *Wisdom is too high for a fool* (*Proverbs* 24:7)

"Swift as a deer," to perform all *mitzvos*, be they light or difficult, and "strong as a lion," to rise up and contest sinners when one is able to protest their actions, as the verse states, וּבִתְקוֹמְמֶיךָ אֶתְקוֹטָט, *and I quarrel with those who rise up against You* (*Psalms* 139:21).

"The brazen" person is one who is impervious to reproof, even when it is delivered in the appropriate manner. Now, being that brazenness may be practiced when necessary in order to fulfill the commandment of our Creator, but otherwise is to be avoided, we therefore pray, "May it be Your will. . .that the Holy Temple be rebuilt," and there, our eyes be illuminated

NOTES

"even a hundred times" (*Bava Metzia* 31). The *Sforno* understands the initial advice of Yehudah ben Teima, "be bold as a leopard," as reflecting this Talmudic dictum. To admonish a person repeatedly is difficult and unpleasant, but one must be bold and persistent. He understands "light as an eagle" as referring to man's inherent aspiration to soar heavenward and reach elevated spiritual levels, and not to despair of ever attaining such heights, for such a defeatist attitude is the mark of a fool. He applies the expression "swift as a deer" to total observance of *mitzvos*, not being judgmental regarding their relative importance.

As for "strong as a lion," the *Sforno* is of the opinion that it refers to the strength required to confront and challenge sinners, providing there is a realistic chance of success. He implies that otherwise, it would be better to follow the advice of our Sages, that there are times when one is rewarded for desisting rather than chastising.

5
20

used to say: The brazen goes to Gehinnom, but the shamefaced goes to the Garden of Eden. May it be Your will, HASHEM, our God and the God of our forefathers, that the Holy Temple be rebuilt, speedily in our days, and grant us our share in Your Torah.

20. **H***e used to say: A five-year-old begins Scripture; a ten-year-old begins Mishnah; a thirteen-year-old becomes obliged to observe the commandments; a fifteen-year-old begins the study of Gemara; an eighteen-year-old goes to the marriage canopy; a twenty-year-old begins pursuit [of a livelihood]; a thirty-year-old attains full strength; a forty-year-old attains understanding; a fifty-year-old can*

פירוש לרבי עובדיה ספורנו

באופן שנבדיל בין העזות הטוב והעזות הרע ודומיהם:

ה:כ. אמר שעם זה שחיי האדם קצרים בכלל, הנה מלבד זה ראוי להתבונן שהעתים הראויים להשתדלות בתוכם הם קצרים מאד מאחרים לבוא ומקדימים לצאת

SFORNO'S COMMENTARY

in Your Torah, in such a manner that we will be able to differentiate between "good" [acceptable] insolence and "bad" [objectionable] brazenness; and similar distinctions [in the realm of character traits].

5:20

בֶּן חָמֵשׁ . . . בֶּן מֵאָה . . . — *A five-year-old . . . a hundred-year-old.* The Tanna is saying that not only is man's life brief, in general, but man must consider and contemplate that those periods of life meant for certain endeavors are

NOTES

יְהִי רָצוֹן . . . שֶׁיִּבָּנֶה בהמ״ק — *May it be Your will . . . that the Holy Temple be rebuilt . . .* The *Sforno* explains the insertion of the יְהִי רָצוֹן by Yehudah ben Teima at the conclusion of the Mishnah. For in the absence of the Holy Temple (*Beis HaMikdash*), and the Torah instruction which emanates from there, as well as its spiritual influence upon the Jewish mind and heart, one cannot reach the intellectual level to be able to discern between proper and improper use of *chutzpah*. This is also true of other traits, such as anger, jealousy, etc., which can be channeled in a constructive, positive manner, through man's wise judgment. This explains why this יְהִי רָצוֹן is injected into our Mishnah, for at first glance, it seems incongruous.

Other commentaries suggest that this Mishnah of Yehudah ben Teima should be placed at the *end* of this chapter, which concludes *Mesechta Avos* (since chapter 6 does not consist of *Mishnayos*, but of *Beraisos*). If this is the case, then it is most appropriate to conclude this tractate with a prayer for the rebuilding of the Holy Temple, and the request to grant every person his portion in the Torah.

5:20

בֶּן חָמֵשׁ . . . בֶּן מֵאָה . . . — *A five-year-old . . . a hundred-year-old . . .* The *Sforno* interprets this concluding instruction of Yehudah ben

לְעֵצָה, בֶּן שִׁשִּׁים לְזִקְנָה, בֶּן שִׁבְעִים לְשֵׂיבָה, בֶּן שְׁמוֹנִים לִגְבוּרָה, בֶּן תִּשְׁעִים לָשׁוּחַ, בֶּן מֵאָה כְּאִלּוּ מֵת וְעָבַר וּבָטֵל מִן הָעוֹלָם.

[כא] **בֶּן** בַּג בַּג אוֹמֵר: הֲפָךְ בָּהּ וַהֲפָךְ בָּהּ, דְּכֹלָּא בָהּ; וּבָהּ תֶּחֱזֵי, וְסִיב וּבְלֵה בָהּ, וּמִנָּהּ לָא תָזוּעַ, שֶׁאֵין לְךָ מִדָּה טוֹבָה הֵימֶנָּה בֶּן הֵא הֵא אוֹמֵר: לְפוּם צַעֲרָא אַגְרָא.

פירוש לרבי עובדיה ספורנו

ולפיכך צריך שימהר האדם כי אמנם לא יהיה ראוי לתלמוד עד ט״ו שנה, ולא יבונן אל נכון עד ארבעים שנה ואחר החמשים תהיה ירידת הכחות מבוארת, כאמרו „ומבן חמשים שנה ישוב מצבא העבודה״, ובזה העיר אזן על החריצות להשיג חיי עולם בעוד הכוחות המשרתות בתקפם, כמו שהעיד שלמה באמרו „וזכור את בוראך בימי בחורותיך עד אשר לא יבואו ימי הרעה״:

ה:כא. הפוך בתורה להבין ולהביט נפלאות ממנה ולא תצטרך לספרי פילוסופי האומות וחוקריהם, דכולא בה, ובה תחזי תראה

SFORNO'S COMMENTARY

limited, "late in coming and early in leaving." Therefore, one must hasten to act appropriately (in the proper time period of one's life). For example, he is not yet ready to study Talmud properly until he is fifteen years old; and he is not established fully (in his discernment) until he is forty years old; and once past fifty, he is on the decline, as it is written (*Numbers* 8:25), וּמִבֶּן חֲמִשִּׁים שָׁנָה יָשׁוּב מִצְּבָא הָעֲבֹדָה, *At fifty years of age, he shall withdraw from the legion of work.* All this is told to us in order to sensitize and encourage us to be diligent in attaining eternal life while the powers and energies that serve us are still at full strength, as Solomon admonishes us: וּזְכֹר אֶת בּוֹרְאֶךָ בִּימֵי בְּחוּרֹתֶיךָ עַד אֲשֶׁר לֹא יָבֹאוּ יְמֵי הָרָעָה, *And remember your Creator in the days of your youth, before the evil days come* (*Ecclesiastes* 12:1).

5:21

הֲפָךְ בָּהּ . . . דְּכֹלָּא בָהּ . . . — *Delve in it [the Torah] . . . for everything is in it . . .* "Delve in it [the Torah]" so as to understand it and appreciate its wonders, and you will not find it necessary to study the books of the philosophers and thinkers of the nations of the world.

NOTES

Teima as advice regarding the budgeting of one's time, and the need to utilize each period of life properly. He explains that the reason why the Tanna lists these instructions according to years is to heighten one's awareness and sensitivity to the brevity of life, and the importance of utilizing time wisely and appropriately.

5:21

הֲפָךְ בָּהּ . . . דְּכֹלָּא בָהּ — *Delve in it [the Torah] . . . for everything is in it . . .* Considering that the *Sforno* himself was extremely well versed in science and medicine, we must understand his interpretation of this Mishnah as referring only to the philosophical and theological works of the wise men of

offer counsel; a sixty-year-old attains seniority; a seventy-year-old attains a ripe old age; an eighty-year-old shows strength; a ninety-year-old becomes stooped over; a hundred-year-old is as if he were dead, passed away and ceased from the world.

21. *Ben Bag Bag says: Delve in it [the Torah] and continue to delve in it [the Torah] for everything is in it; look deeply into it; grow old and gray over it, and do not stir from it, for you can have no better portion than it. Ben Hei Hei says: The reward is in proportion to the exertion.*

פירוש לרבי עובדיה ספורנו

מופתים שכליים על דעות אמתיות בענין האלקי ובהשארות הנפש וזולתם, שהם עקרי המחקר הראוי, לאהבה וליראה את האל יתברך כי זה כל האדם וכל עיקר כוונת התורה. ובהיות כי לא יראה לך ולא ימצא כל זה מדברי התורה זולתי אחר השתדלות ועמל, כאמרו „אם תבקשנה ככסף וכמטמונים תחפשנה אז תבין יראת יי ודעת קדושים תמצא", אמר בן הא הא שלא ימנע האדם מזה העמל כלל, כי אמנם כל מה שיגדל העמל תגדל מעלת הנפש השכלית לחיי עולם כאמרו אף חכמתי עמדה לי:

SFORNO'S COMMENTARY

"For everything is in it; look deeply into it," and you will find intellectual proof regarding true and authentic opinions of Godly matters and the immortality of the soul, and similar things, which represent the essential subjects of theological research. This deliberation brings one to love and revere the Almighty, Blessed is He, כִּי זֶה כָּל הָאָדָם, *for that is man's whole duty* (*Ecclesiastes* 12:13), and the basic intent and purpose of Torah.

Now, being that one cannot realize this goal (of discovering these truths and guidance) from Torah, without great toil and exhausting endeavors — as it is said in *Proverbs*, אִם תְּבַקְשֶׁנָּה כַכָּסֶף וְכַמַּטְמֹנִים תַּחְפְּשֶׂנָּה אָז תָּבִין יִרְאַת ה׳ וְדַעַת אֱלֹהִים תִּמְצָא, *If you seek her like silver, and search for her as for hidden treasures, then shall you understand the fear of Hashem, and find knowledge of God* (*Proverbs* 2:4-5) — therefore, Ben Hei Hei says that a man should not desist from this toil, because the greater the toil, the higher will his נֶפֶשׁ הַשִּׂכְלִית, *intellectual soul,* be elevated in eternal life, as it is written, אַף חָכְמָתִי עָמְדָה לִּי, *Still my wisdom stayed with me* (*Ecclesiastes* 2:9).

NOTES

the world. Regarding these disciplines Ben Bag Bag urges us to delve exclusively into the Torah, for all can be found there, providing that one realizes the necessity to apply assiduously to its study. The *Sforno,* therefore, explains that Ben Hei Hei is elaborating on the statement of Ben Bag Bag, and he proves his interpretation of this concluding Mishnah by quoting from the Books of *Proverbs* and *Ecclesiastes,* where the wisest of all men, King Solomon, teaches us that reverence and knowledge of Hashem can only be attained through arduous application and serious searching for the truth. It is, however, well worth the effort, for the attainment of this wisdom is for all eternity.

רַבִּי חֲנַנְיָא בֶּן עֲקַשְׁיָא אוֹמֵר: רָצָה הַקָּדוֹשׁ בָּרוּךְ הוּא לְזַכּוֹת אֶת יִשְׂרָאֵל, לְפִיכָךְ הִרְבָּה לָהֶם תּוֹרָה וּמִצְוֹת, שֶׁנֶּאֱמַר: „יהוה חָפֵץ לְמַעַן צִדְקוֹ, יַגְדִּיל תּוֹרָה וְיַאְדִּיר.״

Rabbi Chanania ben Akashia says: The Holy One, Blessed is He, wished to confer merit upon Israel; therefore He gave them Torah and mitzvos in abundance, as it is said: "HASHEM desired, for the sake of its [Israel's] righteousness, that the Torah be made great and glorious."

פרק ו

Chapter Six

כָּל יִשְׂרָאֵל יֵשׁ לָהֶם חֵלֶק לָעוֹלָם הַבָּא,
שֶׁנֶּאֱמַר: „וְעַמֵּךְ כֻּלָּם צַדִּיקִים, לְעוֹלָם יִירְשׁוּ
אָרֶץ, נֵצֶר מַטָּעַי, מַעֲשֵׂה יָדַי לְהִתְפָּאֵר.״

All Israel has a share in the World to Come, as it is said: "And your people are all righteous; they shall inherit the land forever; they are the branch of My planting, My handiwork, in which to take pride."

ו
א

[א] **רַבִּי** מֵאִיר אוֹמֵר: כָּל הָעוֹסֵק בַּתּוֹרָה לִשְׁמָהּ זוֹכֶה לִדְבָרִים הַרְבֵּה; וְלֹא עוֹד, אֶלָּא שֶׁכָּל הָעוֹלָם כֻּלּוֹ כְּדַאי הוּא לוֹ. נִקְרָא רֵעַ, אָהוּב. אוֹהֵב אֶת הַמָּקוֹם, אוֹהֵב אֶת הַבְּרִיּוֹת, מְשַׂמֵּחַ אֶת הַמָּקוֹם, מְשַׂמֵּחַ אֶת הַבְּרִיּוֹת. וּמַלְבַּשְׁתּוֹ עֲנָוָה וְיִרְאָה; וּמַכְשַׁרְתּוֹ לִהְיוֹת צַדִּיק, חָסִיד, יָשָׁר, וְנֶאֱמָן; וּמְרַחַקְתּוֹ מִן הַחֵטְא, וּמְקָרַבְתּוֹ לִידֵי זְכוּת. וְנֶהֱנִין מִמֶּנּוּ עֵצָה וְתוּשִׁיָּה, בִּינָה וּגְבוּרָה, שֶׁנֶּאֱמַר: „לִי עֵצָה וְתוּשִׁיָּה, אֲנִי בִינָה, לִי גְבוּרָה.״ וְנוֹתֶנֶת לוֹ מַלְכוּת, וּמֶמְשָׁלָה,

פירוש לרבי עובדיה ספורנו

ו:א. נקרא רע – שותף להקדוש ברוך הוא במעשה בראשית בהיותו עוזר להשיג התכלית המכוון מאתו יתברך, כאמרו „ולי מה יקרו רעיך אל״. אוהב את הבריות בהיטיבו להם כמדת בוראו הטוב והמטיב, כאמרו „והלכת בדרכיו״. ומלבשתו ענוה ויראה שהם מיני זהירות, ומכשרתו להיות צדיק וחסיד שהם מיני זריזות, כאמרם ז״ל

SFORNO'S COMMENTARY

6:1

כָּל הָעוֹסֵק בַּתּוֹרָה לִשְׁמָהּ זוֹכֶה לִדְבָרִים הַרְבֵּה — *Whoever engages in Torah study for its own sake merits many things.* "He is called friend" — i.e., a partner to the Holy One, Blessed is He, in the work of Creation — for he helps attain the intended purpose of God [in creation], as it is written, וְלִי מַה יָּקְרוּ רֵעֶיךָ אֵל, *To me — how precious are Your dear ones, O God* (*Psalms* 139:17).

"He loves [His] creatures" by being good to them, and thereby emulating the attribute of His Creator, Who is good and does good, as it is written, וְהָלַכְתָּ בִּדְרָכָיו, *and you shall go in His ways* (*Deuteronomy* 28:9).

"[The Torah] clothes him in humility and fear [of God]," these being characteristics of זְהִירוּת, "watchfulness." It also "makes him fit to be righteous and devout," these being types of זְרִיזוּת, "zeal," as our Sages say,

NOTES

6:1

כָּל הָעוֹסֵק בַּתּוֹרָה לִשְׁמָהּ זוֹכֶה לִדְבָרִים הַרְבֵּה — *Whoever engages in Torah study for its own sake merits many things.* The concept of man becoming a partner with the Almighty in creation is found in the Talmud (*Shabbos* 10a), where our Sages teach us that one who judges equitably, honestly, and fairly becomes a "partner" to God, as does one who recites וַיְכֻלּוּ ("and he finished, etc.") in his Shabbos prayers (ibid. 119b). By emulating Hashem, Who is the Righteous Judge, and by acknowledging God's creation of the world in six days, man joins the Almighty in Creation, for he sustains and strengthens the work of creation.

A רֵעַ is a "friend," or, in the context of our Mishnah, an assistant, a helper, an associate. By studying and living Torah, man adds to the stability and purpose of

1. Rabbi Meir said: *Whoever engages in Torah study for its own sake merits many things; furthermore, [the creation of] the entire world is worthwhile for his sake alone. He is called, "Friend, Beloved." He loves the Omnipresent, he loves [His] creatures, he gladdens the Omnipresent, he gladdens [His] creatures. [The Torah] clothes him in humility and fear [of God]; it makes him fit to be righteous, devout, fair and faithful. It moves him away from sin and draws him near to merit. From him people enjoy counsel and wisdom, understanding and strength, as it is said: 'Mine are counsel and wisdom, I am understanding, mine is strength.' [The Torah] gives him kingship and dominion*

פירוש לרבי עובדיה ספורנו

זהירות מביאה לידי זריזות. ונהנין ממנו להבין ולהורות לזולתו דרכי חיי עולם וחיי שעה. ממשלה להישיר זולתו במדיניות, גם כן רזי תורה באלקיות, כמעין להוסיף דעת גם בדברים בלתי נכללים בתורה, ויהא צנוע שקונה בה תכונות מעשים טובים:

SFORNO'S COMMENTARY

זְהִירוּת מְבִיאָה לִידֵי זְרִיזוּת, "watchfulness brings one to zeal." And "from him people enjoy counsel and wisdom," for he instructs others, granting them understanding of the ways of life, both temporal and eternal.

"The Torah gives him . . . dominion," teaching others communal and social skills, as well as Godly secrets of Torah. "He becomes like a steadily strengthening fountain," increasing his knowledge in subject matters which are not included in Torah. "He becomes modest," which means that he acquires traits [that foster] good deeds.

NOTES

the world. The *Sforno* quotes the verse in *Psalms* as proof of this thesis, for King David praises and extols those who are the dear friends of God.

It is interesting to note that the *Sforno,* in his commentary on *Psalms,* explains this verse (*Psalms* 139:17) differently. There, he follows the interpretation of *Ibn Ezra* and *Radak,* who translate רֵעֶיךָ as your "ideas or concepts," which are dear to me. In his commentary on *Psalms,* the *Sforno* adds that by studying Torah and analyzing the depth of *mitzvos,* one becomes familiar with the thoughts and designs of God. Here, however, he chooses to translate רֵעַ as "a friend and helper."

In his introduction to *Avos,* and in his commentary on the first Mishnah of chapter 4, the *Sforno* stated that the purpose of that chapter is to instruct man how to attain traits of "watchfulness" and "zeal," which result when man's intent in all his deeds is for the glory of God. The *Sforno* applies this thought to explain the meaning of "clothing oneself with humility and fear of God" through Torah, which Rabbi Meir includes in the benefits which accrue to one who studies Torah.

The concluding comment of the *Sforno* on the phrase מֶמְשָׁלָה, "dominion," is prompted by the seeming redundance of this phrase, since the student has already

ו ב

וְחִקּוּר דִּין; וּמְגַלִּין לוֹ רָזֵי תוֹרָה; וְנַעֲשֶׂה כְּמַעְיָן הַמִּתְגַּבֵּר, וּכְנָהָר שֶׁאֵינוֹ פוֹסֵק; וְהֹוֶה צָנוּעַ, וְאֶרֶךְ רוּחַ, וּמוֹחֵל עַל עֶלְבּוֹנוֹ. וּמְגַדַּלְתּוֹ וּמְרוֹמַמְתּוֹ עַל כָּל הַמַּעֲשִׂים.

[ב] **אָמַר** רַבִּי יְהוֹשֻׁעַ בֶּן לֵוִי: בְּכָל יוֹם וָיוֹם בַּת קוֹל יוֹצֵאת מֵהַר חוֹרֵב, וּמַכְרֶזֶת וְאוֹמֶרֶת: „אוֹי לָהֶם לַבְּרִיּוֹת, מֵעֶלְבּוֹנָהּ שֶׁל תּוֹרָה!" שֶׁכָּל מִי שֶׁאֵינוֹ עוֹסֵק בַּתּוֹרָה נִקְרָא נָזוּף, שֶׁנֶּאֱמַר: „נֶזֶם זָהָב בְּאַף חֲזִיר, אִשָּׁה יָפָה וְסָרַת טָעַם." וְאוֹמֵר: „וְהַלֻּחֹת מַעֲשֵׂה אֱלֹהִים הֵמָּה

פירוש לרבי עובדיה ספורנו

ו:ב. עלבונה של תורה כשאין האדם מחשיבה להתבונן בה ולהבין התועלת הנמשך ממנה, ולזה נקרא נזוף שיקרה לו שיקראהו הגוער בו בשם פחות, על דרך עיא עיא ראה מי קורא לך בחוץ. והביא ראיה על זה ממה שאמר שהאשה היפה

SFORNO'S COMMENTARY

6:2

בְּכָל יוֹם . . . בַּת קוֹל יוֹצֵאת . . . — *Every day . . . a heavenly voice emanates . . .* "[Their] insult to the Torah" (occurs) when man fails to esteem and value [Torah], to examine and study it, so as to understand the benefit to be derived from it [then the Torah is, as it were, "insulted"]. Therefore, that person "is called 'rebuked' " — meaning, that when he is reprimanded, he may be called by a derogatory name, as we find (in *Moed Katan* 16b): **עַיְּיָא, מִי קוֹרֵא לְךָ בַּחוּץ**, "Aya, see who is calling to you outside."

The Tanna brings proof to his statement from [the analogy of] a beautiful woman whose husband does not appreciate her beauty. She is like **נֶזֶם זָהָב**

NOTES

6:2

בְּכָל יוֹם . . . בַּת קוֹל יוֹצֵאת . . . — *Every day . . . a heavenly voice emanates . . .* The *Sforno* is of the opinion that unless a person contemplates the greatness and unmatched value of Torah, holding it in the highest esteem, he is guilty of shaming it, even though he does nothing overtly to insult its importance.

The phrase **נָזוּף** , translated as "reprobate," or "rebuked," is used in the Talmud to describe one who is under a ban (**חֵרֶם**).

been promised "kingship." He therefore explains that this second phrase refers to talents and skills in the social, communal area, whereas "kingship" refers to knowledge of Torah, in the sense of מַאן מַלְכֵי רַבָּנָן, "who are kings the Rabbis." This idea of developing expertise in subject matters beyond Torah is also found in his commentary on becoming "a strengthening fountain." All this mirrors the *Sforno*'s own development of disciplines and skills in the fields of science and medicine.

and analytical judgment; the secrets of the Torah are revealed to him; he becomes like a steadily strengthening fountain and like an unceasing river. He becomes modest, patient, and forgiving of insult to himself. [The Torah] makes him great and exalts him above all things.

2. *Rabbi Yehoshua ben Levi said: Every single day a heavenly voice emanates from Mount Horeb, proclaiming and saying, "Woe to them, to the people, because of [their] insult to the Torah!" For whoever does not occupy himself with the Torah is called, "Rebuked," as it is said: "Like a golden ring in a swine's snout is a beautiful woman who turns away from good judgment." And it says: "The Tablets are God's handiwork*

פירוש לרבי עובדיה ספורנו

אשר לא יטעם הטועם את יפיה היא כמו נזם זהב באף חזיר שאינו מכיר ערך וחשיבות הזהב, וקרא הבלתי טועם יופי היפה בשם חזיר. וזה אם כן יקרה למי שאינו עוסק בתורה מבלי אין אצלו הכרת מעלתה ותועלתה, ונתן טעם על שם שהנזיפה ראויה לו מפני שהוא בהתרשלותו מאבד ממנו השגת תועלת וכבוד רב:

SFORNO'S COMMENTARY

בְּאַף חֲזִיר, *a gold ring in a swine's snout* (*Proverbs* 11:22), who does not recognize the value and importance of gold. The Tanna therefore calls this man, who doesn't appreciate his wife's beauty, a "swine." And so it is, when one does not occupy himself with Torah, for he fails to recognize its advantages, usefulness, and benefit. The Tanna in this way gives good reason why this person is worthy of rebuke, for it is due to his carelessness that he has deprived himself from attaining the benefits [of Torah] and the great honor [which it brings].

NOTES

The *Sforno* cites the story of Rebbe, who instructed his pupils not to disseminate Torah outside the *Beis HaMedrash.* His disciple, Rabbi Chiya, did not abide by this instruction, and taught his nephews "outside." When Chiya later came to visit Rebbe, he called him עַיָּא (Aya) instead of חִיָּא (Chiya), thereby rebuking him for his disobedience. The *Sforno* proves from this incident that one may call another by a derogatory name to demonstrate his displeasure with that person's conduct.

By the same token, the proof-verse from *Proverbs* (11:22) is understood by him to mean that one is permitted to call a person who treats Torah with disdain and contempt "a swine"! He also explains the concluding part of this *Beraisa* as describing the loss incurred by neglecting Torah study. One could have realized true freedom and honor, had he only pursued the study of Torah, but through his own lethargy and carelessness, he forfeited both of these gifts.

ו וְהַמִּכְתָּב מִכְתַּב אֱלֹהִים הוּא חָרוּת עַל הַלֻּחֹת.״
ג אַל תִּקְרָא ,,חָרוּת״ אֶלָּא ,,חֵרוּת״, שֶׁאֵין לְךָ בֶּן חוֹרִין אֶלָּא מִי שֶׁעוֹסֵק בְּתַלְמוּד תּוֹרָה. וְכָל מִי שֶׁעוֹסֵק בְּתַלְמוּד תּוֹרָה הֲרֵי זֶה מִתְעַלֶּה, שֶׁנֶּאֱמַר: ,,וּמִמַּתָּנָה נַחֲלִיאֵל, וּמִנַּחֲלִיאֵל בָּמוֹת.״

[ג] **הַלּוֹמֵד** מֵחֲבֵרוֹ פֶּרֶק אֶחָד, אוֹ הֲלָכָה אֶחָת, אוֹ פָּסוּק אֶחָד, אוֹ דִּבּוּר אֶחָד, אוֹ אֲפִילוּ אוֹת אֶחָת – צָרִיךְ לִנְהָג בּוֹ כָּבוֹד. שֶׁכֵּן מָצִינוּ בְּדָוִד מֶלֶךְ יִשְׂרָאֵל, שֶׁלֹּא לָמַד מֵאֲחִיתֹפֶל אֶלָּא שְׁנֵי דְבָרִים בִּלְבָד, וּקְרָאוֹ רַבּוֹ, אַלּוּפוֹ, וּמְיֻדָּעוֹ, שֶׁנֶּאֱמַר: ,,וְאַתָּה אֱנוֹשׁ כְּעֶרְכִּי, אַלּוּפִי וּמְיֻדָּעִי.״ וַהֲלֹא דְבָרִים קַל וָחֹמֶר: וּמָה דָּוִד מֶלֶךְ יִשְׂרָאֵל, שֶׁלֹּא מֵאֲחִיתֹפֶל אֶלָּא שְׁנֵי דְבָרִים בִּלְבָד, קְרָאוֹ רַבּוֹ אַלּוּפוֹ וּמְיֻדָּעוֹ – הַלּוֹמֵד מֵחֲבֵרוֹ פֶּרֶק אֶחָד, אוֹ הֲלָכָה אֶחָת, אוֹ פָּסוּק אֶחָד, אוֹ דִּבּוּר אֶחָד, אוֹ אֲפִילוּ אוֹת אֶחָת, עַל אַחַת כַּמָּה

פירוש לרבי עובדיה ספורנו

ו:ג. ומאחר שמי שלא ילמוד תורה ראוי לעלבון הנזיפה, הנה מי שיהיה מקנה לאדם כבוד שהוא הפך העלבון ראוי לכבוד. והביא ראיה שבענין זה ראוי לנהוג כבוד אפילו במי

SFORNO'S COMMENTARY

6:3

הַלּוֹמֵד מֵחֲבֵרוֹ . . . צָרִיךְ לִנְהָג בּוֹ כָּבוֹד . . . — *He who learns from his fellow man . . . must treat him with honor . . .* Since one who does not study Torah is worthy to be rebuked and insulted, it follows that he who brings honor to another (by teaching him Torah), which is the opposite of contempt, is worthy to be honored himself. And the Tanna brings proof from King David, that under these circumstances, it is fitting to pay respect and honor even to

NOTES

6:3

הַלּוֹמֵד מֵחֲבֵרוֹ . . . צָרִיךְ לִנְהָג בּוֹ כָּבוֹד . . . — *He who learns from his fellow man . . . must treat him with honor . . .* The *Sforno* explains this *Beraisa* section by section, elucidating the various proof-verses cited by the Tanna. The first verse, from *Psalm* 55, where David calls Achitophel "a man of my measure, my guide, and my intimate," is in recognition of Achitophel teaching him two lessons: The first, that a person should not study Torah by himself, and the second, that a king should not walk alone to the house of study. This proves that even one who is

and the script was God's script charus (engraved) on the Tablets." Do not read "charus" (engraved) but 'cherus' (freedom), for you can have no freer man than one who engages in the study of the Torah. And anyone who engages in the study of the Torah becomes elevated, as it is said: "From Mattanah to Nachaliel, and from Nachaliel to Bamos."

3. H*e who learns from his fellow man a single chapter, a single halachah, a single verse, a single Torah statement, or even a single letter, must treat him with honor. For thus we find in the case of David, King of Israel, who learned nothing from Achitophel except for two things, yet called him his teacher, his guide, his intimate, as it is said: "You are a man of my measure, my guide and my intimate." One can derive from this the following: If David, King of Israel, who learned nothing from Achitophel except for two things, called him his teacher, his guide, his intimate — one who learns from his fellowman a single chapter, a single halachah, a single verse, a single statement, or even a single letter, how much more*

פירוש לרבי עובדיה ספורנו

שלמטה ממנו מדוד המלך שנהג כבוד באחיתופל שהיה למטה ממנו. והביא ראיה על מה שאמר אפילו אות אחת כאומרו אין כבוד אלא תורה, כלומר שהתורה היא בעצמה כבוד, לא סבת כבוד בלבד. והנה על כל חלק מהכבוד יצדק שם כבוד, כמשפט כל מתדמה

SFORNO'S COMMENTARY

one of inferior status, for King David honored Achitophel, who was inferior to him. He then brings proof to his statement, "even one letter," by saying, "honor comes only for Torah" — meaning, that Torah in itself is honor, and not merely the *cause* of honor. Hence, regarding any part of honor, one is justified to call it "honor," for the whole is the sum of its parts.

NOTES

superior, such as David compared to Achitophel, must pay honor to his inferior if the latter has taught him Torah. However, how do we know that this is true even if he only teaches him one letter, or one single verse?

The *Sforno* answers, that if one recognizes the value of the totality of Torah it follows that any part of Torah is of great value as well, just as any minute portion of a precious metal has value and worth.

The *Sforno* then proceeds to show how the Tanna connects the verses in *Proverbs*, link by link, to prove that the words "honor and good" refer to Torah.

ו וְכַמָּה שֶׁצָּרִיךְ לִנְהָג בּוֹ כָּבוֹד! וְאֵין כָּבוֹד אֶלָּא
ד תּוֹרָה, שֶׁנֶּאֱמַר: „כָּבוֹד חֲכָמִים יִנְחָלוּ״; „וּתְמִימִים
יִנְחֲלוּ טוֹב״ וְאֵין טוֹב אֶלָּא תוֹרָה, שֶׁנֶּאֱמַר: „כִּי
לֶקַח טוֹב נָתַתִּי לָכֶם, תּוֹרָתִי אַל תַּעֲזֹבוּ.״

[ד] **כָּךְ** הִיא דַרְכָּהּ שֶׁל תּוֹרָה: פַּת בַּמֶּלַח תֹּאכֵל, וּמַיִם בַּמְּשׂוּרָה תִּשְׁתֶּה, וְעַל הָאָרֶץ תִּישַׁן, וְחַיֵּי צַעַר תִּחְיֶה, וּבַתּוֹרָה אַתָּה עָמֵל; אִם אַתָּה עוֹשֶׂה כֵּן, „אַשְׁרֶיךָ וְטוֹב לָךְ״: „אַשְׁרֶיךָ״ — בָּעוֹלָם הַזֶּה, „וְטוֹב לָךְ״ — לָעוֹלָם הַבָּא. אַל תְּבַקֵּשׁ גְּדֻלָּה לְעַצְמְךָ, וְאַל תַּחְמֹד כָּבוֹד יוֹתֵר מִלִּמּוּדֶךָ, עֲשֵׂה וְאַל תִּתְאַוֶּה לְשֻׁלְחָנָם שֶׁל

פירוש לרבי עובדיה ספורנו

החלקים. והביא ראיה על זה שהתורה בעצמה היא כבוד ממה שכתב „כבוד חכמים ינחלו״, והביא על שבאומרו ינחלו אמר זה על התורה שקרא אותה כבוד ממה שנאמר „ותמימים ינחלו [טוב]״, שהטוב הגמור לנפש השכלי הנותן לה מציאות וחיי עולם הוא התורה העיונית, והביא ראיה על זה ממה שאמר „כי לקח טוב נתתי לכם״, ובאר שזה הטוב הוא התורה כאמרו „תורתי אל תעזובו״:

ו:ד. הזהיר משני דברים אשר הם על הרוב המונעים האדם מעסוק בתורה בלי

SFORNO'S COMMENTARY

He then brings proof to his assertion that the Torah itself is "honor" from the verse in *Proverbs*, כָּבוֹד חֲכָמִים יִנְחָלוּ, *The wise shall inherit honor* (3:35). This is a reference to Torah, since the expression "shall inherit" is also found in the verse, וּתְמִימִים יִנְחֲלוּ טוֹב, *And the perfect shall inherit good* (ibid. 28:10), which refers to Torah that is analyzed [by perfect scholars], for it is the source of intellectual and spiritual "good," which grants existence and eternal life [to those who pursue Torah]. He proves this thought from the verse, כִּי לֶקַח טוֹב נָתַתִּי לָכֶם, *I have given you a good teaching* (*Proverbs* 4:2), explaining that "good" refers to Torah, as it says at the conclusion of this verse, תּוֹרָתִי אַל תַּעֲזֹבוּ, *Do not forsake My Torah.*

NOTES

6:4

וְאַל תַּחְמֹד כָּבוֹד — *And do not covet honor* . . . Most commentators interpret the statement, "and do not covet honor," as one lesson, and "let your performance exceed your learning" as a separate one. According to this interpretation, there should be a comma or semi-colon between the words כָּבוֹד and יוֹתֵר.

Not so the *Sforno,* who understands the meaning of the *Beraisa* differently. He links the phrase "do not covet honor," with the next two Hebrew words, יוֹתֵר מִלִּמּוּדֶךָ, interpreting it to mean, "Do not covet honor

must he treat him with honor! And honor is due only for Torah, as it is said: "The wise shall inherit honor"; ". . .and the perfect shall inherit good." And only Torah is truly good, as it is said: "I have given you a good teaching, do not forsake My Torah."

4. *This is the way of Torah: Eat bread with salt, drink water in small measure, sleep on the ground, live a life of deprivation — but toil in the Torah! If you do this, "You are praiseworthy, and all is well with you." "You are praiseworthy" — in this world; "and all is well with you" — in the World to Come. Do not seek greatness for yourself, and do not covet honor beyond your wont, do what you are capable of doing [within your] limitations and do not aspire to the table*

פירוש לרבי עובדיה ספורנו

ספק. האחד הוא החפץ בתענוגי הגוף, ואמר שהעוסק בתורה צריך שיסתפק בהכרחי לחיי שעה ולא יאבד זמנו לבקש מותרות, והשני הוא הכוסף אל הגדולה והמעלה בחיי שעה, ואמר שצריך שלא יחמוד להוסיף כבוד בעולם הזה יותר מלימודו, ר״ל יותר ממה שהורגל בו כפי מדרגתו בחיי שעה. ואמר בהשגת התורה „ימצא חיים ... וכבוד״, גדולי המעלה מכל זולתם:

SFORNO'S COMMENTARY

6:4

כַּךְ הִיא דַּרְכָּהּ שֶׁל תּוֹרָה . . . — *This is the way of Torah . . .* The Tanna cautions us regarding two things which usually prevent man from occupying himself with Torah study. One is the desire for physical pleasure. He therefore tells us that one who wishes to occupy himself with Torah must be satisfied with the basic necessities of life, and not squander his time in the pursuit of luxuries. The second [failing] is the longing for position and prominence in this world. The Tanna therefore teaches us not to covet honor in this world beyond the status and station to which he is accustomed in this transitory world.

He concludes by stating that in the attainment and mastery of Torah, man will realize a life of honor and prestige superior to all others.

NOTES

beyond your wont" — i.e., more than what you are accustomed to, in keeping with your station in life. He puts the comma after מִלִּמּוּדֶךָ. Consequently, the next section must be read עֲשֵׂה וְאַל תִּתְאַוֶּה וכו׳, "Do what you are capable of doing [within your limitations], and do not aspire to the table of kings."

ו מְלָכִים, שֶׁשֻּׁלְחָנְךָ גָּדוֹל מִשֻּׁלְחָנָם, וְכִתְרְךָ גָּדוֹל
ה מִכִּתְרָם; וְנֶאֱמָן הוּא בַּעַל מְלַאכְתְּךָ, שֶׁיְּשַׁלֶּם לְךָ
שְׂכַר פְּעֻלָּתֶךָ.

[ה] **גְּדוֹלָה** תּוֹרָה יוֹתֵר מִן הַכְּהֻנָּה וּמִן הַמַּלְכוּת, שֶׁהַמַּלְכוּת נִקְנֵית בִּשְׁלֹשִׁים מַעֲלוֹת, וְהַכְּהֻנָּה נִקְנֵית בְּעֶשְׂרִים וְאַרְבָּעָה, וְהַתּוֹרָה נִקְנֵית בְּאַרְבָּעִים וּשְׁמוֹנָה

פירוש לרבי עובדיה ספורנו

ו:ה. כבר אמרו שלשה כתרים הם כתר תורה כתר כהנה וכתר מלכות, ובזה אמר שכתר התורה גדול מן השני כתרים הנשארים. וזה כי אמנם כתר המלכות נקנה בשלשים מעלות כלם גשמיות מסבבות כבוד בחיי שעה, והם הנזכרות במשפט המלוכה אשר בהם שרשים מתפשטים לענפים רבים, והמלך מותר בהם לפחות לצורך מלחמה. וכן כתר הכהנה נקנה בכ״ד מתנות כהנה אשר בהן תהיה כבוד הכהנה,

SFORNO'S COMMENTARY

6:5

גְּדוֹלָה תּוֹרָה יוֹתֵר מִן הַכְּהֻנָּה וּמִן הַמַּלְכוּת — *Torah is even greater than priesthood or royalty.* It has already been taught (chapter 4) that there are three crowns: the crown of Torah, the crown of priesthood, and the crown of royalty. In this *Beraisa*, we are told that the crown of Torah is greater than the other two crowns. Because the crown of royalty "is acquired along with thirty prerogatives" [of office], all of which are material, bringing honor to man in this temporal life. These are enumerated in the "laws of royalty," and from these roots many other privileges branch out. Now, the king is empowered to exercise all these rights, especially in a time of war.

Also, the crown of priesthood, acquired along with "twenty-four gifts" — these being the מַתְּנוֹת כְּהוּנָּה, "the gifts of priesthood" — are for the purpose of granting honor to the *Kohanim,* as it says, לְךָ נְתַתִּים לְמָשְׁחָה, *I have given*

NOTES

6:5

גְּדוֹלָה תּוֹרָה יוֹתֵר מִן הַכְּהֻנָּה וּמִן הַמַּלְכוּת — *Torah is even greater than priesthood or royalty.* The *Sforno* does not interpret the thirty and twenty-four items, associated with kingship and priesthood respectively, as being the *means* by which these crowns are acquired. Rather, he understands them as being the *privileges* of royalty and priesthood. These prerogatives, however, are inferior to those gained by the man of Torah because they are all *material* gains, and thus, transitory. Not so Torah. The forty-eight qualities and virtues enumerated by the Tanna, resulting from Torah study, are *spiritual* and *intellectual* in nature, and bring man to a level of ethical and moral excellence. Hence, the crown of Torah is far superior to the crowns of royalty and priesthood.

The reason why the *Sforno* introduces the idea of a "crown" is not only because of the Mishnah in chapter 4, but also because he links our *Beraisa* to the previous one,

of kings, for your table is greater than theirs, and your crown is greater than their crown; and your Employer is trustworthy to pay you remuneration for your deeds.

5. *Torah is even greater than priesthood or royalty; for royalty is acquired along with thirty prerogatives, and the priesthood with twenty-four [gifts], but the Torah is acquired by means of forty-eight qualities,*

פירוש לרבי עובדיה ספורנו

באמרו „לך נתתים למשחה", וכלן גשמיות מקנות כבוד בחיי שעה. אמנם כתר תורה נקנה בהפך זה, כי אמנם כל אלה שהזכיר אינם מעלות אבל דברים מבדילים ומפרישים האדם מן החמריות ומכבוד חיי שעה, ותכלית זה בהכרח הוא להקנות כבוד לחיי עולם אשר אין בינו ובין כבוד חיי שעה שום ערך והדמות. ואמר שמתנות הכבוד לחיי עולם היא אמירת הדבר בשם אומרו, כמו שאמרו ז"ל ששפתיו דובבות בקבר, ומכאן אתה למד שזאת המדה מביאה גאולה לעולם בחיי שעה ובחיי

SFORNO'S COMMENTARY

them to you for distinction [by reason of the anointing] (*Numbers* 18:8). These are also material gifts, bringing with them temporary honor in this life.

However, the crown of Torah is acquired contrary (to those of kingship and priesthood). For all the items listed (regarding Torah) are not prerogatives but qualities which differentiate and separate man from the material (aspects of life) and from the honor of this world. The purpose [of Torah] must therefore be to grant man honor in his *eternal life,* and there is no comparison or quantitative parallel between that honor and the honors of transitory life.

(The Tanna) tells us that among the gifts of honor in eternal life is "repeating a saying in the name of the one who said it," as our Sages taught שְׂפָתָיו דּוֹבְבוֹת בַּקֶּבֶר, *"His lips whisper in the grave"* (*Yevamos* 97). And from this we also learn that this quality brings redemption to the world, be it the

NOTES

which stated, "and your crown is greater than their crown."

The thirty prerogatives of the king mentioned by the Tanna are based on the episode in the Book of *I Samuel,* Chapter 8, when the people of Israel requested of Samuel the Prophet to appoint a king to rule over them. He cautioned them that the king would be empowered to draft their sons as soldiers, and their daughters as cooks and bakers. He would also be entitled to take a tenth of their seed and sheep, and appropriate their fields and vineyards for his officers and servants. The *Rambam* in *Hilchos Melachim,* Chapter 4, lists the far-reaching powers and entitlements of a king. These add up to thirty, as stated in our *Beraisa.*

The twenty-four gifts of priesthood are enumerated in the Talmud, Tractate *Bava Kamma* 110: "Ten are in the Temple, four in Jerusalem, and ten throughout the land." The *Rambam* in *Hilchos Bikkurim,* Chapter One, lists the twenty-four gifts given to the children of Aaron from the sacrificial offerings, all first-born animals, first fruits, and *terumah* and *challah,* among others.

ו דְבָרִים, וְאֵלּוּ הֵן: בְּתַלְמוּד, בִּשְׁמִיעַת הָאֹזֶן, בַּעֲרִיכַת
ה שְׂפָתָיִם, בְּבִינַת הַלֵּב, בְּשִׂכְלוּת הַלֵּב, בְּאֵימָה,
בְּיִרְאָה, בַּעֲנָוָה, בְּשִׂמְחָה, בְּטָהֳרָה, בְּשִׁמּוּשׁ חֲכָמִים,
בְּדִקְדּוּק חֲבֵרִים, בְּפִלְפּוּל הַתַּלְמִידִים, בְּיִשּׁוּב,
בְּמִקְרָא, בְּמִשְׁנָה, בְּמִעוּט סְחוֹרָה, בְּמִעוּט דֶּרֶךְ
אֶרֶץ, בְּמִעוּט תַּעֲנוּג, בְּמִעוּט שֵׁנָה, בְּמִעוּט שִׂיחָה,
בְּמִעוּט שְׂחוֹק, בְּאֶרֶךְ אַפַּיִם, בְּלֵב טוֹב, בֶּאֱמוּנַת
חֲכָמִים, בְּקַבָּלַת הַיִּסּוּרִין, הַמַּכִּיר אֶת מְקוֹמוֹ,
וְהַשָּׂמֵחַ בְּחֶלְקוֹ, וְהָעוֹשֶׂה סְיָג לִדְבָרָיו, וְאֵינוֹ מַחֲזִיק
טוֹבָה לְעַצְמוֹ, אָהוּב, אוֹהֵב אֶת הַמָּקוֹם, אוֹהֵב אֶת
הַבְּרִיּוֹת, אוֹהֵב אֶת הַצְּדָקוֹת, אוֹהֵב אֶת הַמֵּישָׁרִים,
אוֹהֵב אֶת הַתּוֹכָחוֹת, וּמִתְרַחֵק מִן הַכָּבוֹד, וְלֹא מֵגִיס
לִבּוֹ בְּתַלְמוּדוֹ, וְאֵינוֹ שָׂמֵחַ בְּהוֹרָאָה, נוֹשֵׂא בְעֹל עִם
חֲבֵרוֹ, וּמַכְרִיעוֹ לְכַף זְכוּת, וּמַעֲמִידוֹ עַל הָאֱמֶת,
וּמַעֲמִידוֹ עַל הַשָּׁלוֹם, וּמִתְיַשֵּׁב לִבּוֹ בְּתַלְמוּדוֹ, שׁוֹאֵל
וּמֵשִׁיב, שׁוֹמֵעַ וּמוֹסִיף, הַלּוֹמֵד עַל מְנָת לְלַמֵּד,
וְהַלּוֹמֵד עַל מְנָת לַעֲשׂוֹת, הַמַּחְכִּים אֶת רַבּוֹ, וְהַמְכַוֵּן
אֶת שְׁמוּעָתוֹ, וְהָאוֹמֵר דָּבָר בְּשֵׁם אוֹמְרוֹ. הָא לָמַדְתָּ,
כָּל הָאוֹמֵר דָּבָר בְּשֵׁם אוֹמְרוֹ, מֵבִיא גְאֻלָּה לָעוֹלָם,
שֶׁנֶּאֱמַר: „וַתֹּאמֶר אֶסְתֵּר לַמֶּלֶךְ בְּשֵׁם מָרְדֳּכָי.״

פירוש לרבי עובדיה ספורנו

עולם, שהרי מענין „דובב שפתי ישנים״ למדנו למדת גאולתה לחיי עולם מיד המקטרגים וממדת הדין, ועל הגאולה הנמשכת מזאת המדה לחיי שעה הביא ראיה ממה שנאמר ותאמר אסתר למלך בשם מרדכי שהיה זה סבה לגאולה בחיי שעה:

SFORNO'S COMMENTARY

transitory or permanent (eternal) one, for the verse, דּוֹבֵב שִׂפְתֵי יְשֵׁנִים, *The lips of those who softly murmur* (*Song of Songs* 7:10), refers to one's redemption from the "accusers" and the "attribute of justice" in the eternal world. And

NOTES

The *Sforno* interprets the statement, "Whoever repeats a thing in the name of the one who said it. . .," as meaning that, be it in this world or the World to Come, redemption is the reward for this quality. The verse quoted from *Megillas Esther* is the

6 *which are: Study, attentive listening, articulate speech,*
5 *intuitive understanding, discernment, awe, reverence,*
modesty, joy, purity, ministering to the sages, closeness with colleagues, sharp discussion with students, deliberation, [knowledge of] Scripture, Mishnah, limited business activity, limited sexual activity, limited pleasure, limited sleep, limited conversation, limited laughter, slowness to anger, a good heart, faith in the sages, acceptance of suffering, knowing one's place, being happy with one's lot, making a protective fence around his personal matters, claiming no credit for himself, being beloved, loving the Omnipresent, loving [His] creatures, loving righteous ways, loving justice, loving reproof, keeping far from honor, not being arrogant with his learning, not enjoying halachic decision-making, sharing his fellow's yoke, judging him favorably, setting him on the truthful course, setting him on the peaceful course, thinking deliberately in his study, asking and answering, listening and contributing to the discussion, learning in order to teach, learning in order to practice, making his teacher wiser, pondering over what he has learned, and repeating a saying in the name of the one who said it. For you have learned this: Whoever repeats a thing in the name of the one who said it brings redemption to the world, as it is said: "And Esther reported it to the king in the name of Mordechai."

SFORNO'S COMMENTARY

as for redemption in this world (transitory life), which results from this quality, he brings proof from the verse in *Esther*, וַתֹּאמֶר אֶסְתֵּר לַמֶּלֶךְ בְּשֵׁם מָרְדֳּכָי, *And Esther reported it to the king in the name of Mordechai* (2:22), which was the cause of the redemption in this transitory life.

NOTES

proof-verse for the reward of redemption in this world, since the Jews were saved and redeemed in the time of Mordechai and Esther as a result of her telling the king that it was Mordechai's report of the plot against the king that saved his life. As for redemption in "eternal life," he explains that this refers to the protection afforded the Torah scholar from the "heavenly accusers" after his demise, as a consequence of the scholar's ongoing merit, even in the grave, whenever the living repeat Torah in his name. Our Sages teach us this lesson in *Mesechta Yevamos* 97, based on the verse in *Shir HaShirim*, quoted by the *Sforno* in his commentary on this *Beraisa*.

ו
ו־ז

[ו] **גְּדוֹלָה** תוֹרָה, שֶׁהִיא נוֹתֶנֶת חַיִּים לְעוֹשֶׂיהָ בָּעוֹלָם הַזֶּה וּבָעוֹלָם הַבָּא, שֶׁנֶּאֱמַר: „כִּי חַיִּים הֵם לְמֹצְאֵיהֶם, וּלְכָל בְּשָׂרוֹ מַרְפֵּא." וְאוֹמֵר: „רִפְאוּת תְּהִי לְשָׁרֶּךָ, וְשִׁקּוּי לְעַצְמוֹתֶיךָ." וְאוֹמֵר: „עֵץ חַיִּים הִיא לַמַּחֲזִיקִים בָּהּ וְתֹמְכֶיהָ מְאֻשָּׁר." וְאוֹמֵר: „כִּי לִוְיַת חֵן הֵם לְרֹאשֶׁךָ, וַעֲנָקִים לְגַרְגְּרֹתֶיךָ." וְאוֹמֵר: „תִּתֵּן לְרֹאשְׁךָ לִוְיַת חֵן, עֲטֶרֶת תִּפְאֶרֶת תְּמַגְּנֶךָּ." וְאוֹמֵר: „כִּי בִי יִרְבּוּ יָמֶיךָ, וְיוֹסִיפוּ לְךָ שְׁנוֹת חַיִּים." וְאוֹמֵר: „אֹרֶךְ יָמִים בִּימִינָהּ, בִּשְׂמֹאולָהּ עֹשֶׁר וְכָבוֹד." וְאוֹמֵר: „כִּי אֹרֶךְ יָמִים וּשְׁנוֹת חַיִּים, וְשָׁלוֹם יוֹסִיפוּ לָךְ."

[ז] **רַבִּי** שִׁמְעוֹן בֶּן יְהוּדָה מִשּׁוּם רַבִּי שִׁמְעוֹן בֶּן יוֹחַאי אוֹמֵר: הַנּוֹי, וְהַכֹּחַ, וְהָעֹשֶׁר, וְהַכָּבוֹד, וְהַחָכְמָה, וְהַזִּקְנָה, וְהַשֵּׂיבָה, וְהַבָּנִים — נָאֶה לַצַּדִּיקִים וְנָאֶה לָעוֹלָם, שֶׁנֶּאֱמַר:

פירוש לרבי עובדיה ספורנו

ו:ו. כבר מנו חכמים קצת מצות שאדם אוכל פירותיהן בעולם הזה והקרן קיימת לו לעולם הבא, ובתוכם אמרו תלמוד תורה כנגד כלם, ובזה אמר שהתורה נותנת חיים ואישור במדרגות שונות בעולם הזה ובעולם הבא. והביא ראיה באלו הכתובים על היותה מסבבת חיי העולם הזה, וכן על האישור בם ועל היותה מסבבת חיי עולם,

SFORNO'S COMMENTARY

6:6

גְּדוֹלָה תוֹרָה, שֶׁהִיא נוֹתֶנֶת חַיִּים לְעוֹשֶׂיהָ — *Great is Torah, for it confers life upon its practitioners.* The Sages enumerate a number of *mitzvos* which אָדָם אוֹכֵל פֵּרוֹתֵיהֶן בָּעוֹלָם הַזֶּה וְהַקֶּרֶן קַיֶּמֶת לוֹ לָעוֹלָם הַבָּא, *A person enjoys its fruits in this world, but its principal remains intact for him in the World to Come* (*Peah* 1:1). Among them, the Mishnah states: וְתַלְמוּד תּוֹרָה כְּנֶגֶד כֻּלָּם, *the study of Torah is equivalent to them all.* Hence, our *Beraisa* teaches us that Torah confers life and happiness, on different levels in this world and the World to Come. The Tanna brings proof from these verses (in *Proverbs*) that Torah is the cause of

NOTES

6:6

גְּדוֹלָה תוֹרָה, שֶׁהִיא נוֹתֶנֶת חַיִּים לְעוֹשֶׂיהָ — *Great is Torah, for it confers life upon its practitioners.* The *Sforno,* by quoting from the Mishnah in *Mesechta Peah,* focuses on the phraseology of our Tanna, who states that both this world and the World to Come are affected by one's study of Torah. The

6. *Great is Torah, for it confers life upon its practitioners, both in this world and in the World to Come, as it is said: "For they [the teachings of the Torah] are life to those who find them, and a healing to his entire flesh." And it says: "It shall be healing to your body, and marrow to your bones." And it says: "It is a tree of life to those who grasp it, and its supporters are praiseworthy." And it says: "They are a garland of grace for your head, and necklaces for your neck." And it says: "It will give to your head a garland of grace, a crown of glory it will deliver to you." And it says: "Indeed, through me [the Torah] your days shall be increased, and years of life shall be added to you." And it says: "Lengthy days are at its right, and at its left are wealth and honor." And it says: "For lengthy days and years of life, and peace shall they add to you."*

7. *Rabbi Shimon ben Yehudah says in the name of Rabbi Shimon ben Yochai: Beauty, strength, wealth, honor, wisdom, old age, hoary age, and children — these befit the righteous and befit the world, as*

פירוש לרבי עובדיה ספורנו

ועל מיני האישור בם כפי טוב כוונת העוסק בה וכפי רב השתדלותו:

ו:ז. אמר שהוא נאה לצדיקים ונאה לעולם שיהיו לצדיקים אלו ההצלחות ויתמיד בהם

SFORNO'S COMMENTARY

life and happiness in this world, and that it is also the source of life and happiness in the World to Come, all according to the quality of one's occupation with Torah, and commensurate with the extent of one's efforts.

6:7

. . . נָאֶה לַצַּדִּיקִים וְנָאֶה לָעוֹלָם — . . . *These befit the righteous and befit the world.* The Tanna says that it "befits the righteous and befits the world" when the

NOTES

Tanna in *Peah* extols Torah beyond all other *mitzvos,* and assures us that it benefits man in both worlds. In our *Beraisa,* proof that the power of Torah can effectuate a multitude of blessings is brought from eight different verses in *Proverbs.* The *Sforno* points out, however, that these blessings are on various levels, depending upon the motivation and the degree of one's application to the pursuit of Torah scholarship.

6:7

. . . וְהַזִּקְנָה . . . נָאֶה לַצַּדִּיקִים וְנָאֶה לָעוֹלָם — . . . *Old age . . . these befit the righteous and befit the world.* Among the seven qualities listed

ו „עֲטֶרֶת תִּפְאֶרֶת שֵׂיבָה, בְּדֶרֶךְ צְדָקָה תִּמָּצֵא.״
ח וְאוֹמֵר: „עֲטֶרֶת זְקֵנִים בְּנֵי בָנִים, וְתִפְאֶרֶת בָּנִים
אֲבוֹתָם.״ וְאוֹמֵר: „תִּפְאֶרֶת בַּחוּרִים כֹּחָם, וַהֲדַר
זְקֵנִים שֵׂיבָה.״ וְאוֹמֵר „וְחָפְרָה הַלְּבָנָה וּבוֹשָׁה
הַחַמָּה, כִּי מָלַךְ יהוה צְבָאוֹת בְּהַר צִיּוֹן
וּבִירוּשָׁלַיִם, וְנֶגֶד זְקֵנָיו כָּבוֹד.״ רַבִּי שִׁמְעוֹן בֶּן
מְנַסְיָא אוֹמֵר: אֵלּוּ שֶׁבַע מִדּוֹת, שֶׁמָּנוּ חֲכָמִים
לַצַּדִּיקִים, כֻּלָּם נִתְקַיְּמוּ בְּרַבִּי וּבְבָנָיו.

[ח] **אָמַר** רַבִּי יוֹסֵי בֶּן קִסְמָא: פַּעַם אַחַת הָיִיתִי
מְהַלֵּךְ בַּדֶּרֶךְ, וּפָגַע בִּי אָדָם אֶחָד.
וְנָתַן לִי שָׁלוֹם, וְהֶחֱזַרְתִּי לוֹ שָׁלוֹם. אָמַר לִי: „רַבִּי,
מֵאֵיזֶה מָקוֹם אָתָּה?״ אָמַרְתִּי לוֹ: „מֵעִיר גְּדוֹלָה שֶׁל
חֲכָמִים וְשֶׁל סוֹפְרִים אָנִי.״ אָמַר לִי: „רַבִּי, רְצוֹנְךָ
שֶׁתָּדוּר עִמָּנוּ בִּמְקוֹמֵנוּ וַאֲנִי אֶתֵּן לְךָ אֶלֶף אֲלָפִים
דִּינְרֵי זָהָב וַאֲבָנִים טוֹבוֹת וּמַרְגָּלִיּוֹת?״ אָמַרְתִּי
לוֹ: „אִם אַתָּה נוֹתֵן לִי כָּל כֶּסֶף וְזָהָב וַאֲבָנִים
טוֹבוֹת וּמַרְגָּלִיּוֹת שֶׁבָּעוֹלָם, אֵינִי דָר אֶלָּא בִּמְקוֹם
תּוֹרָה.״ וְכֵן כָּתוּב בְּסֵפֶר תְּהִלִּים עַל יְדֵי דָוִד מֶלֶךְ
יִשְׂרָאֵל: „טוֹב לִי תוֹרַת פִּיךָ מֵאַלְפֵי זָהָב וָכָסֶף.״

פירוש לרבי עובדיה ספורנו

זמן ארוך כדי שיוכלו להיטיב לזולתם, וראוי להתפלל על צדיקי הדור שישיגו כל אלה ההצלחות לטובתם ולתועלת בני דורם. והביא ראיה על קצתם מן המקראות,

SFORNO'S COMMENTARY

righteous meet with this success [i.e., beauty, strength, etc.] and enjoy them for a long period of time, for they will then be able to do good unto others. It is [therefore] fitting that one pray on behalf of the righteous of one's generation, that they should attain these successes, for their own benefit and for the sake of the people of their generation. The Tanna brings proof to

NOTES

in our *Beraisa* is "old age." Hence, the *Sforno* understands the Tanna to mean that these attributes of success, in order to be fully experienced by the righteous and shared with others, should be of long duration. From the phrase, "befit the righteous and befit the world," the *Sforno* deduces that these qualities are not

it is said: "Ripe old age is a crown of splendor, it can be found in the path of righteousness." And it says: "The crown of the aged is grandchildren, and the splendor of children is their fathers." And it says: "The splendor of young men is their strength, and the glory of old men is hoary age." And it says: "The moon will grow pale and the sun be shamed, when HASHEM, *Master of Legions, will have reigned on Mount Zion and in Jerusalem, and honor shall be before His elders." Rabbi Shimon ben Menasya said: These seven qualities that the Sages attributed to the righteous were all realized in Rabbi and his sons.*

8. *Rabbi Yose ben Kisma said: Once I was walking on the road, when a certain man met me. He greeted me and I returned his greeting. He said to me, "Rabbi, from what place are you?" I said to him, "I am from a great city of scholars and sages." He said to me, "Rabbi, would you be willing to live with us in our place? I would give you thousands upon thousands of golden dinars, precious stones and pearls." I replied, "Even if you were to give me all the silver and gold, precious stones and pearls in the world, I would dwell nowhere but in a place of Torah." And so it is written in the Book of Psalms by David, King of Israel: "I prefer the Torah of Your mouth above thousands in gold and silver."*

פירוש לרבי עובדיה ספורנו

והעיד רבי שמעון בן מנסיא שאין זה איפשר רחוק שימצאו כל אלה ההצלחות יחדו בצדיקים, והעיד כי אמנם כלם יחד נמצאו בדורו ברבי ובניו:

SFORNO'S COMMENTARY

this teaching from a number of verses. Rabbi Shimon ben Menasya then testified that it is not impossible for all these attributes of success to be found in one righteous person and his family, for indeed, in his generation this was the case with "Rabbi and his sons."

NOTES

granted to man exclusively for his own enjoyment, but are to be used for the benefit of others as well. The reason for the inclusion of Rabbi Shimon ben Menasia's statement is to emphasize that all these qualities can be found in one person and his family, and hence, it is a realistic goal toward which man should strive.

ו וְלֹא עוֹד אֶלָּא שֶׁבִּשְׁעַת פְּטִירָתוֹ שֶׁל אָדָם אֵין
ח מְלַוִּין לוֹ לְאָדָם לֹא כֶסֶף וְלֹא זָהָב וְלֹא אֲבָנִים
טוֹבוֹת וּמַרְגָּלִיּוֹת, אֶלָּא תוֹרָה וּמַעֲשִׂים טוֹבִים
בִּלְבָד, שֶׁנֶּאֱמַר: „בְּהִתְהַלֶּכְךָ תַּנְחֶה אֹתָךְ,
בְּשָׁכְבְּךָ תִּשְׁמֹר עָלֶיךָ, וַהֲקִיצוֹתָ הִיא תְשִׂיחֶךָ.״
„בְּהִתְהַלֶּכְךָ תַּנְחֶה אֹתָךְ״ – בָּעוֹלָם הַזֶּה;
„בְּשָׁכְבְּךָ תִּשְׁמֹר עָלֶיךָ״ – בַּקֶּבֶר; „וַהֲקִיצוֹתָ
הִיא תְשִׂיחֶךָ״ – לָעוֹלָם הַבָּא. וְאוֹמֵר: „לִי
הַכֶּסֶף וְלִי הַזָּהָב, נְאֻם יהוה צְבָאוֹת.״

פירוש לרבי עובדיה ספורנו

ו:ח. אלא תורה ומעשים טובים בלבד, ושתי אלה לא יושגו על השלמות זולתי בחברת תופשי התורה העוסקים בתורה ובמעשים טובים, וזה כי בחברתם יוסיף דעת בתורה וירגיל עצמו במעשים טובים כמותם, וכשייטיב האדם שם לזולתו תהיה הטבתו לבני אדם מהוגנים. ומביא ראיה על שהתורה מלוה את האדם בשעת פטירתו ממה שכתוב „בשכבך תשמור עליך״ שלא יצטער בקבר. והביא ראיה על היות הזהב

SFORNO'S COMMENTARY

6:8

אֵין מְלַוִּין לוֹ . . . לֹא כֶסֶף . . . אֶלָּא תוֹרָה וּמַעֲשִׂים טוֹבִים — *Neither silver . . . escort him, but only Torah study and good deeds.* "Only Torah study and good deeds" [escort a person when he departs this world], and these can only be fully attained in the company of those "who grasp the Torah" and occupy themselves with Torah and good deeds. This is so because, in their company, one will increase his knowledge of Torah and train himself to habitually perform good deeds in the same manner as they. Also, when he does good for others, it will be on behalf of people who are worthy [to be the recipients of his good deeds].

The Tanna brings proof that the Torah accompanies a person when he departs from this world from the verse, בְּשָׁכְבְּךָ תִּשְׁמֹר עָלֶיךָ, *When you lie down, it shall guard you* (*Proverbs* 6:22) — meaning, that you will suffer no

NOTES

6:8

אֵין מְלַוִּין לוֹ . . . לֹא כֶסֶף . . . אֶלָּא תוֹרָה וּמַעֲשִׂים טוֹבִים — *Neither silver . . . escort him, but only Torah study and good deeds.* The *Sforno* explains why Rabbi Yose declined the invitation extended to him to dwell in a community which he assumed was devoid of Torah. Since man's mission and purpose in life is to attain Torah and perform good deeds, could not Rabbi Yose have done so in any community? Nonetheless, he believed that he could not realize perfection in his Torah study without the intellectual stimulation of others and the opportunity to learn from other scholars.

6
8 *Furthermore, when a man departs from this world, neither silver, nor gold, nor precious stones nor pearls escort him, but only Torah study and good deeds, as it is said: "When you walk, it shall guide you; when you lie down, it shall guard you; and when you awake, it shall speak on your behalf." "When you walk, it shall guide you" — in this world; "when you lie down, it shall guard you" — in the grave; "and when you awake, it shall speak on your behalf" — in the World to Come. And it says: "Mine is the silver, and Mine is the gold, says* HASHEM, *Master of Legions."*

פירוש לרבי עובדיה ספורנו

והכסף בלתי נחשבים אצל בעל הנסיון בערך אל התורה מדברי דוד המלך שנסה זה ברב עשרו ואמר „טוב לי תורת פיך מאלפי זהב וכסף", והביא ראיה שאין ראוי להשתמש בכסף וזהב הבלתי הכרחיים לחיי שעה אלא כשנשתמש בהן לכבודו יתברך, ממה שכתוב „לי הכסף ולי הזהב אמר יי צבאות":

SFORNO'S COMMENTARY

pain in the grave. And he brings proof that gold and silver are unimportant in comparison to Torah from one [i.e., David] who experienced both, for although King David enjoyed great wealth, he said, טוֹב לִי תוֹרַת פִּיךָ מֵאַלְפֵי זָהָב וָכָסֶף, *I prefer the Torah of Your mouth more than thousands in gold and silver* (*Psalms* 119:72). And he brings proof that it is improper to use silver and gold, that is not necessary in this transitory life, from the verse in *Hagai* 2:8, לִי הַכֶּסֶף וְלִי הַזָּהָב נְאֻם ה׳ צְבָאוֹת, *Mine is the silver and Mine is the gold, says Hashem, Master of Legions,* unless it be for the honor of God, Blessed is He.

NOTES

The same is true regarding good deeds, for only in the environment of a "good society" will one habitually do good deeds. The *Sforno* also adds that even when doing good for others, it is proper to do so only on behalf of those who deserve to be the recipients of these good deeds.

Regarding the value of gold and silver as compared to Torah, the *Sforno* points out that the proof-verse cited by Rabbi Yose is selected most carefully. A person who has never been wealthy has no way of judging the relative value and worth of Torah compared to riches. That is why proof is brought from King David, who possessed both, and has the credibility to attest to the superiority of Torah!

The *Sforno* also interprets the verse from *Hagai* as an admonition not to use one's excess wealth for frivolous and mundane purposes, since "gold and silver" are not really his to do with as he sees fit. Rather, they are God's, and as such, should only be used for His honor and glory.

ו
ט

[ט] **חֲמִשָּׁה** קִנְיָנִים קָנָה הַקָּדוֹשׁ בָּרוּךְ הוּא בְּעוֹלָמוֹ, וְאֵלּוּ הֵן: תּוֹרָה – קִנְיָן אֶחָד, שָׁמַיִם וָאָרֶץ – קִנְיָן אֶחָד, אַבְרָהָם – קִנְיָן אֶחָד, יִשְׂרָאֵל – קִנְיָן אֶחָד, בֵּית הַמִּקְדָּשׁ – קִנְיָן אֶחָד. תּוֹרָה מִנַּיִן? דִּכְתִיב: „יהוה קָנָנִי רֵאשִׁית דַּרְכּוֹ, קֶדֶם מִפְעָלָיו מֵאָז.״ שָׁמַיִם וָאָרֶץ מִנַּיִן? דִּכְתִיב: „כֹּה אָמַר יהוה, הַשָּׁמַיִם כִּסְאִי, וְהָאָרֶץ הֲדֹם רַגְלָי, אֵי זֶה בַיִת אֲשֶׁר תִּבְנוּ לִי, וְאֵי זֶה מָקוֹם מְנוּחָתִי״; וְאוֹמֵר: „מָה רַבּוּ מַעֲשֶׂיךָ יהוה, כֻּלָּם בְּחָכְמָה עָשִׂיתָ, מָלְאָה הָאָרֶץ קִנְיָנֶךָ.״ אַבְרָהָם

פירוש לרבי עובדיה ספורנו

ו:ט. אמר שהתכלית שכיון האל יתברך לקנותו ולהשיג במה שברא נשלם בחמשה דברים. ואמר שהראשון הוא התורה שהיא לשלמות נמצא בחיריי שיהיה בצלמו יתברך ובדמותו, הביא ראיה על זה ממה שנאמר „אני חכמה״ כולי „יי קנני ראשית דרכו״: והשני הוא מציאות שמים וארץ אשר במציאותם נמצא המין האנושי המוכן

SFORNO'S COMMENTARY

6:9

חֲמִשָּׁה קִנְיָנִים קָנָה הקב״ה בְּעוֹלָמוֹ — *Five possessions did the Holy One, Blessed is He, acquire for Himself in His world.* The Tanna states that the ultimate goal the Almighty wished to reach and attain through creation was completed with these five possessions. He states that the first one is Torah, which serves to perfect and complete the being who has free choice (i.e. the human being) so that he be in His image and likeness. He brings proof to this from the verses in *Proverbs*, אֲנִי חָכְמָה... ה׳ קָנָנִי רֵאשִׁית דַּרְכּוֹ, *I am wisdom ... HASHEM acquired me [the Torah] at the beginning of His way* (8:12-22).

The second is the existence of heaven and earth, for through their existence the human species is able to realize that perfection, which was the

NOTES

6:9

חֲמִשָּׁה קִנְיָנִים קָנָה הקב״ה בְּעוֹלָמוֹ — *Five possessions did the Holy One, Blessed is He, acquire for Himself in His world.* The *Sforno* explains that the word קִנְיָן, *possession,* used by the Tanna of this *Beraisa,* is meant to depict God in His role as Creator. Everything the Almighty created has purpose, and is the fulfillment of His will. As His will is perfect and complete, so is His creation. The five things enumerated in the *Beraisa* complete the process of creation and bring it to its perfection. The *Sforno* analyzes God's five possessions, which are: Torah; heaven and earth; Abraham, who represents the ideal man visualized by Hashem; and the people chosen by God to effectuate His Divine plan here on earth, these being the people of Israel; and the Holy Temple in Jerusalem.

The *Sforno* explains the reason for bringing additional proof-verses for two of these Godly possessions, for in each case the additional verse amplifies and clarifies the

9. *Five possessions did the Holy One, Blessed is He, acquire for Himself in His world, and they are: Torah, one possession; heaven and earth, one possession; Abraham, one possession; Israel, one possession; the Holy Temple, one possession. From where do we know this about the Torah? Since it is written: "HASHEM acquired me [the Torah] at the beginning of His way, before His works in time of yore." From where do we know this about heaven and earth? Since it is written: "So says HASHEM. The heaven is My throne, and the earth is My footstool; what House can you build for Me, and where is the place of My rest?" And it says: "How abundant are Your works, HASHEM, with wisdom You made them all, the earth is full of Your possessions."*

פירוש לרבי עובדיה ספורנו

להיות אותו השלם אשר כיון הוא יתברך בבריאה, והביא ראיה על זה ממה שנאמ׳ „השמים כסאי והארץ הדום רגלי״ כולי „ואל זה אביט אל עני ונכה רוח וחרד על דברי״, ומזה התבאר שזה הנמצא החרד ומשתדל בדבר האל יתברך שהוא התורה הוא המכוון במציאות שמים וארץ. וכן הביא ראיה ממה שנאמר „מה רבו מעשיך יי כלם בחכמה עשית״ הנאמר אחר שספר חדוש שמים וארץ, כלומר שכל מה

SFORNO'S COMMENTARY

intent of God's creation. He brings proof to this from the verses in *Isaiah*: הַשָּׁמַיִם כִּסְאִי וְהָאָרֶץ הֲדֹם רַגְלָי . . . וְאֶל זֶה אַבִּיט אֶל עָנִי וּנְכֵה רוּחַ וְחָרֵד עַל דְּבָרִי, *The heaven is My throne and the earth is My footstool . . . but it is to this that I look; to the poor and broken-spirited person who is zealous regarding My word* (66:1-2). From this it is established clearly that the person who is zealous in his endeavors regarding the word of God — i.e., the Torah — is [the one who represents] the purpose and aim of the existence of heaven and earth. He also brings proof from the verse in *Psalms*, מָה רַבּוּ מַעֲשֶׂיךָ ה׳ כֻּלָּם בְּחָכְמָה עָשִׂיתָ מָלְאָה הָאָרֶץ קִנְיָנֶךָ, *How abundant are Your works, Hashem, with wisdom You made them all, the earth is full of Your possessions* (104:24), which follows [the Psalmist's] story of the creation of heaven and earth. Meaning, all that

NOTES

teaching of the Tanna. Regarding heaven and earth, the *Sforno* explains that this creation was for the benefit of mankind, the crown of Creation, and that man in turn can only realize his purpose and potential through the wisdom of Torah, which is the wisdom of God. This concept is expressed by David in *Psalms* (Chap. 104). The people of Israel and the Holy Sanctuary represent the completion of God's aim and purpose insofar as perfection of people and place are concerned.

The second proof-verse, regarding Israel (*Psalms* 16:3), is not explained by the *Sforno*. The *Midrash Shmuel,* however, does offer a reasonable explanation for the

ו מִנַּיִן? דִּכְתִיב: „וַיְבָרְכֵהוּ וַיֹּאמַר, בָּרוּךְ אַבְרָם לְאֵל
ט עֶלְיוֹן, קֹנֵה שָׁמַיִם וָאָרֶץ.״ יִשְׂרָאֵל מִנַּיִן? דִּכְתִיב:
„עַד יַעֲבֹר עַמְּךָ יהוה, עַד יַעֲבֹר עַם זוּ קָנִיתָ״;
וְאוֹמֵר: „לִקְדוֹשִׁים אֲשֶׁר בָּאָרֶץ הֵמָּה, וְאַדִּירֵי כָּל
חֶפְצִי בָם.״ בֵּית הַמִּקְדָּשׁ מִנַּיִן? דִּכְתִיב: „מָכוֹן
לְשִׁבְתְּךָ פָּעַלְתָּ יהוה, מִקְּדָשׁ אֲדֹנָי כּוֹנְנוּ
יָדֶיךָ״; וְאוֹמֵר: „וַיְבִיאֵם אֶל גְּבוּל קָדְשׁוֹ, הַר זֶה
קָנְתָה יְמִינוֹ.״ כָּל מַה שֶּׁבָּרָא הַקָּדוֹשׁ בָּרוּךְ הוּא
בְּעוֹלָמוֹ לֹא בְרָאוֹ אֶלָּא לִכְבוֹדוֹ, שֶׁנֶּאֱמַר: „כֹּל
הַנִּקְרָא בִשְׁמִי וְלִכְבוֹדִי בְּרָאתִיו, יְצַרְתִּיו אַף
עֲשִׂיתִיו״; וְאוֹמֵר: „יהוה יִמְלֹךְ לְעֹלָם וָעֶד.״

פירוש לרבי עובדיה ספורנו

שהמציא היה בשביל החכמה אשר התכלית המכוון בה נשלם בארץ, כאמרו „מלאה הארץ קנינך״: והקנין השלישי היה אברהם אשר הוא לבדו בדורו היה אותו הנמצא המכוון, והביא ראיה על זה ממה שנאמר „ברוך אברם לאל עליון קונה שמים וארץ״, כלומר שבמציאות אברהם נעשה האל יתברך עליון קונה שמים וארץ בהשיגו יתברך בחם התכלית המכוון: והקנין הרביעי היה ישראל, שבין כל העמים לא נשלם תכלית כוונתו – ונשלם בישראל, והביא ראיה ממה שנאמר „עם זו קנית״,

SFORNO'S COMMENTARY

He brought into existence was for the wisdom [Torah], whose aim and purpose can only be completely attained here on earth, as it is written, *The earth is full of Your possessions.*

The third possession was Abraham who, alone in his generation, was the one who realized [in his being] the intent [of Hashem]. He brings proof to this from the verse in *Genesis*: בָּרוּךְ אַבְרָם לְאֵל עֶלְיוֹן קֹנֵה שָׁמַיִם וָאָרֶץ, *Blessed is Abram of God the most high, Who acquired heaven and earth* (14:19) — meaning, that through Abraham's being, God, the Blessed One, became *Most high, Who acquired heaven and earth,* by attaining and reaching His aim [in the creation of man].

The fourth possession is Israel, for of all the nations, His intent and purpose was not realized except through Israel. And he brings proof from the verse in *Exodus,* עַם זוּ קָנִיתָ, *these people that You acquired* (15:16) —

NOTES

inclusion of this verse in *Psalms,* to teach us that even at those times in Jewish history when Israel is not worthy, the merit of the holy ones, who have passed away, will grant their descendants a special status. The *Sforno* explains that the second verse, quoted by the Tanna, regarding the Holy Temple is for the purpose of clarifying

6 9 *From where do we know this about Abraham? Since it is written: "And He blessed him and said: Blessed is Abram of God the Most High, Who acquired heaven and earth." From where do we know this about the people Israel? Since it is written: "Until Your people passes through, HASHEM, until it passes through — this people You acquired," and it [also] says, "But for the holy ones who are in the earth and for the mighty all my desires are due to them." From where do we know this about the Holy Temple? Since it is written: "Your dwelling-place which You, HASHEM, have made; the Sanctuary, my Lord, that Your hands established." And it says: "And He brought them to His sacred boundary, to this mountain which His right hand acquired." All that the Holy One, Blessed is He, created in His world, He created solely for His glory, as it is said: "All that is called by My Name, indeed, it is for My glory that I have created it, formed it, and made it." And it says: "HASHEM shall reign for all eternity."*

פירוש לרבי עובדיה ספורנו

כלומר שבזה העם לבדו בין כל העמים נשלם השגת החפץ האלקי וקנינו: והקנין החמישי היה בית המקדש אשר בו לבדו בין כל המקומות נשלם החפץ והתכלית האלקי, והביא ראיה על זה ממה שנאמר הר זה קנתה ימינו, ובהיות

SFORNO'S COMMENTARY

meaning, that only through this people, among all the people of the earth, was the Divine desire and purpose fulfilled and acquired.

The fifth possession was the Holy Temple, for in that place alone, among all places, was the desire and purpose of the Almighty completed and fulfilled. He brings proof to this from the verse in *Exodus*: מִקְּדָשׁ ה׳ כּוֹנְנוּ יָדֶיךָ, *The Sanctuary, my Lord, that Your hands established* (15:17) — meaning, that for the Sanctuary which He made, His hands did establish all other material things. To show that this refers to the Holy Temple [in Jerusalem] and not to the Sanctuary in Shiloh, he brings proof from the verse in *Psalms*: הַר זֶה קָנְתָה יְמִינוֹ, *This mountain which His right hand acquired* (78:54).

NOTES

that the Sanctuary listed by him refers to the one in Jerusalem, for only that one is situated on a mountain, unlike the one in Shiloh. The concluding phrase (*may all the earth* etc.) is based on a verse in *Psalms* (72:19). The *Sforno* uses this expression at the conclusion of his other writings, as he does here.

❦ ❦ ❦

רַבִּי חֲנַנְיָא בֶּן עֲקַשְׁיָא אוֹמֵר: רָצָה הַקָּדוֹשׁ בָּרוּךְ הוּא לְזַכּוֹת אֶת יִשְׂרָאֵל, לְפִיכָךְ הִרְבָּה לָהֶם תּוֹרָה וּמִצְוֹת, שֶׁנֶּאֱמַר: „יהוה חָפֵץ לְמַעַן צִדְקוֹ יַגְדִּיל תּוֹרָה וְיַאְדִּיר.״

פירוש לרבי עובדיה ספורנו

כבודו יתברך השלם בכל מיני התכלית היה זה בהכרח תכלית כוונתו, והביא ראיה על זה ממה שנאמר „כל הנקרא בשמי ולכבודי בראתיו״ וממה שנאמר

SFORNO'S COMMENTARY

Now, since the glory [honor] of the Blessed One is utterly complete and perfect, this was perforce the end purpose and intent [of His creation]. He brings proof to this from the verse in *Isaiah*: כֹּל הַנִּקְרָא בִשְׁמִי וְלִכְבוֹדִי בְּרָאתִיו, *All that is called by My Name, indeed it is for My Glory that I have created it* (43:7), and also from the verse in *Exodus*: כּוֹנְנוּ יָדֶיךָ ה׳ יִמְלֹךְ לְעֹלָם

Rabbi Chanania ben Akashia says: The Holy One, Blessed is He, wished to confer merit upon Israel; therefore He gave them Torah and mitzvos in abundance, as it is said: "HASHEM desired, for the sake of its [Israel's] righteousness, that the Torah be made great and glorious."

פירוש לרבי עובדיה ספורנו

ועד „כוננו ידיך, יי ימלוך״, כלומר שכוונת כל מה שכוננו ידיו היה שימלוך לעולם ויםלא כבודו את כל הארץ אמן ואמן:

SFORNO'S COMMENTARY

וָעֶד, *That your hands established . . . Hashem shall reign for all eternity* (15:17-18) — meaning, that the intent of all that His hands established was for the purpose that He reign for all eternity. וְיִמָּלֵא כְבוֹדוֹ אֶת כָּל הָאָרֶץ אָמֵן וְאָמֵן, *and may all the earth be filled with His glory, Amen and Amen* (*Psalms* 72:19).